The
Essential
Guide to
Psychiatric Drugs

The
Essential
Guide to
Psychiatric Drugs

JACK M. GORMAN, M.D.

Columbia University College of Physicians and Surgeons

St. Martin's Press/New York

Library of Congress Cataloging-in-Publication Data

Gorman, Jack M.
    The essential guide to psychiatric drugs / Jack M. Gorman. —
Updated ed.
        p.   cm.
    Includes bibliographical references and index.
    ISBN 0-312-06967-7 (pbk.)
    1. Psychotropic drugs—Handbooks, manuals, etc.   2. Psychotropic
drugs—Popular works.   3. Consumer education.   I. Title.
    [DNLM: 1. Psychotropic Drugs.   QV 77 G671e]
    RM315.G67   1992
    615'.788—dc20
    DNLM/DLC
    for Library of Congress   91-35978
                                                                 CIP

First U.S. Paperback Edition: January 1992
10 9 8 7 6 5 4

Medical Caution

Contents

Who Should Use This Book and How Should It Be Used?   ix

Acknowledgments   xiii

Drug Directory   xv

Part I: Essential Information About Psychiatric Drugs

   1. Be an Informed Consumer!   3

   2. How Do I Know If I Need a Psychiatric Drug?   9

   3. Psychotherapy, Drugs, or Both?   15

   4. How Do I Get Psychiatric Drugs?   21

   5. What Are Side Effects?   31

   6. How Long Should I Take a Psychiatric Drug?   35

Part II: Psychiatric Drug Reference Guide

   7. Drugs Used to Treat Depression   47

   8. Drugs Used to Treat Anxiety   117

   9. Drugs Used to Treat Manic Depression/Bipolar
      Affective Disorder   175

  10. Drugs Used to Treat Schizophrenia   201

  11. Sleeping Pills   253

  12. Drugs Used to Treat Drug Abuse   285

Part III: Special Topics About Psychiatric Drugs

  13. Treating the Violent Patient   309

  14. Family, Environment, and Genetics   315

  15. Weight Loss and Weight Gain   323

  16. Sex and Psychiatric Drugs   331

  17. Treating the Elderly   337

  18. Psychiatric Drugs and Pregnancy   345

  19. AIDS: Dealing with Psychiatric Problems   351

20. Generic Versus Brand: What's in a Name?   359
21. How Psychiatric Drugs Work   365
A Final Note   377
Glossary of Terms   381
Suggestions for Further Reading   387
Index   391

Who Should Use This Book and How Should It Be Used?

Bookshelves in libraries and bookstores across the United States are loaded with psychological self-help books and home health care manuals. Everybody seems to have access to information about health and medical treatment.

But over the years, as a practicing psychiatrist and scientist, I have been surprised by the number of patients with psychiatric problems and their families who have almost no idea of what psychiatric drugs are supposed to do or why they are taking them. Many times I function as a consultant for patients who have already received psychiatric treatment, and I have found that most patients do not know if they are taking the right medication or even if they should be on medication at all. Nor do they recognize the side effects caused by the drugs.

I find that most patients and their families crave information about the reasons for taking psychiatric drugs, the benefits the drugs produce, and the risks the drugs entail. And they are quite able to grasp explanations that are neither condescending nor overly technical.

Despite popular myth, even very depressed or anxious patients can absorb great amounts of information about their illness and treatment options. I feel that all patients have a right and a responsibility to know why they are taking a drug, whether other options are available, and what the risks are. A fully informed patient is usually a doctor's ally, not an enemy.

This book is *not* intended to substitute for a personal psychiatrist, who will prescribe medication and monitor its effects. Because people are so different from each other and psychiatric drugs so complex, it is important that you ask your doctor about the information you read here, as not everything I have written could possibly fit every situation.

This guide will, however, help the person with a psychiatric problem. It will also help friends, relatives, and spouses of people who suffer from psychiatric illness to understand when drug therapy should be considered for their loved ones and which drug should be used, how long should treatment last, and what side effects should be expected.

It is important to stress that this book is not an attempt to "sell" psychiatric drugs. I hope I have clearly outlined the many situations in which drugs are *not* the best choice in treatment of a psychiatric problem and situations in which drugs may even be harmful.

Many books cover a specific psychiatric syndrome, like depression or panic disorder or obsessive-compulsive disorder, and describe the drugs useful in that particular condition. This guide is the only book I know of that includes all psychiatric drugs. There are two ways to use the book.

First, it can be used as a reference book that provides information about individual psychiatric drugs. The middle section comprises separate descriptions of most available psychiatric drugs. You can simply look up the drug in which you are interested and read about its use, correct dose, special properties, and side effects. If you use the book in this way, it is not necessary to read all of the chapters to get the information you need about a particular drug.

Second, the book can be used to obtain a better general understanding of when and how to use psychiatric drugs. Part I tells you how to know if you should take medication for an emotional problem, how long to take the drug, how to stop use of psychiatric drugs, and how to choose the right doctor. Part III provides information on special topics concerning psychiatric drugs, for example, drugs given to the elderly, drugs used during pregnancy, and drugs that affect weight and sexual function.

The *Essential Guide to Psychiatric Drugs* is intended for three main groups: people who suffer from psychiatric problems, family members and friends of patients with psychiatric illnesses, and nonpsychiatric therapists and physicians who have clients and patients with emotional disorders. Although medical students, psychiatric residents, and even psychiatrists may find the book useful, it is deliberately written in a nontechnical manner. Essentially, I imagined that I was talking to a new patient and his or her relatives in my consulting room. This book should sound as if you had asked your doctor a question and he or she is taking the time to give you an answer you can understand.

A word about the cost of psychiatric drugs. Each price listed here is the *wholesale price per pill,* taken from the 1991 edition of *Drug Topics Red Guide* (Medical Economics Inc., Oradell, NJ), the book your pharmacist regularly consults. Drug stores usually mark up the price an average of 40%, but the actual price you pay will vary greatly from store to store and from city to city. Therefore, the prices given here are most useful when used to compare the cost of one drug with that of another.

The case histories provided are of course fictional to protect the identities of my patients. They represent composites of actual cases and hence may be taken as accurate examples of common psychiatric problems.

Both generic and brand names are used throughout the book. Sometimes, brand names are so commonly used that it would be confusing to neglect them. The first letter of a brand name is always capitalized.

It is estimated that one out of every five Americans may at some point in his or her life suffer from a psychiatric problem, but only a very small number of these people will receive treatment. This book will help you decide if drug treatment might help you, or someone you care about, combat mental illness.

Acknowledgments

In my career as a doctor and scientist, many important and influential figures have shaped how I view my patients and my work. I have been fortunate to be guided by some truly outstanding mentors. Among these I especially acknowledge Dr. Donald F. Klein, the dean of American psychopharmacology; Dr. Roger MacKinnon, who teaches young psychiatrists the art of interviewing patients in the most elegant way possible; my father-in-law, Dr. Howard I. Kantor, one of the most caring physicians I have had the privilege to know; and Dr. Herbert Pardes, whose dedication to finding new treatments for psychiatric illness is an inspiration to all psychiatrists.

I also want to thank Drs. Stuart Yudofsky, Michael Sheehy, Fred Quitkin, Alexander Glassman, Jerome Steiner, Robert Gould, Anke Ehrhardt, and Donald Kornfeld for all they taught me. Physicians ultimately learn most from their patients, and I thank my own patients for their patience and courage.

Special gratitude is extended to my assistants Barbara Barnett and Fanchea Jordan, my editor Bob Weil, and my agent Vicki Bijur.

Many people in my personal life were extremely helpful to me in writing this book. They include my parents, Kate and Elliot Gorman; my mother and father-in-law, Howard and Gloria Kantor; my brother, Howard Gorman; and my sister, Amy Gorman Leon.

Three people were more helpful than anyone else: my beautiful daughters Rachel Lisa and Sara Elizabeth, whose cheerfulness and good humor are better antidepressants than any I could ever prescribe; and most of all, my wife, Dr. Lauren Kantor Gorman, who among many brilliant talents is clearly the world's best psychiatrist.

Drug Directory

The following alphabetical list covers the drugs comprehensively described in this book. The numbers on the right designate the page(s) where the drug is fully explained. Note that brand names are printed in capital letters and generic names in lowercase letters.

DRUG NAME	PAGE DESCRIBED
ADAPIN (doxepin hydrochloride)	73
alprazolam (XANAX)	105, 142
amitriptyline (ELAVIL, ENDEP)	69
amoxapine (ASENDIN)	104
amphetamine (DEXEDRINE, BIPHETAMINE, DESOXYN)	108
ANAFRANIL (chlomipramine)	164
ANTABUSE (disulfiram)	297
ASENDIN (amoxapine)	104
atenolol (TENORMIN)	160
ATIVAN (lorazepam)	140
BIPHETAMINE (amphetamine)	108
buproprion (WELBUTRIN)	105
BUSPAR (buspirone)	144
buspirone (BUSPAR)	144
carbamazepine (Tegretol)	191
CATAPRES (clonidine)	299
CENTRAX (prazepam)	139
chlomipramine (ANAFRANIL)	164
chlordiazepoxide (LIBRIUM)	138, 295
chlorpromazine (THORAZINE)	230
clonazepam (KLONOPIN)	197
clonidine (CATAPRES)	299
clorazepate (TRANXENE)	139
clozapine (CLOZARIL)	248
CLOZARIL (clozapine)	248

DRUG NAME	PAGE DESCRIBED
CYLERT (pemoline)	111
DALMANE (flurazepam)	272
DEPAKENE (valproic acid)	195
desipramine (NORPRAMIN, PERTOFRANE)	67
DESOXYN (amphetamine)	108
DESYREL (trazodone)	103
DEXEDRINE (amphetamine)	108
diazepam (VALIUM)	137
disulfiram (ANTABUSE)	297
DOLOPHINE (methadone)	303
DORAL (quazepam)	278
doxepin (ADAPIN, SINEQUAN)	73
ELAVIL (amitriptyline)	69
ELDEPRYL (selegiline)	99
ENDEP (amitriptyline)	69
estazolam (PROSOM)	277
EUTONYL (pargyline)	96
fluoxetine (PROZAC)	100
fluphenazine (PROLIXIN, PERMITIL)	237
flurazepam (DALMANE)	272
halazepam (PAXIPAM)	139
HALCION (triazolam)	275
HALDOL (haloperidol)	228
haloperidol (HALDOL)	228
imipramine (TOFRANIL)	65, 304
INDERAL (propranolol)	159
isocarboxazid (MARPLAN)	93
KLONOPIN (clonazepam)	197
LIBRIUM (chlordiazepoxide)	138, 295
LIDONE (molindone)	244
lithium (ESKALITH, LITHOBID, LITHONATE, LITHOTABS)	189
lorazepam (ATIVAN)	140
loxapine (LOXITANE)	242
LOXITANE (loxapine)	242

DRUG NAME	PAGE DESCRIBED
LUDIOMIL (maprotiline)	80
maprotiline (LUDIOMIL)	80
MARPLAN (isocarboxazid)	93
MELLARIL (thioridazine)	232
mesoridazine (SERENTIL)	235
methadone (DOLOPHINE)	303
methylphenidate (RITALIN)	110
MOBAN (molindone)	244
molindone (LIDONE, MOBAN)	244
naltrexone (TREXAN)	301
NARDIL (phenelzine)	86
NAVANE (thiothixene)	241
NICORETTE (nicotine polacrilex)	301
NORPRAMIN (desipramine)	67
nortriptyline (AVENTYL, PAMELOR)	71
ORAP (pimozide)	246
oxazepam (SERAX)	141
PAMELOR (nortriptyline)	71
pargyline (EUTONYL)	96
PARNATE (tranylcypromine)	89
PAXIPAM (halazepam)	139
pemoline (CYLERT)	111
PERMITIL (fluphenazine)	237
perphenazine (TRILAFON)	239
PERTOFRANE (desipramine)	67
phenelzine (NARDIL)	86
pimozide (ORAP)	246
prazepam (CENTRAX)	139
PROLIXIN (fluphenazine)	237
propranolol (INDERAL)	159
PROSOM (estazolam)	277
protriptyline (VIVACTIL)	78
PROZAC (fluoxetine)	100
quazepam (DORAL)	278

DRUG NAME	PAGE DESCRIBED
RESTORIL (temazepam)	274
RITALIN (methylphenidate)	110
selegiline (ELDEPRYL)	99
SERAX (oxazepam)	141
SERENTIL (mesoridazine)	235
SINEQUAN (doxepin)	73
STELAZINE (trifluoperazine)	235
SURMONTIL (trimipramine)	76
TEGRETOL (carbamazepine)	193
temazepam (RESTORIL)	274
TENORMIN (atenolol)	160
thioridazine (MELLARIL)	232
thiothixene (NAVANE)	241
THORAZINE (chlorpromazine)	230
TOFRANIL (imipramine)	65, 304
TRANXENE (clorazepate)	139
tranylcypromine (PARNATE)	89
trazodone (DESYREL)	103
TREXAN (naltrexone)	301
triazolam (HALCION)	275
trifluoperazine (STELAZINE)	235
TRILAFON (perphenazine)	239
trimipramine (SURMONTIL)	76
tryptophan (TROFAN)	281
VALIUM (diazepam)	137
valproic acid (DEPAKENE)	195
VIVACTIL (protriptyline)	78
WELBUTRIN (buproprion)	105
XANAX (alprazolam)	105, 142

Part I

ESSENTIAL INFORMATION
ABOUT PSYCHIATRIC DRUGS

1. Be an Informed Consumer!   3

2. How Do I Know If I Need a Psychiatric Drug?   9

3. Psychotherapy, Drugs, or Both?   15

4. How Do I Get Psychiatric Drugs ?   21

5. What Are Side Effects?   31

6. How Long Should I Take a Psychiatric Drug?   35

Chapter 1

Be an Informed Consumer!

A psychiatrist practicing in a large northeastern city recently received a phone call from a surgeon. One of the surgeon's patients, who had had his gall bladder removed two days earlier, was found in tears lying in his hospital bed by a staff nurse. The patient reluctantly told the nurse he believed he was about to die and wanted to say good-bye to his wife and children. Without another word the nurse called the surgeon, who immediately called the psychiatrist.

"Please get my patient on an antidepressant right away," the surgeon demanded.

"Are there any medical problems that might interfere with the safe use of antidepressants?" the psychiatrist asked.

"None," the surgeon quickly answered, and went on to state with clear anxiety in his voice, "but he is very depressed, maybe suicidal, and you better give him a drug right away."

The surgeon sounded nervous, but his assessment of the situation was probably correct. At least that was the psychiatrist's initial impression after the phone call. Within an hour the psychiatrist was at the bedside of the tearful patient, who looked healthy and robust, but thoroughly despondent. Already, the psychiatrist was running through his mind the many antidepressant medications currently available. Perhaps imipramine. No, that might cause constipation and it takes four weeks to work. Phenelzine? No, too many blood pressure problems. And so on.

In fact, this patient was never placed on antidepressant medication. As the psychiatrist reviewed the patient's chart, he overheard a nurse discussing the case. Apparently, the patient had been admitted with severe jaundice, a yellowing of the skin caused by excess amounts of bilirubin in the blood. A tumor blocking the bile duct was suspected first, ruled out, then suspected again. Because none of the tests were definitive, a decision was made to operate on the patient to see if a tumor was compressing any part of the system that connects the gall bladder to the liver. At the time of operation, no tumor was found, but the surgeon had felt some stones in the gall bladder he thought might be causing the problem and therefore removed the gall bladder. Two days later, the patient's jaundice resolved.

"How did he react when he was told it wasn't cancer?" the psychiatrist wondered.

"I don't know," the nurse answered, "I'm not even sure who told him that no tumor was found."

In fact, no one had told the patient that only gallstones, no tumor, had been found. In one of those breakdowns in communication that occur all too often in large hospitals today, the surgeon thought the resident was going to explain things. The resident thought it was the intern's job, but the intern was barely awake to remember which patient was which. And the nurses expected that one of the doctors would certainly have set the patient straight.

Thirty minutes later, the patient was sitting up in bed, smiling and complaining that he wanted dinner. It took only that long—four weeks sooner than imipramine—for the psychiatrist to find out that the patient had assumed that he had cancer, that no one wanted to break the news to him, and that he would never leave the hospital. He wanted to be brave, then found himself distraught and angry at himself for being so emotional. Mental images of his bereaved wife and children were torturing him and he wondered whether his life insurance company would find out he had told a small lie fifteen years earlier on his application.

Without administering a single drug, the psychiatrist "cured" this man's "suicidal depression." Most likely, the psychiatrist did not take much credit for the lifesaving intervention. This treatment was seemingly a matter of simple common sense. Yet, without this intervention, which took a good bit of detective work, we can imagine how horrible things might have gotten for the poor patient.

It may seem odd to begin a book about medications used to treat psychiatric disorders by telling a story in which drugs clearly were not the right treatment. I do this to drive home one of the central points behind this explanation of psychiatric drugs: medicine is not the answer for many situations of depression, anxiety, and even psychosis. *Talking to patients with problems is absolutely essential and sometimes is curative.* If a patient feels that a doctor has decided to start a medication to treat a psychiatric problem very quickly, without taking a detailed personal history, he or she should get another opinion before taking a single pill.

Let me tell another story that gives the opposite perspective. A sixty-year-old woman was brought by relatives to the hospital emergency room. A month earlier, the woman's husband had died after a two-year battle with cancer. At first, she seemed stoic and perhaps even relieved that her husband's protracted suffering was at last over. But then she became increasingly depressed and withdrawn. She stopped eating and bathing, seemed confused and easily distracted, and refused to leave her apartment. The doctor in the emergency room recognized that the woman was depressed and reassured her family that this was a "natural" consequence of bereavement. "Just stay with her and be supportive," the doctor advised the family, "and she will soon pull out of it." The doctor seemed empathetic and wise to the family; they believed his advice and took the depressed widow home.

Two weeks later the widow was brought by ambulance to the same emergency room, semicomatose, after an overdose of sleeping pills. Fortunately, she was revived and admitted to the hospital. She was immediately started on antidepressant medication and improved dramatically over the next two weeks. Although she remained very sad about her husband's death, she once again engaged her family, ate meals, took baths, and went shopping. She never again contemplated taking her own life.

The surgical patient and the widow had virtually the same symptoms of depression. To the casual observer, their complaints would have been indistinguishable. Yet, in the first case drugs would have been useless; without antidepressants, the second patient probably would have ultimately killed herself.

WHAT IS PSYCHOPHARMACOLOGY?

Psychopharmacology is the branch of medicine that specializes in the use of medication to correct psychiatric illness. A skilled psychiatrist must know a great deal about a wide variety of drugs. Because all of these drugs have different side effects, the psychiatrist must also understand a great deal of general clinical medicine. Much of this knowledge is highly technical and complex. There is a great deal of science underlying the drugs used to treat psychiatric patients.

Yet no amount of science could possibly help the doctor decide not to treat the surgical patient I have described with antidepressants but to immediately treat the widow. No x-ray, blood test, or finding on physical examination can be used to help make this decision. Nothing will show up in the urine, sputum, or blood of either patient that would tell which one will respond to medication and which one will not.

Psychiatrists make these decisions based largely on a combination of clinical lore, experience, and intuition. In only a few instances do we have scientifically indisputable facts on which to rely. Hence, the patient and his family must be involved in every step of the decision-making process. A correct decision can produce substantial, even dramatic, benefit; a mistake can lead to prolongation of suffering, adverse physical side effects, and sometimes even disaster. It is no wonder, then, that many patients and doctors alike avoid drug treatment of psychiatric disorders or even insist that drugs are universally bad and dangerous.

THE MANY CONTROVERSIES

In any human endeavor, and medicine is a cardinal example, whenever facts are sparse, strongly held theories proliferate. Because the pros and cons for the use of medicine in psychiatry are not absolutely clear or agreed upon, strong arguments have arisen on all sides. Radical biologists insist that all psychiatric illnesses result from abnormalities in the brain. Drugs are almost always seen as the answer and the adverse side effects as simply inconvenient. To these practitioners, "talking" therapies of whatever variety are simply a waste of time. Diametrically opposed to the radical biologists are the dogmatic psychologists who insist that psychiatric problems are not medical problems but rather the products of unconscious conflict, bad life experiences, incorrect thinking, or adverse social circumstances. These theorists are fond of claiming that medications only "cover up" psychiatric symptoms, whereas psychological treatments—be they psychoanalysis, behavioral modification, cognitive restructuring, and so on—get to the true "root" of the problem. To the dogmatic psychologists, medications actually prevent patients from working on their problems and are almost always dangerous.

Many different kinds of professionals are involved in mental health care, including psychiatrists, psychologists, social workers, and nurses. Only psychiatrists are medical doctors, however, with the legal right to prescribe medication for psychiatric illness. Nevertheless, it is a clear mistake to see the conflict between biologists and psychologists as purely a matter of professional rivalry, with psychiatrists attempting to assert the usefulness of drugs to increase their market share of the mental health world. Even psychiatrists are often divided along biological and psychological lines, and plenty of nonmedical mental health practitioners strongly favor the use of medication in the treatment of mental disorders. Iconoclasts come with many different degrees.

7

DECIDING THE BEST TREATMENT

I have often felt sympathy for the patient suffering from depression, panic attacks, or bulimia who must decide what kind of treatment to get and from whom. Often, patients feel that if they go to a psychiatrist they will automatically be prescribed drugs, if they go to a psychoanalyst they will be prescribed psychoanalysis, and if they go to a behaviorist they will be prescribed behavioral treatment. Imagine if a person complaining of stomachache was offered digitalis by a cardiologist, steroid cream by a dermatologist, and eye glasses by an ophthalmologist!

Thus, the purpose behind this book. As I will describe, medications can be extremely helpful—even lifesaving—in treating mental disorders. But the patient with a psychiatric problem must be an informed consumer and understand some guidelines before agreeing to take a drug. It is not my intention to justify psychiatric drugs or to argue in favor of medication for every psychiatric problem. Rather, I intend to explain situations in which careful consideration should be given to the use of medication and situations in which drugs should be rejected as treatment. In addition, it is important to know something about how these drugs work, what side effects they produce, and what benefits can and cannot legitimately be expected. Finally, patients should have some way of judging whether they are getting proper care and consideration from their physician.

The advertising slogan of a large chemical corporation, "better living through chemicals," has been proposed sarcastically as the motto for psychiatrists who prescribe drugs. This book is intended as a primer in how to avoid the "better living through chemicals" approach in favor of application of sound clinical and scientific principles to the medical treatment of some very serious illnesses.

Chapter 2

How Do I Know If I Need a Psychiatric Drug?

Let's say you haven't been feeling quite like yourself for the past few weeks. It's hard to get out of bed when the alarm clock goes off, even though you have been lying awake for a few hours. Nothing seems to interest you much including sex and your favorite foods. Work suddenly seems impossible and you just cannot concentrate. Recently, you have started to wonder if you really haven't made a mess of things. Maybe life isn't worthwhile? Maybe it would be better to be dead.

Or another example. Everything seems to be going just fine in your life when suddenly one day while you are driving the car, your heart starts to pound, you feel as if you can't catch your breath, you sweat, feel dizzy and faint, and are sure you must be having a heart attack. Maybe just a bad day, you think, until you get another of these attacks two days later while at work. A third attack wakes you up in the middle of the night, and another hits while you are playing with your children.

Or one more. Your twenty-year-old son has always been a model student, athlete, and popular with other kids his age. Lately he seems to be acting strangely. He paces around the house at all hours of the night and sounds as if he is muttering to an imaginary person. He tells you he thinks the food you serve him is poisoned. Sometimes when he talks, he goes on and on without making any sense. Then, in the middle of a tranquil evening as the family is watching television, he suddenly screams and threatens to kill his father.

These are all examples of psychiatric conditions that may respond to drugs. The first is an obvious case of depression, the second is called panic disorder, and the third is the tragic but all too familiar early stage of schizophrenia. Many people feel unhappy from time to time; everybody experiences anxiety and a few palpitations when there are things to worry about; and what teenager or young adult does not go through a period of acting strangely as far as his or her parents are concerned? Obviously, we do not recommend drugs, or psychiatric intervention for that matter, for the routine ups and downs of everyday life. How then to decide to see a psychiatrist and consider taking medicine?

RULES TO CONSIDER BEFORE SEEING A PSYCHIATRIST

Here are some general rules to consider in trying to make that decision:

1. It is perfectly normal to feel sad or nervous sometimes, but usually there is an obvious reason. If you just received bad news, it is not abnormal to be unhappy; if you have a major presentation to make at work tomorrow you will probably feel anxious and even have trouble falling asleep. But if you find yourself depressed, anxious, or panicky for no obvious reason, you may be suffering from a psychiatric disorder.

2. Even when people feel blue or worried with good cause, it usually does not completely ruin their ability to work, take care of their children, and function socially. When depression or anxiety have a big impact on the job or in the ability to perform your usual tasks at home, it's a good time to think about seeing a psychiatrist.

10

3. Normal worries and bad moods usually last only a day or two; if you can't shrug it off, especially when others tell you things aren't really as bad as you think they are, you might need help.

4. Take seriously the concern expressed by people close to you or that you trust. A husband or wife comments that you don't seem like yourself lately. Your boss or secretary mentions that you seem distracted and bothered. Your family doctor points out that you seem unduly worried about having a heart attack even though you are in perfectly good health. Many times, a person suffering from depression or anxiety disorder is the last to admit something is wrong.

5. Watch out for "home remedies." If you start taking a drink every night because otherwise you'll never fall asleep, or if you borrow someone else's tranquilizers or think that aspirins or antihistamines are necessary for your "nerves," you are probably doing a poor job at self-medication. There are better medications for depression and insomnia than scotch and soda.

6. Anytime you seriously entertain the thought "I would be better off dead" or "my life is worthless and my family might be in better shape collecting my life insurance," you should pick up the phone and get help.

7. People are entitled to act strangely, entertain "unusual" ideas or opinions, or follow a "different drummer." You do no favor for a loved one, however, by allowing him to become lost in hallucinations, to be tortured by paranoid ideas, or to threaten harm to others. One out of every hundred people in the United States has schizophrenia; it is a devastating disease without a cure. But running away from schizophrenia only delays getting the help that is available. Instead of worrying about the stigma some people associate with seeing a psychiatrist, worry instead of what may happen if you do not follow your instinct that your son or daughter is acting in a bizarre manner and get help quickly.

To summarize these seven points, you (or someone close to you) may be a candidate to take a psychiatric drug if you have symptoms of anxiety or depression for no good reason; if your symptoms interfere with your ability to function at home or work; if your symptoms persist longer than a few days; if others tell you that you seem unusually moody, stressed, or anxious; if you have suicidal thoughts; if you use alcohol, street drugs, or unprescribed medications to ease tension, improve your mood, or help you sleep; or if you persistently exhibit odd, bizarre behavior, often to the point that others feel threatened (Table 1).

Remember, there is very little to be lost, and an awful lot to be gained, by consulting a psychiatrist in these circumstances. Don't succumb to the common myths about psychiatrists. We really are not interested in drumming up business by convincing people they are crazy; like most physicians, I like nothing better than to tell someone that nothing is seriously wrong and no treatment is necessary. Psychiatric illness is not a sign of personal weakness. Great scientists (S.E. Luria), heads of countries (Abraham Lincoln), sports figures (Jimmy Piersall), and famous artists (Van Gogh) have suffered from psychiatric illnesses.

Table 1:

Warning Signs That a Psychiatric Drug May Be Needed

1. You feel depressed, anxious, or panicky for no obvious reason.
2. Depression or anxiety makes it difficult to do your usual work.
3. Even though others tell you things are not that bad, you cannot stop worrying.
4. Others tell you that you do not seem your usual self.
5. You take other people's medication or over-the-counter drugs or drink more to "calm your nerves" or help you sleep.
6. You have thoughts of suicide or feel that life isn't worth it.
7. You are acting in a bizarre or frightening manner.

Finally, it is not true that everybody will know if you see a psychiatrist. Psychiatrists take the promise of confidentiality very seriously and are bound never to reveal to anyone that they saw you or what your problem is. I remember one young woman suffering from depression who burst into tears when I recommended she take medication for her illness. "If my boss ever finds out I am taking drugs for depression, he'll fire me in a minute!" she sobbed. As much as I wanted to relieve her unfounded fears, I, of course, could not tell her that her boss was, coincidentally, also a patient of mine and that he himself was taking antidepressants. There is no reason that anyone has to know that you see a psychiatrist.

GETTING HELP

Now that you have decided you may have a problem requiring professional help, the next step is to decide what kind of help to get. Here, you might become confused. Pick up any newspaper and you'll find advertisements from therapists promising cures for depression, anxiety, alcoholism, and cigarette smoking. Your best friend may recommend vitamins and exercise. Your family doctor may want to give you tranquilizers.

What you need is the advice of an expert in psychiatric illness who is familiar with the variety of treatments available and who can tailor a remedy to your personal situation. To get that, I advise first consulting a psychiatrist. The best way to find one is the same procedure you would use in choosing a dentist, pediatrician, or gynecologist. Ask your family doctor, call the local hospital or medical school, or rely on recommendations from family or friends.

In general, there are two kinds of treatment for psychiatric illness: medications and talking therapies. Sometimes a person needs one or the other, and sometimes both. In the next chapter, I consider how to decide which route is best for you.

Chapter 3

Psychotherapy, Drugs, or Both?

Surprisingly, some people are treated for emotional problems for many years without ever being told what is wrong with them. Some patients come to me after years of psychotherapy completely unable to explain how their treatment is affecting their symptoms.

The first task in deciding whether a psychiatric drug is appropriate is the diagnosis. This is no different from what happens when you go to the family doctor complaining of a stomachache or fever. The doctor asks many questions, sometimes performs a physical examination, and may obtain laboratory tests and x-rays. The only difference with psychiatric care is that psychiatrists rely more on answers to questions asked of the patient and family than on physical examinations or test results.

To diagnose, psychiatrists in the United States now use the *American Psychiatric Association Diagnostic and Statistical Manual,* revised third edition, It's called *DSM-III-R* for short and essentially gives very specific instructions on how to put together different kinds of emotional symptoms to make a psychiatric diagnosis. The DSM-III-R forces the doctor to ask detailed questions about the nature of symptoms and how long they have lasted to figure out what is wrong. A new edition of this manual (DSM–IV) is due out shortly.

The diagnosis then guides the psychiatrist in treatment. There are some psychiatric conditions that are almost always treated with medications, some for which medications are optional, and some for which medications are useless. Similarly, psychotherapy helps in some circumstances, is helpful but not required in others, and is a waste of time for still others. Let me give some examples.

THE IMPORTANCE OF DIAGNOSIS

First, let's take the case of Roger P., a 57-year-old insurance sales-man who is married, owns his own home, and enjoys playing golf on the weekends. He was doing very nicely at work until about six months ago, when he started feeling tired a lot of the time, then noticed he was waking up at three or four in the morning without being able to fall asleep again. Over the next few months he began to lose interest in playing golf, found he could not concentrate on what his co-workers or clients were saying to him, and began worry-ing that his business was nearly bankrupt, even though his partners assured him there was no danger of this. Four weeks before seeing a psychiatrist, his wife noticed that he had lost almost 20 pounds and asked him why he seemed so worried and tired all the time. Two weeks earlier he had had the first passing thought that he might be better off dead and after that could not get the thought out of his head. By the time he saw the psychiatrist, he was too depressed to get out of bed in the morning to go to work, stopped shaving or taking showers, and gave only one-word answers after long pauses when asked questions. He admitted that given the opportunity, he would probably kill himself.

Roger P. is an obvious candidate for psychiatric drug treatment. Even though a detailed exploration might reveal the events in his life that triggered his severe depression, he is so withdrawn and uncommunicative that it is unlikely much psychotherapy could be conducted. Furthermore, his condition is life threatening. If he doesn't actually kill himself he might ultimately starve to death unless something is done to improve his appetite and make him start eating again. Roger P. should be put on antidepressant medication immediately. Incidentally, the official diagnosis we would give Roger P. is *major depressive disorder.*

Now let us turn to a less obvious case involving a different type of depression. Virginia M. is 36 and single but has lived with her boyfriend for the last three years. She is an architect, is well respected by her colleagues, and has many close friends. Still, Virginia M. has suspected more and more in recent years that she does not look at life the way other people do. She is successful but never happy. Most of the time she is convinced her boyfriend is about to leave her or she will lose her job. When these thoughts get very strong she tends to eat everything in sight, often to the point of feeling sick to her stomach. Consequently, she is constantly battling her weight. Sometimes she gets horrible anxiety attacks and feels as if her heart is going to pop right out of her chest. On weekends she often spends most of the day in bed, complaining she is too tired to go out. If her friends convince her to go out, she usually has a good time and feels cheerful while she is with them. No one except her boyfriend and closest friends have any idea that she suffers from depression.

There is a very good chance that Virginia M. would get substantial benefit from medication for depression, but unlike the case of Roger P., this is not an emergency. She is not suicidal, her life is not in jeopardy, and she is perfectly able to function at work. Psychotherapy might be helpful if the therapist can identify the causes of the depression. In this case, before making a definite decision on treatment, a psychiatrist might recommend a few more meetings to determine whether psychotherapy has potential benefit and might ultimately recommend a combination of talking therapy and drug therapy. Virginia M. suffers from *atypical depression.*

Now to the opposite end of the spectrum from Roger P. Donna J. is an English professor at a University and is about to find out whether she will get a promotion. She is anxious and moody just thinking about the meeting she must have with her department chairman in two weeks when she will be told her professional fate. But there is more than this simple anxiety and moodiness. As the big meeting approaches Donna J. realizes that she really hasn't done everything she could to improve her chances. She knows she is bright and qualified, but she always avoids making the right political moves. Consequently, she seems to be passed up for less qualified professors on many occasions. Donna J. wonders why she can't push ahead those last few inches and put herself over the top. What holds her back from expending the extra effort to ensure professional success?

Donna J. does not suffer from depression or anxiety disorder. She has a *conflict* about success. Drugs will not help. Of course, a tranquilizer might help her sleep better the night before the big meeting with the chairman, but that is not her real problem. Donna J. will benefit most from one of a variety of psychotherapies aimed at improving her self-confidence, making her assertive, and removing her conflicts about success.

I have deliberately made these examples somewhat extreme to illustrate the main point: diagnosis is as essential when dealing with psychiatric disorders as it is in dealing with any medical problem. The question of what treatment—psychotherapy, drugs, or both—is best can be answered only when the symptoms are clear and the diagnosis made.

Psychiatrists are obviously not the only specialists in emotional problems who know how to make diagnoses or provide useful treatment. A few features of psychiatrists should be kept in mind, however.

First, psychiatrists are medical doctors who must first graduate from medical school just like internists, surgeons, and pediatricians. Medical illnesses can sometimes cause psychiatric illnesses and psychiatrists are specially trained to recognize the situations in which physical disease is the cause of emotional problems. Many people therefore feel most comfortable seeing a psychiatrist at least once to be sure they are not suffering from a neurological or medical problem.

Second, only psychiatrists among the many mental health practitioners are legally qualified to prescribe drugs. Remember, prescribing drugs means much more than simply writing a prescription. Only a physician can appreciate the side effects, dose requirements, and drug interactions involved in administering psychiatric drugs.

Third, in deciding whether a drug might help a psychiatric problem, one of the best guidelines is how well similar patients have done with drugs in the past. Although that information can be obtained from textbooks, the truth is that most doctors and therapists find experience to be the best teacher. By observing how patients with different emotional problems react to the various psychiatric drugs, the psychiatrist learns which patient is the best candidate for a specific treatment. As only psychiatrists have this training and experience, they are often in the best position to recognize who might benefit from drug treatment.

If drug therapy is not required, a referral should be made to a qualified psychotherapist. Psychiatrists are often very skilled in psychotherapy; indeed, some psychiatrists are much more comfortable treating patients with psychotherapy than with drugs. Many psychologists and social workers are also excellent psychotherapists.

Psychologists do graduate work in clinical psychology after college. This usually includes at least a one-year internship in which they evaluate and treat patients. Many also do dissertations and receive a Ph.D. They are often highly qualified to make diagnoses and conduct psychotherapy. Social workers receive a graduate master of social work degree (M.S.W.), usually requiring two years of course work and patient contact. Many do extra training in psychotherapy after getting the M.S.W. degree and some do dissertations and receive a doctorate of social work.

In most states, there is no legal definition of "psychotherapist." Anyone who thinks they have an understanding ear and good advice to give can call him- or herself a psychotherapist. Studies have shown that the best predictor of how well a psychotherapy will work is the "fit" or relationship between patient and therapist at the start of the therapy. I recommend getting a referral from a physician or someone who has been in therapy before, selecting only therapists with a degree in a mental health field (a psychiatrist with an M.D., a psychologist with a Ph.D., or a social worker with an

M.S.W.), and then interviewing two, three, or more therapists until you find one with whom you feel comfortable.

If drug therapy is recommended, there are many things you will need to know before putting the first pill in your mouth. In the next chapter, I offer some guidelines to help you ensure that you are receiving the best possible drug treatment.

Chapter 4

How Do I Get Psychiatric Drugs?

The task of finding a competent practitioner to prescribe and manage psychiatric medication may seem perilous. You may reasonably wonder how to avoid falling into the hands of a doctor who "drugs" everybody who walks into the office.

In many respects, choosing a psychiatrist is not very different from choosing a physician. A doctor with good credentials who seems to listen carefully, explain things, weigh all of the options out loud, and promise easy access during the treatment period is obviously required. This is probably what someone would look for if they needed a doctor to prescribe eye glasses, remove a gall bladder, or treat the flu.

There is, of course, an important aspect of psychiatric illness that makes choosing a proper physician more difficult. By its very nature, mental illness affects a person's judgment and motivation to get help. Psychiatric patients often suffer from excessive guilt; thus, they are prone to avoid challenging a doctor's advice or asking for a second opinion. Some psychiatrists unfortunately promote this attitude, acting as if they have all the answers and reacting angrily if a patient questions the treatment or requests a consultation. Patients with high levels of anxiety may grab at the first suggestion of a cure without thinking things over; they may feel that a strong-willed physician is just what they need to relieve their worries, even if the treatment plan doesn't sound right. Psychotic patients usually have serious distortions of reality and use little logic to make many of their decisions, including their choice of doctor or commitment to adhere to a treatment plan.

TEN POINTS TO REMEMBER

So, in choosing a doctor to prescribe psychiatric drugs, keep these ten guidelines in mind:

1. *Only doctors with an M.D. or D.O. degree, that is, medical doctors, are licensed to prescribe psychoactive medication.* Psychiatrists are mental health experts who went to medical school; many now specialize in prescribing drugs, and in general, they are the most knowledgeable and experienced in prescribing psychiatric medications. At present, there are no specific requirements that a psychiatrist must meet to specialize in drug treatment. Almost all medical school departments of psychiatry can refer you to a psychiatrist with special experience in medication treatment, and this is often a good place to start.

In any event, it is perfectly reasonable to ask psychiatrists if they have special interest and experience in prescribing psychiatric drugs, what proportion of their patients actually receive drugs, where they learned to do this, and if they treat specific types of patients. In answering these questions, the psychiatrist should be direct and clear. A psychiatrist who becomes defensive or tries to "interpret" the questions as hostile or representing an unconscious "conflict" is probably trying to cover up a lack of expertise in psychopharmacology.

2. *Do not take drugs from a non-M.D. practitioner who gets the prescription for you from a doctor.* A patient may be in therapy with a social worker, nurse, or psychologist who thinks that medication is required. Many such therapists are extremely knowledgeable about psychiatric drugs and are in fact very qualified to recognize a need for medication. The proper procedure in this case is for the patient

22

to consult a psychiatrist to decide whether medication is needed and for the psychiatrist to then manage the medication side of treatment.

Unfortunately, some therapists are afraid to refer their patients to other practitioners for fear of losing the patient and therefore merely describe the case to a psychiatrist who writes a prescription without ever seeing the patient. When side effects or questions arise, the therapist asks the doctor and relays the answer to the patient. This would be like having your dentist take out your appendix under the direction of a surgeon in the next room.

Incidentally, the failure to refer patients is hardly limited to non-M.D. therapists. Very often, a psychiatrist will feel that a patient treated with drugs isn't getting better or has additional problems that drugs won't solve. Instead of getting a consultation from a skilled professional in psychotherapy, the psychiatrist may react by blaming the patient for not trying hard enough or by trying to change the medications.

This brings up a very important principle of all health care: there is nothing wrong with a doctor asking a patient to consult another doctor for another opinion. The best doctors do this regularly. No one doctor can know everything. Furthermore, it is entirely possible for the best, smartest, most conscientious doctor to miss some aspect of a case. I am not talking here about doctors who miss heart attacks, strokes, cancer, or mania. Many more subtle problems can arise in treatment that can be misinterpreted or missed entirely. Physicians should always know when to ask for help and patients should always respect a doctor who has the sense to request advice.

3. *Do not take psychiatric medications prescribed by a nonpsychiatric physician longer than a few weeks.* Most prescriptions for antianxiety drugs like diazepam (Valium) and chlordiazepoxide (Librium) are written by family practitioners, internists, and gynecologists, not psychiatrists. There is nothing wrong with this. A patient often develops a close relationship with these primary caregivers and when emotional problems arise, they are sometimes in the best position to know when a medication may be helpful. Taking an antianxiety drug in these circumstances for a week or two can be very helpful and is rarely harmful (see Chapter 8 for more information).

These doctors have no special training or experience in psychiatric illness, however, and should not undertake to treat a patient with psychiatric drugs for a prolonged period. What seems like simple stress to a general practitioner may actually be symptoms of serious depression. A little overexcitement may be the early signs of mania. Alcoholic patients often convince physicians to prescribe tranquilizers, which help them to avoid alcohol withdrawal symptoms but do nothing to deal with alcoholism. Studies have shown that many patients who commit suicide see their primary physician the week or two before, but no diagnosis of depression is made. Once again, good physicians know what they can and cannot treat themselves. No competent psychiatrist would try to treat chest pain or a broken arm; a good family practitioner or internist always refers the patient to a psychiatrist if there is need for prolonged prescription of psychiatric drugs.

4. *When consulting a psychiatrist, make sure the initial appointment lasts at least an hour and that you have an opportunity to explain your situation in depth.* There is no way to take an adequate medical and psychiatric history in a short period. Without such a history, a doctor cannot possibly determine the psychiatric diagnosis and the need for medication.

Remember, except in rare instances, psychiatrists do not yet have the luxury of laboratory tests and x-rays to help them make a diagnosis or design a treatment strategy. Sometimes, very subtle differences in symptom patterns make a large difference. For example, two very depressed people may see a psychiatrist to inquire about the possible benefit of antidepressants. The psychiatrist may quickly determine that medication is indicated, but then face the difficult problem of deciding which of the many available medications should be tried first. In one case, further history reveals that the patient has a specific abnormality on the electrocardiogram that makes the use of one class of antidepressants risky. In the second case, the patient reveals after close questioning that the depressed mood is occasionally alleviated when good things happen to him. This suggests the use of different kinds of antidepressants. It takes time to tease apart the various life situations and emotional symptoms to determine the right treatment; a patient is entitled to that time.

5. *It is very important that you feel that the doctor has tailored his or her treatment recommendations to your specific needs.* I have seen patients in consultation who believe that the psychiatrist they previously saw gave everybody lithium regardless of the specifics, or that the doctor didn't listen carefully to a specific request that medication likely to cause weight gain be avoided. You must feel that the doctor has taken your situation into account and is willing to be as flexible as possible in designing treatment. Sometimes, of course, flexibility is not possible. Patients often wish for medication with absolutely no side effects. No such drugs exist for the treatment of any medical condition and definitely not for the treatment of psychiatric disorders; however, it is often possible to come up with a treatment plan that comes close to meeting a particular person's specific needs, and this should always be attempted.

6. *The psychiatrist should always be willing to justify the choice of treatment.* As much as possible, the patient should be made to feel like an "informed consumer." Brain science is indeed a complicated field, but a good psychiatrist knows how to simplify things sufficiently—without being condescending—so that a patient can understand how the various drugs recommended work. More importantly, the doctor should be able to detail all of the possible alternatives to drug treatment and why they were not chosen.

For every psychiatric condition there is a nondrug treatment that someone, somewhere will recommend. With more than one hundred different psychotherapies, there are obviously many alternatives to drugs. And many times, the psychiatrist, after taking a careful history, decides that psychotherapy is a superior choice to drugs. The patient should feel free to ask about alternatives to drug treatment and should be completely satisfied that the doctor has considered them and is not dogmatically opposed to them.

7. *Unless there is an emergency, consider getting a second opinion before starting medication.* This does not mean that the first doctor should not be trusted. Two doctors are very likely to have slightly different opinions of a person's psychiatric problems and to recommend slightly different treatments. In such a case, it is probably wise to stick with the original physician. For example, if both consultants agree that the diagnosis of depression is correct and that antidepressants are warranted, it probably does not make a great deal of

25

difference if one doctor recommends imipramine (Tofranil) and the other recommends nortriptyline (Aventyl, Pamelor), as both belong to the same class of drugs, cyclic antidepressants. Such differences usually have more to do with which drug the psychiatrist is used to prescribing than with diagnosis or recommended treatment.

On the other hand, if one consultant feels a patient is depressed and should seek psychotherapy, and the other feels the diagnosis is depression as part of manic-depressive illness and long-term treatment with lithium is indicated, obviously there is a serious difference. In later chapters, I explain how to decide what to do in these situations, but for now it is important to stress that to a limit, obtaining more information and opinions is usually a good idea. No one should avoid getting additional facts.

8. *Psychiatric drug treatment is not a "take two aspirins and call me in the morning" situation.* If medication is prescribed after the initial consultation, there should be an arrangement for regular follow-up. Often, patients think they can simply take medication for a few weeks and that will be the end of it. Unfortunately, health insurance coverage for psychiatric care is shockingly inadequate, so patients avoid making further visits to see the doctor. But psychiatric drug treatment is complex and patients must be regularly followed.

For example, antidepressants of the monoamine oxidase inhibitor class are extremely useful and powerful drugs for relief of depression. Sometimes, however, patients actually become "high" from the drug after several weeks, a condition technically called "hypomania." Unfortunately, this "high" is often missed by patients and their families, who are so glad the patient is no longer depressed that they fail to recognize that something new is wrong. The signs of hypomania include rapid speech, excess energy, inappropriate optimism, and decreased sleep requirement. It can often be treated simply by reducing the dose of medication, but it must first be recognized. For that reason, doctors are correct in insisting that the patient on monoamine oxidase inhibitors be seen in the office about once a month, even after the depression has resolved.

In addition to regular office visits, patients need to know that they can contact the doctor or an associate twenty-four hours a day, seven days a week, twelve months a year (even in August, when many psychiatrists seem to take their vacation). Psychiatrists must have the same kind of around-the-clock availability as internists, obstetricians, and cardiologists because psychiatric illness severe enough to require drug treatment may produce complications at any time and psychiatric drugs can produce side effects that need immediate attention. If your doctor is hard to get hold of, switch to a different doctor.

9. *Make sure important side effects are described before you start taking a drug.* This guideline applies to any medical treatment. But special problems arise with psychiatric illness. First, psychiatric patients worry so much in general that the last thing they need is to worry about the rare side effects of drugs. Second, some psychiatric patients suffer from temporary impairment of judgment and may therefore overestimate the risk of a side effect and make an incorrect decision to refuse drug treatment. Third, some psychiatric patients cannot understand the implications of various side effects and make an informed decision.

All of this has led some psychiatrists to adopt a paternalistic approach and edit what they tell patients about the "down side" of a particular drug. Although understandable, this attitude is rarely correct. We all have a right to know the adverse consequences of a treatment. We also have the right to refuse treatment. Hence, it is hard to think of instances in which the doctor should not explain the common and most important side effects. A patient should never feel that a doctor is withholding information about the adverse effects of drugs.

10. *It is appropriate, and often desirable, for family members and "significant others" to be involved in drug treatment of psychiatric disorders.* There are many reasons for this. First, by their very nature psychiatric illnesses often make it difficult for patients to give a complete and accurate history of the problem and symptoms. Manic patients usually talk so fast and give so many extraneous details that the doctor has a hard time figuring out what happened at what time without a family member to help. Depressed patients have trouble concentrating and often omit important facts. It is also very hard for psychiatric patients to remember ever feeling well, so that the doctor may not get a true picture of when the trouble began.

Second, having a regular observer available to help chart the progress of a patient taking medication is very useful. Many antidepressants, for example, improve sleep and appetite before improving mood. The patient may feel nothing is happening because he or she still feels depressed, but the family member may notice that the patient has started sleeping through the night and eating regular meals. Without hearing from this family member, the patient and the doctor might miss the early evidence of a positive drug effect and prematurely discontinue the medication. Finally, it is important to review side effects with family members so that they also know what to watch for. Psychiatric patients may feel so terrible in general that they will not bother to call the doctor if a rash develops or nausea occurs, symptoms of which the doctor must be aware.

Of course, maintaining confidentiality is always crucial in treating patients with mental illness. The psychiatrist, like all mental health practitioners, is absolutely bound never to divulge information about a patient to anyone without permission. Sometimes, family members make intrusive and inappropriate demands for information about a patient's progress. There exist situations in which family members have a vested interest in seeing that the patient does not recover. For example, I have seen many husbands who are threatened by the idea of having their depressed or phobic wives suddenly become happier and therefore more assertive and independent. Thus, it is best that the patient select family members who can be part of the treatment effort and decide with the doctor exactly what role these members will have and what information they should be given access to. Always be wary of a doctor who flatly refuses to discuss anything with a patient's family, even at the patient's request.

Table 2 summarizes the ten guidelines for choosing a psychiatrist and starting drug treatment. In general, the first person to ask is a trusted family doctor, who often will know a good psychiatrist with expertise in managing psychiatric drugs. A person already in therapy with a non-M.D. practitioner will often have the names of psychiatrists who can prescribe medication and who have done a good job in the past. A phone call to the nearest medical school department of psychiatry is often fruitful. Psychiatrists who specialize in drug treatment tend to be on university medical school facul-

Table 2:

Guidelines for Getting Psychiatric Drugs

1. Only medical doctors (with an M.D. or D.O. degree) can prescribe medication.
2. See the psychiatrist yourself; don't get the medication from a non-M.D. therapist who speaks to the psychiatrist and gets the prescription for you.
3. Do not take psychiatric medication from a physician who is not a psychiatrist for longer than a few weeks.
4. The first consultation with the psychiatrist should be long enough (usually at least an hour) for you to completely explain all your symptoms.
5. Treatment should feel as if it is designed to your particular situation and needs.
6. The psychiatrist should be able to explain and justify the particular choice of drug recommended for you.
7. Feel free to get a second opinion from another psychiatrist before you swallow the first pill.
8. Follow-up visits are necessary. You cannot see the doctor once, get a prescription, and do the rest on your own.
9. Get a description of important side effects before you start the medication.
10. Don't hesitate to have your family or "significant others" be with you when you see the psychiatrist and be involved with your treatment.

ties. Finally, to the extent possible, be open with family members and friends when contemplating seeing a psychiatrist. Unfortunately, in some circles there remains a stigma attached to psychiatric illness that dissuades people from discussing their problems. Studies have shown that 20% of the American population suffers from psychiatric illness; in other words, an awful lot of people have psychiatric problems and many have sought treatment. Often, it is the successfully treated patients who keep their experience with psychiatry a secret, and only the relatively few disgruntled patients who openly describe their experience. Many people have had a good experience with psychiatric medication treatment and this is probably the best recommendation one could receive in selecting a doctor.

Once you make the first appointment, review the ten guidelines to determine whether you have chosen the right doctor. Above all, never be afraid to ask questions and expect serious, well-thought-out answers.

Chapter 5

What Are Side Effects?

Every drug, psychiatric or otherwise, has side effects. Some side effects are serious. Some may seem worse than the illness for which the drug was prescribed. Other side effects are merely inconvenient. Side effects may occur early in drug treatment or may not start until many months into treatment. Most side effects are alleviated when the patient stops taking the drug, but in a few instances side effects persist.

Chapters 7 to 12 list the side effects for each drug. Here, I make some general comments about side effects.

Side effects are unwanted physical and emotional changes caused by drugs that usually have nothing to do with the drugs' ability to cure illnesses. No drug is specific enough to affect only the sick part of the body; all drugs do at least one thing more than what we want them to do.

It is important to find out what side effects may be expected before putting the first pill in your mouth. There are basically two ways to obtain this information.

USING *PDR* SELECTIVELY

The first way is to look up the side effects in a reference book. I usually encourage patients to read whatever they want to about drug treatment.

Sometimes, patients may unnecessarily worry themselves by referring to such books as the *Physicians Desk Reference (PDR)*. For example, one patient who had been taking a drug for about a month told me the medication was giving her headaches. "I've never heard or observed that to be a side effect of this particular drug," I told her.

Now, she thought she had me. "Oh yes, it says right in the *PDR* that headaches are a side effect of this drug you have me on."

That was news to me so I got out my copy of the *PDR* and looked it up. What we found was a table listing about twenty different side effects. There were two columns in the table: one column showed the number of patients who took the drug and experienced each side effect and the other column showed the number of patients who took a placebo pill—an identical sugar pill used in drug studies—and manifested the side effects. For the side effect *headache,* the number of patients in the placebo column was higher than the number of patients in the active drug column. This means that the drug is not anymore responsible for causing headaches than is a sugar pill.

This is one of the pitfalls of reading a book like the *PDR*. Much of the language is technical and often refers to findings from scientific tests of drugs rather than actual clinical experience.

Another problem with these reference books is that they often list every side effect ever reported for a drug, even if it occurred in only one of a thousand cases. Doctors who treat a large number of patients need to know that information; they might run into that one in a thousand patient who develops a very rare side effect. An individual patient, however, has a very small chance of experiencing that side effect.

Also consider what can be found with respect to very common drugs in the *PDR* or similar books. Although penicillin is a highly effective antibiotic that rarely hurts anyone, there are those rare cases in which patients have a severe allergic reaction that can be fatal. The risk is so small, however, that few people refuse to take such an effective drug as penicillin. Even aspirin has some pretty serious side effects in some people. A listing for aspirin in *PDR* or similar books would include such side effects as ulcers and uncontrolled bleeding. Aspirin overdose can even be fatal! So merely reading through a list of side effects could deter a person from taking an aspirin when she has a headache.

ASK THE DOCTOR

The second way to get information is to ask the doctor prescribing the medication to explain all of the side effects and to give you an idea of how likely they are to occur in a given individual. This can vary from person to person. Some antidepressants can make it difficult for a person to urinate. For a 20-year-old woman who is otherwise perfectly healthy, this effect is usually very mild and hardly noticeable; however, a 60-year-old man with an enlarged prostate gland might end up in the emergency room and have a catheter inserted.

The best advice is to read books like the *PDR* and also to ask the psychiatrist prescribing the medication to give you a list of the more common side effects. The doctor should alert you to the serious effects that need immediate attention and also reassure you about those effects for which there is no need to worry. Above all, don't hesitate to call the doctor if you are not sure whether a new symptom is serious. A good doctor would rather be called than find out that something bad has happened to his or her patient, but the patient was too embarrassed to call. Naturally, we all like to sleep through the night. It will always be worth my while to get out of bed at four in the morning to decide if some possible drug side effect is serious rather than have one of my patients unnecessarily become sick.

33

Chapter 6

How Long Should I Take a Psychiatric Drug?

You should continue to take a drug as long as it helps and you should keep taking it until the illness is gone.

For each psychiatric drug described in Chapters 7 to 12, you will find information on how long to stay on the drug and what to do to discontinue use of the drug. Some general principles are useful.

We usually start out with very small doses of psychiatric medication and build up to the full therapeutic dose over a few days or even weeks. This gradual buildup minimizes the side effects and gives the body a chance to adjust. Then, some drugs take weeks before they start to work, especially antidepressants, lithium, and an antianxiety drug called BuSpar. You should definitely give the drug a fair chance to know if it is going to help.

Many people are concerned that the effects of a psychiatric drug will wear off. Technically, this is called "tolerance." A patient becomes tolerant to a drug when a dose that has worked for a while stops working. In such situations it is necessary to increase the dose or switch to a different drug.

Fortunately, tolerance is almost never a factor with psychiatric drugs. Once a dose of antidepressant, lithium, or antianxiety drug is found that works, it usually remains effective as long as drug treatment is required. The exceptions are sleeping pills, which frequently lose their effectiveness after two to three weeks, and amphetamines, which are only rarely used as antidepressants.

Now, let's say the drug works and you are feeling much better. You might want to stop taking the medication, and, in certain situations, that is exactly the right thing to do (Table 3).

Table 3:

How Long to Stay on Psychiatric Drugs

DRUG	RECOMMENDED TREATMENT LENGTH
Antidepressants	Six months after remission
Lithium	Indefinitely for bipolar (manic-depressive) patients
Antipsychotics	One year after first episode; indefinitely after second episode
Antianxiety drugs	Shortest possible period (except when treating panic disorder)
Antipanic drugs	Six months after remission
Sleeping pills	Shortest possible period

SHORT-TERM TREATMENT

A 34-year-old man who had always been a bit on the nervous side learned one morning that the company at which he had worked for the last five years had just lost a great deal of money. Rumors around the office convinced him the company was about to go out of business and he would soon lose his job. Over the next few weeks, despite the lack of official confirmation from his boss of these rumors, he found himself paralyzed with worry, fear, and anxiety. Unable to sleep, he could not concentrate on looking for a new job. A psychiatrist prescribed an antianxiety medication at a low dose and recommended counseling. The man took the medication every morning for a week, and met with the psychiatrist two more times. He focused on the need to formulate a plan of action to find out if his job was secure and, if not, to find a new one. At the end of the week he felt more relaxed and was determined to take control of the situation. The psychiatrist recommended that he stop the medication, but continue the counseling sessions a few more weeks. Within a month he was working at a new and better job.

In this case, a medication that took action very quickly was prescribed, and combined drug therapy and relatively simple counseling allowed the patient to calm down quickly and get his life under control. Long-term drug therapy was not necessary.

MEDIUM-LENGTH TREATMENT

After the death of her mother, a 46-year-old woman developed a deep depression that continued several months. It quickly became apparent to her family and friends that the depression went beyond normal bereavement. The woman lost twenty pounds, slept only two or three hours a night, complained constantly of muscle pain and headache, and burst into tears almost daily at work. One day she explained to her husband that she was sure she was responsible for her mother's death, even though she fully recognized that her

37

mother had died of an inoperable tumor. A psychiatrist placed the woman on an antidepressant medication. The medication caused side effects for the first two weeks; then the woman's husband noticed she was sleeping through the night and eating again. After four weeks she became noticeably less depressed, stopped complaining of physical ailments, and no longer cried at work. She asked the psychiatrist if she could stop taking the medication. The doctor advised her that the risk of relapse is relatively high during the six months after a depression has resolved. The patient remained on the antidepressant six months and then discontinued use; she has remained free of depression.

Even though a patient may feel better after a few weeks on a medication, there is good evidence that for many psychiatric illnesses, at least six months of treatment is required to avoid relapse.

At the other extreme are situations in which medication should be taken indefinitely. Many such situations exist in other areas of medicine as well. We would not criticize the diabetic for taking insulin for the rest of her life; without it, she would die. Some people with high blood pressure or thyroid conditions take medications for years because the underlying illness can only be controlled, never cured, by the continuous ingestion of drugs.

For some reason, however, many people are horrified by the idea of taking a psychiatric drug for many years. Nevertheless, the next description is of a patient for whom this was clearly necessary.

LONG-TERM TREATMENT

A well-known movie actor in his early thirties was brought to the emergency room in coma after having ingested about one hundred of his friend's sleeping pills. Fortunately, his friend found him lying on the living room floor only a few minutes after he passed out and called an ambulance. His stomach was pumped and he was transferred to the intensive care unit. After more than twenty-four hours he woke up, angry that he had survived his suicide attempt. Friends told the hospital psychiatrist that the actor had been increasingly despondent during the last six months, but that before that, he had exhibited the completely opposite behavior. In fact, prior to becoming depressed the actor had gone through six months of nonstop activity. He had been to five or six auditions a week, stayed up very late almost every night writing screenplays and letters, spent enormous amounts of money on clothes and gifts, and told everybody he was a sure shot for an Academy Award. He irritated even close friends with his nonstop talking and bragging, his drinking, and his quick temper.

The hospital psychiatrist called the actor's parents and learned that he had repeatedly exhibited such highs and lows since he was nineteen years old and that he had one previous serious suicide attempt. The parents revealed that the actor's older brother and one paternal uncle had similar problems. The psychiatrist easily diagnosed manic depression—now known officially as bipolar affective disorder—and recommended treatment with the mood-stabilizing drug lithium. Once it was established that lithium was helpful, the doctor recommended that the patient continue treatment at least five years, because the risk of a relapse, which might lead to a successful suicide attempt, far outweighed the inconvenience of taking the pills every day.

WHEN TO STOP DRUGS QUICKLY

There are three main reasons to stop a medication as soon as possible. First, if a drug does no good, it should be stopped immediately. Patients and doctors should constantly ask themselves and each other what good the medicine is doing. It is wrong to keep taking pills when the symptoms persist.

Second, if a drug causes intolerable side effects it should be stopped. For example, an antidepressant that cures a patient's depression but makes him so sleepy he cannot work or makes it impossible for him to have sex is simply substitution of one set of problems for another. Usually it is possible to find a drug that alleviates a psychiatric problem without producing side effects worse than the illness.

Third, some drugs are habit forming (Table 4) and those drugs

Table 4:

Are Psychiatric Drugs Habit Forming?

DRUG CLASS	EXAMPLE	HABIT FORMING	NOT HABIT FORMING
Antidepressants	Tofranil		X
	Pamelor		
	Prozac		
	Nardil		
Amphetamines	Dexedrine	X	X
Antipsychotics	Thorazine		X
	Mellaril		
	Stelazine		
Lithium	Eskalith		X
	Lithobid		
Antianxiety	Valium	X	
	Librium		
	Ativan	X	
	BuSpar		X
Sleeping pills	Dalmane	X	
	Halcion	X	
	Restoril	X	

become harder to stop the longer they are used. This is especially true of some medications of the benzodiazepine class used to treat anxiety, for example, diazepam (Valium) and clorazepate (Tranxene), and of most sleeping pills. Although these drugs are usually very safe and useful, it is best to discontinue use as soon as possible. Antidepressants (except amphetamines), lithium, and antipsychotic drugs are generally not habit forming.

Prematurely stopping a psychiatric drug often leads to the return of symptoms. Patients with depression or panic attacks, for example, usually need to take the medication at least six months to avoid relapse. Patients with schizophrenia or bipolar affective disorder may need to stay on the drugs the rest of their lives or risk very serious symptoms that necessitate hospitalization. Thus, patients should ask their doctors if they can stop the medication. They should not give in to pressure from others who think that taking drugs reflects a "weakness" or "only covers up the problem" and stop taking the drugs too soon. The goal is to take the drug long enough to control the illness.

GETTING OFF PSYCHIATRIC DRUGS

After you and your doctor decide that you should stop taking a psychiatric drug, one word can usually sum up how to do it: slowly.

With few exceptions it is always best to reduce the dose of a psychiatric drug over several days or even weeks, rather than stop abruptly. Stopping a drug too quickly may produce withdrawal or rebound symptoms.

Many changes occur in the brain and the rest of the body after medications have been taken for a long time. In a sense, the body gets used to the drug and makes changes to accommodate it. If a drug is then withdrawn too quickly, the body may not have enough time to prepare for the change and may, therefore, react in what seems a chaotic way.

For example, some drugs produce "anticholinergic" side effects. These drugs actively inhibit a part of the nervous system called the cholinergic nervous system. If the drug is stopped suddenly, the cholinergic nervous system loses its brakes and may overreact for several days. The patient feels as if he has the flu; there is discomfort, but not danger.

The anticholinergic drugs with which this can be a problem include imipramine (Tofranil), amitriptyline (Elavil), doxepin (Sinequan), nortriptyline (Aventyl), protriptyline (Vivactil), desipramine (Norpramin), maprotiline (Ludiomil), chlomipramine (Anafranil), phenelzine (Nardil), chlorpromazine (Thorazine), thioridazine (Mellaril), loxapine (Loxitane), and perphenazine (Trilafon).

More uncomfortable is what happens if an antianxiety drug like Valium, Ativan, Xanax, Serax, or Librium is suddenly stopped. The whole nervous system may suddenly become very active. The patient develops a withdrawal syndrome with shakiness, anxiety, difficulty sleeping, ringing in the ears, and, although very rarely, convulsions. This is described in more detail in Chapter 8.

The only psychiatric drugs that routinely cause serious withdrawal effects are the stimulant drugs very occasionally prescribed to treat depression that has not responded to other treatment. These drugs include amphetamines (for example, Dexedrine), Ritalin and Cylert. Abrupt cessation of stimulant drugs can cause severe, often suicidal, depression.

The special factors to consider in deciding when to stop antipsychotic medications are discussed in Chapter 10.

In this respect, psychiatric drugs are really no different than other medications. If a person who has taken medication for high blood pressure for many years stops taking it too quickly her blood pressure can shoot way up, even higher than it was before she started taking the drug. After taking thyroid hormone medication for a few weeks, a patient's own thyroid gland may completely shut down and stop producing hormone. Again, if the patient stops the thyroid medication abruptly, his thyroid gland may not have time to start working again, leaving the patient with no thyroid hormone at all.

Except in the case of emergencies or surgery with general anesthesia, there is usually no reason to discontinue a psychiatric drug suddenly. In general, the longer a person has been on medication and the higher the dose, the longer it will take to safely stop it. The doctor usually outlines a schedule for gradual reduction of the dose of the drug, called a tapering schedule, until zero medication is reached. When this is done, there may be slight discomfort, but rarely danger. Withdrawal syndromes usually disappear entirely within two weeks of the last dose.

This is why psychiatrists want patients to tell them every time they change their dose of medication. I always warn patients not to stop a drug suddenly and to call me if they think they want or need to lower the dose.

Many patients taking psychiatric drugs worry about what will happen if they require emergency surgery. Suppose an appendix needs to be removed or a broken bone must be repaired in an operation? There would be no time to stop the psychiatric drug.

There is, fortunately, little need to worry. In these emergency situations, operations can proceed safely. The anesthesiologist will have to work a bit harder to take into account the effects of the psychiatric drug on blood pressure, heart rate, and breathing during the surgery. Sometimes, the anesthesiologist stops the psychiatric drug and administers other medications to prevent drug withdrawal symptoms; at other times, the anesthesiologist continues the psychiatric drug and makes the necessary compensations during the operation. There is now a convincing literature that in emergency situations, even patients taking monoamine oxidase inhibitor antidepressants—which have very important effects on blood pressure—can safely undergo general anesthesia and surgery.

Hospitalization to stop use of psychiatric drugs is rarely needed; however, a very small percentage of psychiatric patients abuse their medication, usually the benzodiazepine antianxiety drugs (for example, Valium and Librium), and take much higher doses than prescribed. These patients often see several different doctors at the same time. Each doctor writes a prescription, thinking he is the patient's only doctor. Patients who abuse benzodiazepines usually have alcohol and other drug abuse problems as well. Patients who take extremely high doses of benzodiazepines, such as 40 or 50 mg a day of Valium or 10 mg a day of Ativan, can still often be tapered off the drug as long as it is done very slowly. Some, however, cannot comply with the tapering regimen and are best hospitalized. This situation is rare and involves less than 1% of patients who are prescribed antianxiety drugs.

Part II

PSYCHIATRIC DRUG REFERENCE GUIDE

7. Drugs Used to Treat Depression   47
8. Drugs Used to Treat Anxiety   117
9. Drugs Used to Treat Manic Depression/Bipolar
   Affective Disorder   175
10. Drugs Used to Treat Schizophrenia   201
11. Sleeping Pills   253
12. Drugs Used to Treat Drug Abuse   285

Chapter 7

Drugs Used to Treat Depression

No one should ever decide to live with depression. In fact, it is now comparatively rare—although unfortunately not rare enough—for a depressed patient to be unable to realize substantial improvement through psychiatric treatment. One of the saddest things a doctor sees is a patient who has suffered from depression for years, believing the situation was "all my fault," "something I just needed to get over," or "the way things are in life, nothing is perfect."

Depression as an illness is extremely common. Good scientific studies indicate that about eight percent (almost one in ten) of Americans will develop depression serious enough to warrant treatment sometime in their lifetime. It is possible, although not certain, that having a parent or a first-degree relative with a history of depression may increase the lifetime risk of suffering a severe depression. Like red hair or blue eyes, various forms of depression, such as manic depression, seem to run in families, and children show a higher risk of inheriting the gene from a parent with strong depressive tendencies. Some, but not all, research studies have indicated that the same may be true of a family history of alcoholism.

Depression is also very serious. This may sound simple, but I once saw an otherwise rather good article titled "Depression: The Common Cold of Psychiatry" in the magazine section of a Sunday newspaper. Although depression may be analogous to the common cold in terms of frequency of occurrence, the two are hardly similar in terms of severity and the headline seriously trivialized the illness. People get over colds with no lasting problems. Depression, on the other hand, can be fatal. The ominous complication of depression is, of course, suicide. Most suicides are committed by people who had a depression that should and could have been diagnosed. In this country, suicide remains a leading cause of death; third among all causes of death for people 25 to 34 years of age and tenth for adults overall. The highest risk group is elderly men, especially those with other medical problems. Teenage suicide is an increasing problem; even children commit suicide. Thus, depression must be taken seriously as a potential killer by patients, their families, and their doctors.

Even when it doesn't result in death, depression is an awful illness. The depressed person feels consistently down, blue, and sad. There is no glimmer of hope and everything that happens seems to be wrong. The patient with depression usually wishes he or she were dead and may voice these feelings, for example "I wouldn't mind if a truck hit me." Appetite, concentration, sleep, and energy are usually grossly altered. In short, to be depressed is often to experience a living hell.

The decision to use drugs to treat depression depends largely on the answers to two questions: Does the patient have a form of depression that is likely to respond to medication? How quickly must the depression be relieved?

DIFFERENT KINDS OF DEPRESSION

There are innumerable systems for classification of depression. Despite popular belief, depression comes in many varieties, with great variation in the associated symptoms. Unfortunately, many of the classification systems used by doctors are not particularly helpful in deciding the best treatment for a particular patient. A number of terms used in the classification of depression are given in Table 5 so that the reader can gain some familiarity with these different systems; however, most of these terms have only limited usefulness.

At present, two classes of depression in which there is a real difference in treatment decisions are *atypical* and *major* depression. Although not without controversy, there is good scientific evidence that these types of depression respond differently to different classes of antidepressants. Two other classifications of depression that are useful in deciding the right treatment are *bipolar* and *psychotic.* Table 6 lists important features of these four different forms of depression.

MAJOR VERSUS ATYPICAL DEPRESSION

The terms *major* and *atypical* are actually poor terms, but they are so ingrained in the psychiatric literature that the use of new words here would probably only increase confusion. The problem is that "major" sounds like "serious," but major depression is not more serious than atypical depression. In fact, some patients with atypical depression are more depressed than those with major depression. "Atypical," on the other hand, sounds like something unusual, but atypical depression may actually be more common in the general population than major depression.

Major depression is depression in which there is almost a complete loss of ability to derive pleasure from anything. Mood is no longer reactive; that is, no one or no event can cheer the patient up, even briefly. Assessing a patient as having a reactive or a nonreactive mood does not imply anything about the cause of the depression. By reactive mood is meant the capacity of the patient to be cheered up.

FEATURES OF MAJOR DEPRESSION

People who compliment a patient with major depression find that their kind words fall on deaf ears. The patient with major depression who suddenly gets good news will somehow attach a negative

49

Table 5:

Some Terms Used to Classify Depression

TERM	DESCRIPTION
Unipolar	Depression that occurs in a person who never experiences manic highs
Bipolar[a]	Depression that occurs in a person who sometimes also experiences manic highs
Reactive	Depression that is supposedly caused by an obvious traumatic life event, like death of a family member or dismissal from a job
Endogenous	Depression that supposedly comes out of the blue, with no obvious cause
Primary	Depression that is unaccompanied by other psychiatric illness
Secondary	Depression that occurs after the onset of another illness, like alcoholism, drug dependency, or medical illness
Postpartum	Depression that occurs in a woman who has recently had a baby; generally the same as major depression
Involutional	Depression that occurs in an elderly person; generally the same as major depression
Atypical[a]	Depression characterized by an ability to be cheered up by some things (see text for a more detailed description of this form of depression)
Major[a]	Depression characterized by an inability to be cheered up
Psychotic[a]	Depression accompanied by hallucinations and/or delusions

[a]Clinically useful terms; see Table 6. *Note:* A person can suffer form *several* forms of depression at the same time.

interpretation to it and never crack a smile. Everything that happens seems only to make these patients feel more guilty, more worried, and sadder.

Along with this loss of mood reactivity and of interest in life, the patient with major depression usually exhibits a characteristic group of symptoms. First, the patient tends to have a sleep disturbance called early morning awakening: although often able to fall asleep without trouble, the patient wakes up very early in the morning and finds himself totally unable to fall asleep. There is loss of appetite, usually leading to some degree of weight loss, and difficulty in concentrating. In trying to read a newspaper article, for example, the patient with major depression may find that he reads and rereads the same paragraph five times and still can't follow the story. This problem can get so bad that the patient appears to have dementia. The lack of concentration and difficulty in remembering exhibited by these people are sometimes called *pseudodementia.*

Major depression tends to occur in discrete episodes. The patient is usually well and then slowly begins to show signs of depressed mood, loss of interest in life, and the other symptoms already described. Suicide is always a risk in these patients. An example of a patient suffering from major depression follows:

Mr. Thomas (not his real name) is a very successful 55-year-old businessman, who built his small investment company into a multimillion dollar business. He has been happily married for almost 30 years and has three children who are happy and love him. About two months after his last birthday, Mr. Thomas began complaining of insomnia; he would wake up at three or four in the morning and then toss and turn without returning to sleep until the alarm clock went off. He began to lose weight and suffered from various aches and pains including headaches and stomachaches. His family doctor performed a thorough physical examination and blood tests; Mr. Thomas was the picture of physical health. Then, he started to make mistakes at work, looked dreary and distracted to his co-workers, and lacked energy. His wife noticed that his usually robust sex drive had dwindled to complete lack of interest and that nothing, includ-

Table 6

Features of Different Forms of Depression

	MAJOR	ATYPICAL
Reactive Mood	No	Yes
Course	Episodic	Chronic
Worst time of day	Morning	Evening
Appetite	Decreased	Increased
Sleep	Disturbed (early morning awakening)	Increased
Energy	Decreased	Very decreased
Psychotic signs	No	Very rarely
Anxiety symptoms	Common	Common, especially panic attacks
Hospitalization required	Sometimes	Occasionally
Effective treatments	Cyclic antidepressants, electroconvulsant therapy	Monoamine oxidase inhibitors, Prozac, psychotherapy

ing visits from his children, favorable financial news, and his favorite hobbies, seemed to cheer him up.

One day, Mr. Thomas let slip to his wife "I wonder how much longer I'll be able to go on?" He explained to her that he knew he was a "fraud" as a businessman, an inadequate husband and father, and a boring person. After much persuasion and pleading, Mr. Thomas was convinced to see a psychiatrist who diagnosed major depressive disorder and recommended an antidepressant. Four weeks later, Mr. Thomas was again sleeping through the night, his appetite returned to normal, and he was noticeably more interested in life and more energetic.

BIPOLAR	PSYCHOTIC
No	No
Episodic	Episodic
Morning	Morning
Increased or decreased	Decreased
Increased or decreased	Decreased
Extremely decreased	Decreased but agitated
Sometimes	Always
Common	Common
Often	Usually
Lithium, thyroid hormone, antidepressants	Cyclic antidepressants plus antipsychotic or electroconvulsant therapy

FEATURES OF PSYCHOTIC DEPRESSION

Sometimes, major depression can become so severe that the patient begins to show signs of psychosis. That is, the patient exhibits symptoms otherwise associated with diseases such as schizophrenia in which there is a major break with reality. So-called psychotic depression involves hallucinations—hearing or seeing things that are not really there—or delusions—developing false ideas in which the patient believes. A psychotically depressed patient may hear a voice telling him that he is a bad person, has committed terrible crimes, or should die. To the patient these voices sound real, and he is sometimes surprised that no one else can hear them.

In typical delusions, a psychotically depressed patient may believe that she has an incurable disease even though all medical tests are normal, that she has caused a terrible event like an automobile crash or a war, or that someone close to her has died even though the person is really alive. It is important to emphasize that these hallucinations and delusions are all depressing in nature and quality; psychotically depressed patients do not hear friendly or encouraging voices talking to them and they do not believe they are kings or presidents or millionaires.

Studies and clinical practice have indicated that major depression responds best to antidepressants of the *cyclic* class, described later in this chapter, and to electroconvulsive therapy discussed at the end of this chapter. When psychotic features coexist with major depression, an antipsychotic medication (for example, Thorazine and Haldol) is often added to the cyclic antidepressant or electroconvulsive therapy is given. Unless there is an urgent need to resolve the depression immediately, such as an extreme suicide threat or severe weight loss, most psychiatrists treat the patient with major depression with a tricyclic antidepressants first. If this treatment fails, electroconvulsive therapy may be considered.

FEATURES OF BIPOLAR DEPRESSION

An episode of what seems to be major depression may actually be part of the illness now called *bipolar affective disorder.* Bipolar patients suffer from recurrent cycles of depression and mania. When they are depressed, they have most of the features of major depression, although sometimes they overeat and oversleep instead of experience insomnia and loss of appetite. The suicide rate during bipolar depression is extremely high. In addition to treatment with an antidepressant, patients with bipolar depression should usually receive lithium. Such treatment will help resolve the current depression and, more importantly, will greatly reduce the risk of experiencing future depressions and manic episodes.

It is important to distinguish bipolar or psychotic depression from major depression. Bipolar depression usually requires the institution of lithium therapy; psychotic depression requires addition of antipsychotic medication to the antidepressant. Bipolar affective disorder and its treatment are described in more detail in Chapter 9.

FEATURES OF ATYPICAL DEPRESSION

Patients with atypical depression maintain a reactive mood throughout their depression. Again, this has nothing to do with how deeply depressed they may feel; their suffering is real. Rather, from time to time something good will happen that temporarily cheers the patient up to the point that she actually experiences pleasure. Unless this illness is treated, however, the depression usually returns all too quickly.

Many of the vegetative signs observed in major depression are reversed in atypical depression. Patients with atypical depression tend to overeat and oversleep. Some say they develop a particular craving for sweet food; others say they eat more because it seems to calm them down. Weight gain is not uncommon with this group. The patient with atypical depression often has no trouble falling asleep or staying asleep; in fact, they sleep whenever they can, sometimes twelve to fourteen hours a day, including multiple naps. The patient may explain the sleeping as his only escape from feeling depressed.

Along with this oversleeping come a very pronounced decrease in energy and constant complaints of fatigue and lack of motivation. The patient with major depression usually feels worst in the morning; the patient with atypical depression finds the end of the day the hardest part.

As already described, the patient with major depression seems oblivious to what is going on in the world. Nobody or nothing can make any difference in the relentlessly depressed mood. Atypical depression is often the complete opposite. The patient feels as if he or she is entirely under the influence of external events. Everything that even hints of criticism or rejection immediately makes the patient feel horribly depressed and creates a desire to go to bed or even die. Praise and attention can temporarily lift the patient's mood, which is why I think this illness is particularly common in performers who have the unique opportunity to get on stage, receive applause, and temporarily get better.

In his ground-breaking work on classifying depression, Donald F. Klein, M.D., has likened the life of a patient with atypical depression to being on a roller coaster. Getting attention is like taking a stimulant drug such as amphetamine or cocaine; there is a temporary high almost like euphoria, followed by a deep crash when the effect of the applause wears off. In fact, I have noted that many patients with atypical depression have used amphetamines or cocaine in the past and seem to get particular mood benefit from their use.

Again, unlike the discrete episodic nature of major depression, atypical depression seems to last for years and sometimes, if untreated, for a lifetime. Patients may tell the doctor they cannot remember a time in their life, going back to adolescence, when they did not feel depressed. Here is an example of a patient with atypical depression:

Dr. Marjorie Cross is a 34-year-old dermatologist with a successful practice and many hobbies and interests. She is highly regarded as a competent and caring doctor. For as long as she can remember, however, she has been plagued by feeling "blue," lonely, and abandoned for periods lasting a few days to a few months. Many times she has contemplated talking to a professional person about this, but usually something has occurred to cheer her up. Most recently, for example, she became very depressed when a man she had been dating for three months decided to end their relationship. After hearing the news she stayed in bed an entire weekend, getting up only to binge on chocolate ice cream and peanut butter sandwiches. She alternated between crying and feeling murderously angry. Although she was able to go to work on Monday morning, she felt tired and listless. All of this changed, however, when a man she had met a few months before at a party called and asked her to dinner. A few hours later her mood was much better and she felt very energetic again.

The reason for spending so much time in making this distinction between major and atypical depression is the difference in drug responsivity of the two syndromes. Cyclic antidepressant drugs may sometimes produce an improvement in patients with atypical depression, but clinical experience and some very good studies, especially by my colleague Frederick Quitkin, show that atypical depression responds best to the class of antidepressants called monoamine oxidase inhibitors (MAOIs), (described on later in this chapter). The new antidepressant Prozac may also be particularly effective for atypical depression. In a clear-cut case of atypical depression, many psychiatrists start the patient immediately on an MAOI or Prozac, rather than a cyclic antidepressant. Thus, the distinction between types of depression makes an important difference in the treatment plan.

Of course, no single individual's illness in any branch of clinical medicine is ever entirely pure. A patient with major depression may eat too much or may not have that much trouble sleeping, or a patient with atypical depression may feel worse in the morning than in the evening or actually lose his/her appetite. It is not uncommon for a person with a long history of atypical depression to develop major depression at some point. This is sometimes called "double depression." Hence, the differential diagnosis between the two, and consequently the decision about drug choice, is not always straightforward. A very careful history and description of symptoms and course of illness are clearly required.

SEVERITY OF DEPRESSION

The second issue in deciding whether drug treatment is necessary for depression—how quickly must the depression be resolved—is really one of severity. A person who has been depressed for more than two weeks, does not eat, cannot sleep beyond three in the morning, and constantly thinks of committing suicide should be treated with medication immediately. Remember that antidepressant medications usually work after four weeks, sometimes sooner, whereas psychotherapies may take months or longer, so it is impor-

57

tant not to delay the start of treatment too long. On the other hand, a person who has an occasional bad day and once in a while gets into a bad mood probably won't respond to antidepressants and doesn't need them anyway. Patients who have tried various forms of psychotherapy and still feel depressed should seek consultation from a psychiatrist.

There are two basic rules of thumb. First, if a depression lasts longer than two weeks, interferes with the ability to function in school or work, and disturbs vegetative functions like sleeping and eating, then drug treatment should be considered. Second, even when depression is clearly the product of some adverse life event, like loss of a job, death of a family member, or divorce, if mood does not improve with reassurance and support and persists over time, drug treatment should be considered. Studies have shown over and over again that these so-called "reactive depressions" actually do respond to antidepressants. Finally, whenever a patient feels suicidal there should be a psychopharmacologic consultation.

STEPS INVOLVED IN GETTING TREATMENT

Now let us suppose you and your doctor have decided that drug treatment of depression is a good idea. Here is what needs to be done.

1. Your psychiatrist should establish the type(s) of depression you are suffering from (major, bipolar, psychotic, atypical).

2. All possible medical causes of depression should be ruled out. Many medical conditions can masquerade as depression, including thyroid problems, certain types of cancer, neurological problems like small strokes that otherwise go unrecognized, AIDS, and diseases of the immune system such as lupus. Some medications used to treat medical problems are also known to cause depression, for example, many drugs used to treat high blood pressure and steroid

drugs like prednisone. Medical illness is more likely to be the cause of depression in elderly patients. A careful medical history is always needed and sometimes a physical examination and laboratory tests are advisable. Some psychiatrists do this themselves; others request a consultation with an internist or family practitioner. Remember, however, that most depressed patients do not have underlying medical problems. It is wrong to spend months undergoing complex medical tests to find the cause of depression. This only delays effective treatment.

3. Blood tests, x-rays, or other medical tests may be necessary either to help confirm that an underlying medical problem is causing your depression or that antidepressants are safe for you to take.

4. You and your doctor should discuss the exact drug recommended—the dose, the side effects, and when you should expect to start feeling better.

5. You should discuss with the psychiatrist whether medication alone is the recommended treatment or if some form of psychotherapy along with the drugs will be beneficial. Make sure you are satisfied the doctor has thought about this carefully and given you a recommendation that makes sense for your own personal situation.

6. Make another appointment to see the doctor in about a week so your progress can be checked. Some suggested treatment plans for four different forms of depression are shown in Tables 7 to 10. Please remember that these are only blueprints: the treatment you need can only be decided on by you and your doctor.

REVIEW OF ANTIDEPRESSANTS

We are now ready to review all of the drugs used in the treatment of depression. These are divided into four classes: cyclic antidepressants, monoamine oxidase inhibitors, stimulants, and the "new" antidepressants (Table 11).

59

Table 7:

Suggested Treatment Plan for Major Depression

1. Rule out underlying medical illnesses that may be causing depression.
2. If over 50 years old, have an electrocardiogram.
3. Begin a cyclic antidepressant: imipramine or desipramine are good choices to start with for younger patients; nortriptyline is a good start for people over 65.
4. Start at a low dose and gradually increase the dose to the therapeutic level.
5. Wait four to six weeks for a response. If there is no response, consider adding lithium or thyroid hormone.

Table 8:

Suggested Treatment Plan for Bipolar Depression

1. Rule out underlying medical illnesses that may be causing depression.
2. Carefully evaluate for suicide potential; hospitalize if necessary.
3. Begin lithium and cyclic antidepressant (imipramine, desipramine, and nortriptyline are all reasonable choices).
4. Watch for development of signs of mania.
5. Stop the cyclic antidepressant as soon as the depression resolves, but remain on lithium indefinitely to prevent future depressions and manic episodes.

Table 9:

Suggested Treatment Plan for Psychotic Depression

1. Rule out underlying medical illnesses that may be causing depression.
2. Carefully evaluate for suicide potential; hospitalization often is advised.
3. Begin a cyclic antidepressant (imipramine, desipramine, and nortriptyline are good choices) and an antipsychotic drug (Trilafon, Haldol, or Stelazine)
4. Wait four to six weeks for a response. Stop the antipsychotic drug when the hallucinations and delusions are completely resolved.
5. If there is no response, consider electroconvulsive therapy.

Table 10:

Suggested Treatment Plan for Atypical Depression

1. Rule out underlying medical illnesses that may be causing depression.
2. Begin Prozac or a monoamine oxidase inhibitor (Nardil or Parnate).
3. Start at a low dose and gradually increase the dose to the therapeutic level.
4. Consider psychotherapy in addition to medication.

Table 11:

Checklist for Antidepressants

I. Cyclic Antidepressants

DRUG	USE	ANTICHOLINERGIC[a]	SEDATIVE	INSOMNIA	WEIGHT GAIN	DIZZINESS[b]
Tofranil	MD,PD,BD[c]	XX[d]	X	X	XX	XX
Norpramin, Pertofrane	MD,PD,BD	X	—	X	X	XX
Elavil	MD,PD,BD	XXX	XX	—	XX	XX
Pamelor	MD,PD,BD	X	X	X	X	X
Sinequan, Adapin	MD	XX	XX	—	XX	XX
Surmontil	MD	XX	XX	—	XX	XX
Vivactil	MD,AD	XXX	—	XX	—	X
Ludiomil	MD	X	XX	—	X	X

Table 11, *continued*

DRUG	USE	ANTICHOLINERGIC[a]	SEDATIVE	INSOMNIA	WEIGHT GAIN	DIZZINESS[b]
II. Monoamine Oxidase Inhibitors						
Nardil	AD	X	X	X	XXX	XXX
Parnate	AD	—	—	XX	—	XXX
Marplan	AD	X	X	X	XX	XXX
Eutonyl	AD	X	X	X	XX	XXX
III. New Antidepressants						
Prozac	MD,AD	—	—	XX	—	—
Desyrel	MD	—	XX	—	—	XX
Asendin	MD	—	—	XX	—	—
Welbutrin	MD,BD	—	—	XX	—	—

Table 11, continued

DRUG	USE	ANTICHOLINERGIC[a]	SEDATIVE	INSOMNIA	WEIGHT GAIN	DIZZINESS[b]
IV. Stimulants						
Dexedrine	AD	—	—	XX	—	—
Ritalin	AD	—	—	XX	—	

[a]Anticholinergic side effects are mainly dry mouth, constipation, blurry vision, and difficulty urinating.
[b]Refers to the drug's capacity to cause dizziness by lowering blood pressure.
[c]MD, major depression; BD, bipolar depression; PD, psychotic depression; AD, atypical depression.
[d]X, mild; XX, moderate; XXX, a great deal; —, none or almost none.

64

CYCLIC ANTIDEPRESSANTS

IMIPRAMINE

Brand Names: Tofranil, Janimine, others.

Used for: Mostly major depression. Also some of the anxiety disorders (see Chapter 8). In children, imipramine is used to treat bedwetting (enuresis).

Do Not Use if: You have narrow-angle glaucoma, you have certain abnormal heart rhythms (your doctor will tell you if you have these), or your prostate gland is very enlarged.

Tests to Take First: You may need an electrocardiogram first, especially if you are over age 50.

Tests to Take While You Are on It: A blood test can tell how much of the drug is actually getting into your body. Called an imipramine level, this test is necessary only if you are not responding to the usual dose of the drug and your doctor is considering an increase in dose.

Usual Dose: Will probably start between 25 and 75 mg a day and build up to 100 to 200 mg. Sometimes, psychiatrists prescribe 300 mg daily or more as long as side effects are not a problem. You should probably have an electrocardiogram before taking more than 300 mg. The entire day's medication can be taken in a single dose at bedtime.

How Long Until It Works: Usually after about four weeks of taking the drug daily. Sometimes, an effect is seen as early as two weeks; other times, it takes as long as six weeks. Usually, sleep and appetite return to normal before the actual depressed mood returns.

Common Side Effects: The following effects occur in 10% or more of patients who take Tofranil: dry mouth, constipation, blurry vision, difficulty urinating, increased sensitivity to the sun, dizziness after standing up quickly, weight gain, increased sweating, drowsiness.

Less Common Side Effects: Confusion, agitation, memory impairment, nausea, drowsiness.

What to Do About Side Effects: (1) Dry mouth—don't suck on hard candies containing sugar as you will ruin your teeth; try sugarless hard candies or mouthwash. (2) Constipation—drink at least six glasses of water or juice daily. Laxatives may be prescribed. (3) Blurry vision—normal vision usually returns in a couple of weeks, but a change in eyeglass prescription can help. (4) Difficulty urinating—this problem is greater in men than women and can become a serious problem in older men; usually it is only annoying. The drug bethanechol (Urecholine) can be prescribed to counteract this effect. (5) Increased sensitivity to the sun—use very good suntan lotion, at least No. 15, when out in the sun. You should do this even if you aren't taking imipramine. (6) Dizziness after standing up quickly—this is caused by a brief drop in blood pressure. The best remedy is to sit down and get up slowly. In elderly people this side effect can be more serious and for that reason imipramine is not always the best antidepressant for people over age 65. (7) Weight gain—this can range from just a few pounds to twenty or more pounds. No one knows why imipramine does this and not a lot can be done except to diet. Severe weight gain is sometimes a reason to switch to a different antidepressant. (8) Drowsiness— taking the whole dose at night, right before bedtime, minimizes daytime sleepiness. (9) Less common side effects—these are generally only a problem in elderly people, in whom confusion, agitation, and memory impairment may necessitate switching to another drug. For younger patients these side effects are rarely of concern. (See Table 13 for a summary of the common side effects of cyclic antidepressants and remedies.)

If It Doesn't Work: After four to six weeks at a good dose (at least 200 mg), the doctor may first add another drug to try to increase imipramine's effectiveness. The two used most often are thyroid hormone and lithium. If this doesn't work the doctor will probably recommend switching to another antidepressant.

If It Does Work: Once the depression is lifted it is usually recommended to keep taking the medication for six months, at which time the dose is reduced and stopped over about two weeks. You should see your doctor about once a month for medication management, more often if there are other complications. Tofranil should be tapered rather than abruptly stopped to avoid withdrawal symptoms (similar to those of flu); however, Tofranil is not addictive and is easy to stop.

Cost: Brand, 62 cents/50-mg pill. Generic, 5 cents/50-mg pill.

Special Comments: Imipramine was the first tricyclic (meaning "three-ringed") antidepressant introduced in the United States. It is a tried and true drug that is very effective in relieving major depression. It has relatively more side effects than some of the other drugs discussed here, but remains the "gold standard" against which other antidepressants are usually judged.

DESIPRAMINE

Brand Names: Norpramin, Pertofrane.
Used for: Major depression.
Do Not Use if: You have narrow-angle glaucoma or certain abnormal heart rhythms (your doctor will tell you if you have these).
Tests to Take First: You may need an electrocardiogram first, especially if you are over age 50.
Tests to Take While You Are on It: A blood test can tell how much of the drug is actually getting into your body. Called a desipramine level, this test is necessary only if you are not responding to the usual dose of the drug and your doctor is considering an increase in dose.
Usual Dose: Usually starts at 25 to 75 mg a day and is increased over one to two weeks to about 200 mg. Doses up to 300 mg are often administered and occasionally doctors prescribe more than 300 mg. The entire day's medication can be taken in one dose at night.
How Long Until It Works: Usually after about four weeks of taking the drug daily. Sometimes an effect may be seen as early as two weeks and other times it takes as long as six weeks. Usually, sleep and appetite return to normal before the actual depressed mood returns.
Common Side Effects: Dry mouth, constipation, difficulty urinating, blurry vision, increased sensitivity to the sun, weight gain, increased sweating, dizziness after standing up quickly. Side effects occur less frequently with desipramine than with imipramine.
Less Common Side Effects: Confusion, agitation, memory impairment, nausea. These side effects are the same as those for imipramine, although less likely to occur.
What to Do About Side Effects: (1) Dry mouth—don't suck on hard candies containing sugar as you will ruin your teeth; try sugarless hard candies or mouthwash. (2) Constipation—drink at least six glasses of water or juice daily. Laxatives may be prescribed. (3)

Blurry vision—normal vision usually returns in a couple of weeks, but a change in eyeglass prescription can help. (4) Difficulty urinating—this problem is greater in men than women and can become a serious problem in older men. Usually it is only annoying. The drug bethanechol (Urecholine) can be prescribed to counteract this effect. (5) Increased sensitivity to the sun—use very good suntan lotion, at least No. 15, when out in the sun. You should do this even if you aren't taking desipramine. (6) Dizziness after standing up quickly—this is caused by a brief drop in blood pressure. The best remedy is to sit down and get up slowly. In elderly people this side effect can be more serious and for that reason desipramine is not always the best antidepressant for people over age 65. (7) Weight gain—this can range from just a few pounds to twenty or more pounds. No one knows why desipramine does this and not a lot can be done except to diet. Severe weight gain is sometimes a reason to switch to a different antidepressant. (8) Less common side effects—these are generally only a problem in elderly people, in whom confusion, agitation, and memory impairment may necessitate switching to another drug. For younger patients these side effects are rarely of concern.

If It Doesn't Work: After four to six weeks at a good dose (at least 200 mg), the doctor may first try adding another drug to try to increase desipramine's effectiveness. The two most often used are thyroid hormone and lithium. If this doesn't work the doctor will probably recommend switching to another antidepressant.

If It Does Work: Once the depression is lifted it is usually recommended to keep taking the medication for six months, at which time it is reduced and stopped over about two weeks. You should see your doctor about once a month for medication management, more often if there are other complications. It is best to taper desipramine instead of abruptly stopping, but withdrawal symptoms are usually not a problem and it is easy to get off the drug.

Cost: Brand, 85 cents/50-mg pill. Generic, 35 cents/50-mg pill.

Special Comments: Desipramine is actually a derivative of imipramine. In fact, the body naturally turns imipramine into desipramine. Desipramine generally has milder side effects than imipramine, especially with respect to dry mouth, constipation, difficulty urinating, and blurry vision. For that reason, many clinicians and patients prefer it to imipramine. Desipramine has different chemical effects on the brain than imipramine and for that reason some psychiatrists believe it is less effective in some circumstances than imipramine. The choice between imipramine and desipramine is often a tossup.

AMITRIPTYLINE

Brand Names: Elavil, Endep, others.

Used for: Major depression. Control of certain kinds of chronic pain.

Do Not Use if: You have narrow-angle glaucoma, you have a very enlarged prostate, or you have certain abnormal heart rhythms (your doctor will determine if this is an important consideration for you).

Tests to Take First: You may need an electrocardiogram first, especially if you are over age 50.

Tests to Take While You Are on It: None at present, but blood level monitoring similar to that used with imipramine is now being developed.

Usual Dose: Starts at 25 to 75 mg daily and is raised over one to two weeks to about 200 mg. Doses of 300 mg are often given and occasionally doctors prescribe higher doses. The entire day's medication can be taken in one dose at bedtime.

How Long Until It Works: Elavil is very sedating so a depressed patient with insomnia will experience an improvement in sleep after a day or two. The antidepressant effect takes two to six weeks, with appetite improving before alleviation of the depressed mood.

Common Side Effects: The following effects occur in at least 10% of patients who take Elavil: dry mouth, constipation, blurry vision, difficulty urinating, increased sensitivity to the sun, dizziness after standing up quickly, weight gain, sleepiness, increased sweating.

Less Common Side Effects: Confusion, agitation, memory impairment, and nausea are generally only a problem in elderly people who take Elavil. In older people these side effects may necessitate switching to another drug. For younger patients these side effects are rarely of concern.

What to Do About Side Effects: (1) Dry mouth—don't suck on hard candies containing sugar as you will ruin your teeth; try sugarless hard candies or mouthwash. (2) Constipation—drink at least six glasses of water or juice daily. Laxatives may be prescribed. (3) Blurry vision—normal vision usually returns in a couple of weeks, but a change in eyeglass prescription can help. (4) Difficulty urinating—this problem is greater in men than women and can become a serious problem in older men. Usually it is only annoying. The drug bethanechol (Urecholine) can be prescribed to counteract this effect. (5) Increased sensitivity to the sun—use very good sun tan lotion, at least No. 15, when out in the sun. You should do this even if you aren't taking Elavil. (6) Dizziness after standing up quickly—this is caused by a brief drop in blood pressure. The best remedy is to sit down and get up slowly. In elderly people this side effect can be more serious and for that reason amitriptyline is not always the best antidepressant for people over age 65. (7) Weight gain—this can range from just a few pounds to twenty or more pounds. No one knows why Elavil does this and not a lot can be done except to diet. Severe weight gain is sometimes a reason to switch to a different antidepressant. (8) Sleepiness or sedation—the best approach is to take the medication as close to bedtime as possible; however, many patients still complain of feeling drowsy during the day and this sometimes limits the drug's usefulness.

If It Doesn't Work: After four to six weeks at a good dose (at least 200 mg), the doctor may first try adding another drug to try to increase Elavil's effectiveness. The two most often used are thyroid hormone and lithium. If this doesn't work the doctor will probably recommend switching to another antidepressant.

If It Does Work: Once the depression is lifted it is usually recommended to keep taking the medication for six months, at which time it is reduced and stopped over about two weeks. You should see your doctor about once a month for medication management, more often if there are other complications. Elavil should be tapered rather than abruptly stopped to avoid withdrawal symptoms (flulike symptoms); however, it is relatively easy to withdraw from this drug.

Cost: Brand, 59 cents/50-mg pill. Generic, 3 cents/50-mg pill.

Special Comments: The main difference between imipramine and Elavil is that Elavil has more side effects. It causes more dry mouth, constipation, blurry vision, and difficulty urinating than either imipramine or desipramine, and, unlike those two drugs, it makes patients feel sleepy. For patients with extreme agitation the sedating property of Elavil is sometimes desirable, but for the most part Elavil is not the drug of first choice for depressed patients who want to continue working and concentrating during the day.

NORTRIPTYLINE

Brand Names: Pamelor.
Used for: Major depression.
Do Not Use if: You have narrow-angle glaucoma, you have certain heart rhythm irregularities that can be easily detected with a standard electrocardiogram (ECG), or you have a very enlarged prostate gland.
Tests to Take First: Your doctor may want you to have an ECG before starting the medication, especially if you are over 50 years old.
Tests to Take While You Are on It: In contrast to imipramine, desipramine, Elavil, and almost every other antidepressant, blood tests to determine the amount or level of nortriptyline in you are almost always required. The reason is that nortriptyline is effective only when the amount of drug in the blood is maintained within a narrow range. If there is too little or too much, the drug will simply not work against depression. So the doctor usually requests a blood level a few weeks after you start taking nortriptyline to make sure that the dose is right. This has nothing to do with side effect control.
Usual Dose: Doses of nortriptyline are lower than those of imipramine, desipramine, and Elavil. The starting dose is between 10 and 25 mg and the usual therapeutic dose ranges from as low as 50 to 75 mg to as high as 150 mg. The blood level of the drug determines the dose the patient should take. The entire day's medication can be taken in a single dose at bedtime.
How Long Until It Works: On average, four weeks, but sometimes as quickly as two weeks. Don't give up if it takes a little longer. Six weeks is long enough to know whether it will help.
Common Side Effects: Dry mouth occurs in about 20% of people who take nortriptyline. Unlike imipramine, desipramine, and Elavil, nortriptyline does not seem to lower blood pressure much when a

person rises quickly. Although this effect usually poses no problem for younger people, blood pressure drops can sometimes cause the elderly to pass out and fall. A few elderly people have sustained hip fractures while on cyclic antidepressants. Because this side effect occurs less often with nortriptyline, it is often recommended as the best cyclic antidepressant for elderly patients. Difficulty urinating, constipation, and blurry vision occur in 10% or less of patients who take nortriptyline. Weight gain and increased sensitivity to the sun can also occur.

Less Common Side Effects: Confusion, agitation, memory impairment, nausea. These side effects are the same as those for imipramine, although less likely to occur.

What to Do About Side Effects: (1) Dry mouth—don't suck on hard candies containing sugar as you will ruin your teeth; try sugarless hard candies or mouthwash. (2) Constipation—drink at least six glasses of water or juice daily. Laxatives may be prescribed. (3) Blurry vision—normal vision usually returns in a couple of weeks, but a change in eyeglass prescription can help. (4) Difficulty urinating—this problem is greater in men than women and can become a serious problem in older men. Usually it is only annoying. The drug bethanechol (Urecholine) can be prescribed to counteract this effect. (5) Increased sensitivity to the sun—use very good suntan lotion, at least No. 15, when out in the sun. You should do this even if you aren't taking nortriptyline. (6) Dizziness after standing up quickly—this is caused by a brief drop in blood pressure. The best remedy is to sit down and get up slowly. (7) Weight gain—this ranges from just a few pounds to twenty or more pounds. No one knows why nortriptyline does this and not a lot can be done except to diet. Severe weight gain is sometimes a reason to switch to a different antidepressant. (8) Less common side effects—these are generally only a problem in elderly people, in whom confusion, agitation, and memory impairment may necessitate switching to another drug. For younger patients these side effects are rarely of concern.

If It Doesn't Work: After four to six weeks at a therapeutic blood level, the doctor may first add another drug to try to increase nortriptyline's effectiveness. The two most often used are thyroid hormone and lithium. If this doesn't work the doctor will probably recommend switching to another antidepressant.

If It Does Work: Once the depression is lifted it is usually recommended to keep taking the medication for six months, at which time it is reduced and stopped over about two weeks. You should see your doctor about once a month for medication management, more often if there are other complications. Nortriptyline should be tapered instead of abruptly stopped to avoid withdrawal symptoms (flulike symptoms); however, nortriptyline causes very mild withdrawal and it is very easy to stop use.

Cost: Brand, 60 cents/25-mg pill. Generic, not available.

Special Comments: Nortriptyline is the drug of choice for elderly people with major depression who do not have certain specific heart problems. The need to get blood levels a few times during treatment is only a minor inconvenience. Because the effective dose is lower for nortriptyline than for some of the other cyclic antidepressants, even younger people sometimes find it has less side effects.

DOXEPIN

Brand Names: Sinequan, Adapin.

Used for: Major depression.

Do Not Use if: You have narrow-angle glaucoma, you have a very enlarged prostate, you have certain heart rhythm abnormalities (your doctor will determine if this is an important consideration for you).

Tests to Take First: You may need an electrocardiogram first, especially if you are over age 50.

Tests to Take While You Are on It: None at present.

Usual Dose: Starts at 25 to 75 mg daily and is raised over one to two weeks to about 200 mg. Doses of 300 mg are often given and occasionally doctors will prescribe even higher doses. The entire day's medication can be given as a single dose at bedtime.

How Long Until It Works: Sinequan is very sedating so a depressed patient with insomnia will experience improved sleep after a day or

Table 12.

Common Side Effects of Cyclic Antidepressants

SIDE EFFECT	SPECIAL PRECAUTIONS	POSSIBLE REMEDIES
Dry mouth[a]	Can cause tooth decay	Suck on sugarless hard candies, use mouthwash
Constipation[a]	Rarely causes complete inability to move bowels	Increase fluid intake, eat raw bran, take laxatives
Difficulty urinating[a]	Dangerous for men with enlarged prostates	Physician may add the drug bethanechol (Urecholine)
Blurry vision[a]	Not dangerous, but these drugs should never be given to patients with narrow-angle glaucoma	Usually transient, may require glasses
Increased sensitivity to sun	Can lead to severe sunburn	Use sunblock when outside in strong sunlight
Increased sweating	Mild dehydration in very hot weather	Increase fluid intake in warm weather

Table 12, *continued*

SIDE EFFECT	SPECIAL PRECAUTIONS	POSSIBLE REMEDIES
Increased heart rate	Usually not a problem	Physician may want to check electro-cardiogram
Weight gain	Usually only a few pounds but can be more	Try to restrict calories when on the drug

[a]These are called "anticholinergic" side effects.

two. The antidepressant effect takes two to six weeks, with appetite improving before alleviation of the depressed mood.

Common Side Effects: Dry mouth, constipation, blurry vision, difficulty urinating, increased sensitivity to the sun, dizziness after standing up quickly, weight gain, sleepiness, increased sweating.

Less Common Side Effects: Confusion, agitation, memory impairment, nausea. Generally only a problem in elderly people, in whom these side effects may necessitate switching to another drug. For younger patients these side effects are rarely of concern.

What to Do About Side Effects: (1) Dry mouth—don't suck on hard candies containing sugar as you will ruin your teeth; try sugarless hard candies or mouthwash. (2) Constipation—drink at least six glasses of water or juice daily. Laxatives may be prescribed. (3) Blurry vision—normal vision usually returns in a couple of weeks, but a change in eyeglass prescription can help. (4) Difficulty urinating—this problem is greater in men than women and can become a serious problem in older men. Usually it is only annoying. The drug bethanechol (Urecholine) can be prescribed to counteract this effect. (5) Increased sensitivity to the sun—use very good suntan lotion, at least No. 15, when out in the sun. You should do this even if you aren't taking doxepin. (6) Dizziness after standing up quickly—this is caused by a brief drop in blood pressure. The best remedy is to sit down and get up slowly. In elderly people this side effect can be more serious and for that reason doxepin is not always the best antidepressant for people over age 65. (7) Weight gain—this ranges from just a few pounds to twenty or more pounds. No one knows why doxepin does this and not a lot can be done except to diet. Severe weight gain is sometimes a reason to switch to a different antidepressant. (8) Sleepiness or sedation—the best approach is to take the medication as close to bedtime as possible; however, many patients still complain of feeling drowsy during the day and this sometimes limits the drug's usefulness.

If It Doesn't Work: Switch to a different antidepressant (see Special Comments).

If It Does Work: Once the depression is lifted it is usually recommended to keep taking the medication for six months, at which time it is reduced and stopped over about two weeks. You should see your doctor about once a month for medication management, more often if there are other complications.

Cost: Brand, 48 cents/50-mg pill. Generic, 18 cents/50-mg pill.

Special Comments: Doxepin has an interesting history. It was originally advertised as having fewer important side effects than other cyclic antidepressants and was supposed to be especially gentle on the heart. This made it a very popular antidepressant. We now know that the heart-related side effects of cyclic antidepressants are easy to predict by getting an electrocardiogram and are not generally a problem. It turns out that doxepin really has no fewer heart-related side effects than the other cyclic antidepressants but it does cause sedation, dizziness after standing quickly, and dry mouth. Many psychiatrists also insist it doesn't work all that well against depression. Consequently, it has fallen a great deal out of favor in recent years. Imipramine, desipramine, amitriptyline, and nortriptyline are better choices.

TRIMIPRAMINE

Brand Name: Surmontil.
Used for: Major depression.
Do Not Use if: You have narrow-angle glaucoma, you have certain abnormal heart rhythms (your doctor will be able to tell you if you

have these), your prostate gland is very enlarged, or you have a history of seizures (epilepsy).

Tests to Take First: You may need an electrocardiogram first, especially if you are over age 50.

Tests to Take While You Are on It: None required.

Usual Dose: Probably starts between 25 and 75 mg daily and builds up to 100 to 200 mg. Sometimes psychiatrists prescribe 300 mg or more daily as long as side effects are not a problem. You should probably have an electrocardiogram before taking doses greater than 300 mg.

How Long Until It Works: Usually after about four weeks of taking the drug daily. Sometimes an effect may be seen as early as two weeks; at other times, it takes as long as six weeks. Usually, sleep and appetite return to normal before alleviation of the depressed mood.

Common Side Effects: Dry mouth, constipation, blurry vision, difficulty urinating, increased sensitivity to the sun, dizziness after standing up quickly, weight gain, increased sweating, drowsiness.

Less Common Side Effects: Confusion, agitation, memory impairment, nausea.

What to Do About Side Effects: (1) Dry mouth—don't suck on hard candies containing sugar as you will ruin your teeth; try sugarless hard candies or mouthwash. (2) Constipation—drink at least six glasses of water or juice daily. Laxatives may be prescribed. (3) Blurry vision—normal vision usually returns in a couple of weeks, but a change in eyeglass prescription can help. (4) Difficulty urinating—this problem is greater in men than women and can become a serious problem in older men. Usually it is only annoying. The drug bethanechol (Urecholine) can be prescribed to counteract this effect. (5) Increased sensitivity to the sun—use a very good suntan lotion, at least No. 15, when out in the sun. You should do this even if you aren't taking trimipramine. (6) Dizziness after standing up quickly—this is caused by a brief drop in blood pressure. The best remedy is to sit down and get up slowly. In elderly people this side effect can be more serious and for that reason trimipramine is not always the best antidepressant for people over age 65. (7) Weight gain—this ranges from just a few pounds to twenty or more pounds. No one knows why trimipramine does this and not a lot can be done except to diet. Severe weight gain is sometimes a reason to switch to a different antidepressant. (8) Drowsiness—taking the whole dose at bedtime reduces the amount of daytime sleepiness, but patients still feel to drowsy during the day and prefer a different antidepressant. (9) Less common side effects—these are generally only a problem in elderly people, in whom confusion, agitation, and memory impairment may necessitate switching to another drug. For younger patients these side effects are rarely of concern.

If It Doesn't Work: After four to six weeks at a good dose (at least 200 mg), the doctor may first add another drug to try to increase trimipramine's effectiveness. The two most often used are thyroid hormone and lithium. If this doesn't work the doctor will probably recommend switching to another antidepressant.

If It Does Work: Once the depression is lifted it is usually recommended to keep taking the medication for six months, at which time it is reduced and stopped over about two weeks. You should see your doctor about once a month for medication management, more often if there are other complications.

Cost: Brand, 78 cents/50-mg pill. Generic, 57 cents/50-mg pill.

Special Comments: Obviously, trimipramine is pretty much the same as imipramine—a perfectly good antidepressant with no special features. Consequently, it never caught on much in the United States and is infrequently prescribed.

PROTRIPTYLINE

Brand Name: Vivactil.

Used for: Major depression. Unlike other cyclic drugs, it may also have particular usefulness in treating atypical depression.

Do Not Use if: You have narrow-angle glaucoma, certain heart rhythm abnormalities, very bad insomnia, or an enlarged prostate.

Tests to Take First: If you are over 50 and in certain other situations your doctor will probably want an electrocardiogram first.

Tests to Take While You Are on It: None required.

Usual Dose: Starts at 5 to 10 mg daily and is increased as high as 60 mg. It is best to take the medication in two divided doses, one in the morning and one in the afternoon. Vivactil lasts a long time in the body, so even after stopping use, it will remain in the body for about a week.

How Long Until It Works: The antidepressant effect takes the usual four weeks that is common to all drugs in this class; However, this is a very "activating" drug and patients may feel a burst of energy from Vivactil after being on it only a few days.

Common Side Effects: Dry mouth, constipation, blurry vision, and difficulty urinating are especially common with Vivactil; increased sensitivity to the sun and dizziness after getting up fast may occur. Vivactil also causes insomnia and may temporarily make a patient feel jittery or even anxious. It does not produce weight gain and may even induce a modest weight loss.

Less Common Side Effects: Confusion, agitation, memory impairment.

What to Do About Side Effects: (1) Dry mouth—don't suck on hard candies containing sugar as you will ruin your teeth; try sugarless hard candies or mouthwash. (2) Constipation—drink at least six glasses of water or juice daily. Laxatives may be prescribed. (3) Blurry vision—normal vision usually returns in a couple of weeks, but a change in eyeglass prescription can help. (4) Difficulty urinating—this problem is greater in men than women and can become a serious problem in older men. Usually it is only annoying. The drug bethanechol (Urecholine) can be prescribed to counteract this effect. (5) Increased sensitivity to the sun—use very good suntan lotion, at least No. 15, when out in the sun. You should do this even if you aren't taking Vivactil. (6) Dizziness after standing up quickly—this is caused by a brief drop in blood pressure. The best remedy is to sit down and get up slowly. In elderly people this side effect can be more serious. (7) Less common side effects—these are generally only a problem in elderly people, in whom confusion, agitation, and memory impairment may necessitate switching to another drug. For younger patients these side effects are rarely of concern.

As mentioned earlier, Vivactil has unique side effects. The modest amount of weight loss is usually not regarded as a problem by most patients and nothing needs to be done about this. The occasional jitteriness and anxiety are temporary; tranquilizers can be prescribed although if this is done it should only be for a week or less in low doses. Insomnia can be a problem; patients complain it takes more an hour to fall asleep and they wake up in the middle of the night. Taking the medication in the morning may help. Sleeping pills also help, but this is to be avoided whenever possible.

If It Doesn't Work: Usually it's best to switch to a different medication in this case.

If It Does Work: Once the depression is lifted it is usually recommended to keep taking the medication for six months, at which time it is reduced and stopped over about two weeks. You should see your doctor about once a month for medication management, more often if there are other complications. It is best to taper off Vivactil rather than stop abruptly to minimize withdrawal symptoms (flulike symptoms); however, Vivactil is relatively easy to stop taking.

Cost: Brand, 38 cents/5-mg pill. Generic, not available.

Special Comments: Vivactil isn't prescribed very much any more because the side effects of dry mouth, constipation, urinary difficulties, and so on, are about the worst among the cyclic drugs and because some patients complain of anxiety. The one advantage it has over the other cyclic drugs is its "activating" property, which makes the patient feel more energetic and thus is not bad for someone with depression. It also doesn't produce weight gain. It has been suggested that Vivactil is similar to monoamine oxidase inhibitor antidepressants in having a particular effect in cases of atypical depression. Overall, Vivactil's advantages are usually outweighed by its disadvantages.

MAPROTILINE

Brand Name: Ludiomil.

Used for: Major depression.

Do Not Use if: You have narrow-angle glaucoma, you have certain abnormal heart rhythms (your doctor will be able to tell you if you have these), your prostate gland is very enlarged, or you have a history of seizures (epilepsy).

Tests to Take First: You may need an electrocardiogram first, especially if you are over age 50.

Tests to Take While You Are on It: None required.

Usual Dose: Starts at about 50 mg daily and goes as high as 225 mg daily. Dose should not exceed 225 mg because this increases the risk of causing a seizure.

How Long Until It Works: Usually after about four weeks of taking the drug daily. Sometimes an effect may be seen as early as two weeks; at other times, it takes as long as six weeks. Usually, sleep and appetite return to normal before alleviation of depressed mood.

Common Side Effects: Dry mouth, constipation, increased sensitivity to the sun, dizziness after standing up quickly, weight gain, drowsiness. These side effects are pretty much the same as those for imipramine, although they may be slightly milder.

Less Common Side Effects: Confusion, agitation, memory impairment, nausea, difficulty urinating, blurry vision. These side effects are pretty much the same as those for imipramine, although they may be slightly milder. Although not common, convulsions may occur in about one in a thousand people. This risk is higher than that with other cyclic drugs. The risk is probably greater for patients with a history of seizures. Risk is reduced by keeping the dose below 225 mg.

What to Do About Side Effects: (1) Dry mouth—don't suck on hard candies containing sugar as you will ruin your teeth; try sugarless hard candies or mouthwash. (2) Constipation—drink at least six glasses of water or juice daily. Laxatives may be prescribed. (3) Blurry vision—normal vision usually returns in a couple of weeks, but a change in eyeglass prescription can help. (4) Increased sensitivity to the sun—use very good suntan lotion, at least No. 15, when out in the sun. You should do this even if you aren't taking Ludiomil. (5) Dizziness after standing up quickly—this is caused by a brief drop in blood pressure. The best remedy is to sit down and get up slowly. In elderly people this side effect can be more serious and for that reason Ludiomil is not always the best antidepressant for people over age 65. (6) Drowsiness—taking the whole dose at bedtime should reduce daytime sleepiness. (7) Weight gain—this ranges from just a few pounds to twenty or more pounds. No one knows why Ludiomil does this and not a lot can be done except to diet. (8) Less common side effects—these are generally only a problem in elderly people, in whom confusion, agitation, and memory impairment may necessitate switching to another drug. For younger patients these side effects are rarely of concern.

If It Doesn't Work: After four to six weeks at a good dose (not above 225 mg), the doctor may first try adding another drug to try to increase Ludiomil's effectiveness. The two most often used are thyroid hormone and lithium. If this doesn't work the doctor will probably recommend switching to another antidepressant.

If It Does Work: Once the depression is lifted it is usually recommended to keep taking the medication for six months, at which time it is reduced and stopped over about two weeks. During this "maintenance" period the dose should be kept below 200 mg/day. You should see your doctor about once a month for medication management, more often if there are other complications. Ludiomil should be tapered, not stopped abruptly, but it is not hard to stop.

Cost: Brand, 55 cents/50-mg pill. Generic, 32 cents/50-mg pill.

Special Comments: The chemical structure of all the cyclic drugs described so far has three rings, hence they are called tricylics. Ludiomil has four rings and so is called a tetracylic. The company that makes Ludiomil emphasized its chemical composition in its advertising when it first released the drug onto the American market. As it turns out, this change in chemical structure does not make Ludiomil act much differently in people than imipramine or the other tricylic drugs. It works perfectly but has virtually nothing that distinguishes it from imipramine.

Summary of Cyclic Antidepressant Drugs

Imipramine (Tofranil), desipramine (Norpramin), amitriptyline (Elavil, Endep), and nortriptyline (Aventyl, Pamelor) are the standard drugs in this class and the drugs that generally should be prescribed first to treat major depression. Of these four, amitriptyline has more side effects and is probably the poorest choice for outpatients who want to keep on working and functioning without feeling sedated. Thus, when a cyclic antidepressant is called for, most psychiatrists will probably prescribe imipramine, desipramine, or nortriptyline, with a preference for nortriptyline in the elderly.

MONOAMINE OXIDASE INHIBITORS

Monoamine oxidase inhibitors, or MAOIs, are powerful antidepressants that produce dramatic improvement in some cases of depression. They also have many side effects and require a special diet. Therefore, these drugs should be prescribed only by a psychiatrist who is experienced in giving them to patients.

Before describing the five drugs in this class, it is important to explain the need for the special diet. MAOIs block or inhibit the work of an important brain chemical. Readers interested in understanding more about this should read Chapter 20. One of the consequences of the way these drugs work is that a person taking an MAOI will not be able to handle a substance called tyramine found in specific foods. After eating a tyramine-containing food, a person taking an MAOI can develop a very high level of tyramine, which can cause the blood pressure to soar out of control. This is called a "hypertensive crisis" and can cause severe headache, stiff neck, nausea, stroke, or even death.

To prevent a hypertensive crisis, certain foods and medications should be eliminated from the diet. The list of foods and drugs to avoid that I use is shown in Table 13, but you should ask your doctor for a complete explanation before taking an MAOI.

There are two main reasons for prescribing an MAOI:

1. Although some patients with atypical depression may improve if given a cyclic antidepressant, research studies have shown that MAOI antidepressants work best for this kind of depression. Many psychiatrists are trying Prozac, a new antidepressant for patients with atypical depression, before an MAOI. Prozac is described under New Antidepressants later in this chapter.

2. Many patients who do not respond to a six-week trial of a cyclic antidepressant will go on to have a good response to an MAOI.

The typical person placed on an MAOI has a long-standing depression, often dating to childhood or adolescence. These patients tend to function more or less adequately on a daily basis and are not generally candidates for emergency hospitalization. They are

Table 13:

Food and Drugs to Avoid While Taking Monoamine Oxidase Inhibitors[a]

I. Food to Avoid
Cheese, except cottage cheese, cream cheese, and farmer cheese

Homemade yogurt (commercial yogurt is okay)

Aged meats and fish (e.g., aged corned beef. salami, fermented sausage, pepperoni, summer sausage, pickled herring, smoked lox)

Liver and liverwurst

Broad beans (Italian green beans, Chinese pea pods, English pea pods)

Bovril or Marmite yeast extract (baked products like bread and cake made with yeast are perfectly safe)

Meat tenderizers

Overripe bananas and banana skins

Red wine, chianti, vermouth, liquors, beer, ale, sherry, cognac

II. Foods to Eat in Moderation
White wine and distilled alcoholic beverages (e.g., gin, vodka, whiskey)

Caffeinated drinks (coffee, tea, soda)

Avocados

Chocolate

Figs, raisins, and dates

Soy sauce

III. Drugs to Avoid
Cocaine

Demerol (meperidine)

Cold medications (aspirin, ibuprofen, and acetaminophen are okay)

continued

Table 13, *continued*

> Nasal decongestants (cromolyn sodium, Nasalcrom, and
>   Intal are okay)
> Sinus, allergy, hay fever, and asthma medications (check
>   with your doctor, because some may be permitted)
> Amphetamines
> Diet pills
> Local anesthetics containing epinephrine (your dentist can
>   give you Novocain without epinephrine)
>
> [a] (Please review this with your doctor and make additions that he
> or she recommends).

often unusually sensitive to criticism and rejection, complain of chronic fatigue and lethargy, overeat when they feel depressed, and sleep whenever possible. They also commonly are anxious and may experience panic attacks.

Nardil and Parnate are the two most common MAOIs used for these people. Nardil causes more weight gain than Parnate, but Parnate disturbs sleep more than Nardil. In other respects, the medications are very similar, so the decision about which to take depends mainly on what side effects are more acceptable to the individual patient and with which drug the physician is most familiar. Marplan is not used in the United States very much, Eutonyl may be soon discontinued by the manufacturer (no generic form is available), and Eldepryl is not yet approved for depression (only for Parkinson's disease) in the United States. Doctors may, however, prescribe Eldepryl for depression if they wish.

MAOIs are also used to treat some anxiety disorders, as discussed in the next chapter. Now for the specific drugs in this class.

PHENELZINE

Brand Name: Nardil.

Used for: Atypical depression. Major depression that has not responded to a cyclic antidepressant.

Do Not Use if: You do not think you can stick to the diet restrictions, you use cocaine (which may precipitate a hypertensive crisis), or you ever have to take the pain-killing drug meperidine (Demerol).

Tests to Take First: It is probably a good idea for the doctor to record your blood pressure before you start taking the drug to know how the drug affects it.

Tests to Take While You Are on It: There is a blood test that shows how effectively the drug is blocking the work of the brain chemical monoamine oxidase, which Nardil is supposed to inhibit. This is sometimes done if a person doesn't seem to be responding and the doctor wants to know if increasing the dose would be helpful. Usually, however, the simplest thing is to increase the dose and see what happens.

Usual Dose: Nardil is available in 15-mg tablets. The starting dose is usually one or two pills, taken either together or divided. The therapeutic dose can be 45 or 60 mg, but some patients need 90 mg or even higher doses to get a good response. After the first week or two, the whole day's dose can be taken at bedtime.

How Long Until It Works: At least two weeks, usually four weeks, and sometimes as long as six weeks.

Common Side Effects: Low blood pressure and dizziness after standing up fast (at least 10% of the patients); weight gain, sometimes as much as twenty pounds, in at least 10% of patients and probably more; swelling around the ankles from fluid retention; sleep disturbance, which can be insomnia for some people or sleepiness for others; trouble having an orgasm, for both men and women, in about 20% of patients.

Less Common Side Effects: Hypertensive crisis is actually quite rare as long as the patient sticks to the dietary and medication restrictions. It is really not very hard to do this and very rarely does a patient object to these restrictions. Some of the side effects caused by the cyclic antidepressants—dry mouth, constipation, blurry vision, difficulty urinating—can also occur with Nardil, but to a much smaller degree. Patients may experience a "hypomania" (opposite of depression) high; such patients feel happy all the time, without a care in the world, and are very self-confident. They experience little need for sleep and have tremendous energy and a high sex drive. Some patients actually enjoy this effect, but those around such patients complain that they are irritable, intrusive, and grandiose and talk too much. Because patients may not identify hypomania as a problem, it is important to enlist the aid of a spouse, parent, sibling, close friend, or adult child to monitor the progress of the patient on phenelzine. Tingling or shocklike sensations in fingers and toes, nausea or diarrhea, and muscle twitching are also common side effects.

What to Do About Side Effects: (1) Low blood pressure and dizziness—even younger people find these effects troublesome. The best remedies are to rise slowly from a lying or sitting position; to avoid saunas and dehydration, which lower blood pressure further; and to drink fluids throughout the day. Some doctors prescribe salt tablets or recommend extra salt intake during meals to keep blood pressure up. Special surgical stockings that compress the legs may also help, but most people hate to wear them. Finally, a pill called Florinef can be prescribed for a few weeks to keep blood pressure up. Occasionally, this side effect is bad enough to warrant stopping the drug. (2) Weight gain—like low pressure, this side effect sometimes limits the ability of people to use Nardil. Calorie restrictions and exercise help. Most people lose the weight once they stop the drug. (3) Swelling—fingers and ankles sometimes swell as a result of water retention. The swelling usually goes down; a water pill (called a diuretic) may help, but it may lower blood pressure further and should therefore be prescribed cautiously. (4) Sleep disturbances—these usually level out in time. One strategy in battling insomnia is to take the medication in the morning. If sleepiness is the problem, the drug can be taken at bedtime. The daytime sleepiness sometimes caused by Nardil is difficult to eliminate, but usually lasts only an hour or two in the afternoon. It is best to avoid prescribing sleeping pills to counteract insomnia and to avoid drinking a lot of coffee to counteract sedation. (5) Trouble with orgasm—both men and women frequently complain that the length of time to orgasm is longer. As this effect usually goes away with time, patience is important. If it persists, lowering the dose may help. Finally, two drugs have been used with some success: bethanechol (Urecholine) and cyproheptadine (Periactin). (6) Hypertensive crisis—this can be avoided because the patient taking an MAOI should follow a very strict diet. If dietary restrictions are violated and the blood pressure suddenly increases, the first symptom is usually a severe, throbbing headache. In this medical emergency, the patient should go to an emergency room immediately because rapid treatment can bring the blood pressure back down before anything serious happens. Some psychiatrists give patients a medication called nifedipine (Procardia, Adalat) to carry with them at all times. At the first sign of a headache the patient is instructed to place a capsule under the tongue. This can bring the blood pressure down again very quickly (see Table 14 to learn what to do if you get a headache). (7) Hypomania—the dose of the drug should be lowered or the drug stopped. Sometimes, counteracting medications are prescribed. (8) Tingling and shocklike feelings—as a decrease in vitamin B_6 causes this effect, vitamin B_6 pills are usually administered.

Table 14:

What to Do if You Have a Headache While on Monoamine Oxidase Inhibitors

1. Don't panic.
2. Call your doctor immediately.
3. Put a nifedipine capsule under your tongue.
4. Proceed to the nearest emergency room, preferably accompanied by another person.
5. Tell the staff in the emergency room you are on a monoamine oxidase inhibitor (Nardil, Parnate, Eutonyl, Eldepryl, or Marplan). They should check your blood pressure immediately, begin treatment if it is too high, and call your doctor.

If It Doesn't Work: There are several strategies available to the person who does not respond to Nardil after six weeks. Thyroid pills and lithium are sometimes added to boost the response. Very experienced psychiatrists may try to combine Nardil with other antidepressants, but this must be done with great caution. Patients should *never* do this on their own. Often, a failure to respond to Nardil means that more intense efforts at psychotherapy will be required.

If It Does Work: Nardil almost always works, so the major issue is usually surviving the side effects. Most patients find the benefits of freedom from depression far outweigh the side effects. Patients on Nardil should be seen about once a month by the doctor and will usually need to raise and lower the dose many times to maintain as much freedom from side effects as possible without sacrificing the antidepressant effect. The usual rule of remaining on the drug at least six symptom free months applies. Atypical depression, however, is often a chronic condition and some patients find they slump right back into depression when they try to stop the medicine. For that reason, many patients elect to stay on Nardil for years. There are no known long-term health risks.

Cost: Brand, 24 cents/15-mg pill. Generic, not available.

Special Comments: From the list of side effects, patients may wonder who would be bold enough to try Nardil. But for people who get relief after years of chronic depression the side effects are usually tolerable. MAOIs should be prescribed cautiously but not avoided when necessary.

TRANYLCYPROMINE

Brand Name: Parnate.

Used for: Atypical depression. Major depression that has not responded to cyclic antidepressants.

Do Not Use if: You don't think you can stick to the diet restrictions, you suffer from severe insomnia, you use cocaine, or you need the pain-killing drug meperidine (Demerol).

Tests to Take First: It is probably a good idea for the doctor to record your blood pressure before you start taking the drug to know how the drug affects it.

Tests to Take While You Are on It: There is a blood test that shows how effectively the drug is blocking the work of the brain chemical monoamine oxidase, which Parnate is supposed to inhibit. This is sometimes done if a person doesn't seem to be responding and the doctor wants to know if increasing the dose would be helpful. Usually, however, the simplest thing is just to increase the dose and see what happens.

Usual Dose: Parnate comes in 10-mg tablets. The usual starting dose is one or two tablets. It may take from 30 mg to as much as 60 mg to get a good response. The dose should be raised slowly by about one pill every three to four days. It is usually taken as one or two doses in the morning or early afternoon.

How Long Until It Works: May be faster than Nardil, often in about two weeks, but may take up to six weeks. Some people experience a "speeded up," amphetamine-like effect first, but this passes in about a week.

Common Side Effects: (1) Low blood pressure and dizziness after standing up quickly (more common than with Nardil). (2) weight gain, but less than that with Nardil. (3) swelling around the ankles from fluid retention. (4) sleep disturbance (usually insomnia) that is often troublesome. (5) trouble having an orgasm, for both men and women, but less than with Nardil.

Less Common Side Effects: Hypertensive crisis is actually quite rare as long as the patient sticks to the dietary and medication restrictions. It is really not very hard to do this and very rarely does a patient object to these restrictions. Hypertensive crisis has been reported with Parnate when the dietary and medication restrictions were not broken. Some of the side effects caused by the cyclic antidepressants—dry mouth, constipation, blurry vision, difficulty urinating—can also occur with Parnate to a much smaller degree. Patients may experience a "hypomania" (opposite of depression) high; such patients feel happy all the time, without a care in the world, and are very self-confident. They experience little need for sleep and have tremendous energy and a high sex drive. Some patients may actually enjoy this effect, but others around them complain that they are irritable, intrusive, and grandiose, and talk too much. Because patients may not identify hypomania as a problem, it is important to enlist the aid of a spouse, parent, sibling, close friend, or adult child to monitor the progress of someone on Parnate. Tingling or shock-like sensations in fingers and toes and muscle twitching are also side effects.

What to Do About Side Effects: (1) Low blood pressure and dizziness—even younger people find these effects troublesome. The best remedies are to rise slowly from a lying or sitting position; avoid saunas and dehydration, which lower blood pressure further; and drink fluids throughout the day. Some doctors prescribe salt tablets or recommend extra salt intake during meals to keep blood pressure up. Special surgical stockings that compress the legs may also help, but most people hate to wear them. Finally, a pill called Florinef can be prescribed for a few weeks to keep the blood pressure up. Occasionally, this side effect is bad enough to warrant stopping the drug. (2) Weight gain—like low blood pressure, this side effect sometimes limits the ability of people to use Parnate. It occurs less often with Parnate than with Nardil. Calorie restriction and exercise help. Most people lose the weight once they stop the drug. (3) Swelling—fingers and ankles swell from water retention. The swelling usually goes down; a water pill (called a diuretic) may help, but it may lower blood pressure further and should therefore be prescribed cautiously. (4) Sleep disturbances—these usually level out in time. Parnate often produces insomnia. The new antidepressant Desyrel, which is very sedating, is sometimes prescribed for the insomnia (50 mg at night). Some doctors prescribe sleeping pills (Restoril, Halcion, or Dalmane). Parnate should be taken early in the day. (5) Trouble with orgasm—both men and women frequently complain that the length of time to orgasm is longer than usual, but this is less of a problem than with Nardil. As this effect usually goes away in time, patience is important. If it persists, lowering the dose can help. Finally, two drugs have been used with some success: bethanechol (Urecholine) and cyproheptadine (Periactin). (6) Hypertensive crisis—this can be avoided because the patient taking an MAOI should follow a very strict diet. If dietary restrictions are violated and blood pressure suddenly increases, the first symptom is usually a severe, throbbing headache. Rarely, hypertensive crisis can occur to a patient on Parnate even without violating the dietary restrictions. In this medical emergency, the patient should go to an emergency room immediately because rapid treatment can bring the blood pressure back down before anything serious occurs. Some psychiatrists give patients a medication called nifedipine (Procardia, Adalat) to carry with them at all times. At the first sign of a headache the patient is instructed to place a capsule under the tongue. This can bring the blood pressure down again very quickly (see Table 14 to learn what to do if you get a headache while on Parnate). (7) Hypomania—the dose should be lowered or the drug stopped. Sometimes, counteracting medications are prescribed. (8) Tingling or shocklike feelings—as a decrease in vitamin B_6 causes this effect, vitamin B_6 pills are usually administered.

What to Do if It Doesn't Work: Several strategies are available to the person who does not respond to Parnate after six weeks. Thyroid hormone or lithium is sometimes added to boost the response. Very experienced psychiatrists may try to combine phenelzine with other antidepressants, but this must be done with great caution. Patients should *never* do this on their own. Often, a failure to respond to Parnate means that more intense efforts at psychotherapy are required.

If It Does Work: Parnate almost always works, so the major issue is usually surviving the side effects. Most patients find the benefits of freedom from depression far outweigh the side effects. Patients on Parnate should be seen about once a month by the doctor; the dose usually needs to be raised and lowered many times to maintain as much freedom from side effects as possible without sacrificing the antidepressant effect. The usual rule of remaining on the drug at least six symptom-free months applies. Atypical depression, however, is often a chronic condition and some patients find they slump right back into depression when the try to stop the medicine. For that reason, many patients elect to stay on Parnate for years. There are no known long-term health risks.

Cost: Brand, 33 cents/10-mg pill. Generic, not available.

Special Comments: Parnate is very similar to Nardil, but tends to be more "activating." Some people experience fewer side effects on it than with Nardil and some people experience more. A very thin person not too worried about weight gain might prefer Nardil; a patient who feels sleepy and lethargic often because of their depression may prefer Parnate. The MAOI special diet (see Table 12) is again of crucial importance.

ISOCARBOXAZID

Brand Name: Marplan.
Used for: Atypical depression. Major depression that has not responded to cyclic antidepressants.
Do Not Use if: You do not think you can stick to the diet restrictions, you use cocaine, or you ever have to take the pain-killing drug meperidine (Demerol).
Tests to Take First: It is probably a good idea for the doctor to record your blood pressure before you start taking the drug to know how the drug affects it.
Tests to Take While You Are on It: There is a blood test that shows how effectively the drug is blocking the work of the brain chemical monoamine oxidase, which it is supposed to inhibit. This is sometimes done if a person doesn't seem to be responding and the doctor wants to know if increasing the dose would be helpful. Usually, however, the simplest thing is just to increase the dose and see what happens.
Usual Dose: Starts at 10 or 20 mg daily and can be raised to about 50 mg.
How Long Until It Works: At least two weeks, usually four weeks, and sometimes as long as six weeks.
Common Side Effects: Basically the same effects as with Nardil (dizziness, weight gain, sexual problems). Some clinicians insist that Marplan has fewer overall side effects, although this has never been proven.
Less Common Side Effects: Hypertensive crisis is actually quite rare as long as the patient sticks to the dietary and medication restrictions. It is really not very hard to do this, and very rarely does a patient object to the restrictions. (2) some of the side effects caused by the cyclic antidepressants—dry mouth, constipation, blurry vision, difficulty urinating—can also occur with Marplan, but to a much smaller degree. Some patients may experience a "hypomania" (opposite of depression) high; such patients feel happy all the time,

without a care in the world, and are very self-confident. They experience little need for sleep and have tremendous energy and a high sex drive. Patients may actually enjoy this effect, but others around them complain that they are irritable, intrusive and grandiose and talk too much. Because patients may not identify hypomania as a problem, it is important to enlist the aid of a spouse, parent, sibling, close friend, or adult child to monitor the progress of someone on Marplan. Tingling or shocklike sensations in fingers and toes and muscle twitching are also side effects.

What to Do About Side Effects: (1) Low blood pressure and dizziness—even younger people find these effects troublesome. The best remedies are to rise slowly from a lying or sitting position; avoid saunas and dehydration, which lower blood pressure further; and drink fluids throughout the day. Some doctors prescribe salt tablets or recommend extra salt intake during meals to keep blood pressure up. Special surgical stockings that compress the legs may also help, but most people hate to wear them. Finally, a pill called Florinef can be prescribed for a few weeks to keep blood pressure up. Occasionally, this side effect is bad enough to warrant stopping the drug. (2) Weight gain—like low pressure, this side effect sometimes limits the ability of people to use Marplan. Calorie restrictions and exercise help. Most people lose the weight once they stop the drug. (3) Swelling—fingers and ankles swell from water retention. The swelling usually goes down; a water pill (called a diuretic) may help, but it may lower blood pressure further and should therefore be prescribed cautiously. (4) Sleep disturbances—these usually level out in time. For people who experience insomnia from the medication, one strategy is to take the medication in the morning. Patients who become sleepy, can take the medication at bedtime. It is best to avoid prescribing sleeping pills to counteract insomnia and to avoid drinking a lot of coffee to counteract sedation. (5) Trouble with orgasm—both men and women frequently complain that the length of time to orgasm is longer than usual. As this effect usually goes away with time, patience is important. If it persists, lowering the dose can help. Finally, two drugs have been used with some success: bethanechol (Urecholine) and cyproheptadine (Periactin). (6) Hypertensive crisis—this can be avoided because the patient taking an MAOI should follow a very strict diet. If dietary restrictions are violated and blood pressure suddenly increases, the first symptom is usually a severe, throbbing headache. In this medical emergency, the patient should go to an emergency room immediately because rapid treatment can bring the blood pressure back down before anything serious happen. Some psychiatrists give patients a medication called nifedipine (Procardia, Adalat) to carry with them at all times. At the first sign of a headache the patient is instructed to place a capsule under the tongue. This can bring the blood pressure down again very quickly. (7) Hypomania—the dose of the drug should be lowered or the drug stopped. Sometimes, counteracting medications are prescribed. (8) Tingling or shock-like feelings—as a decrease in vitamin B_6 causes this effect, vitamin B_6 pills are usually administered.

If It Doesn't Work: Several strategies are available to the person who does not respond to isocarboxazid after six weeks. Thyroid hormone or lithium is sometimes added to boost the response. Very experienced psychiatrists may try to combine Marplan with other antidepressants, but this must be done with great caution. Patients should *never* do this on their own. Often, a failure to respond to Marplan means that more intense efforts at psychotherapy are required.

If It Does Work: The major issue is usually surviving the side effects. Most patients find that the benefits of freedom from depression far outweigh the side effects. Patients on Marplan should be seen about once a month by the doctor; the dose usually needs to be raised and lowered many times to maintain as much freedom from side effects as possible without sacrificing the antidepressant effect. The usual rule of remaining on the drug for at least six symptom-free months applies. Atypical depression, however, is often a chronic condition and some patients find they slump right back into depression when the try to stop the medicine. For that reason, many patients elect to stay on Marplan for years. There are no known long-term health risks.

Cost: Brand, 47 cents/10-mg pill. Generic, not available.

Special Comments: Marplan is not very different from Nardil and is rarely prescribed in the United States. It is worth trying if someone has responded well to Nardil or Parnate but experiences severe side effects. In such cases Marplan might be better tolerated.

PARGYLINE

Brand Name: Eutonyl.

Used for: Pargyline is actually advertised as a drug for high blood pressure, but it is a monoamine oxidase inhibitor and is very rarely prescribed for atypical depression.

Do Not Use if: You do not think you can stick to the diet restrictions, you use cocaine, you ever have to take the pain-killing drug meperidine (Demerol), or you have very low blood pressure.

Tests to Take First: It is probably a good idea for the doctor to record your blood pressure before you start taking the drug to know how the drug affects it.

Tests to Take While You Are on It: There is a blood test that shows how effectively the drug is blocking the work of the brain chemical monoamine oxidase, which pargyline is supposed to inhibit. This is sometimes done if a person doesn't seem to be responding and the doctor wants to know if increasing the dose would be helpful. Usually, however, the simplest thing is just to increase the dose and see what happens.

Usual Dose: Pargyline comes in 25-mg tablets and one pill at night is the usual starting dose. Because it lowers blood pressure quite a bit, the dose should be raised slowly, by about one pill a week, to between 75 and 150 mg to obtain the antidepressant response. The total daily dose should be divided into two equal doses.

How Long Until It Works: At least two weeks, usually four weeks, and sometimes as long as six weeks.

Common Side Effects: Low blood pressure and dizziness after standing up quickly. It is important to watch for too great a drop in blood pressure, especially as the dose is increased. Weight gain, sometimes as much as twenty pounds. Swelling around the ankles from fluid retention. Sleep disturbance, which can be insomnia for some people or sleepiness for others. Trouble having an orgasm, for both men and women.

Less Common Side Effects: Hypertensive crisis is actually quite rare as long as the patient sticks to the dietary and medication restrictions. It is really not very hard to do this, and very rarely does a patient object to these restrictions. Some of the side effects caused by the cyclic antidepressants—dry mouth, constipation, blurry vision, difficulty urinating—can also occur with pargyline, but to a much smaller degree. Patients may experience a hypomania (opposite of depression) high; such patients feel happy all the time, without a care in the world, and are very self-confident. They experience little need for sleep and have tremendous energy and a high sex drive. Patients may actually enjoy this effect, but others around them complain that they are irritable, intrusive, and grandiose and talk too much. Because patients may not identify hypomania as a problem, it is important to enlist the aid of a spouse, parent, sibling, close friend, or adult child to monitor the progress of someone taking pargyline. Tingling or shocklike sensations in fingers and toes and muscle twitching are also side effects.

What to Do About Side Effects: (1) Low blood pressure and dizziness— even younger people find these effects troublesome. The best remedies are to rise slowly from a lying or sitting position; avoid saunas and dehydration, which lower blood pressure further; and drink fluids throughout the day. Some doctors prescribe salt tablets or recommend extra salt intake during meals to keep blood pressure up. Special surgical stockings that compress the legs may also help, but most people hate to wear them. Finally, a pill called Florinef can be prescribed for a few weeks to keep blood pressure up. Occasionally, this side effect is bad enough to warrant stopping the drug. (2) Weight gain—like low blood pressure, this side effect sometimes limits the ability of people to use pargyline. Calorie restrictions and exercise help. Most people lose the weight once they stop the drug. (3) Swelling—fingers and ankles swell from water retention. The swelling usually goes down; a water pill (called a diuretic) may help, but it may lower blood pressure further and should therefore be prescribed cautiously. (4) Sleep disturbances—these usually level out in time. For people who experience insomnia from the medication, one strategy is to take the medication in the morning. Patients who become sleepy can take the medication at bedtime. It is best to avoid prescribing sleeping pills to counteract insomnia and to avoid drinking a lot of coffee to counteract sedation. (5) Trouble with orgasm—both men and women frequently complain that the length of time to orgasm is longer than usual. As this effect usually goes away with time, patience is important. If it persists, lowering the dose may help. Finally, two drugs have been used with some success:

bethanechol (Urecholine) and cyproheptadine (Periactin). (6) Hypertensive crisis—this can be avoided because the patient taking an MAOI should follow a very strict diet. If dietary restrictions are violated and blood pressure suddenly increases, the first symptom is usually a severe, throbbing headache. In this medical emergency, the patient should go to an emergency room immediately because rapid treatment can bring the blood pressure back down before anything serious happens. Some psychiatrists give patients a medication called nifedipine (Procardia, Adalat) to carry with them at all times. At the first sign of a headache the patient is instructed to place a capsule under the tongue. This can bring the blood pressure down again very quickly. (7) Hypomania—the dose of the drug should be lowered or the drug stopped. Sometimes, counteracting medications are prescribed. (8) Tingling or shocklike feelings—as a decrease in vitamin B_6 causes these effects vitamin B_6 pills are usually administered.

If It Doesn't Work: Several strategies are available to the person who does not respond to pargyline after six weeks. Thyroid hormone or lithium is sometimes added to boost the response. Very experienced psychiatrists may try to combine Eutonyl with other antidepressants, but this must be done with great caution. Patients should *never* do this on their own. Often, a failure to respond to pargyline means that more intense efforts at psychotherapy are required.

If It Does Work: The major issue is usually surviving the side effects. Most patients find that the benefits of freedom from depression far outweigh the side effects. Patients on pargyline should be seen about once a month by the doctor; the dose usually needs to be raised and lowered many times to maintain as much freedom from side effects as possible without sacrificing the antidepressant effect. The usual rule of remaining on the drug for at least six symptom-free months applies. Atypical depression, however, is often a chronic condition, and some patients find they slump right back into depression when they try to stop the medicine. For that reason, many patients elect to stay on pargyline for years. There are no known long-term health risks.

Cost: Brand, 28 cents/25-mg pill. Generic, not available.

Special Comments: Like isocarboxazid, pargyline is rarely prescribed for depression. A patient who has responded to phenelzine (Nardil) or tranylcypromine (Parnate) but is very bothered by side effects may find pargyline more tolerable. It is also a good choice for depressed patients with high blood pressure. The manufacturer of pargyline may soon discontinue it. Unless a generic manufacturer steps in, it may be very hard to obtain pargyline in the future.

SELEGILINE (FORMERLY DEPRENYL)

Brand Name: Eldepryl.
Used for: Parkinson's disease. Has also been tested for treatment of depression.
Special Comments: Eldepryl is a monoamine oxidase inhibitor that became available in the United States for the treatment of Parkinson's disease in September 1989. It was first thought that patients taking Eldepryl could get by without adhering to the MAOI diet, but this applies only when used for Parkinson's disease. At least for the present, the dietary restrictions should be scrupulously followed if it is used as an antidepressant. The advantage of Eldepryl is that it appears to have fewer side effects than phenelzine (Nardil) or tranylcypromine (Parnate). As the big problem with those standard MAOI drugs is the side effects, Eldepryl may be a real advance. It will be a while before we are sure if it works as well as the other MAOIs to treat depression, but it is definitely something to look forward to.
Cost: Brand, 54 cents/5-mg pill. Generic, not available.

THE "NEWER" ANTIDEPRESSANTS

The drugs in this category have been introduced into the American market in the 1980s, and each has unique properties.

These antidepressants have a chemical structure different from that of the cyclic antidepressants, and they have different biological effects on the brain as well. As each was introduced, its manufacturer insisted the new drug represented a "major breakthrough" that would revolutionize the treatment of depression. Only one,

Prozac (fluoxetine), appears to be a true advance in antidepressant treatment.

Prozac has virtually swept the nation since its introduction in 1988. It is in contention to be the best-selling antidepressant in the United States. The reasons are clear. Compared with the cyclic antidepressants, it has several advantages: (1) It has many fewer side effects (although, of course, it is not free of side effects); (2) it has little capacity to cause death if taken in overdose; and (3) most patients need only take one capsule daily, instead of the many pills per day usually required for other drugs.

Most importantly, Prozac, unlike the other "new antidepressants," clearly works to resolve depression. It is highly effective, something that cannot always be said of Desyrel and Asendin in my (and many other psychopharmacologists') experience.

Because Prozac is relatively new, many of us are reluctant to state just yet that it is the drug of choice in treating depression. I envision, however, that someday it will be. Table 15 lists some situations in which Prozac might be the first drug prescribed in treating depression. The major problem with Prozac is its price: a 20-mg capsule is listed in the "Red Book" as $1.32, compared with $0.20 for a 15-mg Nardil pill or $0.55 for a 50-mg Tofranil pill (remember, however, that most patients take as many as six Nardil or Tofranil tablets a day). Drug stores charge as much as $3.50 for a Prozac capsule, and a monthly medication bill can exceed $100.00.

FLUOXETINE

Brand Name: Prozac.
Used for: All types of depression and several anxiety disorders.
Do Not Use if: You are bothered by severe insomnia or your weight is dangerously low. Even these conditions do not always preclude the use of Prozac, which is a very safe drug.
Tests to Take First: None, because there are no known medical problems that make taking Prozac a risk.
Tests to Take While You Are on It: None required.
Usual Dose: Prozac comes in 20-mg capsules. The manufacturer says that most people get the maximum antidepressant effect from just one capsule daily. Many clinicians find, however, that an occasional

Table 15:

When Is Prozac a Good First Choice for Treatment of Depression?

1. The diagnosis is atypical depression (Prozac may be tried before an MAOI).
2. There are panic attacks in addition to the depression.
3. There are obsessions and compulsions in addition to the depression.
4. The patient has heart disease, which makes the use of cyclic antidepressants risky.
5. The patient is obese and cannot tolerate additional weight gain (Prozac may even promote some weight loss).

patient needs a higher dose and people seem to tolerate at least 80 mg daily fairly well. Other people may experience more side effects, such as agitation, at the higher doses. The drug has a long length of action; it takes several days for a single capsule to be completely eliminated from the body. This means that the whole dose can be taken once a day, usually in the morning. If for some reason 20 mg a day is too much, the patient may do well on one pill every other day. Some patients who are better off with less than 20 mg a day, at least to start, open the capsule and spill a quarter (5 mg) or a half (10 mg) into a glass of juice or water and drink it. That way, the patient can take as little as 5 mg a day. This can be raised to 20 mg daily over the next two weeks.

How Long Until It Works: Some patients may start to feel better after two weeks, but the full antidepressant effect takes about four weeks.

Common Side Effects: Prozac clearly has fewer side effects than the previously available antidepressants. The major common side effects are insomnia (trouble falling asleep or frequent awakening during the night); nausea, diarrhea, or stomach cramps; headache; and nervousness.

Less Common Side Effects: (1) Drowsiness. (2) serious weight loss, (3) difficulty having an orgasm. (4) hypomania (opposite of depression;

101

patients become hyperactive, overly optimistic, and extremely talkative).

What to Do About Side Effects: Most of Prozac's side effects are mild and go away completely after the first week or two on the drug. The best thing to do about all the effects is to wait because they will probably disappear. Sleep problems are made easier by taking Prozac in the morning. Some people think the weight loss it promotes is actually a plus, but overweight people should not count on Prozac for weight reduction; the most lost is usually about five pounds and it is often regained. If Prozac makes a patient very anxious it is best to take half a capsule a day or one capsule every other day. When hypomania occurs, the dose is lowered or the drug is stopped temporarily. Sometimes, counteracting medication is necessary.

If It Doesn't Work: Attempts can be made to boost the antidepressant response by adding other drugs if Prozac hasn't worked by six weeks and the dose has been pushed to 80 mg. Some doctors add a cyclic antidepressant like desipramine or nortriptyline, but this must be done cautiously. Thyroid hormone or lithium might work. After that, it is probably best to try a different antidepressant.

If It Does Work: A patient should remain on Prozac for six months after relief from depression, and then try to stop it. A patient on 20 mg a day can stop abruptly; those on higher doses should taper off, but there is not much of a problem with withdrawal. Some patients suffering from chronic atypical depression may stay on drugs like Prozac much longer. Fortunately, this does not seem to be harmful.

Cost: Brand, $1.68/20-mg capsule. Generic, not available.

Special Comments: When Prozac was first released it was hailed in the media as a wonder drug. Then reports that some people committed violent acts or developed suicidal ideas while taking Prozac lead the media to swing in the opposite direction and make Prozac look like poison. Neither extreme is close to the truth. Prozac has side effects and doesn't help everyone, so it isn't a wonder drug. On the other hand, there is still no convincing evidence that Prozac is anything more than an innocent bystander in those cases in which patients supposedly became suicidal. Prozac remains a safe and effective antidepressant, but patients who take it should still see their doctor regularly and stop taking it if their condition worsens or if it doesn't work.

TRAZODONE

Brand Name: Desyrel.

Used for: Major depression.

Do Not Use if: You have certain heart rhythm abnormalities (which your doctor will tell you about).

Tests to Take First: An electrocardiogram may be required by your doctor.

Tests to Take While You Are on It: None required.

Usual Dose: Starts at about 50 mg a day and may be increased to between 200 and 400 mg. Occasionally, a doctor will prescribe as much as 600 mg. The dose is usually taken at night after a meal or a light snack.

How Long Until It Works: About four weeks.

Common Side Effects: Sleepiness, dizziness after standing up quickly, and nausea and vomiting.

Uncommon Side Effects: (1) Priapism, or sustained erection of the penis, has been reported in some patients taking trazodone. It is estimated to occur in between 1 in 1,000 and 1 in 10,000 men who take the drug. This is a serious emergency because severe damage can occur to a penis that has been erect for several hours. One third of the men who develop priapism require surgery. (2) disturbances in heart rhythms can occur in people with underlying heart disease.

What to Do About Side Effects: For the sedation caused by trazodone, it is best to take the medicine in one dose before bedtime so you will be sleeping anyway. Dizziness can be controlled by getting up slowly. Nausea usually goes away on its own. Sustained erection of the penis is an emergency and you should call your doctor immediately. Patients with heart disease should probably not be given trazodone in most cases.

If It Doesn't Work: Switch to a different drug.

If It Does Work: Remain on it for six months and then try to discontinue use.

Cost: Brand, 94 cents/50-mg pill. Generic, 13 cents/50-mg pill.

Special Comments: Trazodone is very popular with doctors because it doesn't cause any dangerous side effects and makes agitated, depressed patients sleepy, but many psychiatrists complain that their patients don't seem to get much better taking trazodone. It's safe and well tolerated, but there are serious questions about its effectiveness. Consequently, many psychiatrists have lost faith in trazodone.

AMOXAPINE

Brand Name: Asendin.
Used for: Major depression.
Do Not Use if: You are very anxious along with being depressed, you have a lot of trouble sleeping, or you have a history of seizures (epilepsy).
Tests to Take First: None required.
Tests to Take While You Are on It: None required.
Usual Dose: Starts with 100 mg two or three times daily and can be increased to between 300 and 600 mg to obtain an antidepressant effect. Usually taken early in the day.
How Long Until It Works: There are claims that Ascendin works very quickly, in about a week, but some patients may not feel the full effect for about three weeks.
Common Side Effects: Nervousness, agitation, and insomnia are the most troublesome, but 14% of patients experience drowsiness.
Less Common Side Effects: Alone among the antidepressant drugs, Asendin has the *potential* to produce a serious and sometimes permanent side effect called tardive dyskinesia. This involves involuntary movements of various muscles, usually beginning with chewing and lip-smacking. Tardive dyskinesia is a potential side effect of most drugs used to treat schizophrenia, but Asendin is the only antidepressant known to produce it.
What to Do About Side Effects: Taking the medication early in the day may counteract some of the insomnia. Lowering the dose can reduce the agitation, but may also reduce the chance of the drug working. Because of its potential to cause tardive dyskinesia, Asendin should not be taken longer than six months and should be stopped at the first sign of abnormal body movements.
If It Doesn't Work: Try a different antidepressant.
If It Does Work: Take it for about six months and then taper off over about two weeks.

Cost: Brand, 85 cents/50-mg pill. Generic, 68 cents/50-mg pill.

Special Comments: Because Asendin energizes people, it may make a sluggish depressed patient feel better in a week; it also makes some patients feel anxious and irritable. The risk of developing tardive dyskinesia is probably small, but because this effect is so awful and there are so many other drugs that work just as well, Asendin is losing favor rapidly.

ALPRAZOLAM

Brand Name: Xanax.

Used for: Treatment of anxiety disorders and anxiety with accompanying depressive symptoms, but may be used occasionally to treat mild depression alone or serious depression in a patient with serious medical problems.

Special Comments: Xanax is used mainly to treat anxiety and a fuller description is found in Chapter 8. While the drug was being tested, however, some scientists observed that it seemed to relieve depression. It is not officially recommended by the company that makes it or by the Food and Drug Administration for depression, but some clinicians find it helpful. It is medically safe to give and, therefore, is sometimes the only option for a depressed patient with serious medical problems who can't take anything else. There are two problems with its use as an antidepressant: (1) it probably doesn't work nearly as well as the regular antidepressants, and (2) it can be hard to stop use after it has been taken for several weeks, unless discontinued slowly.

BUPROPION

Brand Name: Welbutrin.

Used for: Major depression. Bipolar depression.

Do Not Use if: You have a history of seizures (epilepsy), you suffer from severe insomnia, or you are very underweight.

Tests to Take First: None recommended.

Tests to Take While You Are on It: None recommended.

Usual Dose: Start with 100 mg twice daily and increase to 100 mg three times a day after four days. If there is no response in three to four weeks, the dose can be raised to a maximum of 450 mg per day, given in three doses of 150 mg each. Never take more than 150 mg in any one dose.

How Long Until It Works: About four weeks.

Common Side Effects: Restlessness, agitation, and insomnia may occur in one third of patients treated with Welbutrin. About one fourth of patients lose as much as five pounds (almost no one gains weight). Some patients also experience headache, nausea and vomiting, and rashes.

Less Common Side Effects: The major worry is the precipitation of seizures. Approximately 4 of 1,000 people treated with Welbutrin had a convulsion during the testing phase of the drug.

What to Do About Side Effects: Because Welbutrin was only released onto the American market in the summer of 1989, it is still too early to know the tricks it will take to minimize side effects. Such problems as restlessness and insomnia probably disappear on their own after a few weeks; some clinicians may add small amounts of the antianxiety benzodiazepine drugs (like Xanax) to reduce these problems. Most patients welcome the small amount of weight loss. The risk of seizures, however, is a problem. Clearly, patients with a history of seizures should not take Welbutrin. The dose should be kept as low as possible and should never exceed 450 mg.

If It Doesn't Work: Try a different antidepressant.

If It Does Work: Remain on it for six depression-free months, but lower the dose as much as possible to minimize the seizure risk. The medication should then be tapered over several weeks. Withdrawal symptoms should not be a major problem.

Cost: Brand, 41 cents/75-mg pill. Generic, not available.

Special Comments: Welbutrin was about to be released on the market several years ago when several cases of convulsions were reported in patients with an eating disorder called bulimia. The government halted its release until the summer of 1989. Apparently, the Food and Drug Administration is satisfied that the risk of precipitating a seizure is acceptable at the 0.4% level. Many clinicians, however, are likely to be reluctant to prescribe Welbutrin until there is more general experience with the drug. It is said to have less tendency to produce hypomania and mania than other antidepressants and therefore may be especially useful in patients with bipolar depression who often get high when treated with antidepressants.

Summary of the "New" Antidepressants

Of the drugs included in this category, only Prozac truly offers advantages over the cyclic and MAOI antidepressants. In time, Prozac will be prescribed more and more. Eventually, it may become the "first"-choice drug for all forms of depression. Welbutrin may also prove a welcome addition, but this awaits more clinical experience.

STIMULANT ANTIDEPRESSANT DRUGS

Depression may also be treated with drugs called psychostimulants. Use of such drugs is reserved for only two situations: (1) patients who have failed to respond to at least two other antidepressants and psychotherapy and who are seriously depressed, and (2) patients with serious and usually terminal medical illnesses such as cancer or AIDS who are depressed and too sick to take other kinds of antidepressants.

The reason for these restrictions is that the stimulant drugs are addictive. They include amphetamines, sometimes called "speed" or "uppers," methylphenidate (Ritalin), and pemoline (Cylert). The drugs produce a short-term mood elevation even in people who are not depressed. College students take them to stay awake all night and finish term papers.

In most people the effects of these stimulant drugs are short-lived and there is often a letdown or "crash" after they wear off. During this "crash" the patient can feel very depressed, sleepy, and sluggish. Furthermore, and very much unlike the other drugs discussed so far in this chapter, stimulant drugs have the potential to induce "tolerance." People who abuse amphetamines and other stimulants—usually in attempts to lose weight or stay awake for prolonged periods—often find that a dose that had worked for a while is suddenly ineffective and they need a higher dose. They then become "tolerant" to the higher dose and have to increase the dose again. Soon, the person is addicted to the drug. Stopping it suddenly leads to a severe withdrawal reaction characterized by bad depression and extreme fatigue. Suicides have been reported in people who suddenly stop taking amphetamines.

Given all these problems, why even mention the stimulant drugs? Simply because they are the only drugs that work for some depressed patients. A very small group of usually chronically depressed patients seems to be resistant to every other treatment for depression. These people usually function at a fairly low level relative to their ability and they feel sad and blue all of the time. They complain of fatigue, low interest in life, and inability to concentrate. Many say they have been depressed since childhood.

Another small group of patients with very serious medical problems also develops depression. Sometimes the medical problems they have make other antidepressant drugs unsafe, or the medical problems so magnify the side effects of the other antidepressants that the dying patient is made even more uncomfortable. Stimulant drugs may actually be the safest choice in this situation.

For these two groups of patients stimulant drugs may be the only answer, even though the patient will probably become addicted. This is not to be taken lightly. The decision to place a patient on a stimulant drug for depression is serious and must be done only after all other efforts are declared either unsafe or ineffective. The patient must understand that he will probably become addicted to the medication and that he should never stop taking it abruptly.

AMPHETAMINES

Brand Names: Dexedrine, Biphetamine, Desoxyn, various other preparations.
Used for: Officially, for three conditions: (1) narcolepsy, a condition in which the patient falls asleep suddenly during the day; (2) obesity, and (3) hyperactivity in children. Unofficially, it is sometimes used for chronic depression that fails to respond to all other treatments and for very ill medical patients with depression.

Do Not Use if: You haven't tried other antidepressants and psycho-therapy, you have high blood pressure, you are very nervous or have severe insomnia, you have a history of addiction to drugs or alcohol, or you have Tourette's syndrome.

Tests to Take First: You should probably have an electrocardiogram to be sure nothing is wrong with your heart and your blood pressure should be recorded.

Tests to Take While You Are on It: Blood pressure and pulse should be taken every day for the first week, then once a week for a month, and then at least every month.

Usual Dose: Usually starts with 5 or 10 mg per day and can be raised, sometimes to 50 mg or higher. The higher the dose, the worse will be the addiction. Amphetamines should not be taken at bedtime.

How Long Until It Works: Usually almost immediately, sometimes an hour after the first dose. The effect also wears off quickly, lasting only a few hours. Therefore the drug is usually taken in divided doses two or three times daily. After it has worked for a while the effect may wear off and the patient may require a higher dose. This is called tolerance. At this point a decision must be made either to keep raising the dose or to stop the drug because it is not working adequately.

Common Side Effects: (1) Nervousness. (2) Insomnia. (3) Loss of appetite. (4) Addiction.

Less Common Side Effects: (1) High blood pressure. (2) Rapid pulse rate. (3) Tolerance (constant need to raise the dose). (4) Feelings of suspicion and paranoia.

What to Do About Side Effects: The last dose of the drug every day should be taken several hours before bedtime to prevent insomnia. Nervousness usually goes away and appetite returns so that weight loss is rarely dangerous. Nothing can be done about the addiction except to remember not to stop taking amphetamines abruptly. If high blood pressure, rapid pulse, paranoia, or tolerance becomes a problem, the drug is usually stopped.

If It Doesn't Work: The drug should be slowly tapered. Fortunately, the withdrawal symptoms are psychological and not medical.

If It Does Work: Some people decide to stay on the drug indefinitely.

A very sick medical patient may legitimately stay on it for the rest of her life.

Cost: Brand, 15 cents/5-mg pill. Generic, 3 cents/5-mg pill.

Special Comments: Amphetamines are given only in special situations by very experienced psychiatrists. They are medically safe but usually produce addiction. There is also a good chance they will provide only temporary help.

METHYLPHENIDATE

Brand Name: Ritalin.

Used for: Officially, children with a condition called "attention deficit hyperactivity disorder," formerly called hyperactivity. Unofficially, Ritalin is sometimes prescribed for depression when nothing else has worked, or is added to other antidepressants when they have only worked partially, or is given to very medically sick people with depression. Ritalin is occasionally prescribed for elderly patients with depression and medical problems.

Do Not Use if: You have high blood pressure, you are very nervous, you have severe insomnia, or you have a history of addiction to drugs and alcohol.

Tests to Take First: Your pulse and blood pressure should be recorded. Some doctors will want an electrocardiogram (ECG, EKG).

Tests to Take While You Are on It: Pulse and blood pressure should be monitored frequently.

Usual Dose: Begins at about 5 mg twice daily and may go as high as 60 mg to obtain a response. Should not be taken at bedtime.

How Long Until It Works: The antidepressant effect may be felt immediately, after the first dose, but usually lasts only several hours. For this reason it should be taken two to three times daily.

Common Side Effects: (1) Nervousness. (2) Insomnia. (3) Loss of appetite. (4) Addiction (although it may be less addicting than amphetamines).

Less Common Side Effects: (1) High blood pressure (but less likely with Ritalin than with amphetamines). (2) rapid pulse rate. (3) Tolerance (constant need to raise the dose). (4) feelings of suspicion and paranoia (but less likely than with amphetamines).

110

What to Do About Side Effects: The last dose of the drug every day should be taken several hours before bedtime to prevent insomnia. Nervousness usually goes away and appetite often returns so that weight loss is rarely dangerous. Nothing can be done about the addiction except to remember not to stop taking Ritalin abruptly. If high blood pressure, rapid pulse, paranoia, or tolerance becomes a problem the drug is usually stopped.

If It Doesn't Work: The drug should be slowly tapered. Fortunately, the withdrawal symptoms are psychological and not medical.

If It Does Work: Some people decide to remain on the drug indefinitely. A very sick medical patient may legitimately stay on it for the rest of his life.

Cost: Brand, 26 cents/5-mg pill. Generic, 21 cents/5-mg pill.

Special Comments: Ritalin is best known as the somewhat controversial but highly safe and effective treatment for the childhood psychiatric condition called attention deficit hyperactivity disorder. Ritalin calms these children down, whereas, in adults, it has the opposite effect and is a stimulant. It is less powerful than amphetamines and therefore somewhat less addicting.

PEMOLINE

Brand Name: Cylert.

Special Comments: Pemoline is very similar to methylphenidate (Ritalin) except that it works longer and therefore needs to be taken only once daily. It is not used in adults very often. Liver function tests should be done periodically if it is prescribed. It often takes weeks before Pemoline works.

ELECTROCONVULSIVE THERAPY

"Shock treatment" easily ranks as the most controversial treatment in psychiatry. So many people have seen the movie *One Flew Over the Cuckoo's Nest,* and have derived from it an image of what electroconvulsive therapy (ECT) involves. To most people, shock treat-

111

ments mean strapping a resistant patient to a stretcher, slapping electrodes on his head, and sadistically releasing painful electrical current to the brain. The whole procedure is viewed as an exercise in mind control, like a lobotomy (which the "hero," played by Jack Nicholson, in *One Flew Over the Cuckoo's Nest,* also received).

ECT is obviously not a drug and therefore it would be easy to avoid talking about it in a book about psychiatric drugs. Somehow that seems a cowardly approach to a very heated and controversial area. So without undertaking a lengthy discussion, I will make a few statements about ECT.

First, it is an inescapable fact that for the treatment of major depression, ECT is by far the most successful method. The problem is that ECT does not work for most cases of atypical depression, for anxiety disorders, or for personality problems that involve occasional states of depression (Table 16). The diagnosis is again crucial. If the patient is properly diagnosed with major depressive disorder there is approximately a 90% chance that ECT will cure the patient.

Table 16:

Reasons to Administer Electroconvulsive Therapy to the Patient With Major Depression

1. Patient is extremely suicidal and it is dangerous to wait the weeks it usually takes for medication to work.
2. Patient refuses to eat and is severely malnourished; waiting for an antidepressant drug to work may be dangerous.
3. Patient has psychotic depression.
4. Patient has medical problems that make antidepressant medications risky (often true for elderly depressed patients).
5. Patient with major depression has not responded to at least a four-week trial of a cyclic antidepressant and then a four-week trial of a monoamine oxidase inhibitor antidepressant.

112

Second, ECT, as it is now performed, resembles what was depicted in *One Flew Over the Cuckoo's Nest* about as much as a game of chess resembles a heavyweight boxing match. People who observe ECT are usually surprised at how boring and routine the procedure really is. The patient must first, agree to undergo ECT, and many hospitals now require the consent of both the patient and at least one family member. So there is no strapping of people by force onto stretchers. Next, an intravenous line is inserted and the patient is given a short-acting anesthetic that puts her to sleep. After this, a small dose of a drug that temporarily paralyzes the muscles is given and a bag is placed around the patient's mouth and nose so that air can be given mechanically until the muscle paralyzer wears off. In many hospitals, these drugs are now administered by anesthesiologists. Complications from any of these procedures are almost nonexistent. Finally, the electrodes are placed on the scalp and a brief pulse of electrical current is administered. The patient does not actually move or convulse physically; all that usually happens is an instantaneous twitching of the toes. After a few minutes, the patient wakes up and returns to his room. More and more patients are undergoing ECT as an outpatient procedure, without being admitted even overnight to the hospital.

Third, ECT is not mind control. The major side effect of ECT is memory loss. All patients forget what happened during the time immediately before each ECT treatment. After a few treatments many patients develop varying degrees of amnesia; they forget things that have just happened or people they have just met. Most usually remember remote events, things that occurred months and years before the treatment began, without any problem. Numerous good scientific studies have shown that in the great majority of patients, any memory problems caused by ECT disappear in time, usually well within a month. Careful neuropsychological testing in a number of studies has failed to show any long-lasting memory problems in most patients who have received ECT.

Sometimes, memory problems can last longer, although six months is generally the upper limit. What about those who insist they have "permanent brain damage" from ECT? Once again, it must be stated that careful scientific studies have never been able to find any evidence of permanent memory loss resulting from

ECT. It may be that patients with preexisting memory problems, such as occur with certain neurological illnesses, blame their problems on their ECT treatments. Recurrences of depression or other psychiatric illness after ECT treatment can also interfere with memory, but the patient may nevertheless mistakenly associate the memory problem with ECT. Finally, we must always entertain the possibility that for a *rare* patient, ECT might produce long-term memory problems, but this has simply never been picked up by research studies. The risk of permanent memory defect from ECT seems so remote that individual patients should probably disregard it.

A few clinicians recommend "maintenance ECT" to depressed patients in which the patient receives a treatment every week or every other week as an outpatient. Some patients have received as many as 100 ECT treatments using this procedure. The indications and effectiveness of this procedure have never been rigorously studied. Furthermore, it is possible that such a large number of treatments might produce more long-term memory loss than the standard six to twelve ECT treatments generally recommended. Consequently, I feel that "maintenance ECT" should first be scientifically studied in research protocols before it is recommended in general clinical practice.

In the past, two electrodes were placed on the patient's head for ECT, one on each temple. This is called bilateral ECT. In the last few years, researchers have found that placing the electrodes on only one side results in less memory disturbance. This is called unilateral ECT. There is some controversy about whether unilateral ECT is as effective as bilateral ECT, but many clinicians now elect to try unilateral first and use bilateral only in patients who are unresponsive after several treatments.

Medically speaking, ECT is extremely safe. It is recommended for depressed patients who are too sick to take antidepressant medications and for depressed pregnant women, in whom antidepressant drugs could conceivably harm the unborn child. This may surprise some people, but it is generally believed by clinicians that shock treatment is less likely to harm an unborn child than is the administration of antidepressant drugs to the pregnant women. It is known that women with epilepsy who have seizures during their pregnancies usually deliver normal babies. There are very few instances in which ECT is ruled out on medical grounds.

Thus, ECT is a treatment of great effectiveness and very small risk. Why, then, is it so controversial?

First, the treatment is admittedly mysterious. One of my colleagues, Dr. Stuart Yudofsky, once likened it to kicking the television set when the picture is fuzzy. We still haven't the slightest clue why it works. All that is known is that causing a convulsion in the brain relieves depression. Interestingly, ECT also relieves mania and reduces psychotic symptoms in some patients with schizophrenia, although it is rarely used in these situations anymore.

Second, it is probable that ECT was abused in the past. It may have been administered to patients with a form of depression for which ECT is not effective. These patients generally do not respond, but sometimes clinicians continue to administer ECT treatments long after it is clear there is not going to be a response.

There are very specific instances in which ECT is a lifesaver: the patient who is extremely suicidal but does not respond to antidepressant drugs; the patient who refuses to eat because of depression and again does not respond to or will not agree to take antidepressant drugs; and the patient with psychotic depression. These are patients whose lives are at risk. Nothing about ECT is so bad to justify denying such patients an effective treatment.

For less emergency situations, most clinicians reserve the use of ECT for patients who have not responded to at least two antidepressant drugs, usually first a good try at a cyclic antidepressant and then a good try at a monoamine oxidase inhibitor. Many of these drug refractory patients respond very well to ECT.

ECT is usually given in a series of six to twelve treatments, each treatment separated by at least one day. After completing ECT, the patient is generally placed on an antidepressant drug for several more months for maintenance of the normal mood.

Chapter 8

Drugs Used to Treat Anxiety

Anxiety is not only normal, it is necessary. Anxiety makes us run away from a burning building, bring our children to the doctor when they complain of earaches, check the bindings on our skis every winter, and declare all our income on our tax returns. Worrying is a part of everyday life and although it may be unpleasant, it is a powerful mechanism to ensure that we avoid danger.

So why do we need drugs to make anxiety go away? Unlike depression, which seems to serve no useful purpose and therefore is best done away with, anxiety can be beneficial. Wouldn't drugs that eliminate anxiety do more harm than good? Do we really want to go through life entirely carefree without worries or fears?

These are absolutely legitimate questions. In fact, prescribing drugs to block anxiety can sometimes be very harmful. There is no question that unrestrained use of tranquilizers, street drugs, and alcohol to reduce life's normal cares and worries is dangerous.

Yet the recent and very extensive scientific survey conducted by the National Institute of Mental Health surprised many people—professionals and laymen alike—by showing that anxiety *disorders* are the most common psychiatric illnesses in the United States today. At least one out of every twenty Americans in any six-month period will suffer from an anxiety disorder that should be treated by a mental health professional. And in many instances medication is the best and safest way to treat those anxiety disorders.

THREE FORMS OF ANXIETY

The first and perhaps most important thing to know about anxiety is that it takes many forms; some require treatment and some are better left alone. I like to divide anxiety into three categories: (1) normal anxiety, (2) excessive anxiety, and (3) anxiety disorders. Let me explain a bit more what I mean.

Normal Anxiety

There are many good reasons to feel anxious, even though feeling anxious doesn't feel particularly good. If your daughter complains of a sore throat, you may well worry that it could be strep throat, that she might miss school, and that you may have to miss time from work to get her to the pediatrician. If you get into your car in the morning and the engine doesn't turn over, you will probably worry that the repair bill may be expensive, that you might have to do without the car for a few days, and that it could take hours for the tow truck to show up.

This kind of anxiety actually is helpful, because it will motivate you to take action. You worry about your daughter's sore throat, so you go to the phone and make an appointment to get a throat culture. The car may be in bad shape, so you start making arrangements for a tow truck and a rental car. In these situations the anxiety disappears when the stressful situation clears up. Once the pediatrician tells you nothing is seriously wrong with your child, you breathe a sigh of relief and stop worrying. When your friendly mechanic says the only problem with your car is that the battery is old and he'll have a new one in within an hour, you realize that it's only a minor inconvenience. So normal anxiety is related to a

118

real-life event, motivates you to take appropriate action, and goes away when the stressful situation clears up. You shouldn't waste your money on psychiatrists for this and certainly don't take drugs.

Excessive Anxiety

Sometimes a stressful situation arises that would make anyone feel anxious, but the anxiety grows out of proportion to the real threat involved. For example, many people feel anxious before meeting with their boss. They may worry about what the boss might say or do several hours before the meeting. Some may even have a little trouble getting their work done for a few hours. Once the meeting is over and nothing serious has happened, the person will normally relax and go on with things. Let's look, however, at an example where such anxiety becomes exaggerated:

Allen, a 33-year-old investment banker with a large firm, receives a call one morning from his boss' secretary, who said that the boss wanted to meet with him at three that afternoon. "What is it about?" Allen asks the secretary. "I think it's about the car company deal you just finished," she answers, although she obviously isn't sure. Instantly, our banker is in a panic. The deal he worked on had been successfully completed for the firm, but now he wonders if he left something out that has just come to light. Maybe the boss thinks he didn't work hard enough on the deal. After all, one night last week he left work before midnight, right in the middle of a crucial part of the transaction. Allen is unable to work the rest of the day. He feels nauseous, gets a headache, and suddenly starts worrying that he may have cancer, that his wife might be having an affair, that his tax return is going to be audited, and so on.

The meeting with the boss actually goes well, although Allen shakes the whole time. The boss thinks he did a good job, makes a few suggestions on things he might have been done better, tells Allen he is doing well with the firm, and then gets to the real purpose of the meeting: going over the next big deal he wants Allen to work on. But Allen's anxiety is unrelieved. He focuses only on the few suggestions for improvement the boss gives him, insisting to himself that unless he does better on the next deal he will certainly be fired. He spends the next week unable to sleep, fighting with his wife, and constantly worried. Eventually, as he becomes involved in the new deal he calms down. But his wife, who somehow puts up with all of this, points out to him that he seems to get into this state of high anxiety very often since he began working at the firm.

Obviously, Allen took normal anxiety about a meeting with his boss and blew it way out of proportion. He focused on the one slightly negative comment made by his boss and ignored all the praise. Instead of recognizing that the boss was obviously so satisfied with his work that he was putting him on another big deal, Allen turned things completely around to make it appear that he was on the brink of being fired. And Allen brought in all kinds of extraneous worries. Why should a meeting with his boss make him suddenly worry about his relationship with his wife, his physical health, or his income tax return? Finally, he suffered several physical signs of anxiety, like headache and upset stomach.

Excessive anxiety is anxiety that arises from a life stress but soon goes beyond what is called for. It serves no purpose and doesn't go away once the stress is over. Note, however, that Allen's anxiety eventually did go away; it lasted only about a week, and did not really impair his ability to work too much. Mostly, it was unpleasant and unnecessary and probably annoying to his wife.

Excessive anxiety often requires treatment, but rarely drug treatment. Various forms of psychotherapy are very useful for people like Allen to help them look at things more realistically and stop turning everyday life events into mental catastrophes. Sometimes people want to know more about what causes them to be so anxious and therefore may choose to have long-term psychotherapy. Other people use short-term psychotherapies to learn how to cope better with stress and to think more logically about things that happen. Either way, medications are usually not necessary.

Anxiety Disorders

Anxiety disorders are forms of anxiety that arise without any obvious life stress provocation. And then they don't go away, sometimes for life, if they are not treated. Unlike normal anxiety or excessive anxiety, anxiety disorders can have very great impact on the ability to function in day-to-day life. Although some doctors and scientists think that anxiety is nothing to be concerned about, some anxiety disorders can absolutely ruin a life.

In the last ten years scientists have made great progress in categorizing anxiety disorders and finding effective treatments. Some of these treatments do involve drugs. Like depression, anxiety disorders can almost always be treated successfully and sometimes the symptoms can be completely eliminated.

THE ANXIETY DISORDERS

There are four anxiety disorders, each with a very unique treatment requirement: generalized anxiety disorder (or GAD for short), panic disorder, the phobias, and obsessive-compulsive disorder (or OCD). A little description of each is necessary so that the patient with an anxiety disorder can understand the very different drug treatments that may be recommended.

Generalized Anxiety Disorder

A form of chronic anxiety, generalized anxiety disorder lasts at least six months; the patient is constantly anxious, tense, and worried. Usually it is difficult to fall asleep and there are lots of aches and pains like headache, stomachache, menstrual cramps, and backache. Although stressful events may make this condition worse, people with GAD are anxious even if everything is going great in their lives. Many drink excessively to try and calm down or fall asleep, so the risk of developing a problem with alcohol is high with GAD. Often, after many months or years with chronic anxiety, the patient develops a full-blown depression requiring antidepressant treatment. People with GAD usually have a lot of trouble at work. They don't have a lot of fun because they are always on edge and usually very fatigued. The most common medications that work for GAD, if medication is elected, are the benzodiazepines, which include familiar names like Valium, Xanax, Ativan, and Librium.

121

A new drug called buspirone (BuSpar) is also effective for GAD. Many other drugs have been tried, but are less effective. Many psychotherapies are also used to treat GAD.

Panic Disorder

The best way to describe panic disorder, which probably affects two million Americans at any given moment, is through a clinical example:

Jane, a neurosurgeon, is driving to work one day over a bridge when traffic gets a bit heavy and she wonders for a moment if she will get to the hospital on time. All of a sudden she feels her heart start to pound, she feels as if she can't catch her breath, and she shakes, trembles, and is sure she must be having a heart attack. Convinced she is about to die or lose control of the car, she drives very slowly in the right-hand lane. When Jane gets to the hospital her symptoms are relieved but she still goes to the emergency room and tells the nurse there that she thinks she is having a heart attack. The nurse is skeptical; Jane is, after all, a perfectly healthy-appearing 35-year-old woman. Nevertheless, she is seen immediately by an emergency room doctor who orders an electrocardiogram and several blood tests. Everything is normal.

Jane feels relieved. Her symptoms are now gone. Perhaps she simply has been working too hard. Maybe she needs a vacation. Everything goes back to normal until two days later when, while sitting at home reading, it happens again. Her heart pounds, she breathes too fast, and she feels dizzy and lightheaded. The symptoms last twenty minutes; by then Jane is back in the emergency room. This time a neurologist is called. Maybe it's a brain tumor. She is admitted to the hospital and undergoes many tests, but nothing abnormal is found. Jane is relieved to find she is not suffering from a deadly disease. But she keeps having attacks, each lasting about twenty minutes, and each terrifying. They happen in the car, at work, and at home.

Now Jane starts worrying about when the next attack might strike. She has what we call *anticipatory anxiety,* worrying between attacks. She also starts avoiding situations in which she might not be able to get help right away if an attack occurs. She doesn't want to drive across the bridge during rush hour for fear of being trapped in the car during a traffic jam; she turns down a chance to fly to Hawaii for a conference; she sits near the door in church and the movies so she can get out fast. Soon, Jane becomes so afraid of getting an attack that she avoids going anywhere unless accompanied by a close friend.

Jane has developed panic disorder. The attacks are called panic attacks. Unlike a person with generalized anxiety disorder who is more or less always anxious, the patient with panic disorder becomes anxious in sudden and unpredictable bursts. Scientists believe that the cause of this disorder is partly medical and partly psychological. It is believed that panic disorder has a biological basis, but that stressful life events contribute to the severity of the illness. Some patients get so fearful of having attacks that they avoid places where help will not be immediately available; this is called *agoraphobia*.

Medications have been known for over twenty years to be very successful in blocking the panic attacks. Most of these medications are also antidepressants. Many of the effective antipanic drugs are also antidepressants, including cyclic antidepressants (Tofranil, Norpramin, and Aventyl), monoamine oxidase inhibitors (Nardil and Parnate), and Prozac. Desyrel, Asendin, and Welbutrin are not generally effective for panic disorder. Xanax, a benzodiazepine antianxiety drug, has also been shown to be effective in treating panic attacks. Other benzodiazepines, including Klonopin and Ativan, are now being studied for effectiveness against panic. BuSpar, however, is almost certainly not an antipanic drug even though it is effective for generalized anxiety. In addition to drugs, there are now reports that some forms of psychotherapy are also effective in blocking panic attacks. In any event, panic disorder almost always requires treatment.

Phobias

Phobias are irrational fears of things or situations that become so extreme the person avoids them. To be classified as a phobia, the avoidance must seriously interfere with the ability to function. A person who is afraid of skydiving does not have a phobia, because most of us live very nicely without jumping out of airplanes. There are three types of phobias. *Agoraphobia* is really a complication of panic disorder and is treated along with panic attacks.

Simple phobia is a fear of a specific situation or object, for example, fear of heights, fear of closed-in spaces (claustrophobia), and fear of animals. Simple phobias are very normal in childhood. There are no drug treatments for simple phobias, which usually respond nicely to psychotherapy.

Social phobia is a fear of social situations. These patients have severe anxiety attacks if they have to talk in front of a group, speak up in class, call someone for a date, or even sign a check when the bank teller is watching. Whenever they feel they are being watched or have to perform, people with social phobia become extremely anxious, have palpitations, shake, blush, and tremble. Then they think people can see them shaking and blushing and they get even more nervous. Let me give an example of social phobia:

Jonathan was a very popular and outgoing teenager until one day when he had to give a speech in front of his high school class. As he approached the podium he noticed that his heart was pounding. Previously, this stage fright had disappeared once he began, but this time it just got worse as he began talking. In addition to the pounding heart, Jonathan started shaking, felt his voice was going to crack, and began to sweat. He feared that everyone in the audience could see his nervousness and that he would be thoroughly embarrassed. Somehow he got through the speech, but was absolutely convinced he did a terrible job. Afterward, he refused to speak in front of the whole class ever again. Next, it became difficult for him to raise his hand in class because he would experience similar symptoms whenever the teacher called on him. Finally, he started to avoid parties and other social events. Almost any social interaction precipitated an anxiety attack. Now, as an adult, Jonathan rarely attends social events. Although he is very intelligent he has never advanced in his career because he cannot make presentations or withstand job interviews. He feels lonely and frustrated and often gets drunk if he cannot avoid a social encounter.

Social phobia is obviously more than stage fright. Once again, both medications and psychotherapies can relieve the condition to a considerable extent. Effective medications include beta blockers (like propranalol and atenolol), monoamine oxidase inhibitors (Nardil and Parnate), and possibly Prozac.

Obsessive Compulsive Disorder

Formerly thought to be a rare condition, OCD is now felt to affect as many as one in one hundred people. It has recently also become the subject of intense scientific study, and some good treatments are beginning to emerge. These include Prozac and a drug called Anafranil.

Patients with OCD have either one of two problems, or both. An excellent place to read about patients with OCD is in the book by Dr. Judith Rapoport, *The Boy Who Couldn't Stop Washing.* Some examples follow:

If you met Mr. C. at a party or business meeting, you would think he was a pretty ordinary person. He might tell you he works as an accountant, that he is married but has no children, and that he likes watching sporting events on television. You probably wouldn't notice that he refused to eat any food offered him at the party, and that he quietly disappeared to the bathroom five times in the course of only a few hours. And you might not observe that Mr. C's hands are red, raw, and blistered. Mr. C. has had a compulsion to wash his hands as many as forty times a day since he was 16 years old. Anytime he thinks his hands might be dirty, say from touching a piece of food, taking out the garbage, or dusting his apartment, he immediately gets an irresistible urge to wash them hands. He knows that this kind of dirt is not dangerous and that his hand washing is completely excessive.

For entirely mysterious reasons, however, the urge to wash his hands is overwhelming; if he doesn't do it he feels intolerable anxiety. Once he washes he immediately relaxes, until the next time. He can't travel or sit in a movie theater long because he has to know that a sink and soap will always be nearby. Needless to say, he can only hold certain kinds of very restricted jobs where no one will notice. Sometimes he gets so sick of his compulsion that he becomes extremely depressed, but depression is clearly not the

125

major problem. No matter how hard he tries, he cannot stop washing his hands.

Mr. C. has classic compulsions as part of his obsessive-compulsive disorder. Like many patients with this illness, he has had symptoms from adolescence—some people get this as young children—and he is tortured by the compulsions. He does not really want to wash his hands, he does not think the hand washing is necessary, but he cannot stop. Other patients have different compulsions, for example, scrubbing their homes over and over to be sure there is no dirt, checking more than one hundred times that the gas on the stove is turned off before leaving home.

Another example, of a slightly different kind, is Ms. J. who is a secretary in a law firm. She does fairly good work, but is slow and sometimes doesn't complete her work on time. This puzzles her bosses because they think she is unusually intelligent, dedicated, and very organized. Yet sometimes she seems to do everything in slow motion. The reason is that Ms. J. cannot type a document until she first counts all the words in the document. Sometimes she may get almost to the end of counting when she suddenly fears she has made a mistake and must start all over again. If she is interrupted in the middle of counting, she also must begin again. At home, when Ms. J. starts to read a magazine article she forces herself to count all the words beforehand. She never throws out an article she has read because at anytime, she may suddenly doubt she has counted the words correctly and feel compelled to go back and start counting again.

Like Mr. C., Ms. J. hasn't the slightest idea why she needs to conduct these counting rituals or why she has obsessive doubts that she has counted correctly. The obsessive doubts can be terrifying to her; once she thinks she has counted wrong she can think of nothing else until she counts again. At night she may lie awake with various obsessions, like trying to remember how many words were in a document she typed two weeks earlier. Ms. J. has a combination of compulsions—needing to count over and over—and obsessions—thinking in her mind over and over about the number of words in various documents. No one else is aware of her behavior; the bosses simply think Ms. J. is slow. She has never married or conducted a long-term relationship so no other person has seen the piles of magazines on the floors of her apartment. Ms. J. would do anything to stop her compulsions and obsessions, but no amount of effort ever works.

There are behavioral psychotherapies that may work for some patients with OCD, but this is a very hard condition to treat. Almost all patients ultimately take some medication in addition to therapy. The medications that sometimes work are mostly specific antidepressant drugs, including Anafranil and Prozac, even though patients with OCD are not always depressed.

WHEN SHOULD YOU SEEK HELP FOR ANXIETY

We have now identified three broad categories of anxiety—normal anxiety, excessive anxiety, and anxiety disorders—and within these broad categories several subgroups. It may sound complicated: how can anyone figure out where they belong? Here are some guidelines to help you decide when you should consult an expert and when you should consider taking medication:

1. First, try to figure out if there is an obvious reason why you are feeling nervous. Don't grasp at straws; you shouldn't be staying awake all night because you failed a math exam thirty years ago. Ask yourself if the reason you think you feel nervous would make other people feel nervous and if it is likely that your life will calm down soon.

2. Next, try to decide if this is an isolated episode of anxiety or if you are always an anxious person. Do you have a history of letting little setbacks put you into a panic for months?

3. Finally, consider whether the anxiety is helping you stay on top of the situation and take effective action or is impairing your ability to function.

If there is no obvious reason for the anxiety, if you are constantly plagued by anxiety or anxiety-related symptoms, or if anxiety makes it hard for you to function you should consult a psychiatrist for evaluation.

And even more important than the preceding three rules, if you find yourself abusing alcohol, tranquilizers, or any drug to calm yourself down you should seek a consultation immediately. Anxiety disorders can cause alcohol and drug abuse.

What should the consulting psychiatrist tell you? First, the psychiatrist may help you recognize that there is a perfectly good reason for you to be anxious and that you should expect to feel better when things calm down. Let me give an example:

A 45-year-old woman asked me if I would give her a prescription for Valium. She had been feeling very nervous and anxious for several weeks, had difficulty sleeping, and was less able to concentrate at work. It turned out that two of her most trusted assistants had just resigned to take other jobs; she now had to work sixty-hour weeks without much sympathy from either her boss or her husband. Her elderly mother had recently had a stroke and called her daily from the nursing home with new complaints. I felt that this woman, who liked to believe she could cope with anything and resented any emotional problem that might interfere with her usually high performance, had good reason to feel anxious. Giving her Valium would only make her sleepy during the day. Instead, I suggested she was overlooking how much stress she was under and worked out a plan for her to reduce the tension in her life. This included explaining to her boss and husband what the problems were, insisting that she get new assistants, taking a few days off, and asking her sister to help out more with their mother.

In this case, the psychiatrist was expected to hand out a prescription but he didn't. Sometimes, patients are disappointed or angry when told medication is not the right choice; how many internists prescribe antibiotics to patients suffering from viruses just so they can satisfy the patient's wish to get any drug?

On the other hand, there are opposite cases in which the patient may think there is enough stress to explain his symptoms when in fact he is avoiding the fact that a real psychiatric problem exists.

When I first saw Mr. Q., for example, he told me about his recurrent panic attacks. He had to have his wife in the car with him at all times, and even so refused to drive over bridges or through tunnels. He hadn't been in an airplane for five years and couldn't stand shopping malls because the exits are hard to find. So his life was constricted to being driven to his office every day and then driven home. Even so, he had a full-blown panic attack at least once a month and was well known to every emergency room and general practitioner in his home town. Mr. Q. insisted that he was merely suffering from "stress." Things had been hard at work lately, he told me. Sometimes he had fights with his wife. His college-age son was not getting very good grades. All of that might be true, I explained to Mr. Q., but it really sounded like pretty routine stress to me. He had been suffering from panic attacks for five years, but his son started college only six months ago, he had had exactly four arguments with his wife in that period and their marriage seemed solid, and he had been at the same job for almost 15 years. Mr. Q. did not want to face the fact that he was suffering from panic disorder and that mere stress reduction was unlikely to help him. He needed treatment directed toward cessation of the panic attacks and then reduction of his phobias. I prescribed a short course of antipanic medication (imipramine in this case) and some psychotherapy and he did very well.

The psychiatrist, then, must first make a diagnosis. A patient with normal anxiety should be reassured that things will clear up in time. A patient with excessive anxiety should be told that she is overreacting and may need psychotherapy to learn how to keep things within bounds. Occasionally, a very short course of medication is used. A patient with an anxiety disorder requires a combination of specific psychotherapy and medication. Thus, an understanding of the nature of the anxiety problem is very important: the treatment must be tailored to the diagnosis.

THE BENZODIAZEPINES: ARE THEY REALLY DANGEROUS?

By far the drugs most often prescribed to treat anxiety problems belong to the class called *benzodiazepines*. The brand names for these drugs are very familiar to most people and include Valium, Librium, Tranxene, and Xanax. Millions of prescriptions are written

129

for benzodiazepines every year, usually by doctors who are not psychiatrists. In 1981, for example, 54.4 million prescriptions for benzodiazepines were written in the United States (Baum C, Kennedy DL, Forbes MB, et al: Drug use in the United States in 1981. *Journal of the American Medical Association* 1984; 251:1293–1297). Besides being good for anxiety, the benzodiazepines can be used as muscle relaxants and sleeping pills. They are also used to treat seizures in some patients with epilepsy.

The benzodiazepines provoke much heated debate, enough to make the average patient taking a benzodiazepine wonder what is in them. Nowadays it seems there are only two schools of thought, the school that says benzodiazepines are perfectly harmless and the school that says they are disasters. Listen to the first group and you'll think benzodiazepines are as safe as a warm glass of milk before bed. Listen to the second group and you'll think heroin is better.

It is appropriate for experts to fight it out on these issues. But they aren't the ones who are supposed to swallow the pills. So let me try to make some sense of this.

First, the positive side. Benzodiazepines first became available in this country in the early 1960s. They replaced barbiturates and meprobamate (Miltown, Equanil) for treating anxiety. Everybody thought then they represented a major advance. Medically, they are extremely safe. You cannot commit suicide by taking a truckload of benzodiazepines, unless they are combined with other substances. Benzodiazepines don't hurt the brain, heart, liver, or kidneys. They also work very well to relieve anxiety. It is rare that a truly anxious person won't get some help from taking them, and the benefit may be realized after a day or two. Once a stable dose is established, most patients continue to realize benefit from benzodiazepines without needing to increase the dose. That is, contrary to popular belief, several excellent scientific studies show convincingly that tolerance to benzodiazepines—the need to constantly increase the dose to maintain the therapeutic effect—is extremely rare. And stopping use of benzodiazepines has no life-threatening consequences like stopping use of barbiturates. A recent article in the highly respected *New England Journal of Medicine* (1983; 309: 410–416) stated that "The majority of patients taking benzodiazepines appear to derive clinical benefit from them, even when the drugs are taken for prolonged periods. Evidence of drug abuse or excessive escalation of dosage is generally lacking, and there is no consistent evidence that pharmacotherapy of anxiety impairs patients' incentive to seek more definitive solutions.''

BENZODIAZEPINE DEPENDENCE

So benzodiazepines are medically safe, very effective drugs. What could be better?

But here are the negatives. Even though you won't die when you try to stop taking benzodiazepines you won't enjoy the experience very much either. A definite *withdrawal* syndrome is associated with coming off benzodiazepines. At least 50% of patients experience some degree of withdrawal when stopping benzodiazepines. The symptoms are listed in Table 17.

You can read more about withdrawal in general in Chapter 6. As far as the benzodiazepines are concerned, it is important to remember that the severity of the withdrawal symptoms depends directly on several factors:

1. The higher the dose of the benzodiazepine, the worse will be the withdrawal once the drug is stopped.

2. The longer the person has taken benzodiazepines, the worse will be the withdrawal once the drug is stopped.

3. Short-acting benzodiazepines (Xanax, Serax, Ativan) may produce more severe withdrawal symptoms than long-acting benzodiazepines (Valium, Librium, Tranxene), but the difference is very small.

4. Very potent benzodiazepines (Klonopin, Xanax, Ativan) may provide more severe withdrawal symptoms than less potent benzodiazepines (Valium, Librium, Tranxene).

5. Withdrawal symptoms can be reduced a great deal by slow tapering of the medication. Almost all patients experience strong withdrawal symptoms if the medication is stopped suddenly.

Table 17:

Symptoms of Withdrawal From Benzodiazepines

Most Common	Nervousness
	Insomnia
	Loss of appetite
	Metallic taste
	Tingling feelings
	Headache
	Lack of coordination
	Perspiration
	Noises sound very loud
	Muscle aches
	Lack of energy
Least common	Poor concentration

Note: All of these last about two weeks after stopping the medication and are usually completely gone by four weeks.
Source: Lader M: Dependence on benzodiazepines. *Journal of Clinical Psychiatry* 1983; 44:121–127.

6. Withdrawal symptoms usually last two weeks and rarely longer than four weeks after the drug is stopped. They are not life threatening and hospitalization is almost never required.

7. People who abuse other drugs, especially alcohol, generally have a harder time stopping benzodiazepines than non–drug abusers.

8. Withdrawal from benzodiazepines is far easier than from drugs formerly used to treat anxiety, such as barbiturates, meprobamate (Miltown, Equanil), Placidyl, Doriden, and Noludar.

The higher the dose, the more powerful the benzodiazepine, and the longer a person takes the drug the worse will be the withdrawal syndrome when the drug is stopped. So in a sense, patients get "hooked" on benzodiazepines. The term *addiction,* however, should not be applied to benzodiazepine use. Addiction implies a life-style totally consumed with obtaining and taking a drug even if it results in severe injury to the addicted person or others. A cocaine addict will kill to get cocaine and is willing to die for his "coke." People who take Valium do not rearrange their lives or steal or murder to get Valium and they do not disregard their own health. It is medically correct to say that benzodiazepines produce physical and psychological dependence evidenced by the withdrawal syndrome that occurs when they are stopped.

There are a few other problems with benzodiazepines. Their biggest side effect is sleepiness. That's okay if your problem is insomnia, but not so good if you have to drive your car. Some experts say that benzodiazepines are associated with traffic accidents. Also, they may cause memory problems and confusion in elderly people and there is some evidence that benzodiazepines, like a lot of drugs, can increase the risk of an elderly person falling and fracturing a hip.

As in any other debate on a medical topic, the truth about benzodiazepines lies between the two sides. Benzodiazepines are medicines with side effects and potential complications. They are not perfect and are prescribed to many patients who would be better off without them. Once you take them, it is important to try to keep the dose low and to stop as quickly as possible. But it would be tragic for the person suffering from an anxiety disorder who barely gets through the day to be denied these safe and effective drugs. Aspirin causes far more physical harm than benzodiazepines if taken for long periods, and steroid drugs sometimes prescribed for problems as trivial as poison ivy can produce more serious psychological complications.

Let me give some examples of how to use and how *not* to use benzodiazepines:

A recently married woman visits her general practitioner, complaining of stomach cramps, diarrhea, and nausea over the last four weeks. All of the medical tests turn out to be normal. The woman admits to her doctor that she has been worrying a little bit lately about how happy she will be with her marriage. So the doctor gives her a prescription for a one-month supply of Valium, with automatic renewals up to six months. He tells her to try and stop worrying.

This is the classic case of overprescription of benzodiazepines. First, the woman could conceivably take the drug every day for six months without ever seeing a doctor. Second, it is unlikely that Valium will make her marriage any better. Maybe the marriage is fine, but she is having trouble making the adjustment. Maybe the marriage is terrible and the couple should seek counseling. Maybe the marriage isn't the problem at all and the woman has a different psychiatric problem. By the time this woman's prescription runs out she will probably have a hard time getting off Valium without going through withdrawal symptoms.

It is proper for nonpsychiatric doctors to prescribe short courses of anxiety medication. They often know their patients very well and some people confide more in a trusted family doctor or gynecologist than in anyone else. But the general practitioner is not specially trained in psychiatric disorders. Remember the rule: don't take benzodiazepines prescribed by a nonpsychiatric physician longer than a couple of weeks. If you need drugs for anxiety that badly, a short-term prescription won't be enough; you should be seeing a psychiatrist.

Now let me relate an opposite situation. A 40-year-old woman has been taking small doses of the antianxiety drug Librium for 10 years. About once a month she sees her psychiatrist for a prescription renewal. She is working well as an executive at a bank and maintains good social relationships. She has gotten some benefit from psychotherapy, but now wants to go on with life without having to see a therapist on a regular basis. She does not abuse alcohol and reports no side effects from taking Librium.

One weekend her psychiatrist is away and she calls his covering doctor for a prescription renewal. The covering doctor tells her that she is probably addicted to Librium, that she should stop taking it right away, that the drug is only covering up her deep-seated psychological problems, and that she should get into psychotherapy again immediately. So the woman stops the Librium. After two weeks of undergoing a withdrawal syndrome, the insomnia, ringing in the ears, and upset stomach go away, but over the next month, all her old anxiety problems return. She worries incessantly, feels jumpy and tense all the time, and can't concentrate at work. She tries psychotherapy, but finds that all she does in her sessions is worry out loud and complain. Finally, she sees the original doctor who recommends restarting Librium. Within a week, she is back to normal.

In the case of the bank executive, it is very hard to figure out what harm is done by having her take Librium on a regular basis. Without it, she suffers from generalized anxiety disorder to the point where her life is miserable. With it, she functions well and has no side effects.

Obviously, the two cases presented represent extremes. Yet they are entirely realistic and reflect the daily state of affairs. Benzodiazepines should be taken by people who need them for as long as they are needed. They should not be prescribed casually, and attempts to stop them should be made at regular intervals. But they should not be withheld from suffering patients.

When it is time to stop benzodiazepines, the rule is to do it slowly. This is especially important if benzodiazepines have been taken for more than a month. A patient who has taken 15 mg of Valium for two months should reduce the dose to 10 mg for a week and then 5 mg for a week before stopping. In some cases it may even be necessary to taper off in smaller increments. A patient treated for panic disorder with Xanax for six months, for example, will usually feel most comfortable if the medication is slowly tapered over four to six weeks. It is important to work out a tapering schedule with your doctor when the time to stop medication comes.

TREATMENT OF GENERALIZED ANXIETY DISORDER

Two types of drugs are used, the benzodiazepines and a relatively new drug called buspirone (BuSpar), to treat GAD. Most of the benzodiazepines are identical and there are very few good reasons to pick one over the other. They can be divided into two groups, *long-acting* and *short-acting* benzodiazepines (see Table 18).

Long-acting benzodiazepines remain in the body days after the last pill is swallowed. This means that when they are stopped, the amount in the body slowly decreases to zero. This may make withdrawal symptoms less severe because in effect the drug tapers itself.

Short-acting benzodiazepines are completely eliminated from the body a few hours after they are consumed, resulting in an abrupt on–off situation. If a short-acting benzodiazepine is taken before bedtime, by the time the patient wakes up, none will be left in the body. This may be desirable if the patient wants to be completely alert during the day, but it also means that withdrawal symptoms may be worse if the drug is suddenly stopped. Descriptions of all the benzodiazepines and of the new and very different drug BuSpar follow.

Table 18:

Long- and Short-Acting Benzodiazepines

LONG ACTING	SHORT ACTING
Valium	Ativan
Librium	Serax
Tranxene	Xanax
Klonopin	
Centrax	

DIAZEPAM

Brand Name: Valium.

Used for: Generalized anxiety disorder. Sometimes for a condition called night terrors that occurs in children. Also prescribed by general practitioners for muscle relaxation, such as may be needed for people with back problems.

Do Not Use if: You have a history of alcohol abuse or other misuse of addictive drugs, you have liver disease, or you are pregnant or nursing.

Tests to Take First: None required. Valium can be given to patients with very serious medical problems. It has no bad effects on the heart, lungs, or kidneys.

Tests to Take While You Are on It: None. Again, diazepam (Valium) doesn't cause any medical problems that require monitoring by blood tests or x-rays.

Usual Dose: Valium is a *long-acting* benzodiazepine, so one 5 mg dose often lasts the whole day. Patients usually take between 5 and 20 mg daily; the dose can be divided and taken in the morning and evening or taken all at once.

How Long Until It Works: Valium works more quickly than any other benzodiazepine, so relief from anxiety can be felt within thirty minutes to an hour after taking the first pill. For people with generalized anxiety disorder who take it regularly, there usually is a substantial improvement within one week. Once the dose of Valium that controls anxiety is found, most patients remain on that dose indefinitely without experiencing new anxiety symptoms.

Common Side Effects: Drowsiness, potentiation of the effects of drinking alcohol, and withdrawal symptoms when the drug is stopped, especially if stopped abruptly.

Less Common Side Effects: (1) Disinhibition—some patients lose control of their impulses after taking drugs like Valium and do things they wouldn't ordinarily do, like shoplifting, starting arguing with the boss, or driving the car recklessly. (2) dizziness. (3) Confusion and forgetfulness (especially in the elderly).

What to Do About Side Effects: The biggest problem is sleepiness, which usually goes away after a while. Lowering the dose or taking it only at bedtime helps. In general, patients taking Valium should drink very little alcohol, if any, and should never have anything to drink within hours of driving a car. Withdrawal symptoms are reduced by gradually tapering the dose, usually over two to four weeks. It should never be stopped suddenly, especially if it has been taken longer than two weeks. Patients who become disinhibited should probably not take Valium. Dizziness, confusion, and forgetfulness are particular problems in elderly patients, who should be given very small doses of Valium and checked carefully for these side effects. Elderly people should never be put on Valium without being seen regularly by a physician.

If It Doesn't Work: Failure usually means that the diagnosis was wrong and that the patient's main problem isn't generalized anxiety disorder. Sometimes a depression has been missed; Valium won't help depression much. Sometimes the real problems are difficulties in the patient's life that are better dealt with by psychotherapy. Changing from one benzodiazepine to another rarely helps.

If It Does Work: The principle of using the smallest amount of drug for the shortest period possible holds. There is no known medical risk associated with remaining on Valium for life, but the longer a person takes such a drug the harder it is to stop. After a few weeks an attempt should be made to lower the dose. Every month or so, an attempt should be made to stop the drug entirely and see what happens. While a patient is on Valium, every effort should be made to find solutions to anxiety-provoking situations in his life.

Cost: Brand, 48 cents/5-mg pill. Generic, 3 cents/5-mg pill.

Special Comments: Valium is one of the all-time, best-selling medications. There is no better benzodiazepine antianxiety drug. It is safe, works quickly, and helps most patients with anxiety problems a great deal. It is definitely habit forming, and this must always be taken into account before use.

CHLORDIAZEPOXIDE

Brand Name: Librium.
Used for: Generalized anxiety disorders. Alcohol withdrawal.
Usual Dose: 25 to 50 mg two to three times daily, but many people get by with less.

Cost: Brand, 71 cents/25-mg pill. Generic, 4 cents/25-mg pill.

Special Comments: Librium is in almost every respect similar to Valium; some people find Librium less sedating. It is a long-acting benzodiazepine. Besides being used for anxiety, it is sometimes used to help detoxify alcoholics. The side effects are similar to those of Valium. Librium is available in combination with another drug in a preparation called Librax for treatment of upset stomach. Librium also comes combined with the antidepressant drug amitriptyline in a preparation called Limbitrol. I usually recommend staying away from pills that combine different medications, so it is best to take antianxiety drugs and drugs for upset stomach or depression separately.

CLORAZEPATE

Brand Name: Tranxene.

Usual Dose: Starts at 7.5 mg once or twice daily and usually levels off at about 30 mg a day. Some patients take 60 mg daily.

Cost: Brand, 74 cents/7.5-mg pill. Generic, 18 cents/7.5-mg pill.

Special Comments: Another long-acting benzodiazepine, Valium, is turned into Tranxene by the body. It is almost identical to Valium.

PRAZEPAM

Brand Name: Centrax.

Usual Dose: Starts at 10 to 15 mg daily and is increased to between 30 and 60 mg for best results.

Cost: Brand, 54 cents/10-mg pill. Generic, 34 cents/10-mg pill.

Special Comments: Centrax is a long-acting benzodiazepine with the same properties as Valium.

HALAZEPAM

Brand Name: Paxipam.

Usual Dose: Starts at 20 mg once or twice daily to a maximum of about 80 to 160 mg per day.

Cost: Brand, 31 cents/20-mg pill. Generic, not available.

Special Comments: Once again, Paxipam is a long-acting benzodiazepine indistinguishable from Valium.

LORAZEPAM

Brand Name: Ativan.
Used for: Generalized anxiety disorder. Calming agitated patients with mania or schizophrenia. Assisting in detoxification of alcoholics.
Do Not Use if: You have a drinking problem or misuse any other addictive drugs, you have serious liver disease, or you are pregnant or nursing.
Tests to Take First: None required.
Tests to Take While You Are on It: None required.
Usual Dose: Ativan is a short-acting benzodiazepine, so a single dose is eliminated from the body in less than one day. Most patients start with 0.5 mg twice a day. This can then be raised if necessary to a total of 2 to 4 mg daily. Ativan can also be given by injection, although this is rarely necessary when treating patients for anxiety problems.
How Long Until It Works: Some relief from anxiety is usually experienced about an hour after the first dose. Patients who need to take it regularly for severe generalized anxiety disorder will find the illness to be much relieved in the first week. They also find that they need to take the drug at least twice daily, because the effect doesn't last longer than eight to twelve hours.
Common Side Effects: (1) Drowsiness. (2) Potentiation of the effects of drinking alcohol. (3) Withdrawal symptoms when the drug is stopped, especially if stopped abruptly. (4) There is some evidence that short-acting benzodiazepines like Ativan cause even worse withdrawal symptoms when they are stopped.
Less Common Side Effects: (1) Disinhibition—some patients lose control of their impulses after taking drugs like Ativan and do things they wouldn't ordinarily do, like shoplifting, arguing with the boss, or driving the car recklessly. (2) Dizziness. (3) Confusion and forgetfulness (especially in elderly patients).
What to Do About Side Effects: The biggest problem is sleepiness, which usually goes away after a while. Lowering the dose or taking

it only at bedtime helps. In general, patients taking Ativan should drink very little alcohol, if any, and should never have anything to drink within hours of driving a car. Withdrawal symptoms may be even more severe than with Valium, and it is crucial that the dose be gradually reduced over two to four weeks if the patient has taken Ativan longer than two weeks. Patients who become disinhibited should probably not take Ativan. Dizziness, confusion, and forgetfulness are particular problems in elderly patients, who should be given very small doses of Ativan and checked carefully for these side effects. Elderly people should never be put on Ativan without being seen regularly by a physician.

If It Doesn't Work: This usually means that the diagnosis was wrong and that the patient's main problem isn't generalized anxiety disorder. Sometimes a depression has been missed; Ativan won't help depression much. Sometimes the real problems are difficulties in the patient's life that are better dealt with by psychotherapy. Changing from one benzodiazepine to another rarely helps.

If It Does Work: The principle of using the smallest amount of drug for the shortest period possible holds. There is no known medical risk associated with remaining on Ativan for life, but the longer a person takes such a drug, the harder it will be to stop. After a few weeks an attempt should be made to lower the dose. Every month or so an attempt should be made to stop the drug entirely and see what happens. While a patient is on Ativan, every effort should be made to find solutions to anxiety-provoking situations in her life.

Cost: Brand, 45 cents/1-mg pill. Generic, 7 cents/50-mg pill.

Special Comments: Ativan is used in situations where a short-acting drug is desirable. Some patients like to have a pill they can take only occasionally when their symptoms get very bad, knowing that they won't feel sedated more than a few hours. If medication for generalized anxiety is needed longer than a week or two, a long-acting benzodiazepine is probably better.

OXAZEPAM

Brand Name: Serax.

Usual Dose: Serax is one of the shortest acting of all benzodiazepines, so it should be taken three times a day to avoid breakthrough

141

anxiety symptoms. The dose ranges from 10 to 30 mg three to four times daily.

Cost: Brand, 50 cents/10-mg pill. Generic, 16 cents/10-mg pill.

Special Comments: Serax is very similar to Ativan, except that it is even shorter acting. The effects of the drug usually last only about five hours.

ALPRAZOLAM

Brand Name: Xanax.

Used for: Generalized anxiety disorder. Panic disorder. Depression.

Do Not Use if: You have a problem with alcohol or other addictive drugs, you have very advanced liver disease, or you are pregnant or nursing.

Tests to Take First: None required.

Tests to Take While You Are on It: None required.

Usual Dose: Usually begins at 0.5 mg two or three times daily and can be increased to a total of 4.0 mg per day, divided equally in two or three doses. Some doctors prescribe doses up to 10 mg per day, but this usually doesn't help that much. Most patients find they have to take the drug several times a day; it is very powerful but also short-acting. Eight to twelve hours after the last dose, sometimes even earlier, a patient may start to feel some withdrawal symptoms and increased anxiety.

How Long Until It Works: Like all benzodiazepines, Xanax offers some relief within an hour of taking the first pill. After a week of regular use, patients with generalized anxiety disorder feel much better. Panic disorder patients also start feeling better after the first week, but it may take two to four weeks until all of the panic attacks are blocked.

Common Side Effects: (1) Drowsiness. (2) Potentiation of the effects of drinking alcohol, and withdrawal symptoms (as with all of the short-acting benzodiazepines, especially if stopped abruptly).

Less Common Side Effects: (1) Disinhibition—very rarely, some patients lose control of their impulses after taking drugs like Xanax and do things they wouldn't ordinarily do, like shoplifting, arguing with the boss, or driving the car recklessly. (2) Dizziness. (3)

Confusion and forgetfulness (especially in the elderly). (4) There have been a few reports of drug withdrawal seizures, but only in patients who had taken alprazolam for long periods and then stopped abruptly.

What to Do About Side Effects: The biggest problem is sleepiness, which usually goes away after a while. Lowering the dose helps. In general, patients taking Xanax should drink very little alcohol and should never have anything to drink within hours of driving a car. This drug must absolutely never be stopped abruptly by anyone who has taken it regularly for more than a week. Slow tapering, over about four weeks, is necessary for safety and to decrease withdrawal symptoms. Patients who become disinhibited should probably not take Xanax. Dizziness, confusion, and forgetfulness are particular problems in elderly patients, who should be given very small doses of Xanax and checked carefully for these side effects. Elderly people should never be put on Xanax or any other antianxiety drug without being seen regularly by a physician.

If It Doesn't Work: For patients with generalized anxiety disorder, if Xanax doesn't work, usually the original diagnosis was wrong. The true nature of the psychiatric problem should be reconsidered. About 20% of panic disorder patients fail to respond to Xanax; most are then switched to one of the other antipanic drugs (like imipramine or Nardil) discussed in the next section. As explained in Chapter 7, Xanax is sometimes used to treat depressed patients who have serious medical problems because it is so safe. If it doesn't work for depression, however, another antidepressant drug is usually considered.

If It Does Work: Generalized anxiety disorder patients who are placed on Xanax are probably best served by trying to get off it as soon as possible; if it must be continued longer than a few weeks a switch to a longer acting drug to minimize breakthrough symptoms and decrease later withdrawal problems should be considered. Panic disorder patients are usually treated for six months after becoming panic free; then the dose is tapered slowly (over four to six weeks) (treatment of panic disorder is discussed in the next section). The same is true when Xanax is used for depressed patients.

Cost: Brand, 44 cents/0.5-mg pill. Generic, not available.

Special Comments: Xanax is a marvel within the drug industry because of the rapidity with which it became the best-selling antianxiety drug. It is very powerful and very safe. In general, patients like taking it and doctors don't worry that it will cause any harm. Nevertheless, very powerful and very short acting antianxiety drugs (like Xanax) also seem to be the hardest to stop taking, and there has been some backlash against Xanax because of the withdrawal symptoms patients experience upon discontinuation. It is best to keep the dose low and to keep trying to get the patient off the drug. Some people with generalized anxiety disorder need to take Xanax for months or years and patients with panic disorders should stay on it for a least six panic-free months. They need to understand beforehand that although this drug is medically safe, it is not always easy to stop using it. The patient can then decide if he or she wants to worry about future withdrawal problems, which are uncomfortable but not dangerous.

BUSPIRONE

Brand Name: BuSpar.
Used for: Generalized anxiety disorder.
Do Not Use if: You are taking a high dose of a benzodiazepine because buspirone probably won't work in this case.
Tests to Take First: None required.
Tests to Take While You Are on It: None required. BuSpar has no known effects on physical health.
Usual Dose: Most people start taking one pill (5 mg) three times a day. After about a week the dose is raised to four pills and then increased every three days until 30 mg is reached (six pills). If that doesn't work by about four weeks, the dose can be raised in 5-mg increments every three days up to a total dose of 60 mg daily.
How Long Until It Works: About four weeks. Unlike the benzodiazepines, BuSpar does not work right away. You can't take one and expect to feel relaxed in an hour.
Common Side Effects: Few. Mild headache and nausea sometimes occur, but usually go away in a few days.
Less Common Side Effects: Rarely, patients become more anxious. Theoretically, because of some similarities it has to other drugs not

used for anxiety, BuSpar might cause neurological problems (tardive dyskinesia) if taken for many years. In fact, this has not occurred to patients who have taken it, although the drug has been on the market only about three years.

What to Do About Side Effects: The side effects are so mild that nothing much usually has to be done, although lowering the dose can eliminate the headache and nausea.

If It Doesn't Work: Another medication is called for, usually a benzodiazepine.

If It Does Work: BuSpar is not habit forming; patients can pretty much start and stop it at will without worrying about withdrawal symptoms. No one knows yet exactly how long someone should stay on BuSpar, but it is already clear that in at least one third of anxious patients who respond to it, anxiety symptoms return once it is stopped. So, like the benzodiazepines, BuSpar is not a cure, only a treatment. As always, I recommend trying to stop use after a few months.

Cost: Brand, 49 cents/5-mg pill. Generic, not available.

Special Comments: BuSpar is very different from the benzodiazepines listed earlier. It has completely different effects on the brain. It doesn't make the patient sleepy and doesn't relax muscles. It doesn't potentiate the effects of drinking alcohol. Also, BuSpar is not habit forming, and there are no withdrawal symptoms, even if stopped abruptly. All of these are obviously advantages over benzodiazepines. The disadvantages are that it takes about four weeks to work, which may seem an eternity to a severely anxious patient, and it must be taken pretty much two or three times a day to have its full effect. Also, there is reason to believe that patients who have previously responded to one of the benzodiazepines will not be helped by BuSpar. BuSpar cannot be used to reduce the severity of the symptoms of withdrawal from benzodiazepines. Thus, a patient cannot simply stop a benzodiazepine and start BuSpar. Tapering the benzodiazepine is still necessary. Patients who need immediate relief will probably do better with benzodiazepines. A patient who can wait for a response should try BuSpar first.

Some doctors still prescribe a drug called meprobamate (Miltown, Equanil) for treatment of anxiety disorder. Although meprobamate is probably effective in reducing anxiety, it is not more effective than the benzodiazepines and is certainly more dangerous.

The risk of addiction, severe withdrawal after discontinuation, oversedation, and death if taken in overdose is greater with meprobamate than with any of the benzodiazepine drugs. I cannot think of a single clinical situation in which a patient is better off taking Miltown or Equanil than he is taking any of the benzodiazepines. It must be remembered that the Food and Drug Administration does not stop a drug from being prescribed because more effective drugs come along later. Usually, it takes an unexpected and life-threatening side effect to cause federal authorities to pull a medication off the shelves. Therefore, meprobamate can still be prescribed, although I feel it really shouldn't be used.

Summary of Drug Treatment for Generalized Anxiety Disorder

1. If patient can wait for relief (about 4 weeks), try BuSpar first.

2. If more immediate relief is needed, start a short-acting benzodiazepine (Xanax, Ativan, or Serax) for a few days up to two weeks.

3. If long-term treatment is needed, switch to a long-acting benzodiazepine (Valium, Librium, or Tranxene).

4. Keep doses of all drugs as low as possible and try discontinuation periodically.

TREATMENT OF PANIC DISORDER

Panic disorder has three components: the actual panic attack, the anxiety patients experience between panic attacks when they worry about the next one (called "anticipatory anxiety"), and phobias (Table 19). The phobias usually involve the fear of having a panic attack in a situation where help is not immediately available, such as in a car riding over a bridge or in an airplane.

It is important to understand the difference between generalized

Table 19:

Features of Panic Disorder

1. The Panic Attack
   Sudden burst of palpitations, chest discomfort, difficulty breathing or catching breath, dizziness, lightheadedness, sweating, feeling faint, tingling feelings in
   hands and feet, nausea, extreme fear of impending
   death or going crazy or losing control.
2. Anticipatory Anxiety
   Worrying that a panic attack is going to occur at any
   moment
3. Phobic Avoidance (also called Agoraphobia)
   Avoiding situations in which a panic attack may occur
   but help is not immediately available, for example, driving in a car (especially over a bridge), flying in a plane,
   sitting in the middle of the row in a movie theater.

anxiety disorder and panic disorder. In GAD, the patient is almost continuously worried, tense, and anxious. In panic disorder, the main problem is the sudden, episodic bursts of anxiety and physical symptoms (like palpitations, dizziness, and difficulty in breathing) that generally last ten to thirty minutes.

Medications are used mainly to block the panic attack itself. Once this is done, many patients no longer have anticipatory anxiety and also overcome their phobias quickly. Anticipatory anxiety can also be treated with one of the benzodiazepines (Valium, Librium, or Ativan) while waiting for the antipanic drug to work. Once the attacks are eliminated, however, some panic disorder patients continue to have phobias. These patients may require psychological treatment and usually respond well to a few sessions.

Either antidepressants or benzodiazepines are also used to treat panic disorder. Full descriptions of these drugs are found in Chapter 7 and in the section on Drugs Used to Treat Generalized Anxiety Disorder earlier in this chapter. The tried and true drug for treating panic disorder is the cyclic antidepressant drug imipramine (Tofranil), described in detail in Chapter 7. Other cyclic antidepressant drugs that work in treating panic disorder are desipramine (Norpramin or Pertofrane), nortriptyline (Aventyl or Pamelor), and clomipramine (Anafranil). Usually, imipramine or desipramine is chosen. The only difference between treating panic and treating depression with these drugs is that panic patients are sometimes very sensitive to the cyclics and may become even more anxious at the start of treatment. For that reason, I usually prescribe a lower dose to start—about 10 mg a day of imipramine or desipramine, for example—for panic patients than for depressed patients. Then, after the patient is used to the drug, the dose is raised to the same top doses used by depressed patients. Panic attacks are usually blocked completely after imipramine or desipramine is taken for four weeks. Please refer to Chapter 7 for a full discussion of imipramine and desipramine.

The benzodiazepine-like drug alprazolam (Xanax) is very effective in blocking panic attacks. It is also used to treat generalized anxiety disorder and is described in detail earlier in this chapter. Xanax is usually started at 0.5 mg two or three times daily and then increased to between 2 and 4 mg a day to completely block panic attacks. Occasionally, the dose is increased to as much as 10 mg, but I do not recommend this. Xanax works to block panic attacks more quickly than imipramine, in about one to two weeks. It has far fewer side effects, but is more difficult to stop than imipramine.

The use of other benzodiazepines to treat panic attacks, is currently the subject of research. One benzodiazepine drug in particular that seems to work is clonazepam (Klonopin). Klonopin is very similar to Valium, but is advertised by the company that makes it only for the treatment of epilepsy. Nevertheless, it may block panic attacks in patients with panic disorder. Klonopin lasts longer in the body than Xanax, so patients can get by with taking it only once a day. It is about twice as strong as Xanax. The top dose needed is about 2 or 3 mg per day. Unfortunately, some patients develop depression while taking Klonopin. Because of withdrawal symptoms it must be tapered very slowly when discontinued. Klonopin,

148

which is also sometimes used to treat bipolar affective illness, is described in more detail in Chapter 9.

The most powerful antipanic drugs are the antidepressant mono-amine oxidase inhibitors (MAOIs), also described in detail in Chapter 7. Drugs like phenelzine (Nardil) and tranylcypromine (Parnate) work in almost all panic disorder patients. Because of the many side effects they cause and the need for a special diet, however, most psychiatrists will try the patient on imipramine (Tofranil) or Xanax first. Only about 20% of patients do not respond to one of these two; they can then be prescribed an MAOI.

A number of other medications have been reported to work in blocking panic attacks. The new antidepressant Prozac is beneficial for panic attacks; I have had good success treating panic disorder patients with Prozac. The drug has very few side effects and is not habit forming, so it could be the ideal antipanic drug. Unfortunately, as the smallest dose available is a 20-mg capsule and panic disorder patients tend to be more sensitive to Prozac than patients with depression, panic patients may experience increased anxiety and insomnia during the first week of treatment. Until the drug company that makes it provides a smaller-dose capsule, psychiatrists get around the sensitivity problem by asking patients to open the capsule and take only one fourth to one half of the powder inside every morning for the first week. After a week, the patient may take the whole capsule every morning. One capsule is usually enough to block panic attacks; the drug takes effect in about four weeks.

Some drugs used to treat high blood pressure and heart conditions have also been tried in panic disorder. One, verapamil, may work. Beta blockers, for example, propranolol (Inderal), are often prescribed for panic disorder patients because they block the effects of adrenaline and reduce heart rate; however, these drugs usually do not work to block panic attacks. The same is true of the blood pressure drug clonidine (Catapres).

Now that I've listed all of these different drugs, we have one more important question to ask: are drugs really necessary to treat panic disorder?

In earlier years, I would have categorically maintained that the only way to block panic attacks proven effective was treatment with an antipanic drugs. But things change quickly in the mental health field, and exciting developments are now occurring in nondrug treatments of panic disorder. My colleague Dr. David Barlow in Albany, New York, for example, recently developed a method of treatment for panic disorder called "panic control therapy." This treatment is very different from what most people envision when they think of psychotherapy.

Panic control therapy and similar forms of nondrug treatment for panic disorder are very short term: usually, the patient sees the doctor about twelve times over two to three months. The treatment is extremely focused. The patient learns how to breathe correctly, how to stop exaggerating the significance of every palpitation and tingling feeling, how to face anxiety-provoking situations, and how to relax. Between meetings with the doctor there is a lot of home-work. Patients practice breathing without hyperventilating, put themselves into feared situations to become "desensitized," and record all of their anxious thoughts so they they can learn to combat them.

It is too early to tell if this kind of treatment will work as well as antipanic drugs, but outlook for panic control therapy is promis-ing. It does take a little longer to work than medication. With antipanic drugs, panic attacks are usually under control in four weeks, whereas panic control therapy can take three months. And the patient must work at panic control therapy; antipanic drugs merely require remembering to swallow pills. It has been suggested that patients who undergo treatments such as panic control therapy will remain free from panic attacks longer after completion of treat-ment is finished than patients who take antipanic drugs and then discontinue them, but this hypothesis is far from proven.

Another major problem with panic control therapy and similar, focused psychotherapeutic treatments for panic disorder is the scar-city of competent therapists to perform the treatment. Many thera-pists, psychologists and psychiatrists alike, claim they know how to carry out these treatments, but in fact they adapt more traditional forms of psychotherapy and wind up seeing the patient on a regular basis for months or years. Although many psychiatric problems require such lengthy psychotherapy, the specific therapy aimed at stopping panic should not take longer than three months.

For many people the chance to solve a psychiatric problem without taking drugs is an advantage. Therefore, it is crucial that a patient with panic disorder discuss the possibility of focused psychotherapy for panic attacks before deciding to take antipanic medications. Many therapists and patients also believe that a combination of medication and focused psychotherapy is the most effective means of stopping panic.

The treatment of panic disorder can be summarized as follows: (also see Table 20):

1. Get the right diagnosis. This can be tricky with panic disorder. Patients with depression and generalized anxiety disorder sometimes have panic attacks, although usually not often enough (once a week for four weeks) to warrant an additional diagnosis of panic disorder. Careful evaluation by an experienced doctor is required to distinguish panic disorder from other psychiatric problems.

2. Rule out the medical causes of panic attacks. A physical examination, blood tests, thyroid tests, and an electrocardiogram can help confirm that the panic attacks are not caused by a physical illness.

3. Make sure you understand the difference between the three components of panic disorder: panic attacks, anticipatory anxiety, and phobias. The panic attacks should be the focus of treatment in the beginning. Eliminating them is the key to overcoming the problem of panic disorder.

4. Decide between an antipanic drug and one of the new, focused psychotherapies that specifically deal with panic attacks. If you want psychotherapy for panic attacks, make sure you are referred to a doctor who has had specific training in a treatment aimed at panic disorder. Remember that even the best psychotherapy takes about three months to work and requires that you have at least twelve sessions and do homework between sessions. Do not feel ashamed if you decide that you would rather solve the problem as quickly as possible and choose the medication.

5. If you choose drugs, the doctor will probably prescribe either imipramine (or its close relative desipramine) or alprazolam (Xanax) first. This should also be partly your choice. Imipramine

Table 20:

Treatment of Panic Disorder

First Step   Rule out medical conditions that may be the real cause (physical examination and routine blood and thyroid tests).

Second Step   Consider a focused, antipanic psychotherapy by an experienced behavioral/cognitive therapist. This will take at least three months to work.

Or

Begin an antipanic drug. The usual first choices are imipramine (Tofranil) and desipramine (Norpamin or Pertofrane) **which** have several side effects (like dry mouth, constipation, weight gain, and dizziness), take about four weeks to work, and are easy to stop.

Or

Xanax, **which** has few side effects, works in two weeks or less, and is more difficult to stop because of withdrawal.[a]

Third Step   If psychotherapy is chosen, complete a full course and continue to do the exercises even after you stop seeing the therapist.

If medication is chosen, stay on it six panic-free months

continued

Table 20, *continued*

Fourth Step If psychotherapy doesn't work, try a first-line drug (imipramine, desipramine, or Xanax).

If a first-line drug doesn't work, try an MAOI (Nardil or Parnate).[b]

Fifth Step If phobias do not go away even when panic attacks are blocked, get behavioral therapy which usually takes one to ten sessions.

[a]*Note:* Research may soon show that Prozac is also a good first-line antipanic drug. It has few side effects and is easy to stop but takes four to six weeks to work.
[b]*Note:* Research may show that Klonopin, a very potent benzodiazepine, is also a reasonable second-line antipanic drug. It may cause depression in some patients.

takes four weeks to work and may produce such side effects as dry mouth, constipation, and dizziness after standing quickly. It is also relatively easy to stop imipramine without experiencing withdrawal effects. Xanax works in about two weeks and, aside from some sedation, has few side effects. It is harder to stop using Xanax, must be tapered over about a month, and may cause withdrawal effects.

6. If imipramine or Xanax fails to work, which occurs in only 20% of patients with panic disorder, your doctor will ask you to consider an MAOI. These are all described in detail in Chapter 7. Almost all patients respond to one of the MAOIs (Nardil or Parnate), but these drugs must be prescribed carefully by a very experienced psychiatrist because of the many side effects.

7. Remain on the medication for six months once the panic attacks are blocked. This gives you the best chance of staying "panic-free" once the medication is stopped.

8. When the panic attacks stop, push yourself to confront situations you have become phobic about and avoid. Convince yourself that

the panic attacks will not occur after the drug starts working, even if you get caught in your car in a traffic jam or fly in an airplane. If you are still phobic and avoid things even after the panic attacks have stopped, ask your doctor to help you with some exercises to overcome these phobias.

9. Stay in touch with your doctor, even when you are off medication and feeling much better. Panic attacks sometimes return. Fortunately, the same treatment strategy that worked the first time usually works the second time, so there should be little problem getting better again.

Here are some examples of good and bad treatment for panic disorder.

Bad Treatment. When Mrs. Lewis described her anxiety attacks to her doctor, he felt she was under a lot of stress and prescribed Valium 5 mg twice daily. He told Mrs. Lewis to take it for one month and then stop. He reassured her that everything would certainly be better by then. In fact, Mrs. Lewis kept having panic attacks for the whole month. The Valium made her sleepy and a little more relaxed, but that was all. After the month, she stopped taking Valium and for a full week felt more anxiety and had more trouble sleeping than ever before. The problem here is that a relatively low dose of Valium such as 5 mg daily rarely blocks panic attacks. The doctor forgot to tell Mrs. Lewis that she might have withdrawal symptoms if she stopped taking Valium abruptly after regular use for a month. And if he thought she was under stress, why didn't he help her figure out how to make her life less stressful?

Good Treatment. Mrs. Lewis contacted a psychiatrist through the local university-based medical school. The psychiatrist she selected was an expert in anxiety disorders. The psychiatrist felt that stress was not the problem; Mrs. Lewis was suffering from panic disorder with mild phobic avoidance. After thorough discussion of all the treatment options, Mrs. Lewis decided to try imipramine. She started with 10 mg at bedtime every night and increased this to 200 mg over two weeks. After four weeks, her panic attacks were gone. She began to force herself to drive longer and longer distances until she felt completely comfortable with this. Finally, she took a plane ride with her husband, without experiencing an attack.

Bad Treatment. Mr. Lewis also experienced panic attacks. They were so severe that he became completely afraid to ride the train to work. He quit his job and took a much less prestigious job because he could walk to work. He saw a psychotherapist who told him his problem was a deep-seated fear of success. The psychotherapist recommended twice-weekly therapy sessions, and told Mr. Lewis it might take several years to get to the bottom of the problem.

Good Treatment. Fortunately, Mr. Lewis sought another opinion. He was referred to a therapist who specialized in panic disorder treatments and underwent a twelve-session, behaviorally oriented treatment for panic attacks and phobias. After three months his panic attacks were almost completely gone and he was able to ride the train again.

These examples highlight the importance of getting the right diagnosis, seeking out specialists, and not being afraid to question an individual doctor's recommendations. There is one goal for victims of panic disorder: getting rid of the panic attacks. Make sure that whatever treatment you select, drug or nondrug, your doctor agrees that this is the main goal.

TREATMENT OF SOCIAL PHOBIA

Until the mid-1980s, American psychiatrists barely paid any attention to social phobia. Now we know it is quite common and often a serious problem. Unfortunately, we do not yet know what the best treatment is. Some contend that unconscious forces make the patient tremble in social and performance situations; they recommend long-term psychotherapy and psychoanalysis. Others insist that social phobia stems from a passive approach to life, poor social skills, and bad conditioning; they recommend short-term behavioral and cognitive psychotherapy that includes social skills and assertiveness training. Still others believe social phobia is the product of oversecretion of adrenaline or other stress hormones; they prescribe drugs.

No one really knows yet who is right. Probably all three groups are correct, and different patients will do best with treatment tailored to their individual problems. There is a definite lack of expertise in treating the condition, especially with respect to the skillful application of behavioral and cognitive psychotherapy.

Until we have more research, I recommend combining medications and short-term psychotherapy for social phobia. Three medications have so far been noted as effective for social phobia: propranolol (Inderal) for occasional problems and atenolol (Tenormin) or phenelzine (Nardil) for more chronic problems. Long-term psychotherapy and psychoanalysis should be reserved for patients with other personality problems that complicate the social phobia. Here are some examples:

Alfred, an English teacher at a small community college, is a friendly, likable, and generally outgoing man. He has no trouble at parties or in front of his class. Once a month Alfred has to give a talk to about 300 students as part of a special lecture series. On the night before a lecture he can barely sleep. A few hours before the lecture, he feels his heart pounding and he envisions losing his voice and humiliating himself. During the lecture, his mouth becomes very dry and he feels himself tremble and shake. Although he generally gets through the lecture, he hardly inspires the audience and the experience is thoroughly harrowing for him.

Alfred has a very circumscribed problem. It doesn't infect his whole life, but it does have a negative impact on his career. For a professor to advance he or she must be able to speak comfortably in front of large groups. Alfred can get significant relief by taking a simple medication, propranolol (Inderal), about an hour before the big lecture. He should also have a few sessions of therapy to help him stop paying so much attention to his nervousness before the lectures. The treatment is very simple and brief.

Sandra has a slightly more complicated problem. She had been a fellow graduate student of Alfred. Sandra was viewed as the more promising student because her papers were outstanding. But somehow she never promoted herself very strongly and was overlooked for faculty appointments. The reason for this is that Sandra develops overwhelming anxiety whenever she is the center of attention. She dreaded speaking up in class or even having a casual conversation with a professor. She avoids parties and feels relaxed only with her closest friends and relatives. She works as an assistant librarian in a high school library and feels quite unfulfilled.

Sandra will obviously need more intense help than Alfred. She should first try a more focused behavioral treatment program for her anxiety and phobia if she can locate a trained behavioral therapist. If this doesn't work, or works only partially, a trial of medication is indicated. The medication (atenolol or Nardil) will have to be given on a more continuous basis than Alfred's once-a-month schedule because Sandra's anxiety attacks occur in a larger number of social situations.

Finally, there is Richard, a high school friend of Sandra and Alfred's. Richard was considered a very bright student and was a star on the football team. Around age 17 or 18, he began feeling increasingly nervous and uncomfortable around people. He now feels that everything he does is inadequate or doomed to failure. Sometimes he becomes depressed and drinks too much. The most important feature of his problem is the constant feeling that he will make a complete fool of himself. When he calls a woman for a date he stutters and stammers and usually can't get the words out. He hates going to restaurants because he sweats and blushes when he has to order. He doesn't even like telling taxicab drivers where to take him.

Richard will at the very least require formal behavioral psychotherapy and probably medication (atenolol or Nardil) as well. In addition, he may need long-term psychotherapy because his problems are complicated by a deep sense of personal inadequacy and constant pessimism.

Patients with social phobia may have to try a few different treatment approaches to find what works for them. They should start with therapies that promise the quickest help to see if they work. In other words, they should consider medication, which works in two to four weeks, and behavioral therapy, which usually works in about three months. Long-term therapy should be reserved for situations in which these more immediate treatments do not prove helpful.

Two kinds of drugs appear to work in social phobia: the *beta adrenergic blockers* or *beta blockers* and the monoamine oxidase inhibitors, which were described in Chapter 7. Prozac may also work in social phobia.

Beta Blockers and Social Phobia

Beta blockers are very important drugs in the treatment of a wide variety of medical problems including high blood pressure, angina, and migraine headaches. They reduce the amount of nervous system stimulation to such organs as the heart and blood vessels. They also cut down on the ability of adrenaline to make the heart beat faster. People who take beta blockers have less of a tendency to get rapid heartbeat, to shake, to tremble, and to blush in anxious situations. The two beta blockers most often used in treating social phobia are propranolol and atenolol.

For social phobics, the actions of beta blockers can offer great relief. The patient may for the first time be able to stand in front of an audience, and even though she may feel anxious, her heart doesn't pound, she doesn't start sweating or shaking, and she doesn't turn red. All the anxiety is internal, so the patient no longer worries that other people will see her nervousness and laugh at her. With the fear of embarrassment gone, social phobics often get through the performance and their anxiety level drops over time.

Beta blockers are very safe for most patients. They can lower blood pressure and slow heart rate, so people with abnormally low blood pressure or heart conditions may not be able to take them. Beta blockers must not be taken by patients with asthma or any other respiratory illness that causes wheezing. Also, patients with diabetes are often advised not to use them.

The side effects of beta blockers in otherwise healthy people are usually negligible. Nightmares and depression are rare and occur with only some of the beta blockers. Some patients complain of tingling feelings in their fingers and toes, as if their hands and feet were falling asleep; Lowering the dose helps this.

There are many different varieties of beta blocker, but basically they all work in the same way. The two that have been most often prescribed for social phobics are *propranolol* (Inderal) and *atenolol*

(Tenormin). Brand names of other beta blockers are Lopressor, Corgard, Visken, and Blocadren.

There are two ways in which beta blockers are used to treat social phobia. Patients who become anxious in only limited and predictable situations, like Alfred, may want to take propranolol (Inderal) 20 or 40 mg about one hour before they have to perform. Many musicians do this to combat stage fright. The drug usually controls rapid heartbeat, trembling, sweating, and blushing for several hours. If the drug is taken this way, there will probably be few side effects.

Patients who have more generalized anxiety in social situations, like Sandra, may take atenolol (Tenormin) 50 or 100 mg every day. Atenolol (Tenormin) acts much longer than propranolol and generally has fewer side effects. Atenolol (Tenormin) often provides more or less continuous protection against the physical symptoms of anxiety. Most patients who take atenolol (Tenormin) for social phobia also try some form of behavioral therapy, hoping to learn psychological techniques to reduce their anxieties. When this is done they can then taper off the medication over two weeks. There are no withdrawal symptoms, although the drug should be tapered to avoid a short-term rebound increase in blood pressure.

Beta blockers are very safe, have few side effects, and are not habit forming. That is the good news. The bad news is that they often do not work. Despite the decrease in physical symptoms, many social phobics still experience overwhelming psychological symptoms in their feared situations. For these patients the help offered by beta blockers in decreasing the physical manifestations of anxiety is just not enough to make the illness seem much better.

PROPRANOLOL

Brand Name: Inderal.
Used for: Short-term relief of social phobia. Many medical problems such as high blood pressure, angina, and migraine headaches.
Do Not Use if: You have abnormally slow heart rate, you have asthma or allergies that regularly make you wheeze, or you have congestive heart failure.

Tests to Take First: Pulse and blood pressure should be recorded.
Tests to Take While You Are on It: Pulse should be taken occasionally and should not drop below fifty beats per minute (your doctor will give you individual guidelines).
Usual Dose: Most people with severe social anxiety take a 20- or 40-mg tablet about one hour before a stressful situation. It is only taken on an as needed basis for this purpose.
How Long Until It Works: It should work in about one hour to block the physical signs of anxiety (heart pounding, sweating, blushing, and trembling.
Common Side Effects: Taken on this very occasional basis, Inderal has almost no side effects. Some people may feel a little light-headed or sleepy.
Less Common Side Effects: Again, taken occasionally, Inderal has few side effects. Patients with asthma should not take Inderal because it may induce an asthma attack.
What to Do About Side Effects: There really aren't many when the drug is only taken once in a while. If lightheadedness or fatigue is a problem, the dose can be lowered to as little as 5 mg (half of a 10-mg tablet).
If It Doesn't Work: You will probably need more continuous medication treatment or psychotherapy.
If It Does Work: Take it when you need it. Remember, it is intended only as a once-in-a-while treatment before especially frightening, performance-type situations.
Cost: Brand, 32 cents/20-mg pill. Generic, 2 cents/20-mg pill.
Special Comments: Inderal is short acting and a very good choice for the treatment of occasional severe physical anxiety symptoms in patients with social phobia. Patients who take it must, of course, be able to predict what will be a frightening situation. Inderal is not useful after the social phobic experiences symptoms.

ATENOLOL

Brand Name: Tenormin.
Used for: Social phobia. Several medical problems such as high blood pressure and angina.

Do Not Use if: You have an abnormally slow heart rate, asthma, allergies that make you wheeze, congestive heart failure, or diabetes.

Tests to Take First: Blood pressure and heart rate should be recorded.

Tests to Take While You Are on It: Blood pressure and heart rate should be monitored. In general, heart rate should not fall below fifty beats per minute (your doctor will give you individual guidelines).

Usual Dose: One 50-mg tablet a day for the first week. If there is no response, two 50-mg tablets, taken together or divided, should be tried for another week.

How Long Until It Works: After two weeks of 100 mg the patient with social phobia should notice a marked decrease in physical signs of anxiety (palpitations, trembling, blushing, and sweating) in social situations.

Common Side Effects: Cold extremities, dizziness, and tiredness.

Less Common Side Effects: Decrease in heart rate below fifty beats per minute, depression, and nightmares.

What to Do About Side Effects: If side effects are too bothersome, the dose should be lowered to 50 mg every other day. It is rare that side effects are so severe that Tenormin must be discontinued. Asthmatics should not take Tenormin because it may precipitate an asthma attack.

If It Doesn't Work: If there is no response to Tenormin after two weeks of 100 mg and social phobia is a serious problem, consider tapering the medication (it should not be stopped abruptly because the withdrawal effect of very high blood pressure may occur) and try Nardil after being off Tenormin for several days.

If It Does Work: There are no firm guidelines, but we try to treat social phobics for the usual six symptom-free months, then taper off and observe if they remain asymptomatic off medication.

Cost: Brand, 74 cents/50-mg pill. Generic, not available.

Special Comments: Tenormin probably is no better than other beta blockers for long-term treatment of social phobia. It was selected in initial research trials because it needs to be taken only once a day and because it has somewhat less of a tendency to produce wheezing than other beta blockers. Many patients with social phobia do

161

not respond to beta blockers but do respond to Nardil; however, Tenormin is worth a try for the occasional patient who gets a good response because it has relatively few side effects or risks.

Monoamine Oxidase Inhibitors

MAOIs, such as phenelzine (Nardil) and tranylcypromine (Parnate), are extremely effective in relieving social phobia. About 70% of patients with social phobia respond very favorably to MAOIs. After four weeks, they find their social fears almost totally eliminated. We have observed some dramatic improvement in social phobia patients treated with MAOIs.

MAOIs are used for social phobics the same way they are prescribed to patients with depression or panic disorder. They are described in detail in Chapter 7. As you will note from those descriptions, they have many side effects. Patients who take MAOIs *must* stay on a special diet. They may gain weight, feel lightheaded when they stand up fast, develop sexual problems, and have trouble sleeping at night. Sometimes, patients taking MAOIs for social phobia are overstimulated and become high. They actually become too sociable, talking too much, laughing too loud, boasting, and taking too many social risks. Then the dose must be lowered or sometimes the medication stopped completely. The MAOIs are briefly reviewed in Table 21.

Most social phobics who need continuous treatment should probably try a beta blocker first, usually Tenormin 50 or 100 mg. If Tenormin works, stay on it several months as you gradually lose your fear of social situations and performance. If it doesn't work after two or three weeks, however, there is little reason to keep trying. Taper off the drug in about one week and consider trying Nardil. Nardil almost always works, but you will have to maintain the special diet (no cheese, red wine, beer, liver, and so on) and also put up with the annoying side effects. Hopefully, after about six months you will have made great progress in overcoming social phobic symptoms by putting yourself into performance and social situations whenever possible. After a while, the drug therapy will be less important and you may be able to stop it and still feel

Table 21:

MAOIs and Social Phobia

Drug names	Nardil, Parnate, Marplan, Eldepryl, Eutonyl
Most commonly used	Nardil
Usual dose	30 mg (two pills) to 90 mg (six pills) daily of Nardil
Side effects	*Common*—weight gain, dizziness after standing up quickly, trouble sleeping, swelling in ankles and fingers *Less Common*—difficulty having an orgasm, getting high, shocklike feelings in fingers and toes *Rare*—hypertensive crisis (patients on MAOIs must stay on the special diet to avoid a sudden and very dangerous increase in blood pressure)
When does it work	In about four weeks; effects can be dramatic

confident. Patients who cannot stop taking Nardil without a return of the social phobia often lower the dose to about 30 mg a day and take it indefinitely. At this dose, there are fewer side effects, but the MAOI diet must be maintained. Most patients find giving up cheese a small price to pay for relief from social phobia.

TREATMENT OF OBSESSIVE-COMPULSIVE DISORDER

Not so long ago, I would reserve the section on treating obsessive-compulsive disorder for the end of a lecture or chapter on anxiety disorders. No treatment seems beneficial for this condition, not long-term psychotherapy nor behavioral psychotherapy or drug therapy.

The situation is a bit brighter now, although I still must concede that obsessive-compulsive disorder—or OCD as it is usually referred to—is one of the most difficult psychiatric conditions to treat. There are many psychological theories about the cause of this serious illness, but in my opinion it is one of the most biological of all mental disorders. Patients with OCD may seem perfectly normal to the casual observer. They often have none of the odd behaviors or strange mannerisms common to some psychotic or schizophrenic patients. But the obsessive-compulsive patient is a prisoner to senseless thoughts and the need to repeat meaningless rituals. He washes his hands, checks on things, cleans the floors, and thinks about numbers for hours a day. Sometimes he becomes very depressed over this behavior, but patients with OCD rarely attempt suicide. The patient never believes that the obsessions and compulsions are necessary. He doesn't actually *believe* his hands are dirty enough to warrant incessant washing. He often swears he will stop. But he cannot. Something—a brain abnormality, perhaps—forces him to have the obsessions or act out the compulsions over and over.

Almost every psychiatric drug known has been used to treat OCD, including cyclic antidepressants, MAOIs, antipsychotic drugs, amphetamines, clonidine, and tranquilizers. Electroshock treatment is reported to work sometimes, but these treatments work only in the exceptional case, not for most patients. Two drugs are now known to have specific anti–obsessive-compulsive properties: Anafranil and Prozac.

Anafranil (chlorimipramine or clomipramine) is a cyclic antidepressant drug, very similar to Tofranil and Elavil. In fact, it is structurally identical to Tofranil except for the addition of a single chloride atom. It is a very popular antidepressant drug in many European and South American countries, in Mexico, and in Canada. It also works well for panic attacks.

European psychiatrists first noted that obsessive-compulsive disorder patients often respond to Anafranil even if they are not depressed. Apparently, Anafranil does this because of its effect on the brain chemical serotonin. It quickly became obvious that about 50% or more of patients with OCD have a favorable response to Anafranil.

Unfortunately, it was hard to get Anafranil licensed in the United States by the Food and Drug Administration. The reason is unclear. The American manufacturer of Anafranil, Ciba-Geigy, conducted tests of Anafranil with obsessive-compulsive patients, but the government refused to approve the drug at first. Many patients with OCD obtained the drug from pharmacies in Canada and Mexico, but federal authorities made this increasingly difficult and the malpractice insurance company that covers most American psychiatrists refused to pay any claims that arose from the unauthorized use of Anafranil. All of this finally changed in January 1990, when approval was finally granted to market Anafranil in the United States.

Anafranil is prescribed in doses ranging from 150 to 300 mg per day and takes about four to six weeks to work. Usually, the patient is started at a low dose of 25 mg for a few days and then this is increased. The manufacturer recommends that the dose not exceed 250 mg per day because of the risk of seizures at higher doses. There are a number of side effects, but most are tolerable. The most common side effects are dry mouth, constipation, weight gain, dizziness after standing quickly, and sedation. Some patients, especially men, may find it more difficult to urinate. Blurry vision can occur, but usually goes away. Some patients experience decreased ability to have orgasm. Anafranil makes a patient more sensitive to the sun. It should not be taken by patients with certain abnormal electrocardiograms, with narrow-angle glaucoma, or with an enlarged prostate.

Anafranil may not eliminate all obsessions and compulsions, but it can significantly reduce the duration of these symptoms and the amount of anxiety the patient experiences. Many patients with

OCD take Anafranil more or less permanently if it works. Current evidence suggests that OCD patients who respond to Anafranil will relapse very quickly if they stop taking the drug. It may also be useful in treating panic disorder. Anafranil, like most psychiatric drugs, is no more addicting than insulin is to diabetics. The patient is simply not well without taking the medicine.

For patients who do not respond well to Anafranil there are experimental programs in which Anafranil is injected directly into a vein. Intravenous Anafranil is usually given one or more times a week. The procedure is safe when conducted under proper medical supervision. Early reports state that more patients respond to intravenous Anafranil than to oral Anafranil, but these studies are far from being certain.

Prozac (fluoxetine) is the new and very successful antidepressant drug described on page 100. Because Prozac has the same effect on the brain chemical serotonin as Anafranil, scientists reasoned it might also be helpful in obsessive-compulsive disorder. A great deal more research is needed, but it is now clear that many patients with OCD respond to Prozac. Prozac is licensed for prescription in the United States and has remarkably few side effects. The side effects can be likened to drinking too much black coffee at once: jitteriness, nausea, stomach cramps, and diarrhea. Some patients get a headache and have trouble falling asleep while on Prozac. There are scattered reports of difficulty achieving orgasm while taking Prozac. Overall, however, these side effects are usually very mild and often do not occur at all. Patients do not gain weight while taking Prozac and the drug has almost no problematic interactions with other drugs or other medical conditions. Almost everybody can safely take Prozac. It is the rare patient who cannot tolerate Prozac; most patients are quite surprised by the lack of side effects.

Prozac comes in 20-mg capsules and is usually taken in the morning. Some patients respond to as little as one capsule daily. If there is no response to this dose after four weeks, I recommend raising the dose by 20 mg a week until there is a response; the top dose recommended is 80 mg.

One major drawback to Prozac is its expense. Some pharmacies charge as much as $4.00 per capsule, so even taking one pill a day can cost more than $100 a month. There is no generic form of

Prozac available yet, and it is not likely to be available for some time.

Prozac, like Anafranil, takes about four weeks to work. Columbia University psychiatrist Eric Hollander has found that patients who do not respond well to Prozac alone may respond if another drug called Pondomin (fenfluramine) is added. Pondomin is usually prescribed to help obese patients lose weight. It is somewhat similar to amphetamines and can be addicting. There is also the remote chance that Pondomin may cause permanent brain damage if taken for long periods. This is suggested by some preliminary animal research, and it is anybody's guess whether humans react in the same way. Still, the addition of Pondomin should be considered only for patients with OCD who are refractory to every other treatment and who have very severe and debilitating illness.

An experimental drug, fluvoxamine, may also be useful for OCD and may shortly be available.

With few exceptions, patients who have obsessive-compulsive disorder should also have behavioral psychotherapy. Compulsions are treated by a program that restricts the amount of time the patient is permitted to engage in rituals. This is called response blocking. Behavioral psychotherapy may be effective in treating compulsions even without drugs, but the combination appears to be superior. Obsessions are less easily treated by behavioral psychotherapy, but there are techniques that seem useful. Often, separate doctors are needed to conduct the behavioral psychotherapy and monitor the medications. It is best if the two doctors have experience working with each other so they can communicate about your progress during the treatment. The help of family members is important in treating OCD.

Psychoanalysts now acknowledge that long-term psychotherapy is rarely helpful for obsessive compulsives. OCD patients are usually so preoccupied with their symptoms that they cannot concentrate fully on things like dreams, relationships with their parents, and fantasies. It is very important, however, for psychiatrists and therapists who do treat obsessive compulsives to be reassuring and supportive. Often, OCD patients are ashamed of their symptoms and burdened by repetitive thoughts that seem disgusting to them. The doctor must explain that these thoughts and actions are not the patient's fault and that they are no more repulsive than any other medical problem. Although we encourage the patient to exercise as much control as possible over the symptoms, we want them to understand that they are not to blame and will not be condemned.

Some examples of treating OCD patients may be helpful.

Anna, an elementary school teacher who recently graduated from college, had a severe and incapacitating compulsion. At the time she first came for consultation she had been forced to go on a medical leave of absence because her compulsive rituals prevented her from getting to work on time. Often, she had to leave her classroom to wash. The rituals, she told the doctor, had been going on for almost five years. At first she had felt a bit uneasy about dirt and was merely fastidious about keeping clean. Over the years she became preoccupied with the worry that her hands might be dirty. If she believed there was the slightest chance her hands had come in contact with dirt, food, or another person, she would be tortured by anxiety until able to scrub.

Anna came to the consultation with her mother. The mother was worried because a doctor consulting for her daughter's school wrote on a disability form that Anna was schizophrenic. Schizophrenia, the mother knew, is a largely incurable psychiatric condition that usually leads to progressive incapacitation. So the consulting psychiatrist first asked questions relevant to schizophrenia. Had Anna ever heard voices or seen things? Did she believe the dirt she needed to wash from her hands was really dangerous? Was anybody, in her view, trying to harm her? The answer to all of these questions was emphatically no. Anna was not psychotic; there was no break from reality. She understood that there was no logical reason for the hand washing.

Next, because Anna was tearful and glum, the psychiatrist asked about possible signs of depression. But Anna had experienced no change in appetite, no trouble sleeping through the night, and no difficulty laughing during a funny movie or becoming absorbed in a good book. Although she felt her life was a mess, she had no wish to die and no intention of harming herself. Depression therefore seemed an unlikely diagnosis.

Finally, the doctor asked about possible medical problems that could produce this kind of psychiatric symptom pattern, but quickly became convinced that there was no physical illness involved. The diagnosis of obsessive-compulsive disorder was made.

After a thorough description of the illness and the different ways of treating it, the psychiatrist prescribed Prozac 20 mg to be taken in the morning. The dose was raised over the next few weeks to 60 mg daily. He also referred Anna to a colleague who specialized in behavioral psychotherapy. The psychiatrist spoke to his psychotherapy colleague and described the case.

Over the next four weeks, Anna met with the psychiatrist twice and spoke to him several times on the telephone. She experienced mild nausea for the first three days on Prozac, but this then subsided. After three weeks on the drug, she also noted that it took her about 30 minutes longer to fall asleep.

During this time Anna also began the behavioral therapy. The behavioral psychotherapist, a Ph.D. psychologist, began by taking a history. He then designed a program whereby Anna was asked to wait longer and longer before giving in to the urge to washing her hands. Every time she washed she was instructed to make a note in a diary of how long she scrubbed. She was also instructed to record all of her thoughts as she got closer and closer to succumbing and washing. Over the next weeks and months the psychologist helped Anna to control the thoughts that provoked her washing and to wait longer and longer before washing.

Four weeks after starting the drug, Anna's mother reported that she was washing her hands much less frequently. Over the next month, this behavior decreased to the point where Anna could get by with four ten-minute hand washings a day. Admittedly she often felt anxious about dirt during the day and sometimes had to struggle to keep the hand washing in check, but she was now in much better control and much happier. She continued the therapy for a full six-month course, but stayed on Prozac 20 mg even longer. After six months Anna was able to return to work.

Anna obviously represents an example of optimal care and a fortunate result. The care this patient received is no more or less than what any patient should expect. But the result is not necessarily the outcome enjoyed by everyone with OCD, as the next example shows.

Bill had always been a shy and nervous boy and he suffered from a number of nervous tics of the face. One day, shortly after getting his driver's license, he was driving in his car when he suddenly got the idea that he had hit a pedestrian. No, he thought, it can't be. There weren't any screams, no thud, nothing. What if he had just run over the person's foot? There might not have been much noise. Impossible. You don't run over someone's foot without knowing it. But it might be possible. So Bill turned the car around and retraced his route. No bodies on the road, no crowds, no flashing lights or ambulances. Everything seemed all right. But what if they had taken the victim to the hospital already? What if they saw his license plate number? He would be charged with hit and run. So Bill rushed to a pay phone and started calling hospitals to see if anyone who had had a foot run over had been admitted to the emergency room.

This went on for hours. Every time Bill believed he was just making up the hit and run story he would have another doubt and start ruminating more. For days he had these obsessions. He told a few people—his parents, a friend, a teacher—what was on his mind and they thought he was either putting them on or taking drugs. After weeks of worrying to the point where he could no longer do his school work, his parents took him to the family doctor who prescribed Valium. This only made Bill sleepy.

Bill's story from here on is very sad. He eventually was admitted to a psychiatric hospital, received shock treatments (which didn't help), and finally started psychotherapy. Despite twice-weekly sessions centered on his supposed anger at his parents and "unconscious homosexual feelings," he did not improve. From worrying about having hit someone with his car, he went on to worrying that he might stab his mother. Bill had never committed an act of violence in his life and had no conscious anger toward either of his parents, yet he developed a recurrent thought that he might pick up a knife and murder his mother. This is a typical obsession for the patient with OCD. They never act on the thought and they know the thought is senseless. It is as if something forces them to entertain the most repugnant thing imaginable. Bill asked that all the knives in the house be put under lock and key and he developed a phobia of sharp objects.

Through the years, Bill had several psychiatric hospitalizations

170

Table 22:

Drug Treatment of the Anxiety Disorders

DISORDER	FIRST-LINE DRUGS	SECOND-LINE DRUGS[a]
Panic disorder	Imipramine Desipramine Xanax Prozac(?)	Nardil Parnate Klonopin
Generalized anxiety disorder	Valium Librium Tranxene Centrax Paxipam Xanax Serax Ativan BuSpar	None
Social phobia	Inderal Tenormin	Nardil
Obsessive-compulsive disorder (OCD)	Prozac Anafranil	Other anti-depressants

[a]If first-line drug fails.

and was treated with many drugs. Ultimately, he was placed on Anafranil and this helped to some degree. The obsessions became less anxiety provoking and less intense. Bill found for the first time that he could read a book as long as an hour before the obsessions took over. Despite the improvement, which was certainly more than any other drug had provided, Bill remained seriously burdened with obsessions. He now holds a job as a stock room clerk and has a few friends. He enjoys bowling and having a few beers with his buddies, but he has not overcome the obsessions entirely.

Obsessive-compulsive disorder remains one of the challenges for psychiatric research. Medications and behavioral psychotherapy are now able to reduce some of the symptoms. Sometimes a patient is almost entirely cured. Most patients, however, have lingering pathology despite the best medical and psychological care. It is important to remember that many psychiatric conditions resist even the best treatment efforts. Below is a description of Anafranil (chlorimipromine). Prozac is described in detail on pages 100–102.

Table 22 summarizes drug treatment of the anxiety disorders.

CLOMIPRAMINE (ALSO CALLED CLORIMIPRAMINE)

Brand Name: Anafranil.
Used for: Obsessive compulsive disorder. Has also been used successfully to treat major depressive disorder and panic disorder.
Do Not Use if: You have narrow-angle glaucoma, you have a very enlarged prostate, you have certain abnormal heart rhythms (your doctor will determine if this is an important consideration for you), or if you have a history of seizures (unless your doctor takes special precautions).
Tests to Take First: You may need an electrocardiogram first, especially if you are over age 50.
Tests to Take While You Are on It: None are universally required for all patients.
Usual Dose: You will probably be started on 25 mg per day and the dose will be raised over the next two weeks to 100 mg per day, usually taken in one dose. After that, the dose is raised over the next few weeks to 250 mg. Some patients have been treated with higher doses, up to 400 mg per day, but this is not recommended by the manufacturer because of a possible risk of causing seizures at higher doses.
How Long Until It Works: It will take about four weeks to have effect; sometimes six weeks or longer is required.
Common Side Effects: Dry mouth, constipation, nausea, difficulty urinating, weight gain, increased sweating, dizziness upon standing

quickly, sedation, blurred vision, and difficulty having an orgasm. Anafranil will make you more sensitive to the effects of the sun. *Less Common Side Effects:* There may be an increased risk of having a seizure on Anafranil, compared to other drugs of its class (the cyclic antidepressants), especially if the dose is raised too high. For that reason, the top recommended dose is now 250 mg. Elderly patients may experience confusion and memory impairment.

What to Do About Side Effects: (1) Dry mouth—don't suck on hard candies containing sugar as you will ruin your teeth; try sugarless hard candies or mouthwash. (2) Constipation—drink at least six glasses of water or juice daily. Laxatives may be prescribed. (3) Blurry vision—normal vision usually returns in a couple of weeks, but a change in eyeglass prescription can help. (4) Difficulty urinating—this problem is greater in men than women and can become a serious problem in older men. Usually it is only annoying. The drug bethanecol (Urecholine) can be prescribed to counteract this effect. (5) Increased sensitivity to the sun—use very good suntan lotion, with an SPF factor of at least No. 15, when out in the sun. (6) Dizziness after standing up quickly—this is caused by a brief drop in blood pressure. The best remedy is to sit down and get up slowly. In elderly people this side effect can be more serious. (7) Weight gain—this can range from just a few pounds to twenty or more pounds. No one knows why Anafranil does this and not a lot can be done except to diet. (8) Sedation—the best approach is to take the medication as close to bedtime as possible. (9) Difficulty having an orgasm—this problem often goes away on its own in a few weeks. Lowering the dose can sometimes help as can bethanecol (Urecholine) and a drug called cyproheptadine (Periactin) in some cases. (10) Seizures—it is not clear just how much of a problem this is. For now, it is safest to recommend keeping the dose at or below 250 mg and not giving Anafranil to patients with a history of seizures unless they are well controlled on anticonvulsant drugs.

If It Doesn't Work: After six to eight weeks, the drug should have some effect. It usually works best if combined with behavioral treatment. If there is no response the doctor may recommend trying Prozac, adding Pondomin, or trying other antidepressants.

If It Does Work: At least one study suggests that Anafranil treatment may be needed permanently to control obsessions and compulsions. The dose should be reduced after six months to the lowest possible dose that controls the symptoms, but the patient should be kept on drug indefinitely until research proves otherwise.

Cost: Brand, $.89/50-mg capsule; Generic, not available.

Special Comments: Anafranil was finally approved by the Food and Drug Administration in January 1990 after years of trying to get it on the market in the United States and many more years of use throughout the world. The drug is a very useful addition to the limited treatment strategies currently available for obsessive compulsive disorder, but will certainly not "cure" all patients or even eliminate any symptoms in some. It will be used either as the first-line drug, or after a patient has failed to respond to Prozac.

Chapter 9

Drugs Used to Treat Manic Depression (Bipolar Affective Disorder)

When we talk about depression and the anxiety disorders, we generally say that drugs aren't always needed. Sometimes, no treatment is best, sometimes psychotherapy, sometimes drugs alone, and sometimes a combination of drugs and psychotherapy.

But when we talk about the illness psychiatrists now call bipolar affective disorder, there is no debate: the patient should be on medication. The person with bipolar affective disorder is sometimes referred to as being "manic depressive" or having "mood swings." Basically, the bipolar patient is at times depressed, at times high or manic, and at other times perfectly normal. Each patient has his or her own natural cycle of the three states.

Bipolar affective disorder affects men and women equally and usually begins in the twenties. Presently, there is good evidence that this disease is genetic. This doesn't mean that a person with a bipolar parent will automatically develop bipolar affective disorder. Apparently, a host of unknown factors determine whether the gene for mood swings is actually expressed. It is probable, however, that without the inheritance of some abnormal genetic material, the likelihood of developing the illness is small.

Bipolar patients experience some of the most severe depressions seen in psychiatry. Typically, these "bipolar depressions" are characterized by extreme loss of energy and the ability to concentrate, complete inability to enjoy anything, and suicidal ideas. Untreated bipolar patients frequently commit suicide. All the antidepressant drugs discussed in Chapter 7 work for this phase, as does electroconvulsant therapy. But drawing the patient out of the depression is only half the battle.

When high or manic, the bipolar patient feels terrific. She talks constantly, needs almost no sleep, and is continuously active. The manic patient spends more money than she has because she believes that she is so successful and brilliant that riches are around the corner. The manic patient is also very irritable. She doesn't like anyone spoiling her fun or disagreeing with her. While high, the patient has an insatiable sex drive and even the most faithfully married person may have affairs when manic. As the manic phase progresses, the patient may lose touch with reality and become increasingly psychotic. Voices tell her that she is wonderful, that she is going to be elected president, that God is taking a special interest. At this point the patient may become very suspicious as irritability transforms into frank paranoia. She then resembles the person with schizophrenia and, indeed, until recently it was unfortunately very common for psychiatrists to misdiagnose a bipolar patient as schizophrenic.

DIFFERENTIATION FROM SCHIZOPHRENIA

The main difference between bipolar affective disorder and schizophrenia is that the bipolar patient usually passes through a normal phase between highs and lows. Sometimes, the normal period lasts a year or more, sometimes only a few days. Most bipolar patients are able to resume their preillness level of functioning at several points. Schizophrenics, on the other hand, rarely return to normal. After each psychotic break they seem less motivated and less functional than before the break. As I will discuss in more detail in Chapter 10, schizophrenia is usually a disease marked by progressive deterioration.

One of the main reasons for distinguishing bipolar affective disorder from schizophrenia is that treatment for the two conditions is different. Since the introduction of lithium over 30 years ago, most cases of bipolar illness can now be controlled. Therefore, safe and effective treatment to prevent the high and lows is available to most bipolar patients.

Once again, the importance of careful and accurate diagnosis cannot be stressed enough. Sometimes, the diagnosis of bipolar affective disorder is so easy that the elevator operator who transports the patient to the doctor's office can make it. A patient who is talking a mile a minute, believes that she and God are best friends, and just ran up a bill of $10,000 on her American Express card, even though she only makes $30,000 a year, is probably a manic depressive in the manic phase. The same patient may show up two months later deeply depressed, insisting she is the cause of world hunger and deserves to die; she has "flipped" into the depressed phase of the illness.

Other times, however, the diagnosis is more difficult. When depressed, patients may have difficulty remembering their previous manic highs. They may tell the doctor that they never felt well and that life has always been terrible. In this case, the psychiatrist may incorrectly diagnose major depressive disorder instead of the depressed phase of bipolar affective disorder. On the other hand, some chronically depressed patients misinterpret the few days a month when they feel a little less depressed as representing mania. The patient in this circumstance may say "for a few days every month I feel really good, energetic, optimistic, talkative. . . ." What the patient is really describing is temporary relief from depression, not mania.

And of course, despite the great consciousness raising that has occurred in the last two decades about psychiatric diagnosis, differentiating between mania and schizophrenia is still sometimes frankly impossible even for the most experienced clinicians. In fact, psychiatrists recognize a category of illness called *schizoaffective* disorder for patients who seem to straddle the line between schizophrenia and bipolar affective disorder or depression. Although a complete review of the differences between these conditions could be the subject of another book, some examples may be helpful. First, a very obvious case of bipolar affective disorder.

Charles, a 25-year-old waiter and aspiring actor, had been admitted to a suburban hospital psychiatry ward in a floridly psychotic state. Over the previous six months his roommate had started to notice changes in his behavior. Although usually sensible, Charles began talking about his brilliant career as an actor and the likelihood that he would soon be "discovered" for a big movie role. When his roommate pointed out that Charles had never succeeded at a single audition and had never been given any professional parts, Charles got annoyed and said his roommate was merely jealous of his ability.

Then Charles started staying up very late, supposedly reading scripts. His mother became alarmed when he started calling her asking for money to pay off his growing credit card bills. As the months progressed, Charles became progressively more grandiose and irritable. One day he almost got into a fist fight with a friend who disagreed with him about who was the best player in professional football. He also started drinking more and more, complaining that he could not fall asleep unless drunk. A week before being brought to the emergency room Charles attempted to walk into the office of a major movie producer without an appointment, had sex with five different women, spent $2,500 in one afternoon on new clothes, and made six long-distance phone calls to an old girlfriend now living in Paris. Finally, his roommate called his parents one night in terror: Charles had been up all night drinking and making telephone calls. Now he was threatening to bomb the office of the producer for not "realizing I am the greatest actor living in the Western World today who can do Westerns and Easterns and make omelets and eat them faster than anyone else." In short, Charles was talking on and on without making sense and threatening everyone in sight.

The emergency room psychiatrist was able to make a diagnosis of bipolar affective disorder, manic phase, fairly easily after asking Charles' parents a few important questions. At age 18, they told the doctor, Charles had developed a serious depression during his freshman year at college which required psychiatric treatment. Again at age 22, just after graduation, he became depressed, refused to look for a job, and made a suicide gesture by cutting his wrist superficially. He had been admitted to a hospital overnight and then released.

So Charles had had at least two episodes of serious depression and now a bout of mania. Between these periods he had functioned well, working hard, maintaining a relationship with a woman, and attended acting classes at night. During the long intervals between highs and lows he behaved normally. Finally, it turned out that Charles' paternal uncle had a similar illness and had been treated with lithium for many years.

Several interesting features of Charles' case are worth pointing out. First, he had several bouts of depression before the episode of mania. This is usually the case with bipolar patients. Depression usually precedes mania, so at the beginning it is correct to treat only the depression as if the patient is suffering from major depressive disorder. Occasionally, manic periods precede depressed phases.

Second, many manic patients drink alcohol excessively, probably in an attempt to calm themselves down. This makes the situation much worse, of course, because a drunk manic is even more disinhibited than a sober one. Often, the severity of the manic cannot be fully assessed until the patient is sobered up.

Third, without the history of previous depressions and normal functioning between episodes, Charles might have been diagnosed as schizophrenic when he was presented to the emergency room. At that moment he was violent, paranoid, and delusional (he believed he was in direct contact with God). So, the presence of a relative or spouse who can provide the history is invaluable.

Now, a slightly less obvious case.

Patricia, a nurse, was seeing a psychiatrist for the first time at age 30, complaining of depression. She had all the features of depression: loss of energy, decreased sex drive, waking up at 4 AM every morning, weight loss, and suicidal ideas. Years of psychotherapy had been very helpful to her in improving her relationships with men and her ability to get along with her supervisors at work. Her therapist had correctly noted that periods of depression lasting about four weeks seemed to occur regularly two to three times a year. The therapist wondered if medication might not be needed to stabilize Patricia and prevent these regularly occurring depressions.

The depression part was easy to understand, but the consulting psychiatrist had difficulty figuring out what went on in the patient's life when she wasn't depressed. So the psychiatrist asked Patricia to keep a *mood log* like the one shown in Figure 1, a log that can be kept by anyone who suspects he or she might suffer from bipolar disorder. For one month the psychiatrist instructed Patricia to rate her mood daily and to have her husband rate it as well. On the mood log, a score of zero is good; zero means normal mood, not too high or not too low. A score of −10 indicates that the patient is so depressed, she doesn't have the energy to do what she would most like to do: jump out the nearest window. A score of +10 is as manic as one can get: the patient thinks she can walk across water and might try to prove it. Some fluctuation around zero is okay, but the psychiatrist wanted to see how high Patricia was capable of reaching.

As it turned out, Patricia's two or three annual month-long depressions were matched by similar periods of mania—not nearly as manic as Charles, but still not normal. Patricia would recover from a depression, appear normal for a week or two, and then become talkative and provocative at work, behavior that often led to reprimands when she seemed like too much of a know-it-all. During these periods, she was extremely labile, that is, she would laugh raucously at the least funny joke and burst out in tears a few minutes later. She slept poorly, was jittery, and spent too much money. A couple of times during these highs she made sexual advances to doctors at the hospital and one time had an affair. This behavior was uncharacteristic of Patricia, who ordinarily felt very deeply about the need to remain faithful to her husband, whom she loved very much. She was filled with guilt about the affair, but when high, she felt her sexual urges almost uncontrollable.

Unlike Charles, Patricia never become psychotically manic. She didn't hear voices or get delusional ideas or become paranoid. But her mood did become elevated above normal to the point where she did things that she herself believed were wrong.

Thus, after obtaining all the information, the psychiatrist was able

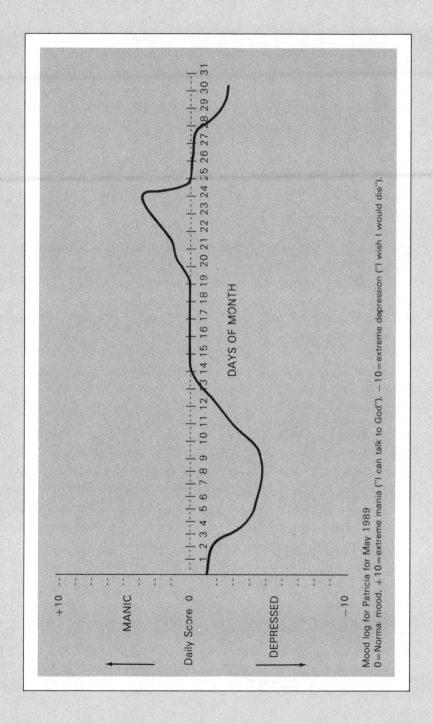

Mood log for Patricia for May 1989
0=Norma mood. +10=extreme mania ("I can talk to God"). −10=extreme depression ("I wish I would die").

to diagnose bipolar affective disorder and prescribe medication to level Patricia's moods.

Here again are important features that must be emphasized. Some might argue that it is wrong to interfere with a person's "good time." Maybe Patricia did know more than the other people at work. After all, nurses often are taken advantage of in hospitals and not treated with proper respect by doctors. Perhaps Patricia is really a liberated woman who should be allowed to have sex with anyone she wants to. People seem much more tolerant of husbands who cheat than of women who do. Isn't treating Patricia's highs a form of psychiatric mind control, an attempt to turn her into a "socially acceptable" person?

I have no doubt that psychiatry has been misused countless times in many countries, including the United States, as a form of social control. The concerns voiced in this area are legitimate; however, before assuming that prescribing lithium is an exercise in mind control, it is important to gain familiarity with what bipolar patients go through.

People like Patricia suffer just as much through the manic periods as they do through the depressed periods. Mania is often a disaster, even though for a while the patient may enjoy the good feeling. More than one manic patient has completely ruined himself financially by reckless spending, only to face the consequences when the mania subsides. Manic patients ruin their marriages and are fired from jobs. They drink too much and always know that at the end of a manic period there looms the possibility of a severe depression.

Medications used to treat manic depressives do not affect their principles or political views. They do not make them incapable of experiencing sadness or joy. What they do is eliminate the extreme swings in mood that destroy lives. If Patricia wants to have affairs or assert herself more at work, lithium or other treatments for bipolar affective disorder will not stop her. The medications will enable her to make up her mind somewhat more free of the disabling and uncontrolled dips or elevations of mood.

Had lithium been available many years ago, it is possible that Virginia Woolf would never have drowned herself in London in 1941 and that Vincent Van Gogh would never have cut off his ear and eventually killed himself in a French asylum in 1890. A study by Dr. Mogens Schou, the psychiatrist who first proved the effectiveness of lithium, showed that of twenty-four bipolar artists, six found that lithium reduced their creativity, six found no effect of lithium on creativity, and twelve found that lithium improved their creativity (Schou M: Artistic productivity and lithium prophylaxis in manic-depressive illness. *British Journal of Psychiatry* 1979;135:-97–103).

Another point to emphasize in Patricia's case is that it took some time to establish the diagnosis. Maintaining a mood log and obtaining information from as many people as possible can be very helpful.

Finally, I want to emphasize the good and close relationship between the psychiatrist and the therapist. Besides her bipolar disorder, Patricia had other problems that responded well to psychotherapy. Even after being placed on medication, Patricia continued her therapy and found it useful.

Finally, a case that presents great diagnostic difficulty.

Richard was a bright college student and graduate student, but always prone to moodiness. From time to time, he would go for weeks without studying or contacting his friends. Few people aside from his family knew him well. His grades grew progressively worse and he never finished his graduate program. Instead he took a job and at first functioned well, but then missed many days of work, complaining he didn't feel well or needed a rest. He finally was fired from and took a new, less appropriate job.

At age 26, Richard began the first of a series of psychiatric hospitalizations. Sometimes, he would feel depressed and suicidal. Other times, he was psychotic, hearing strange voices and insisting that his food was poisoned; during these periods, he giggled and laughed inappropriately, but didn't seem especially happy. Although the episodes seemed to occur in discrete periods, Richard never returned to normal when they were over. He went from job to job, finally ending up on disability and living alone in a cheap apartment.

Richard's case is hard to diagnose. Surely he suffered from highs and lows, but he also had a deteriorating course with more social isolation and less capacity to function over time. And the content of his psychosis was not that of the classically manic patient. The voices did not tell him he was great and wonderful; they said more frightening and sometimes very bizarre things.

Richard was diagnosed as having schizoaffective disorder and treated with both lithium and a powerful drug for schizophrenia (Thorazine) that is described Chapter 10. Unlike Charles and Patricia, he never made a complete recovery and never worked again. The extremes of his depression and psychosis were controlled by the medication, however, and he no longer required multiple hospitalizations every year.

The drugs described in this chapter are useful in preventing a bipolar patient from experiencing *future* highs and lows. Lithium is the standard bearer in this class. Other drugs used to prevent highs and lows are Tegretol, Depakene, Klonopin, and Verapamil. They are not as effective in the immediate treatment of depression or mania. Therefore, there are different ways to treat a bipolar patient with medication depending on the state he is currently in.

There are three states in which a person with bipolar affective disorder may present to the psychiatrist for the first time: depressed, manic, or normal. Each requires a different treatment approach (Table 23).

Table 23:

Treating the Bipolar Patient

1. *If the patient is depressed:* Start an antidepressant (Prozac, Tofranil, or desipramine are probably best) and lithium. Stop the antidepressant about a week or two after the depression is over. Continue lithium.
2. *If the patient is manic:* Start an antipsychotic (Thorazine, Mellaril, or Trilafon) or the antianxiety drug Ativan. Start lithium. Stop the antipsychotic drug or Ativan a few days after the mania is over. Continue lithium.
3. *If the patient is euthymic (normal mood):* Start lithium.

The *Depressed* Bipolar Patient

The first thing to do is get on top of the depression. Usually, one of the antidepressant medications described in Chapter 7 is prescribed. Prozac has become an increasingly popular choice for this purpose. Cyclic antidepressants like Tofranil and Elavil may be prescribed, but there is some concern that these may incite a pattern called *rapid cycling* in the patient. The monoamine oxidase inhibitors can also be prescribed at this point. Monoamine oxidase inhibitors are especially likely to cause the patient to become manic, however, so careful monitoring is needed. The drug Welbutrin is supposed to be an antidepressant with less risk of inducing mania or rapid cycling. It has only very recently been released so that more experience is needed before it is known if this is true. Prozac seems to be the best choice in this situation, although Welbutrin may ultimately prove superior. A psychiatrist will also start the bipolar depressed patient on lithium or another of the specific drugs for bipolar affective disorder (Tegretol, Depakene, Klonopin, Verapamil) at this point. Once the depression has responded to the antidepressant, it can be tapered and the patient maintained on lithium alone.

Rapid Cycling. Rapid cycling is a form of bipolar affective disorder in which the patient has four or more episodes of depression or mania every year. Some rapid cyclers move from depression to mania several times a month. There are even cases in which the patient has mood swings on a daily basis.

Rapid cycling seems to respond less well to lithium than does regular cycling bipolar disorder. There is also reason to fear that many antidepressant drugs, especially the cyclic antidepressants like Tofranil and Elavil, can transform a regular cycler into a rapid cycler. Therefore, psychiatrists are becoming increasingly careful about prescribing antidepressants to bipolar patients. When antidepressants are needed, they are often discontinued as soon as the depression is over, instead of waiting the full six months usually prescribed for an episode of major depression in a non-bipolar patient.

Breakthrough Depressions. What about the patient who is already on lithium or another drug that is supposed to prevent high and lows but who becomes depressed anyway. Breakthrough depressions do occur, even to lithium-treated bipolar patients. They are usually much less frequent and less severe than those occurring in non–lithium-treated patients, but are still worrisome. First, the doctor should check whether the patient is taking the medication as prescribed. Noncompliance, especially with a drug like lithium, which must be taken daily even when the patient feels well, can cause the breakthrough depression. Second, the patient's levels of thyroid hormone should be monitored. Lithium can interfere with the thyroid gland and low thyroid hormone levels can mimic depression. Finally, an antidepressant like Prozac may be prescribed, but should be stopped soon after the depression is alleviated.

The *Manic* Bipolar Patient

The manic bipolar patient often feels so well that he is ambivalent about seeking treatment at all. Friends and relatives have usually had enough by the time they talk the patient into getting help. The acutely manic patient may have a range of problems from simple overactivity, inability to sleep, and irritability to hallucinations, delusions, and a violent temper.

Friends and relatives are usually needed to establish that the patient is indeed bipolar; that is, that the patient has experienced episodes of depression in the past. Usually, an antipsychotic medication such as Thorazine, Haldol, Stelazine, or Navane is prescribed. These drugs work rapidly to calm the patient, reduce the overactivity, and stop psychotic symptoms like hallucinations and delusions. Antipsychotic drugs are complicated and fully described in Chapter 10. For bipolar patients, these drugs are usually taken several times a day for a week or two until the manic symptoms are cleared.

An alternative to antipsychotic drugs is use of some of the antianxiety drugs called benzodiazepines, which are described in Chapter 8. Ativan (lorazepam) is sometimes used for this purpose. It has a rapid sedating effect but is probably not very useful if the patient is also psychotic.

Whether an antipsychotic or a benzodiazepine drug is prescribed, the patient is usually also started on lithium simultaneously. Lithium works too slowly to control acute mania, just as it is not very good for relief of an acute depression. Nevertheless, it is a good time to start the patient on lithium, because when the mania subsides and the antipsychotic drugs are stopped, the patient will be protected by lithium from experiencing another manic outburst.

Not all manic patients can be treated on an outpatient basis. Mania is one of the psychiatric illnesses that often require hospitalization, because manic patients often refuse to comply with treatment or are so hyperactive they don't remember to take the pills properly. A manic patient can get into a lot of trouble, so sometimes it is best to offer the patient the protection of the hospital, where medication can be administered regularly. Remember that mania rarely resolves on its own in a short period. Untreated mania can last months, by which time the patient may have been arrested or bankrupted or may have committed murder. And when the mania does finally go away, the patient often slips into a severe depression which can result in suicide. No matter how wonderful a manic patient thinks he feels, it is no favor to leave him alone.

The *Euthymic* Bipolar Patient

"Euthymic" means normal mood—neither depressed nor manic. A bipolar patient in this state appears completely normal. Studies have shown that even trained mental health professionals cannot tell a bipolar person in the euthymic state from a person with no psychiatric problems. A bipolar patient who presents at this point in the illness should be placed on lithium or one of the other drugs specifically used to prevent the onset of highs and lows.

Once a patient is stabilized on lithium (or one of the other drugs for bipolar affective disorder) the question that always arises is Is it for life? This question is difficult to answer for two reasons. First, no one likes to hear that he or she will have to take medication forever. Second, there is so much variability in the course of bipolar affective disorder that it is difficult to know how long the condition will remain active in an individual patient.

187

Bipolar illness can be devastating and severe, but its treatment is generally well tolerated and safe. So it is best to be cautious about stopping lithium. After a patient has had serious manic and depressive episodes, I usually recommend that she remain on lithium for five to ten years. Then, if the patient has been completely stabilized, she may attempt to stop the lithium. I always make it clear that this is a risk: after about one month the patient could become seriously depressed or manic again. It is helpful if a spouse or relative is available to alert me at the first sign that something is wrong so that treatment can be resumed immediately. Rather than take this risk, some patients elect to continue taking medication indefinitely.

On the other hand, it is rare that the patient who has been successfully treated with lithium for many years is forced to stop taking the drug because medical problems unrelated to lithium use develop. A patient may develop kidney disease, for example, and be forced to stop lithium. In this case, it is not that lithium produces the kidney problem, but that the reduction in kidney function may necessitate stopping lithium. Will such a patient be doomed to a life of highs and lows? Although lithium is the best studied drug for bipolar patients, fortunately, alternative medications, for example, Tegretol, Depakene, and Klonopin, are available. Consequently, if a bipolar patient is forced to stop lithium at some point, the chance is good that an alternative drug can be safely and successfully substituted.

Even if a patient takes lithium or similar medication religiously and has a generally good response, there may be bumps in the road. Breakthrough depression is usually easy to spot because patients don't like it and call the doctor right away. As mentioned earlier, this may mean that lithium has lowered the thyroid hormone level and indicate the need for thyroid medication. Or, a short course of antidepressants may be required. Breakthrough highs are less easily spotted because the patient may confuse this with merely feeling well. One good rule of thumb is that a night or two of sleeping less than five hours without feeling tired the next day means that the doctor should be notified. Breakthrough mania is sometimes treated by increasing the amount of lithium for a while or by administering a brief course of an antipsychotic drug like Trilafon or Thorazine (see Chapter 10).

Bipolar affective disorder is a medical illness requiring skilled medical management. It is also responsive to treatment. It should never be ignored.

Not all bipolar patients respond to lithium. As many as 20% of bipolar patients continue to suffer highs and lows despite taking lithium exactly as prescribed. If this happens, several alternative drugs are available. The first step is usually to combine lithium with a drug ordinarily used to treat seizures, Tegretol (carbamazepine). If the combination of lithium and Tegretol doesn't work, these are discontinued and another antiseizure drug, Depakene (valproic acid) is tried. Several drugs may be tried if Depakene doesn't work, including Klonopin (clonazepam), clonidine, and verapamil. Remember, the purpose of these drugs is to prevent the bipolar patient from experiencing *future* highs and lows. These drugs are not as helpful in treating a patient for an acute depression or mania.

DRUGS USED TO TREAT BIPOLAR AFFECTIVE DISORDER

LITHIUM

Brand Names: Lithonate, Lithane, Lithobid, Eskalith, Eskalith CR, others.

Used For: Long-term treatment of bipolar affective disorder—lithium prevents future highs and lows. To enhance the effectiveness of antidepressant drugs. Possibly to treat alcoholism (experimental).

Do Not Use if: You have kidney disease, you are taking diuretics (water pills) for high blood pressure, or you use anti-inflammatory drugs like Motrin, Naprosyn, and Indocin. It is still possible to use lithium in these situations, but it will require special attention from your doctor. Lithium should not be taken by pregnant women.

Tests to Take First: Before the first lithium tablet goes into your mouth you should have blood tests to measure kidney function and thyroid function. As lithium can affect kidney and thyroid function,

189

it is important that a baseline be established against which later levels can be judged. The doctor should also record your pulse, and, if you are over age 50 and on lithium for the first time, you may need to have an electrocardiogram.

Tests to Take While You Are on It: Blood tests are required frequently, especially after initiation of lithium treatment, because the only way to determine the correct dose (number of pills) for an individual is by monitoring the lithium blood level, which is obtained through a simple blood test. Levels are usually maintained between 0.5 and 1.0mEq/1, although different situations may justify higher or lower levels. The Lithium level is never allowed to rise above 1.2. At this point, serious side effects emerge. Below 0.5, lithium probably doesn't do much good. The first blood level is usually drawn after the first week of lithium treatment, and, if necessary, the dose is adjusted. One week after each change in dose a new level is obtained. When the correct dose is reached, lithium levels can be obtained less frequently. Ultimately, for people under age sixty, levels can be determined four or five times a year. Patients over sixty should have tests at least every month because the body's ability to metabolize lithium starts declining at this point. In addition to these relatively frequent lithium levels, blood tests for kidney and thyroid function are usually obtained every six months. Some doctors also obtain urine tests for kidney function. Finally, and particularly in patients over 60, the doctor should check the patient's pulse once a month; rarely, lithium can produce a dramatic decrease in heart rate.

Usual Dose: Most lithium tablets and capsules come in one strength: 300 mg. A patient is usually started on two or three a day; elderly patients are often started on only one tablet or capsule a day. Once again, it must be emphasized that the final dose can be determined only by measuring the blood level. One patient may take 900 mg a day to reach a "good" level, whereas another patient of exactly the same sex, height, and weight may require 1,500 mg to have the same blood level. After the correct dose is determined it is best that the entire dose be taken once a day, although it makes no difference what time of day it is taken. Many patients prefer to take lithium on a full stomach.

How Long Until It Works: Lithium is given to *prevent* future highs and lows; and once a good blood level is reached, it should start to do this. The only way to determine if lithium is working is to observe the patient over time for further mood swings.

Common Side Effects: (1) Upset stomach and diarrhea, usually in the early phase of treatment. (2) Metallic taste in mouth, also usually in early phase. (3) Increased frequency of urination, but not enough to disrupt a patient's schedule. (4) Weight gain, anywhere from five to twenty or more pounds; the average is about ten pounds, usually in the first year of treatment. (5) Acne. (6) Decrease in thyroid gland function, which occurs in about one fourth of people taking lithium, more often in women than men; in only about 5% of lithium-treated patients does thyroid hormone decrease to the point where treatment with thyroid hormone is essential. (7) Tiredness and difficulty concentrating are reported in about 10% of patients, but may be due, in some cases, to depression. (8) Fine-hand tremor.

Less Common Side Effects: (1) Diabetes insipidus—this has nothing to do with "sugar" diabetes, which is technically called diabetes mellitus. In diabetes insipidus there is a massive increase in thirst and urination. The patient feels as if he must drink almost constantly, and as soon as he drinks he has to urinate. There is a need to wake up almost hourly through the night to urinate. This condition can be treated by adding a special drug or reducing the dose of lithium, but it must be taken care of immediately. (2) Decrease in kidney function—several years ago there were reports of patients developing kidney damage after taking lithium for more than ten years. None of these patients developed kidney failure; that is, dialysis or a kidney transplant was not required. Most experts now doubt that lithium really caused the problem, as those patients were taking many drugs for other medical problems. To be on the safe side, we insist that patients undergo simple blood tests, and sometimes urine tests, that measure kidney function every six months to one year while on lithium. (3) Lithium toxicity—this very serious medical emergency is almost entirely preventable. Two things must be done to avoid lithium toxicity: regularly check the lithium blood level and never become dehydrated. Lithium toxicity occurs when the blood level climbs above 1.5. The patient begins to shake and tremble, feels confused, vomits, and develops diarrhea. The lithium level can be greatly increased by severe dehydration, such as can occur after more than a day without anything to drink, after persistent vomiting and diarrhea, or when mountain climbing in the desert when the temperature is 105°. Elderly people are more prone to develop lithium toxicity than younger people. A lithium treated patient should always drink the equivalent of six glasses of water a day and not start a salt-restricted diet while on lithium. Also, if food poisoning or a stomach virus develops with vomiting or diarrhea, the doctor should be called immediately; the patient will probably be told to stop taking lithium until his stomach settles down.

What to Do About Side Effects: Most of the common side effects go away on their own after a few weeks. Taking lithium on a full stomach usually takes care of the stomach upset. The acne sometimes caused by lithium responds to the same treatments that dermatologists prescribe for teenagers. Thyroid gland underactivity is usually picked up by the lab tests; sometimes, low thyroid function results in depression or enlargement of the thyroid called "goiter." These are easily reversed by prescribing thyroid hormone replacement medication. Tiredness and decreased concentration usually go away in time, but occasionally reduction of the dose of lithium is required. The fine hand tremor is usually barely noticeable. If it becomes annoying, propranolol or atenolol can be added and these usually eliminate the tremor completely. The weight gain is the biggest headache. Dieting can help remove some of this weight, but fluid and salt intake should not be restricted.

If It Doesn't Work: Minor highs and lows may still occur while on lithium, and these are usually treated briefly with appropriate additional medications, such as antidepressants and antipsychotics. If major mood swings continue to occur while on lithium, however, most psychiatrists move to the next level of treatment, which is the addition of Tegretol, described next.

If It Does Work: "How long should one stay on lithium?" Unfortunately, this question remains unanswered because how long the illness remains active in a given patient is not known. After several bouts of life-threatening mania and depression most patients are grateful for the relief lithium offers. After ten years of dutifully taking the medication and remaining symptom free, however, many wonder if they might get away with stopping the drug. I usually recommend that a patient remain on lithium indefinitely, but after many years of stability, I will go along with a try at discontinuation. At the first sign that symptoms are reemerging, however, lithium treatment is resumed.

Cost: 4 cents/300-mg pill in most preparations.

Special Comments: Lithium has proven to be one of the true miracle drugs in psychiatry. About 80% of bipolar patients respond and remain symptom free. Those patients will certainly agree that the discoverer of lithium, Australian physician John Cade, and the man who proved that lithium works in bipolar patients, Scandanavian psychiatrist Mogens Schou, deserve a Nobel Prize. Lithium is safe and effective when administered under proper supervision. Any person with a serious bipolar disorder *deserves* a trial of lithium and should, in no way, fear this drug.

CARBAMAZEPINE

Brand Name: Tegretol.

Used for: Treatment of seizures (epilepsy). Treatment of bipolar affective disorder in patients who fail to respond to lithium alone.

Do Not Use if: You have serious blood or liver disease.

Tests to Take First: A complete blood count (CBC) is required, as are blood tests of liver, kidney, and thyroid function. These tests establish a baseline against which any changes produced by Tegretol can be measured.

Tests to Take While You Are on It: Complete blood counts are performed frequently while patients are on Tegretol. In most patients, there is a small, but insignificant, drop in blood cells. In extremely rare cases (less than one in 50,000 patients), however, a very large drop may occur and Tegretol must be stopped immediately. This condition is called aplastic anemia. If it is going to occur it almost always happens in the first year of treatment. To watch for this, the CBC is obtained once every two weeks during the first two months of treatment and then every three months afterward.

Tegretol can also rarely interfere with liver, kidney, or thyroid function and the appropriate blood tests are obtained every six months to one year. Finally, blood levels of Tegretol can aid in dose adjustment, although such tests are not necessary to avoid toxicity, as are lithium levels. A good Tegretol level ranges from 8.0 to 12.0.

Usual Dose: Tegretol comes in chewable tablets of 100 mg and regular tablets of 200 mg. It is best to start at a low dose of 200 to 400 mg a day, usually divided into two equal doses, and then to raise the dose by about 200 mg every week. The usual dose necessary to treat bipolar patients is 800 to 1200 mg a day. Tegretol is often added to lithium for patients who have not responded to lithium alone, although more and more psychiatrists are finding that Tegretol may be effective by itself.

How Long Until It Works: As with lithium, Tegretol is prescribed to prevent future problems, not to treat acute depression or mania. Once it reaches a level of about 8.0, Tegretol should start to have its preventative effect. Then, it is a matter of waiting to see if mood swings are indeed blocked over the next several months.

Common Side Effects: Dizziness, drowsiness, unsteadiness, nausea, and vomiting usually occur early in treatment and then go away. Most patients tolerate Tegretol well.

Less Common Side Effects: Two problems with Tegretol treatment demand immediate medical attention. First, the very rare (one in 50,000 cases), severe drop in the production of blood cells called aplastic anemia puts patients at great risk of developing serious anemia, infections, and bleeding problems. Warning signs include fever, sore throat, easy bruising, purple spots on the skin, and ulcers in the mouth. To avoid aplastic anemia, CBCs should be drawn frequently and the doctor should check the results. Tegretol must be stopped immediately if the results indicate aplastic anemia. Second, and also extremely rarely, Tegretol can cause a variety of skin reactions that require stopping the drug immediately. Therefore, any new rash should be shown to the doctor right away.

What to Do About Side Effects: The common side effects usually go away on their own, but lowering the dose may temporarily be necessary. The less common side effects are prevented by undergoing the appropriate blood tests and reporting all new symptoms to the doctor promptly.

If It Doesn't Work: Mild highs and lows may still occur on Tegretol and are usually treated symptomatically with brief courses of antidepressants or antipsychotic drugs (for mania). If severe mood swings continue, however, most psychiatrists now recommend discontinuing both lithium and Tegretol and moving on to the next level of treatment, valproic acid (Depakene).

If It Does Work: Follow the same advice given for patients treated with lithium alone: stay on the drug indefinitely. After a few months on Tegretol the risk of serious side effects virtually disappears and most of the common side effects also subside. Patients then hardly notice they are taking Tegretol, so there is usually no urgency to stop it. Discontinuation of the drug always involves the risk of developing a new, serious depression or mania. When it is time to stop taking Tegretol, it should be tapered slowly.

Cost: Brand, 29 cents/200-mg pill. Generic, 19 cents/200-mg pill.

Special Comments: Tegretol has been prescribed by neurologists to treat seizure disorders for many years. Its use to treat bipolar patients who do not respond to lithium is relatively recent. Work by scientists like Dr. Robert Post at the National Institute of Mental Health has shown that Tegretol works for lithium refractory patients, many of whom have the form of the illness called "rapid cycling," that is, they have four or more highs and lows per year. Tegretol represents an important advance in the ability to treat bipolar patients.

VALPROIC ACID

Brand Name: Depakene. Depakote is closely related.

Used for: Seizure disorders. Bipolar affective disorder that fails to respond to lithium and Tegretol.

Do Not Use if: You have serious liver disease.

Tests to Take First: You should undergo blood tests of liver and thyroid function to establish a baseline.

Tests to Take While You Are on It: Liver function, which is determined by a simple blood test, must be monitored frequently in the first few months of treatment, and then once every few months thereafter. Thyroid function tests should also be repeated about once a year. A blood test for determining the level of Depakene is available and is useful in adjusting the dose. It is not used to prevent toxicity the way lithium levels are used.

195

Usual Dose: Depakene is available in 250-mg capsules. The final dose is calculated with a formula based on body weight. Theoretically, a 165-pound person requires a final daily dose of 4,500 mg. Psychiatric patients, however, seem to require lower doses, 2,000 mg or less. Starting treatment at one capsule two or three times daily and increasing the dose by one to two capsules a week constitute the best strategy.

How Long Until It Works: As Depakene is given to prevent future highs and lows, the only way to determine if it is working is to observe the patient over several months to see if mood swings have indeed stopped. It is often useful to keep a daily diary of moods (see Figure 1) to help evaluate how well the drug is working.

Common Side Effects: Depakene is very well tolerated. Nausea, vomiting, indigestion, and drowsiness sometimes occur, but usually go away a week or two after the final dose is achieved.

Less Common Side Effects: If you look up Depakene in the *Physicians Desk Reference (PDR)* and similar books, you will read some terrifying warnings. Depakene has been reported to produce fatal liver damage. What the books don't emphasize is that all of the fatalities were infants with brain damage who had also been taking several other medications. For adults, the risk of serious effects from Depakene is virtually nonexistent. To be on the safe side, liver function is measured every week to every other week after initiation of Depakene treatment and then less frequently after the first three to six months of treatment. The dose is lowered or the drug discontinued if any abnormalities are found. Patients should not fear taking Depakene because of concern that a very rare liver problem could develop.

What to Do About Side Effects: The common side effects go away by themselves. Liver failure probably does not occur at all in adults, but is prevented by careful monitoring of liver function.

If It Doesn't Work: About 80% of bipolar patients respond to lithium alone. Many of the remaining 20% respond to lithium plus Tegretol or to Depakene. The number of treatment failures to all three drugs (lithium, Tegretol, and Depakene) is therefore very small. If all three drugs fail to work the psychiatrist will probably try a variety of recently recommended medications, including clonazepam (Klonopin, described next), verapamil, and clonidine.

If It Does Work: Stay on it for a long time. The side effects are minimal and far better than mania or depression. When it is time to stop Depakene, taper slowly.

Cost: Brand, 68 cents/250-mg pill. Generic, 25 cents/250-mg pill.

Special Comments: Although Depakene has been prescribed for seizure disorders for many years, its use in the treatment of bipolar affective disorder is recent and still the subject of many research studies. We have seen some very dramatic improvements in patients who failed to respond to lithium or Tegretol, and many psychiatrists and scientists are very excited about Depakene's possibilities. At present, until more research is done, it should be reserved only for patients who don't get better with lithium or Tegretol; Someday it may move up on the list.

CLONAZEPAM

Brand Name: Klonopin (formerly, Clonopin).

Used for: Certain seizure disorders. Bipolar affective disorder that fails to respond to other medications. Panic attacks in patients with panic disorder (see Chapter 8).

Do Not Use if: There are hardly any medical conditions or other reasons that prevent a patient from taking Klonopin; however, because it is a member of the class of drugs called "benzodiazepines," which includes Valium, Librium, and Xanax, patients with alcohol abuse problems may also abuse Klonopin.

Tests to Take First: None required.

Tests to Take While You Are on It: None are necessary, although the manufacturer recommends "periodic" liver and blood cell tests for patients who remain on Klonopin for long periods.

Usual Dose: Klonopin comes in tablets of 0.5, 1.0, and 2.0 mg. strength. Patients are usually started on a 0.5-mg tablet two or three times daily and then the dose is raised by 0.5 mg every three to seven days. For seizure patients the dose can be raised as high as 20 mg a day, but bipolar patients usually receive no more than a total of 4 or 5 mg a day.

How Long Until It Works: Unlike lithium, Tegretol, and Depakene, Klonopin may have some immediate effects in calming a manic patient. For the long-term prevention of further highs and lows its effectiveness is still under study, but it should begin to help almost immediately.

Common Side Effects: The main side effect is drowsiness, which usually subsides after a week or two. Like the other benzodiazepines, a withdrawal syndrome is experienced when Klonopin is stopped. This syndrome involves increased anxiety, insomnia, irritability, and sometimes unusual sensory events like ringing in the ears or distorted vision. Withdrawal is minimized by slowly tapering off Klonopin; it should never be stopped abruptly.

Less Common Side Effects: Klonopin has been reported to cause depression, which obviously complicates the situation for bipolar patients whose goal is to *prevent* depression. If a depression should occur in a bipolar patient treated with Klonopin, the doctor is faced with the very difficult problem of determining whether Klonopin is the cause or the underlying illness has simply broken through.

What to Do About Side Effects: Drowsiness can be relieved by lowering the dose, but usually goes away after a week or two. Withdrawal symptoms cannot be prevented, but are minimized by tapering off Klonopin over a period of several weeks.

If It Doesn't Work: Klonopin is used only in bipolar patients who have not responded to lithium, Tegretol, and Depakene. If Klonopin doesn't work, the patient may be one of those rare people who must be treated symptomatically for each depression (with antidepressants or shock treatment) and each mania (with antipsychotic drugs or lorazepam).

If It Does Work: The patient is usually kept on Klonopin indefinitely. This is a patient with bipolar illness that has proven very difficult to control. Klonopin may be the fourth drug tried. In such a complex situation, when something is finally found that works, there is never any rush to stop it. Klonopin has no known long-term side effects and most patients do not mind staying on it.

Cost: Brand, 51 cents/0.5-mg pill. Generic, not available.

Special Comments: Klonopin is another drug used primarily to treat epilepsy that may work for bipolar patients as well. It is not as good as Tegretol or Depakene, but for some reason occasionally works in patients who don't respond to those medications. To scientists, the fact that these antiseizure drugs work for bipolar patients is very interesting, and raises the possibility that mood swings may have some biological relationship to epilepsy.

OTHER DRUGS FOR BIPOLAR PATIENTS

A number of other medications have been tested in the treatment of bipolar affective disorder, including clonidine (Catapres) and verapamil (Calan, Isoptin). Lecithin, a naturally occurring food substance given in very large doses has also been studied. Most of the studies are inconclusive. At the present time, the correct sequence for maintenance treatment of bipolar disorder is to give lithium first, which will usually work. If it doesn't, Tegretol is added. If this is ineffective, both are stopped and Depakene is tried. If Depakene doesn't work, Klonopin may be given. After this the psychiatrist may try clonidine or verapamil or lecithin or even recommend shock treatment (Table 24). The great majority of patients never reach this point because less complicated treatments usually work.

Table 24:

Order in Which Drugs Are Prescribed for Maintenance Treatment of Bipolar Patients

1. Lithium alone
2. Lithium plus Tegretol
3. Depakene alone
4. Klonopin alone
5. Verapamil (Calan, Isoptin) or clonidine (Catapres)
6. Treat each separate depression with antidepressant medication or shock treatment and each separate manic period with antipsychotic drugs or Ativan.

199

Chapter 10

Drugs Used to Treat Schizophrenia

In the 1960s, several books and articles appeared claiming that schizophrenia was not really an illness at all. Some called it an alternative way of viewing the world, "marching to a different drummer," another version of normal. We were told to understand schizophrenics and even to try to learn from them.

I doubt many of these "experts" bothered to ask schizophrenic patients or their families for their opinion of this view. More recently, an editorial in the prestigious British scientific journal *Nature* began, "Schizophrenia is arguably the worst disease affecting mankind."

Although that statement may be an exaggeration, there is no debate that schizophrenia is a horrible illness. It strikes people in late adolescence to early adulthood and often never goes away. Occasionally, schizophrenic patients go into full, spontaneous remission, but this often occurs only after years of devastating illness. In the meantime, most schizophrenics endure many hospitalizations, are unable to work, and have little social interaction. Schizophrenia devastates the early adult years of most patients.

The situation is almost equally grim for families of schizophrenics. Living with a schizophrenic is usually a full-time and harrowing job. The patient lives in his or her own world, entertaining bizarre ideas and listening to voices. He may talk without making sense, pace the floors all night, and occasionally become violent or threatening. Parents, acting as if they have toddlers, are afraid to leave their schizophrenic children alone. They, like the patient, become prisoners of the illness.

So, although schizophrenia may seem romantic or interesting to philosophers, it is plainly awful to its victims. Hence, we want to do whatever we can to relieve the symptoms of schizophrenia.

The different forms of schizophrenia and the different ways in which it begins could be the subject of another book. Here I provide information important in guiding drug treatment. Several books listed under Suggestions for Further Reading provide a more detailed picture.

SYMPTOMS OF SCHIZOPHRENIA

The hallmarks of schizophrenia are hallucinations, delusions, thought disorder, and abnormal affect.

Hallucinations occur when people hear and see things, and less commonly smell or feel things, that are not really there. In schizophrenia, auditory hallucinations—hearing voices—are common. This is not the patient who says "my mind is playing tricks on me and it sounds like someone is talking." This patient really *hears* the voice. Often, the schizophrenic patient is surprised that no one else can hear what she hears. The voices often say bizarre things, tell the patient what to do (so-called "command hallucinations"), or make comments on what the patient is doing. Some schizophrenics like the voices and sit alone in a corner listening; others are tortured by them and plead with others to make them go away.

Delusions are false ideas that the patient passionately insists and believes are true. Paranoid delusions are very common in certain forms of schizophrenia. The patient has the unshakable belief that others are actively planning to harm him. A delusional patient may believe that the FBI is tapping her phone, that people from Mars are communicating with her, that bugs are crawling around inside her, or that someone is poisoning her food. No amount of reasoning with a delusional patient changes their mind; there are no "facts" that will shake the delusion.

Thought disorder involves a number of marked abnormalities in mental processes. Most commonly, the patient talks without making any sense; he strings words together seemingly at random in what is often called a "word salad." This patient is not being "deep" or "esoteric." Paying more careful attention to him will not reveal hidden meanings. What he says is senseless because his brain is simply firing out words that don't fit together. At other times, schizophrenics may be talking sensibly and suddenly stop: the idea they had suddenly disappeared.

Abnormal affect in schizophrenia usually means the absence of normal moods. A patient talks about something sad and laughs or talks about something pleasant without any expression on her face. This is sometimes called "inappropriate" or "flat" or "blunted" affect. The patient seems emotionless and zombielike or inappropriately silly and giggly. It is not that they are depressed or happy; instead, they do not express or feel emotions consistent with their speech or the events around them.

These four symptoms—hallucinations, delusions, thought disorder, and abnormal affect—are called "psychotic" symptoms. Psychotic symptoms can occur in disorders other than schizophrenia. Manic and depressed patients both develop psychotic symptoms. Certain drugs used to treat medical illnesses, for example, steroids, produce psychotic symptoms. Street drugs like cocaine and angel dust (PCP) also induce psychosis. Making the diagnosis of schizophrenia therefore often requires skill and experience.

In most cases, however, the diagnosis of schizophrenia is all too obvious. The reason is that most other psychoses eventually go away, even without treatment. If a psychotically depressed patient doesn't commit suicide, he will get better eventually. Likewise, if a person stops taking steroids or PCP, the psychotic symptoms disappear. The person with schizophrenia, however, suffers from a chronic illness that usually gets worse and worse. Even when the most florid psychotic symptoms go away, the patient feels unmotivated and isolated. He cannot function at work or in social situations. Casual observers find him odd. At one time, chronic schizophrenics used to live in the wards of state psychiatric hospitals; now they all too often live on the streets of big cities.

So the diagnosis of schizophrenia involves the recognition of two factors: acute psychotic symptoms and a deteriorating course of illness. It is difficult to make the diagnosis in someone who has had a single episode of psychosis, which may represent a manic episode or the effect of a drug. The psychosis may never return. But after two or three episodes, especially if the patient doesn't bounce back to normal in between, the diagnosis of schizophrenia can reliably be made.

CAUSES OF SCHIZOPHRENIA

There is now mounting evidence that schizophrenia is at least in part a genetic disease that involves abnormal development of the brain and loss of brain cells. Scientists have shown that in some cases there appears to be an abnormal gene on chromosome 5. Many studies using specialized brain x-rays called CAT scans and MRI scans (see Chapter 19) have shown that schizophrenics basically have less brain tissue than normal people.

We also now know that schizophrenia is not one disease. There are so many different forms, presentations, outcomes, and symptoms that it is likely to be a collection of several different diseases. In this respect, schizophrenia is similar to pneumonia, which can be caused by a number of different bacteria, viruses, and parasites, yet almost always manifests as cough, fever, and chest pain. So too, there are probably many different causes of the hallucinations, delusions, thought disorder, and abnormal affect of schizophrenia. It is encouraging that more research money is now being spent to find the causes of schizophrenia, but the answers probably require many years of research.

One thing that clearly does *not* cause schizophrenia is bad parenting. This does not mean that I am endorsing parental neglect. Psychiatrists' offices are full of people who are the victims of parents who were too busy or self-involved to take proper care of their

204

children. Schizophrenia, however, is not an outcome of an unhappy childhood. We see schizophrenics who had terrible parents and schizophrenics who had good parents. Some schizophrenics are the children of schizophrenics; others are the children of completely normal people. Schizophrenia must be regarded as a tragic disease of uncertain cause that strikes one out of a hundred people in the United States. It can strike anybody.

The news that schizophrenia is not caused by bad parents has helped many family members of schizophrenics shed their guilt and join forces to urge better treatment and more research. Such organizations as the National Alliance for the Mentally Ill have as members many parents of schizophrenics who courageously come forward to make their stories known.

The relatives of schizophrenics, who are often charged with their care, need to know as much as possible about the drug treatment of schizophrenia so they can help guide the treatment. Usually, asking a schizophrenic patient in the middle of a psychotic episode to make a rational decision about taking drugs is not sensible. This does not mean that schizophrenics should routinely be given medication against their will or that information should be withheld from them. It is often surprising to find out how much the psychotic patient actually understands if doctors take the time to explain things to them. And schizophrenics clearly have the right to participate in all treatment decisions. The courts have also insisted that schizophrenics have the right to refuse treatment and stay psychotic, even if it means they must remain hospitalized for years.

Informed family members are a great asset to both patient and doctor. The drugs used to treat schizophrenia are serious medications with many side effects. Family members must serve as advocates for their schizophrenic relatives, as well as assistants to the doctor in identifying side effects.

The drugs used to treat schizophrenia are often referred to as "antipsychotics." I prefer the term *antipsychotic* because these medications are effective against all psychoses, including those caused by schizophrenia, depression, mania, and drug abuse. The term *neuroleptic* is based on the incorrect idea that these drugs work because of certain side effects they produce.

WHEN SHOULD ANTIPSYCHOTIC DRUGS BE PRESCRIBED?

It is important that the general public have some understanding of the antipsychotic drugs. The antipsychotic drugs are sometimes prescribed when they shouldn't be. At one point they were called "major tranquilizers" and were administered indiscriminately to people who were very anxious, agitated, or even annoying. This is almost never justified; antipsychotic drugs are not good antianxiety drugs. Putting an anxious person on an antipsychotic drug exposes them to the risk of developing serious side effects with little payoff. If your doctor wants to prescribe an antipsychotic and you are not suffering from a psychotic illness you should get a second opinion.

Schizophrenia is not the only illness, however, for which antipsychotic drugs are correctly prescribed. Four other conditions are so treated:

1. **Mania, with or without psychotic symptoms.** As I explained in Chapter 9, patients with bipolar affective disorder who are in the manic phase are usually first treated with antipsychotic drugs because lithium takes too long to work. Sometimes, manic patients also have psychotic symptoms, for example, hallucinations and delusions. It is appropriate to treat acute mania with antipsychotic drugs, but these drugs should usually be discontinued in favor of long-term lithium treatment once the acute situation resolves.

2. **Depression with psychotic symptoms.** Most depressed patients do not become psychotic, but occasionally a depressed patient will hear voices telling him he is a horrible person, or he is responsible for terrible crimes, or he should kill himself. Or the depressed patient may develop delusions; for example, he may believe that he has caused someone else's death or is himself dying or that he has lost all of his money. In this case, antipsychotic drugs are usually combined with an antidepressant drug until the psychotic symptoms are eliminated. The antidepressant is then usually continued, but the antipsychotic discontinued.

3. **Dementia with extreme agitation or psychotic symptoms.** Patients with dementias such as occur with Alzheimer's disease

206

(formerly called "senile" dementia), Huntington's disease, or late-stage AIDS sometimes become agitated to the point that they cannot sleep or sit still longer than a minute. They may also develop psychotic symptoms including delusions and hallucinations. Low doses of antipsychotic medications are very effective in calming these patients and eliminating psychotic symptoms. Demented and elderly patients should not be simply be placed on these medications and forgotten about as occurs tragically in too many American nursing homes; there is a constant need for medical supervision and reevaluation.

4. **Certain tics and abnormal movements.** Antipsychotic medications are used, for example in Tourette's syndrome.

Here are some examples of patients who should be placed on antipsychotic medications. All three patients are schizophrenics.

TREATMENT OF SCHIZOPHRENIA

Patti was not a particularly remarkable child. She was neither exceptionally bright nor troublesome. Her teachers liked her, she earned good but not outstanding grades, and she always had plenty of friends without being the most popular girl in school. She got along very well with her older brother. Her parents, hard-working people who made a modest but sufficient income, were justifiably proud of her. After graduation from high school, Patti decided to attend a local community college to try and improve her grades and her chances of getting into a good university.

Things went badly at the college. Patti seemed to lose interest in classes after the first few months, and then began having trouble getting up in the morning. She also seemed listless and preoccupied to her parents, who first wondered if perhaps she was in love, then worried if she might be pregnant or taking drugs or sick. She lost weight and missed meals. One evening, for no apparent reason, she flung a plate of food across the room, yelled out an obscenity, and ran out of the house. She returned several hours later, and when

207

her parents questioned her about her behavior, she screamed "You will never take me alive."

After that, her behavior became more and more strange. She stopped going to college and remained in her room all day. She spoke to almost no one, refused to come to the telephone when somebody called, and picked at her food. Her parents asked her to see the family doctor, but she became angry and refused.

The final crisis occurred when Patti barricaded herself in her room and refused to let anyone in. She screamed incoherently for hours. Her father finally broke down the door to her room and found Patti sitting in the middle of the floor, rocking back and forth and lighting matches. She was taken to the hospital emergency room.

In the emergency room, Patti was first seen by a medical doctor who did her best to conduct a physical examination and obtain blood tests, but Patti thrashed about, insisting she was being persecuted for her "secret knowledge." The blood tests were all normal, including a screen for drugs such as marijuana, cocaine, amphetamines, and angel dust—all drugs that can cause psychotic behavior. Next, a psychiatrist was called in. The psychiatrist asked questions and attempted to gain Patti's confidence. Patti told him that she was being watched closely by "secret forces" and that these "forces" were putting new "thoughts in my head." Patti was hostile and suspicious, but agreed with the psychiatrist that the voices and thoughts she was experiencing were unpleasant. She agreed to drink a solution containing 5 mg of the antipsychotic drug haloperidol (Haldol). An hour later she was calmer and cooperated with the complete physical examination.

Patti was then admitted to the psychiatric ward of the hospital where she was placed on Haldol 5 mg three times daily and a medication called Cogentin to counteract some of the side effects of Haldol. She also underwent extensive medical tests including an electroencephalogram (EEG) and a CAT scan of the brain. The tests were normal, and over a two-week period Patti became calm, started eating, and decided the "secret forces" were only her imagination. She was kept on Haldol and Cogentin several more months, during which time she returned to college. The drug was then discontinued.

Patti's case represents an acute paranoid psychosis—"acute" because it came on relatively quickly and involved many active symptoms; "paranoid" because Patti had delusions that people were persecuting her, beliefs that were obviously false, but unshakable; and "psychosis" because of the presence of hallucinations and delusions. She was treated with a standard antipsychotic drug after medical problems and drug use were ruled out as the cause of her psychotic behavior.

At this point, we do not know whether Patti will go on to meet the diagnostic criteria for schizophrenia. Some patients, for reasons we do not understand, have a single psychotic episode and never become seriously psychiatrically ill again. Should Patti have several similar episodes, she would be diagnosed as having chronic paranoid schizophrenia. Long-term prescription of antipsychotic drugs would then become necessary to control her symptoms.

The next case is quite different. Looking back, Mark's mother remembers that he was always a shy and lonely child. He had few friends in school and was often scapegoated by the other children. He was physically awkward and clumsy. His grades were poor and he seemed to get interested in unusual subjects, like staring at pictures in a book of houseplants for hours on end.

By age 14, the teachers at school were already commenting that Mark was disruptive in school. He would burst out laughing for no good reason or suddenly push another child without provocation. His parents had a hard time getting him to wash or brush his teeth. Most disturbing, he seemed to talk to himself and often, when talking to others, made little sense. By age 16 Mark dropped out of school because his grades were terrible and he was unable to concentrate. He talked about his "friends" who were actually imaginary people with whom he carried on conversations all day long. He watched television most of the time and would describe in great detail the shows he watched as if they were real-life events. Many times his speech was slurred and difficult to understand.

Mark is now thirty years old and admitted to the research psychiatric ward of a University Medical Center hospital. His doctors are studying the causes and treatment of serious mental illnesses. Since age 16, Mark has seen many psychiatrists and undergone many diagnostic tests. He has also been admitted to hospitals from time to time for short periods, usually after he had paced through the night, laughing and talking to himself so loud that people became frightened. He has been treated with many different antipsychotic drugs, including Thorazine, Mellaril, and Stelazine. He usually forgets to take his medication, so he now receives injections once every two weeks of the very long acting antipsychotic drug prolixin decanoate.

Mark is fortunate in some respects. Despite his odd and often frightening behavior, his family has stuck by him, allowing him to live at home and encouraging him to take his medication and see his doctor regularly. After hearing about experimental approaches to treatment of his illness, they have arranged for admission to the Medical Center, but understand that even top experts usually do not produce "cures."

Mark clearly suffers from chronic schizophrenia, "chronic" because the illness has been apparent for many years. Unlike Patti, Mark showed some symptoms of abnormal behavior from a very early age. He never had an abrupt "psychotic" break, but moved slowly into schizophrenia with delusions, hallucinations, abnormal affect, and thought disorder. Antipsychotic drugs may reduce the severity of some symptoms, like hallucinations and delusions, but do not cure the illness. Mark has never held a job and never had a date. When his parents die he may have to be institutionalized permanently because he never developed the capacity to support himself. He is not retarded: IQ tests are normal. He is, however, severely mentally disabled for life.

Now the last case of schizophrenia. Marty is 50 years old. He had his first psychotic break when he was in the army at age 20. Since then he has had fifteen psychiatric hospitalizations. He has worked intermittently as a messenger and as a floor sweeper in an office. Now Marty lives in a group home for chronic schizophrenic patients maintained by a community-based mental health organization.

Marty never laughs and he never cries. He does not look happy and he does not look sad. His face is expressionless. He moves slowly and talks as little as possible. When asked a question he responds in short but appropriate answers. He does not hear voices or see things or have delusions, but he remembers that he did have these symptoms until about ten years ago. Marty makes uncontrollable chewing movements with his mouth and often grimaces involuntarily. These are permanent neurological side effects of the antipsychotic drugs he has taken almost continuously for the last thirty years. Marty now takes no medications.

After many years of psychotic symptoms (hallucinations, delusions, thought disorder), some schizophrenics have a "burnt" out appearance. They no longer exhibit formal psychotic symptoms, but they look and act like "zombies." Some psychiatrists refer to this lack of emotion and motivation as the "negative" symptoms of schizophrenia. These "negative" symptoms do not respond to antipsychotic drugs as well as the "positive" symptoms of hallucinations, delusions, and thought disorder.

Marty also has "tardive dyskinesia," which will be discussed shortly. This neurological side effect of long-term antipsychotic medications involves abnormal and involuntary muscle movements, most pronounced in the face. Usually, they go away when the antipsychotic medication is stopped, but sometimes they become permanent.

The three schizophrenic cases I have presented represent three different aspects of antipsychotic drug use. Patti is an acutely psychotic patient; antipsychotic drugs work very well in this situation. Mark is a chronic schizophrenic who still has psychotic symptoms; antipsychotic drugs may reduce the severity or even eliminate psychotic symptoms, but do not usually return the patient to normal functioning permanently. Marty is also a chronic schizophrenic, but most of his psychotic symptoms have subsided on their own. He has mostly "negative" symptoms and does not respond to antipsychotic drugs. He also has side effects from taking antipsychotic drugs for many years.

Remember, these are only examples. There are rare cases in which even acute psychosis does not respond to antipsychotic drugs. Sometimes, negative symptoms do improve with drug treatment. Not all patients develop tardive dyskinesia, and most of those do get better when the antipsychotic drugs are stopped.

Three important messages should be learned from these cases:

1. Antipsychotic drugs work.

2. Antipsychotic drugs do not "cure" schizophrenia.

3. Antipsychotic drugs can cause serious side effects.

OTHER PSYCHIATRIC ILLNESSES

Now I present two cases in which antipsychotic drugs are appropriately prescribed to patients who do not have schizophrenia.

John is a 42-year-old actor. He was diagnosed with bipolar affective disorder (formerly called manic-depressive illness) at age 25 after a series of manic and depressive episodes. This illness is described in more detail in Chapter 9. For more than ten years John has taken lithium every night and, except for occasional mild depression, has been free of manic highs and depression.

Several months ago, however, he decided he had taken lithium long enough and, without telling his wife or friends or doctor, stopped taking it. He was fine for a month and this convinced him he was completely over the illness. After about six weeks off lithium, friends noticed that he was talking fast, seemed restless, and argued with co-workers frequently. He started writing a play, working far into the night and waking up at the crack of dawn. He felt productive, but his wife read the play and found it to be mostly an endless collection of random ideas and speeches. She mentioned this to John, and he accused her of being envious and not deep enough to understand his talent. He started calling producers in Hollywood and running up enormous phone bills. His wife became alarmed when John told her he had invested most of their savings in an experimental off-Broadway play without consulting her or even checking out the investment.

Finally, John's wife called his psychiatrist and reported his odd and impulsive behavior. The psychiatrist diagnosed acute mania and prescribed an antipsychotic medication called Trilafon. John agreed to take it only because he wanted to get some sleep. After several days he began to calm down; the psychiatrist strongly recommended that he resume taking lithium along with the antipsychotic drug. After three weeks John was back to normal. The antipsychotic drug was discontinued and he remained on lithium another ten years.

As I explained in Chapter 9, during an acute mania in a patient with bipolar affective disorder it is often necessary to prescribe antipsychotic drugs to control the symptoms rapidly. Lithium alone

212

takes too long once the manic episode is in full force. As soon as the episode is under control, the antipsychotic drug is usually stopped. The patient remains on lithium to *prevent* another manic episode.

Virginia is 75 years old and suffers from the degenerative illness Alzheimer's disease. Alzheimer's disease is the most common form of dementia. Patients with Alzheimer's disease gradually lose their memory and ability to perform many intellectual activities. This is not the mild memory loss that sometimes accompanies normal aging, but a progressive loss of mental capacity that usually renders the patient incapacitated before death.

Virginia lives in a nursing home. She reads the newspaper every day, but a few minutes after reading an article cannot explain what it is about. She remembers what she wore to her sweet sixteen party almost sixty years ago, but cannot recall what she had for breakfast an hour after the meal is over. She has difficulty remembering faces and is often confused about whether it is day or night.

Virginia's children and grandchildren visit her frequently. One day her son came to see her and she began yelling at him, accusing him of being an attendant who she insisted had stolen her glasses. It took an aide almost an hour to calm her down and convince her the man was her son. The next day she called her daughter and told her that the attendants were stealing money from her purse and giving her secret injections in the middle of the night. Given the horror stories sometimes heard about nursing homes, her daughter was understandably worried. When she went to check things out her mother yelled at her also and accused *her* of stealing money. Virginia's children then heard the sad news from the nursing home director: Virginia had been making up stories about people stealing things from her for about two weeks. She had reached the point where an aide had to stay with her at all times, because she threatened to walk out of the nursing home in the middle of the night.

A psychiatrist was called in to evaluate Virginia. Virginia ordered the doctor out of the room and accused him of being sent to kill her. At this point Virginia threw her food tray in the garbage, insisting the food was poisoned. The psychiatrist first ordered medical tests to ensure that a medical problem was not causing her psychotic symptoms. The tests showed no change from her checkup

213

six months earlier, so he prescribed a very low dose of an antipsychotic drug. Three days later, Virginia's psychotic symptoms had disappeared, she recognized her son, and ate her meals. Her memory, however, was unimproved.

In Chapter 17, I discuss special considerations in prescribing psychiatric drugs for elderly patients. The case of Virginia illustrates several important points. First, psychotic symptoms like Virginia's paranoid delusions often complicate Alzheimer's disease. These symptoms sometimes jeopardize a patient's well being to the point where there is no choice but to treat. It is crucial that a physician evaluate a patient in this situation because many medical problems; for example, strokes, uncontrolled diabetes, and dehydration can cause psychotic symptoms in elderly people. After a medical doctor has excluded a medical cause, it may be necessary to prescribe antipsychotic drugs. These should be administered in very low doses, because elderly patients—especially demented elderly patients—are very susceptible to side effects. The drugs usually work quickly. They should be stopped and resumed only if the symptoms return. Elderly people should be seen regularly by a doctor once an antipsychotic drug is prescribed. They should never be left on the drugs indefinitely without medical supervision.

IMPROPER USE OF ANTIPSYCHOTIC DRUGS

Having presented these five cases—three schizophrenics, one manic, and one psychotic with Alzheimer's disease—for whom antipsychotic medications were properly prescribed, I now present a case in which drugs were *improperly prescribed.*

Janice is a commercial photographer trying to start her own business after years of taking pictures for weddings. Although she is a very talented photographer, she has little skill for business. Characteristically, she impulsively quit her job and rented studio space that was much too expensive. She got very little advice on the proper way to set up a new business and did not take into consideration the competition she would have.

Consequently, Janice began having serious financial problems. With these, she felt extremely anxious, had trouble falling asleep, and lost weight. Her friends grew tired of listening to her constant preoccupation with the business and her financial problems, and many avoided seeing her. This made Janice feel abandoned, and she angrily thought that the world is simply against a young woman trying to make a go of it on her own.

Worried about her, Janice's parents agreed to lend her some money and also to pay for her to see a psychotherapist. The psychotherapist believed Janice needed to work on two problems: the short-range problem of getting herself out of a tight practical situation and the long-range problem of her continuous refusing to deal with the world in a realistic, adult way. In essence, the therapist explained, Janice maintained a childlike vision of the world in which good intentions and talent alone should be enough to win praise and reward. Whenever things happened to contradict that view, Janice quickly became bitter, accusatory, and angry.

Despite this sound advice, Janice believed she should take some kind of medication. She refused to accept the possibility that she had psychological problems; her main problems, she believes, are anxiety and lack of sleep.

Reluctantly, the therapist referred her to a psychiatrist who put Janice on a medication for anxiety called Tranxene. This helped calm her down and improved her sleep; however, Janice remained angry, frantic, and bent on a course of professional and financial disaster. A month later she returned to the psychiatrist and complained that the medication was not strong enough. She cried a bit and blamed the doctor for not understanding her problems or taking her seriously enough. The doctor consequently told her, "The drug I placed you on is called a 'minor tranquilizer.' It is obviously not strong enough for your problems, so I will give you a 'major tranquilizer' instead."

And so Janice was placed on the antipsychotic drug Thorazine. This made her very sleepy, dizzy, and a little restless. She felt as if she had "cotton balls in my head." One time, when she was about to get a contract for some serious work, she dozed off in the middle of the conversation. Although Janice felt less anxious, she also felt "drugged." After two weeks on Thorazine, she accepted her therapist's recommendation that she get a second opinion from another psychiatrist.

One thing that amazes psychiatrists is the ability of patients with schizophrenia or acute mania to tolerate large doses of antipsychotic drugs like Thorazine. Nonpsychotic patients usually feel terrible and very sedated after taking very small doses. For example, 25 mg of Thorazine will put many nonpsychotic people to sleep for hours; schizophrenic patients sometimes take as much as 1,000 mg a day without showing any signs of sedation.

Janice illustrates a common mistake made with antipsychotic drugs. Because they do calm very psychotic patients, some people, including a few physicians, think they are simply very powerful tranquilizers. If an anxious patient doesn't respond to one of the antianxiety drugs described in Chapter 8, why not try one of these more powerful drugs?

The answer to this question is simple: *antipsychotic drugs are not powerful tranquilizers,* they are medications designed to treat specific sets of psychotic symptoms found in patients with specific diagnoses. Psychosis may occur in a variety of settings, including mania, schizophrenia, psychotic depression, and dementia. In those cases antipsychotic drugs are warranted. They are not to be used for treating anxiety in nonpsychotic patients for two very good reasons. First, they don't work very well in that situation. Second, it is not correct to expose a patient to the risk of severe side effects when drugs with fewer side effects are available.

Janice probably should not be treated with any medication. A short course of Tranxene is not a terrible idea if it temporarily helps her sleep and feel calm enough to deal with her problems rationally. Her therapist had been correct in explaining to Janice that what she needed was counseling and therapy. Giving Janice Thorazine is like performing lung surgery on someone with viral pneumonia. Removing the lung probably would cure the pneumonia, but more conservative treatment is obviously advised.

I must stress again that there are few "absolutes" in treating psychiatric patients with drugs. There are occasional nonpsychotic situations in which antipsychotic drugs may be used with benefit. A severe form of personality disorder, borderline personality disorder, is sometimes best treated with antipsychotic drugs for short periods. Some severe pain caused by medical problems may also respond to antipsychotic drugs. Very low doses of Thorazine and similar antipsychotic drugs are sometimes prescribed for treatment of severe nausea and vomiting. I do not mean to imply that use of an antipsychotic drug in any patient who is not psychotic or manic is automatically wrong. I do mean to warn against the use of antipsychotic drugs for the routine treatment of anxiety and depression. By no means should anybody take these drugs without regular visits to a psychiatrist who understands how to prescribe them.

WHAT ARE THE SERIOUS SIDE EFFECTS OF ANTIPSYCHOTIC DRUGS?

Given the beneficial effects of antipsychotic drugs on some patients why is there so much fuss? I have already said that patients with schizophrenia take as much as 1,000 mg of Thorazine a day sometimes and seem to tolerate it. How dangerous can they be?

Let me start by stating again one of the guiding principles behind the recommendations in this book and the use of medication to treat any medical problem: *the benefit must always clearly outweigh the risk.*

Schizophrenia is a devastating disease. We are willing to accept more risk in treating very serious diseases than in treating less serious diseases. The drugs used to treat cancer, for example, can themselves threaten the lives of patients. But to save a life we often take the risk—with the patient's full consent and understanding—of administering potentially very toxic treatments.

The antipsychotic drugs produce powerful changes in brain chemistry. Many of these changes involve blocking the action of the brain chemical *dopamine.* This is described more fully in Chapter 19. We do not yet know if blocking dopamine is the way in which antipsychotic drugs work to treat psychosis, but we do know that blocking dopamine produces a number of adverse side effects in patients who take antipsychotic drugs. These side effects have technical names and are often confusing to patients and families. Therefore, before proceeding to describe the individual drugs, I want to detail this particular group of side effects:

Acute Dystonic Reaction. Within hours or a few days of starting an antipsychotic drug, some patients, particularly young men, may suddenly experience painful, tightening spasms of the muscles, particularly in the head and neck. The tongue may protrude and the patient drool. Sometimes the eyes appear locked in place. Rarely, muscles of the larynx (windpipe) also begin to spasm and the patient has difficulty breathing. This effect is called dystonia and occurs in between 1% and 8% of patients who take antipsychotic drugs. Acute dystonia can be reversed in a matter of seconds by injection of the proper antidote (Benadryl or Cogentin).

To prevent acute dystonia, many clinicians now place patients on these antidotes, which are taken by mouth, at the same time the antipsychotic drug is started. Several categories of antidotes are available. Some brand names are Cogentin, Artane, Kemadrin, Akineton, and Benadryl (see Table 25).

Parkinsonian Syndrome. After a few weeks of taking antipsychotic medications, some patients develop a neurological syndrome that is very similar to Parkinson's disease, which is seen in the elderly. The most obvious sign of this is tremor, especially of the hands. But patients with drug-induced Parkinsonian syndrome may also have a loss of facial expression, slowed movements, rigidity in arms and legs, drooling, and shuffling gait. It occurs in as many as one third of patients who take antipsychotic drugs. Drugs that treat acute dystonia are also effective in reversing Parkinsonian syndrome. These include Cogentin, Artane, Kemadrin, Akineton, and Symmetrel (see Table 25).

Akathisia. Perhaps as many as 75% of patients treated with antipsychotic drugs develop some degree of akathisia, although it is usually problematic in only about 10% to 20%. Patients with akathisia feel restless and are unable to sit still. They may appear agitated and jumpy, but the problem is not psychological. The restlessness is a direct side effect of the medication. Akathisia is a leading cause of patient refusal to continue taking antipsychotic drugs. Akathisia is also difficult to treat, but some medications may be helpful. These include propranolol (Inderal), clonidine (Catapres), and diazepam (Valium). It is extremely important to treat akathisia vigorously if it is necessary to keep the patient on the antipsychotic drug.

218

Table 25:

Drugs Used to *Counteract* the Side Effects of Antipsychotics

GENERIC NAME	BRAND NAME	USED FOR	DAILY DOSE
Benztropine	Cogentin	Acute dystonia Parkinsonian syndrome Akinesia Akathisia	2–8 mg
Trihexyphenidyl	Artane	Acute dystonia Parkinsonian syndrome Akinesia Akathisia	1–15 mg
Procyclidine	Kemadrin	Acute dystonia Parkinsonian syndrome Akinesia Akathisia	7.5–20 mg
Diphenhydramine	Benadryl	Acute dystonia	25 mg (injection)

continued

Table 25, *continued*

GENERIC NAME	BRAND NAME	USED FOR	DAILY DOSE
Biperiden	Akineton	Acute dystonia	2–6 mg
Amantadine	Symmetrel	Parkinsonian syndrome	100–300 mg
Diazepam	Valium	Akathisia	2–20 mg
Lorazepam	Ativan	Akathisia	0.5–6 mg
Propranolol	Inderal	Akathisia	20–60 mg
Bromocriptine	Parlodel	Neuroleptic malignant syndrome	15–80 mg
Dantrolene	Dantrium	Neuroleptic malignant syndrome	Given by injection
Levodopa	Many	Tardive dyskinesia	Varies
Reserpine	Serpasil	Tardive dyskinesia	Varies

Akinesia. Usually occurring many weeks after initiation of antipsychotic drugs, akinesia involves a decrease in spontaneous movements and apathy. It resembles depression or "negative" symptom schizophrenia, but is actually a drug side effect. It can usually be reversed with the same drugs that reverse acute dystonia and Parkinsonian syndrome (for example, Cogentin, Akineton, Artane, Kemadrin, and Benadryl).

Tardive Dyskinesia. Tardive dyskinesia, or TD, is one of the dreaded, but often unavoidable, outcomes of treatment with antipsychotic drugs and possibly also the antidepressant drug Asendin. Usually developing after a year or more of continuous use of antipsychotic drugs, TD is characterized by involuntary and purposeless movements of the head, neck, trunk, and extremities. TD often begins with wormlike movements of the tongue, grimacing, chewing, and lip smacking. There may also be a variety of sudden or writhing movements of the hands, arms, and legs. The patient cannot control the movements although they may be made worse by stress. TD is especially likely to occur in older people and in people with brain damage who are treated with antipsychotic drugs. The longer the patient is kept on the medication, the more likely TD is to occur.

Most patients do not begin to show signs of TD until they have taken antipsychotic drugs for many years, but signs can emerge more quickly, particularly in the elderly. The risk of developing severe TD from antipsychotic drugs probably lies between 20% and 40%, but mild signs may appear in up to 70% of patients. Patients should be examined carefully by the doctor, at least every six months, for signs of TD. Many psychiatrists use the guidelines for examination found in the Abnormal Involuntary Movements Scales (AIMS) of the National Institutes of Health. When signs of TD are first observed, an attempt is made to lower the dose of drug and even to taper the patient off the medication. In some cases, the movements worsen after the medication is stopped; this is usually temporary and in most instances, especially if caught early, TD goes away after the drug is stopped. There are, however, cases in which stopping the medication results in no decrease, and even a permanent increase, in TD. This difficult-to-treat situation often requires the expertise of neurological specialists in movement disorders.

221

Some drugs may help reverse TD, for example, reserpine and levodopa.

It is impossible to predict which patients will develop TD—studies give different estimates but probably about one in four patients experience some degree of TD—and also impossible to determine how long a given person will be on medication before TD develops. Therefore, it is often hard for psychiatrists to decide how much information to give acutely psychotic patients before starting an antipsychotic drug. On the one hand, we want well-informed patients who make important decisions about their medical care. On the other hand, telling a paranoid patient who hears voices that a drug may cause abnormal movements in a few years is obviously difficult. The patient usually does not understand what he or she is being told and is therefore unable to make an "informed" decision. The following recommendation seems to me the best compromise. Before giving the antipsychotic drug the family should be fully informed about all side effects, but should also be made to understand that TD *virtually never* develops after only a few weeks or months of taking the antipsychotic drugs. As soon as possible, when the patient is calm, an explanation should be given of the long-term risks of taking the medication. Some state laws may apply in this situation. Although the risk of TD is frightening and serious, so is the risk of allowing acute psychosis to remain uncorrected.

Neuroleptic Malignant Syndrome. Neuroleptic malignant syndrome is a very rare but potentially life-threatening side effect of antipsychotic drugs. The patient becomes severely rigid, to the point of not moving at all. Other characteristics are high fever, rapid heart rate, labored breathing, sweating, and abnormalities on blood tests. This syndrome is a medical emergency. Patients with neuroleptic malignant syndrome are usually admitted to the hospital where the antipsychotic drug is immediately stopped. Two medications are recommended to treat this condition, dantrolene and bromocriptine.

These six adverse reactions—acute dystonia, Parkinsonian syndrome, akathisia, akinesia, tardive dyskinesia, and neuroleptic malignant syndrome—are not the only side effects of antipsychotic drugs. Different drugs in this class may cause different side effects, all of which are described in the pages that follow. These six, however, are complex and specific to antipsychotic drugs. All of the antipsychotic drugs have the potential to produce any one of them.

WHICH ANTIPSYCHOTIC DRUG SHOULD THE PATIENT TAKE?

Many types and brands of antipsychotic medication are available. Most of them work as well as the next, so the main difference is usually side effects. In many cases, the acutely psychotic patient is treated on an emergency basis, so the family should know a bit about the different kinds of drugs and the questions they should ask.

In general, there are two types of antipsychotic drugs: *high potency* and *low potency* (see Table 26). They work equally well against psychosis. Low-potency antipsychotic drugs tend to lower blood pressure and cause sedation as their main side effects. Examples are Thorazine and Mellaril. High-potency antipsychotic drugs do not affect blood pressure or produce sleepiness as much, but produce more dystonias and Parkinsonian syndrome. Examples are Haldol and Stelazine.

In the emergency situation, it is now most common to start the patient on high-potency antipsychotic drugs (Haldol, Stelazine, or Prolixin). A typical starting regimen is one 5-mg tablet of Haldol two or three times daily. Patients under age 40 are simultaneously started on medications that cut down on dystonias and Parkinsonian side effects, for example, Cogentin 2 mg or Artane 2 mg, twice daily.

The high-potency antipsychotic is usually continued for several weeks, because a full response may take time. If there is no response after two weeks, the dose is raised. Most clinicians now stress that low doses of antipsychotic drugs should be used whenever possible because they appear to work just as well as high doses and cause fewer side effects.

If one antipsychotic drug does not work after about four weeks, another drug is tried. For reasons that are not at all understood, patients sometimes respond to one but not another.

Table 26:

Summary of Antipsychotic Drugs

CLASS	EXAMPLES	COMMON SIDE EFFECTS
High potency	Haldol, Stelazine, Prolixin, Trilafon, Navane	Dystonia, Parkinsonian syndrome, akinesia
Low potency	Thorazine, Mellaril, Loxitane, Moban	Lower blood pressure, drowsiness, constipation, difficulty urinating, blurry vision, dry mouth

Note: These drugs all work more or less equally well to control the symptoms of schizophrenia. The main reason to choose one over the other is the side effect profile. Besides those listed in the chart, each drug has its own side effects.

Elderly patients with psychotic symptoms are usually given high-potency antipsychotic drugs in very low doses. Haldol 1 or 2 mg daily is a common dose. Elderly patients are not usually given drugs to counteract side effects right away because these anti–side effect drugs may have serious side effects of their own in elderly patients.

The low-potency antipsychotics are used when it is especially important to help the patient sleep, that is, in very agitated patients. They are often given to manic patients who must be calmed down. Thorazine is usually started at 200 to 300 mg daily; this dose is often sufficient but it is routine to go up to 600 mg if necessary. Doses up to 1,000 mg are sometimes used, but are usually not more effective than lower doses.

In very serious emergencies when the patient refuses to swallow pills, but is very ill, antipsychotics can be given by injection. This method is safe, but is discontinued as soon as the patient agrees to swallow the medication. There is little evidence that injected medications work better than oral medications.

HOW LONG SHOULD TREATMENT LAST?

How long should a patient be treated with antipsychotic drugs? For patients with mania, psychotic depression, or dementia who also have psychosis, the answer is easy: the shortest time possible. The antipsychotic drug is usually stopped as soon as the symptoms subside. Manic patients are then kept on lithium and depressed patients on antidepressants. Elderly patients should be kept off medication whenever possible.

The length of treatment for the schizophrenic patient is more difficult to determine. After the first psychotic break, many psychiatrists recommend at least one year of treatment, then discontinuation of the medication and careful observation. After the second psychotic break, the patient should be treated several years. Study after study has shown that schizophrenic patients who discontinue their medication stand a good chance of returning to the hospital. During treatment with an antipsychotic medication, however, the patient should be kept on the lowest possible dose that keeps the symptoms of psychosis in check. The patient should also be observed and examined frequently for any signs of tardive dyskinesia.

Schizophrenic patients often forget or refuse to take their medication. One solution is to give them injections of very long acting antipsychotic medications. Two brands are available in the United States: Prolixin Decanoate and Haldol Decanoate. They can be injected once every two weeks (Prolixin Decanoate) to four weeks (Haldol Decanoate). These injections eliminate the need for the patient to take medication regularly.

Some schizophrenic patients do not respond to standard antipsychotic drugs at all. Until recently, little treatment was available to the person who had tried several different antipsychotic drugs at a range of doses. Some clinicians placed the refractory patient on lithium, Xanax, Inderal, or a wide variety of other drugs. Occasionally these worked.

More recently, the first of the so-called "atypical" antipsychotic drugs has been tested in this country. Clozapine, recently marketed in the United States as Clozaril, does not have many of the effects on human brain chemicals and on animal behavior that the standard antipsychotic drugs do. It also does not seem to produce many of the side effects common to antipsychotic drugs, such as acute dystonia and Parkinsonian syndrome, and may be less likely to produce tardive dyskinesia.

The promising news about clozapine is that it has now been observed to produce dramatic improvements in some schizophrenic patients (about 30%) who have failed to respond to all other drugs. Although all such patients do not respond, enough have to make clozapine the first major breakthrough in the treatment of schizophrenic patients since Thorazine was first introduced in 1952.

Unfortunately, clozapine produces in some patients a severe blood abnormality, which has caused a few deaths. This abnormality (called agranulocytosis) can be prevented by monitoring patients through weekly blood counts, but some patients who might benefit from it simply cannot take clozapine because of this serious side effect. Therefore, clozapine is now restricted to patients who have not responded to other antipsychotic drugs, remain seriously ill, and will comply with the need for weekly blood tests. Scientists and drug companies are working very hard to find other "atypical" antipsychotics that work as well as clozapine without producing serious side effects.

A CHECKLIST FOR THE SCHIZOPHRENIC PATIENT

Treatment of the schizophrenic patient is summarized by the following list.

1. A high-potency antipsychotic medication (Haldol, Prolixin, Navane, Stelazine) should be started at a low dose.

2. A medication to block side effects (Cogentin, Artane, Kemadrin) should be administered if the patient is under 40. Patients over 40 should be given these drugs only if side effects (dystonia, Parkinsonian syndrome, akinesia) occur.

3. The dose of the antipsychotic drug should be increased after one to two weeks only if there has been no response to the lower dose.

4. The dose should be kept as low as possible to control symptoms.

5. A different antipsychotic drug should be prescribed only if the patient does not respond to the first drug after four weeks.

6. Propranolol (Inderal), diazepam (Valium), or lorazepam (Ativan) should be given if the patient develops akathisia (restlessness caused by the antipsychotic drug).

7. A patient who has had only one episode should be kept on the drug for about one year.

8. A patient who has had two or more episodes should be kept on the drug for several years.

9. Patients should see a psychiatrist at least once a month and should be examined regularly for signs of tardive dyskinesia.

10. Patients who persistently forget to take their medication may be switched to long-acting, injectable forms of antipsychotic medications (Prolixin Decanoate or Haldol Decanoate).

Even for a disease like schizophrenia, remember that drugs alone are not enough. Family involvement is extremely helpful; a kind, supportive family, knowledgeable about medications and willing to overlook as much as possible the abnormal behavior of a schizophrenic patient, is very helpful. Schizophrenic patients should be given opportunities to socialize and receive job training whenever possible. Both under- and overstimulation should be avoided. Support and alliance groups for schizophrenic patients are located in most major population areas in the United States; these counseling groups can be very beneficial.

Above all, when treating a schizophrenic, it must be remembered that no matter how distant, nonvolatile, and antisocial the person behaves, she is a suffering human being. It is not the patient's fault that the causes of schizophrenia and its cure have not been found. Although I do not believe that love and kindness can cure schizophrenia any more than I believe abuse and neglect cause the illness, it is clear that mistreatment of the schizophrenic patient can worsen his condition. By the same token, understanding, acceptance, and kindness may make it easier to live with "the worst illness in the world."

Many medications are used to treat psychosis. The following descriptions include only those commonly used in the United States.

HALOPERIDOL

Brand Name: Haldol.
Used for: Psychosis associated with schizophrenia, mania, or depression. Psychosis in elderly people with dementia. Severe tics in patients with the neurological disease Tourette's syndrome.
Do Not Use if: You do not have psychotic symptoms except in rare circumstances. Some psychiatrists believe that Haldol should not be combined with lithium; this topic is controversial, but so many other antipsychotic drugs are available that it is easy to substitute a different one if you are also on lithium. People with a history of epilepsy (convulsions) should use these drugs with caution.
Tests to Take First: None required.
Tests to Take While You Are on It: Tests to determine the blood level of Haldol are now available and sometimes guide the doctor in determining the best dose. These tests are not absolutely necessary, however, and do not help to prevent side effects.
Usual Dose: In very acute, emergency situations Haldol can be given by injection, usually 5 mg every hour up to six doses. Sometimes, a higher dose is given over a shorter time to control dangerously psychotic behavior. In less serious situations, a patient is usually started at 5 mg two or three times daily and watched for about two weeks. If the response is still not good enough, the dose

can be raised as high as 60 mg daily. It is best to keep the dose under 30 mg whenever possible. Elderly patients should be started at 0.5 to 1 mg once or twice a day.

How Long Until It Works: Very psychotic patients may show signs of improvement after a few doses of Haldol, but full relief of symptoms usually takes two to four weeks.

Common Side Effects: Acute dystonia (sudden muscle stiffness). Parkinsonian syndrome (tremors and muscle stiffness). Akathisia (jumpiness). Akinesia (loss of interest and decreased movements). *Note: The preceding side effects are defined more fully earlier in this chapter.* Weight gain.

Less Common Side Effects: Neuroleptic malignant syndrome (serious increase in temperature and muscle rigidity—rare). Tardive dyskinesia (involuntary movements after prolonged use). Production of breast milk in men and women. Seizures in people who already have epilepsy. Loss of menstrual period and sex drive.

What to Do About Side Effects: At the same time Haldol is started, patients under age 40 should also be placed on one of the drugs listed in Table 25 to prevent dystonia, Parkinsonian syndrome, and akinesia. Patients over 40 should be given these drugs only if the side effects actually occur. Akathisia is treated with either Inderal, Valium, or Ativan. The only treatment for weight gain is a diet, which sometimes helps. Neuroleptic malignant syndrome is an emergency that requires immediate medical care. Tardive dyskinesia usually only occurs after years of taking these drugs; in most cases it can be controlled by stopping the drug when the first signs occur. Production of breast milk is very rare and can be treated with special medication.

If It Doesn't Work: After four weeks at high enough doses, the best move is to switch to another antipsychotic drug.

If It Does Work: Except for patients with schizophrenia, Haldol should be discontinued shortly after the psychotic symptoms are under control. Schizophrenic patients must remain on the drug indefinitely, but attempts to lower the dose should be made frequently and the patient should be watched for signs of tardive dyskinesia (described more fully earlier in this chapter).

Cost: Brand, $1.01/5-mg capsule. Generic, 25 cents/5-mg pill.

Special Comments: Haldol is presently one of the most widely prescribed antipsychotic drugs. It is medically safe and very effective, but can cause many uncomfortable and occasionally dangerous nervous system side effects. Therefore, a patient on Haldol must see a physician on a regular basis. Haldol Decanoate is a long-acting form of Haldol that can be injected once every four weeks. It is prescribed mainly for patients who do not remember to take their medicine every day.

CHLORPROMAZINE

Brand Name: Thorazine.
Used for: Psychosis associated with schizophrenia, mania, or depression. Occasionally, in low doses, to control severe nausea or vomiting.
Do Not Use If: You have low blood pressure, an enlarged prostate, narrow-angle glaucoma, or epilepsy, unless your doctor knows about this.
Tests To Take First: None required.
Tests to Take While You Are on It: None required.
Usual Dose: In very severe cases, Thorazine can be given by injection, usually 25 or 50 mg at a time. Most less severely ill patients are started on 100 mg once or twice a day and are then observed for a few days. The dose can be raised to 600 mg a day, sometimes even higher. More and more evidence is now accumulating that for maintenance treatment of schizophrenics, between 300 and 600 mg a day is probably the best dose.
How Long Until It Works: The patient may show some reduction in symptoms, especially violent agitation, after a few doses, but complete relief from psychosis may take up to four weeks.
Common Side Effects: (1) Sedation. (2) Low blood pressure and dizziness. (3) Dry mouth, constipation, difficulty urinating, and blurry vision. (4) Akathisia (jumpiness). (5) Parkinsonian syndrome (tremors and muscle stiffness). (6) Akinesia (loss of motivation and decreased movement). (7) Weight gain. (8) Increased sensitivity to the sun.
Less Common Side Effects: (1) Acute dystonia (sudden muscle stiffness). (2) Tardive dyskinesia (involuntary movements after pro-

longed use). (3) Neuroleptic malignant syndrome (serious muscle rigidity and fever—rare). (4) Production of breast milk in men and women. (5) Seizures in patients with a history of epilepsy. (6) Loss of menstrual period and sex drive.

What to Do About Side Effects: Thorazine makes patients sleepy and lowers blood pressure. There is no way to counteract these effects except by lowering the dose. The sedation produced by Thorazine is sometimes an advantage in quieting violent patients and helping agitated patients sleep better. Reduction of blood pressure produces dizziness, especially after rising from a lying or sitting position. It can cause an elderly person to "black out" and fall, making Thorazine a risky choice in older people.

The neurological side effects of Parkinsonian syndrome and akinesia are seen less often with Thorazine than with Haldol, but still occur and are treated with counteracting drugs (Cogentin and Artane). Akathisia, described in more detail earlier in this chapter, is treated with counteracting medications (Inderal, Valium, or Ativan). It can be very disturbing and sometimes requires reduction of the dose. The quartet of side effects—dry mouth, constipation, difficulty urinating, and blurry vision—are known collectively as *anticholinergic* side effects. They are annoying but not dangerous; the one exception is difficulty urinating, which can be serious in a man with an enlarged prostate. These side effects are usually treated conservatively with laxatives and bran for constipation, sugarless hard candies and mouthwash for dry mouth, the drug bethanechol (Urecholine) for difficulty urinating, and occasionally a new pair of glasses for blurry vision. Because of increased sensitivity to the sun, it is important that people on Thorazine use sun block rated at least No. 15 when exposed to the sun. Drinking plenty of fluids on hot days is also desirable. Weight gain, which can be up to 20 pounds in some people, can sometimes be controlled by calorie reduction.

Of the less common side effects, acute dystonia, is treated with counteracting medications (Cogentin, Artane, or Benadryl). This effect occurs less often with Thorazine than with Haldol. Tardive dyskinesia, the involuntary movements caused by prolonged use of antipsychotic medications, is described more fully earlier in this chapter. TD usually goes away if the medication is stopped as soon as the first signs appear. Therefore, a patient on Thorazine should

231

be examined by a doctor regularly. Neuroleptic malignant syndrome is rare and requires emergency medical care. Production of breast milk is also rare and can be treated. Thorazine increases the chance of having a seizure in patients who have or have had a seizure problem, so the doctor must be informed if the patient has ever had a convulsion or is taking anticonvulsants.

If It Doesn't Work: The patient should first be asked "Are you taking the medication?" Many psychotic patients do not take prescribed medication regularly. If the problem is not noncompliance and the patient has been taking Thorazine for four weeks at a dose of at least 600 mg with no response, then it is usually best to switch to a different drug.

If It Does Work: Manic and depressed patients with psychosis who are given Thorazine should remain on it only until the psychotic symptoms resolve. Schizophrenic patients may have to remain on Thorazine indefinitely, but attempts should always be made to reduce the dose to the lowest possible amount that still controls psychotic symptoms.

Cost: Brand, 57 cents/100-mg pill. Generic, 8 cents/100-mg pill.

Special Comments: Thorazine was one of the first medications for psychosis introduced into clinical practice, in the early 1950s. It is medically safe and very effective, but also makes the patient feel very sleepy and sluggish. Patients on Thorazine often appear "drugged." Therefore, Thorazine is now given mostly to patients in whom some amount of sedation is specifically called for, for example, very agitated or violent patients. It should never be used as a sleeping pill for nonpsychotic patients.

THIORIDAZINE

Brand Name: Mellaril.

Used for: Psychosis associated with schizophrenia, mania, or depression.

Do Not Use If: You have low blood pressure, an enlarged prostate, narrow-angle glaucoma, or epilepsy, unless your doctor knows about this.

Tests to Take First: None required.

Tests to Take While You Are on It: Because Mellaril can rarely produce changes in the retina, patients should be examined by an ophthalmologist every six months to a year while on Mellaril.

Usual Dose: The patient is usually started at 100 mg once or twice daily, and the dose is raised as high as 600 mg over subsequent weeks until psychotic symptoms are resolved. Most patients respond to doses between 300 and 600 mg. More than 800 mg a day should never be given because of the risk of damaging the retina.

How Long Until It Works: The patient will probably become calmer and somewhat less violent after a few doses, but complete relief of psychotic symptoms may take up to four weeks.

Common Side Effects: (1) Sedation. (2) Low blood pressure and dizziness. (3) Dry mouth, constipation, difficulty urinating, and blurry vision. (4) Akathisia (jumpiness). (5) Parkinsonian syndrome (tremors and muscle stiffness). (6) Akinesia (loss of motivation and decreased movement). (7) Weight gain. (8) Increased sensitivity to the sun.

Less Common Side Effects: (1) acute dystonia (sudden muscle stiffness). (2) Tardive dyskinesia (involuntary movements after prolonged use). (3) Neuroleptic malignant syndrome (serious muscle rigidity and fever). (4) Production of breast milk in men and women. (5) Seizures in patients with a history of epilepsy. (6) Loss of menstrual period and sex drive. (7) Damage to the retina, usually only if the dose exceeds 800 mg per day. (8) Changes on the electrocardiogram, probably not of any clinical significance.

What to Do About Side Effects: Mellaril makes patients sleepy and lowers blood pressure. There is no way to counteract these effects except by reducing the dose. The sedation produced by Mellaril is sometimes an advantage in quieting violent patients and helping agitated patients sleep better. Reduction of blood pressure produces dizziness, especially after rising from a lying or sitting position. It can cause an elderly person to "black out" and fall, making Mellaril a risky choice in elderly people.

The neurological side effects of Parkinsonian syndrome and akinesia are seen less often with Mellaril than with Haldol, but still occur and are treated with counteracting drugs (Cogentin and Artane). Akathisia, described in more detail earlier in this chapter, is treated with counteracting medications (Inderal, Valium, or

Ativan). It can be very disturbing and sometimes requires reduction of the dose. The quartet of side effects—dry mouth, constipation, difficulty urinating, and blurry vision—are known collectively as *anticholinergic* side effects. They are annoying but not dangerous; the one exception is difficulty urinating, which can be serious in a man with an enlarged prostate. These side effects are usually treated conservatively with laxatives and bran for constipation, sugarless hard candies and mouthwash for dry mouth, the drug bethanechol (Urecholine) for difficulty urinating, and occasionally a new pair of glasses for blurry vision. Because of increased sensitivity to the sun, it is important that people on Mellaril use sun block rated at least No. 15 when exposed to the sun. Drinking plenty of fluids on hot days is also desirable. Weight gain, which can be up to 20 pounds in some people, can sometimes be controlled by calorie reduction.

Of the less common side effects, acute dystonia is treated with counteracting medications (Cogentin, Artane, or Benadryl). This effect occurs less often with Mellaril than with Haldol. Tardive dyskinesia, the involuntary movements caused by prolonged use of antipsychotic medications, is described more fully earlier in this chapter. It usually goes away if the medication is stopped as soon as the first signs appear. Therefore, a patient on Mellaril should be examined by a doctor regularly. Neuroleptic malignant syndrome is rare and requires emergency medical care. Production of breast milk is also rare and can be treated. Mellaril increases the chance of having a seizure in patients who have or have had a seizure problem, so the doctor must be informed if the patient has ever had a convulsion or is taking anticonvulsants. The patient should see an ophthalmologist about once a year to check for any changes in the retina.

If It Doesn't Work: Assuming that the patient has been taking the medication (often a problem with psychotic patients), if there is no response after four weeks at a dose of at least 600 mg a day, a different antipsychotic drug should be tried.

If It Does Work: Patients treated with Mellaril because of psychotic depression or mania should take the medication only until the psychosis is resolved. Schizophrenic patients may have to remain on

Mellaril indefinitely, but attempts should always be made to keep the dose as low as necessary to control psychotic symptoms.

Cost: Brand, 44 cents/100-mg pill. Generic, 15 cents/100-mg pill.

Special Comments: Mellaril is almost identical to Thorazine. It tends to produce fewer nervous system side effects, like dystonia and akathisia, than Haldol, but more sleepiness and greater reduction of blood pressure. It is prescribed to psychotic patients who are very agitated or violent because in these cases sedation is often desirable. It has been claimed that Mellaril is less likely than other antipsychotic drugs to cause tardive dyskinesia, but this is doubtful.

MESORIDAZINE

Brand Name: Serentil.

Special Comments: Serentil is a little used antipsychotic that is actually the compound the body normally turns Mellaril into. It is perfectly acceptable as an antipsychotic drug and is a bit less sedating than Mellaril and Thorazine. An interesting aspect of Serentil is its supposed specificity in the treatment of the nonpsychotic condition *borderline personality disorder.* Many books have been written about this very severe and difficult-to-treat illness; it is not clear what causes it, how it should be characterized, or whether drugs are useful in treating it.

TRIFLUOPERAZINE

Brand Name: Stelazine.

Used for: Psychosis associated with mania, depression, or schizophrenia. Control of psychotic symptoms in the elderly.

Do Not Use if: You do not have psychotic symptoms, except in rare circumstances. Stelazine will increase the chance of having a seizure in patients with a history of epilepsy.

Tests to Take First: None required.

Tests to Take While You Are on It: None required.

Usual Dose: Patients are usually started at 5 mg two or three times daily and observed for several weeks. If there is no response, the dose can be raised to as high as 60 mg, but a dose between 15 and 40 mg a day is probably optimal for treating schizophrenia.

How Long Until It Works: A severely psychotic patient may feel calmer and be less agitated after a few doses, but full relief of psychotic symptoms usually takes up to four weeks.

Common Side Effects: (1) Acute dystonia (sudden muscle stiffness). (2) Parkinsonian syndrome (tremors and muscle stiffness). (3) Akathisia (jumpiness). (4) Akinesia (loss of interest and decreased movements). *Note: The preceding side effects are defined more fully earlier in this chapter.* (5) Weight gain.

Less Common Side Effects: (1) Neuroleptic malignant syndrome (serious increase in temperature and muscle rigidity—rare). (2) Tardive dyskinesia (involuntary movements after prolonged use). (3) Production of breast milk in men and women. (4) Seizures in people who already have epilepsy. (5) Loss of menstrual period and sex drive.

What to Do About Side Effects: At the same time Stelazine is started, patients under age 40 should also be placed on one of the drugs listed in Table 25 to prevent dystonia, Parkinsonian syndrome, and akinesia. Patients over 40 should be given these drugs only if the side effects actually occur. Akathisia is treated with either Inderal, Valium, or Ativan. The only treatment for weight gain is a diet, which sometimes helps. Neuroleptic malignant syndrome is an emergency that requires immediate medical care. Tardive dyskinesia usually occurs only after years of taking these drugs; in most cases, it can be controlled by stopping the drug when the first signs occur. Production of breast milk is very rare and can be treated with special medication.

If It Doesn't Work: Assuming the patient has been taking the medication as prescribed, if there is no response after four weeks it is best to switch to a different drug.

If It Does Work: Manic or depressed or elderly patients who have been given Stelazine to treat their psychotic symptoms should take it only until those psychotic symptoms go away. Schizophrenic patients may have to stay on Stelazine indefinitely, but attempts should be made often to lower the dose to the minimum required to control psychotic symptoms.

Cost: Brand, 82 cents/5-mg pill. Generic, 7 cents/5-mg pill.
Special Comments: Stelazine is almost identical in action and side effects to Haldol. Like Haldol, it is well suited for treating patients for whom sedation is not desirable. It has been said that Stelazine is also useful for nonpsychotic anxiety, but I feel this is almost always a mistake. Patients with anxiety who are not psychotic and need medication should almost always be given buspirone (BuSpar) or a benzodiazepine (for example, Valium or Xanax) instead of Stelazine.

FLUPHENAZINE

Brand Names: Prolixin, Permitil.
Used for: Psychosis associated with schizophrenia, mania, or depression. Psychosis in elderly patients with dementia.
Do Not Use if: You do not have a psychotic illness.
Tests to Take First: None required.
Tests to Take While You Are on It: None required.
Usual Dose: For severely psychotic patients requiring emergency treatment, Prolixin can be given by injection. Usually, an injection of 5 mg is given first; this can be repeated every fifteen minutes to an hour until a total of six doses have been given. In less emergency situations, the patient is usually given 5 mg two or three times daily and observed for about two weeks. The dose can then be increased to as much as 60 mg a day, but doses of 15 to 30 mg daily are best. Elderly patients should be started at very small doses, sometimes as low as 0.5 mg.
How Long Until It Works: Some decrease in agitation, violent behavior, and psychotic symptoms may be seen after the first few doses, but full control of psychosis usually takes up to four weeks.
Common Side Effects: (1) Acute dystonia (sudden muscle stiffness). (2) Parkinsonian syndrome (tremors and muscle stiffness). (3) Akathisia (jumpiness). (4) Akinesia (loss of interest and decreased movements). *Note: the preceding side effects are defined more fully earlier in this chapter.* (5) Weight gain.
Less Common Side Effects: (1) Neuroleptic malignant syndrome (seri-

ous increase in temperature and muscle rigidity—rare). (2) Tardive dyskinesia (involuntary movements after prolonged use). (3) Production of breast milk in men and women. (4) Loss of menstrual period and sex drive.

What to Do About Side Effects: At the same time Prolixin is started, patients under age 40 should also be placed on one of the drugs listed in Table 25 to prevent dystonia, Parkinsonian syndrome, and akinesia. Patients over 40 should be given these drugs only if the side effects actually occur. Akathisia is treated with either Inderal, Valium, or Ativan. The only treatment for weight gain is a diet, which sometimes helps. Neuroleptic malignant syndrome is an emergency that requires immediate medical care. Tardive dyskinesia usually only occurs after years of taking these drugs; in most cases it can be controlled by stopping the drug when the first signs occur. Production of breast milk is very rare and can be treated with special medication.

If It Doesn't Work: If the patient is not taking the medicine, which is often the case with psychotic patients, one strategy is to switch to Prolixin Decanoate. This long-acting form of Prolixin, similar to Haldol Decanoate, can be given by injection about once every two weeks. If this does not work or noncompliance is not the problem, it is best to try a different antipsychotic drug.

If It Does Work: Patients with mania, depression, or dementia who are given Prolixin or Permitil should remain on it only until the psychotic symptoms resolve. Schizophrenics may have to take Prolixin or long-acting Prolixin Decanoate for a long time, but attempts to lower the dose to the minimum required to control psychotic symptoms should be made frequently.

Cost: Brand, $1.46 cents/5-mg pill. Generic, 67 cents/5-mg pill.

Special Comments: Prolixin is very similar to Haldol and Stelazine and therefore is commonly used to treat psychotic patients who do not want to be sedated. Prolixin (or Permitil) may be less likely to cause seizures in patients who also have epilepsy than are the other antipsychotic drugs. Many community mental health centers and hospitals have clinics devoted to giving schizophrenic patients their biweekly injections of Prolixin Decanoate. Prolixin is one of the most expensive antipsychotic drugs.

238

PERPHENAZINE

Brand Name: Trilafon.

Used for: Psychosis associated with mania, depression, or schizophrenia.

Do Not Use if: You do not have psychotic symptoms, you have epilepsy and your doctor doesn't know it, you have an enlarged prostate, or you have narrow-angle glaucoma.

Tests to Take First: None required.

Tests to Take While You Are on It: None required.

Usual Dose: The patient is usually started on 8 mg once or twice a day. This can be increased up to 64 mg a day until symptoms are relieved.

How Long Until It Works: Some relief from agitation and psychotic symptoms may be obtained after the first few doses, but full remission from psychosis usually takes up to four weeks.

Common Side Effects: (1) Mild sedation. (2) Mild dizziness from lowered blood pressure. (3) Dry mouth, constipation, difficulty urinating, and blurry vision. (4) Akathisia (jumpiness). (5) Parkinsonian syndrome (tremors and stiffness). (6) Akinesia (loss of motivation and decreased movements). (7) Weight gain. (8) Increased sensitivity to the sun.

Less Common Side Effects: (1) Acute dystonia (sudden tightening of muscles). (2) Tardive dyskinesia (involuntary movements after prolonged use). (3) Neuroleptic malignant syndrome (severe muscle rigidity and fever—rare). (4) Loss of menstrual period and sex drive. (5) Breast milk production in men and women. (6) Seizures in people with a history of epilepsy.

What to Do About Side Effects: The only remedy for sedation and dizziness is reduction of the dose. The four anticholinergic side effects—dry mouth, constipation, difficulty urinating, and blurry vision—are usually annoying but not dangerous. Dry mouth is best relieved by mouthwash and sugarless hard candies; constipation by eating bran and using laxatives; difficulty urinating by the drug bethanechol (Urecholine); and blurry vision by a new pair of glasses.

The best way to treat the neurological side effects of Parkinsonian syndrome, acute dystonia and akinesia, is with one of the

239

counteracting medications listed in Table 25, for example, Kemadrin and Benadryl. Some psychiatrists place the patient on these counteracting drugs as soon as Trilafon is started. Weight gain is controlled by diet, and sensitivity to the sun by using at least a No. 15 sunblock and drinking plenty fluids when exposed to the sun. Tardive dyskinesia, the development of involuntary movements in some patients treated with Trilafon for prolonged periods, usually goes away if the drug is stopped after the first signs appear. Therefore, the patient should be checked by the doctor about once a month. Neuroleptic malignant syndrome is very rare and usually requires emergency treatment in the hospital. Breast milk production is similarly very rare and can be treated by counteracting medication. Loss of menstrual period is not necessarily serious, but the patient should be seen by a gynecologist and dose reduction considered. Patients with a history of epilepsy should take all antipsychotic drugs only under the careful supervision of their psychiatrist and neurologist.

If It Doesn't Work: Switching to a different drug is usually the best course of action if Trilafon is ineffective after four weeks.

If It Does Work: Patients with depression or mania who are given Trilafon should take it only until the psychotic symptoms resolve. Schizophrenic patients may have to take Trilafon indefinitely, but attempts to reduce the dose should be made periodically to determine the minimum dose that controls the psychotic symptoms.

Cost: Brand, 66 cents/8-mg pill. Generic, 51 cents/8-mg pill.

Special Comments: Trilafon is a kind of middle-of-the-road drug between the very potent antipsychotics on the one hand (Haldol, Stelazine, and Prolixin) and the lower-potency drugs on the other hand (Thorazine and Mellaril). It produces all of the side effects of the other drugs, but to a milder degree. Thus, it is more sedating than Haldol but less sedating than Thorazine. It is more likely than Thorazine but less likely than Haldol to produce neurological side effects (acute dystonia and Parkinsonian syndrome). Many psychotic patients find it is the most tolerable antipsychotic drug in terms of side effects, and it is often given to patients who find side effects from other drugs too bothersome. Trilafon is also available in combination with the antidepressant drug Elavil in a medication called *Triavil.* This drug is supposedly intended for patients with psychotic depression. As I discussed earlier, I do not generally favor combination drugs because it is usually best to maintain control over the dose of each drug separately.

THIOTHIXENE

Brand Name: Navane.
Used for: Psychosis in patients with schizophrenia, mania, or depression. Psychotic symptoms in elderly patients with dementia.
Do Not Use if: You do not have psychotic symptoms. Navane may precipitate seizures in people with a history of convulsions.
Tests to Take First: None required.
Tests to Take While You Are on It: None required.
Usual Dose: In very severely psychotic patients, Navane can be given by injection. Usually, the patient is given 5 mg and this is repeated as often as every fifteen minutes up to six doses to achieve rapid control of very agitated or violent behavior. In less emergency situations, the patient is usually started at 5 mg two or three times daily and then observed for several weeks. The dose of Navane can be raised as high as 60 mg, but the optimal dose is usually between 15 and 30 mg a day. Elderly patients should take much less, usually starting with 1 mg once or twice a day.
How Long Until It Works: The patient may feel calmer and less agitated after the first few doses, but complete control of psychotic symptoms usually takes up to four weeks.
Common Side Effects: (1) Acute dystonia (sudden muscle stiffness). (2) Parkinsonian syndrome (tremors and muscle stiffness). (3) Akathisia (jumpiness). (4) Akinesia (loss of interest and decreased movements). *Note: the preceding side effects are defined more fully earlier in this chapter.* (5) Weight gain.
Less Common Side Effects: (1) neuroleptic malignant syndrome (serious increase in temperature and muscle rigidity—rare). (2) Tardive dyskinesia (involuntary movements after prolonged use). (3) Production of breast milk in men and women. (4) Seizures in people who already have epilepsy. (5) Loss of menstrual period and sex drive.
What to Do About Side Effects: At the same time Navane is started, patients under age 40 should also be placed on one of the drugs

listed in Table 25 to prevent dystonia, Parkinsonian syndrome, and akinesia. Patients over 40 should be given these drugs only if the side effects actually occur. Akathisia is treated with either Inderal, Valium, or Ativan. The only treatment for weight gain is a diet, which sometimes helps. Neuroleptic malignant syndrome is an emergency that requires immediate medical care. Tardive dyskinesia usually occurs only after years of taking these drugs; in most cases, it can be controlled by stopping the drug when the first signs occur. Production of breast milk is very rare and can be treated with special medication. Patients with a history of epilepsy should take all antipsychotic drugs only under the careful supervision of their psychiatrist and neurologist. Loss of menstrual period is not necessarily serious, but the patient should be seen by a gynecologist and dose reduction considered.

If It Doesn't Work: First, make sure the patient is actually taking the medicine. Psychotic patients have a habit of forgetting, causing everyone to think the drug is ineffective. If noncompliance is not the problem and the patient has not responded after four weeks, it is usually best to change drugs.

If It Does Work: Patients with mania, depression, or dementia who receive Navane should take the drug only until the psychotic symptoms resolve. Schizophrenic patients may have to remain on Navane indefinitely, but attempts to lower the dose to the minimum required to control psychotic symptoms should be made periodically.

Cost: Brand, 62 cents/5-mg pill. Generic, 20 cents/5-mg pill.

Special Comments: Navane, like Stelazine and Prolixin, is very similar to Haldol and generally used for psychotic patients who do not need to be sedated. There are really very few differences among Navane, Haldol, Stelazine, and Prolixin, so psychiatrists usually just pick one and prescribe it to most of their patients with psychotic illnesses.

LOXAPINE

Brand Name: Loxitane.

Used for: Psychosis in patients with schizophrenia, mania, or depression.

Do Not Use If: You do not have psychosis, you have a history of seizures that your doctor doesn't know about, you have an enlarged prostate gland, or you have narrow-angle glaucoma.

Tests to Take First: None required.

Tests to Take While You Are on It: None required.

Usual Dose: Patients are usually started at 10 mg twice a day and then increased to the optimal dose between 60 and 100 mg a day.

How Long Until It Works: The psychotic patient may feel some relief from severe agitation and become less violent after the first few doses, but full control of psychotic symptoms usually takes up to four weeks.

Common Side Effects: (1) Mild sedation. (2) Mild dizziness from lowered blood pressure. (3) Dry mouth, constipation, difficulty urinating, and blurry vision. (4) Akathisia (jumpiness). (5) Parkinsonian syndrome (tremors and stiffness). (6) Akinesia (loss of motivation and decreased movements). (7) Weight gain. (8) Increased sensitivity to the sun.

Less Common Side Effects: (1) Acute dystonia (sudden tightening of muscles). (2) Tardive dyskinesia (involuntary movements after prolonged use). (3) Neuroleptic malignant syndrome (severe muscle rigidity and fever—rare). (4) Loss of menstrual period and sex drive. (5) Breast milk production in men and women. (6) Seizures in people with a history of epilepsy.

What to Do About Side Effects: The only remedy for sedation and dizziness is reduction of the dose. The four anticholinergic side effects—dry mouth, constipation, difficulty urinating, and blurry vision—are usually annoying but not dangerous. Dry mouth is best relieved by mouthwash and sugarless hard candies; constipation by eating bran and using laxatives; difficulty urinating by the drug bethanechol (Urecholine); and blurry vision by a new pair of glasses.

The best way to treat the neurologic side effects of Parkinsonian syndrome, acute dystonia, and akinesia is with one of the counteracting medications listed in Table 25, such as Kemadrin or Benadryl. Some psychiatrists place the patient on these counteracting drugs as soon as Loxitane is started. Weight gain is controlled by diet, and sensitivity to the sun by using at least a No. 15 sunblock and drinking plenty of fluids when exposed to the sun.

Tardive dyskinesia, the development of involuntary movements in some patients treated with Loxitane for prolonged periods, usually goes away if the drug is stopped after the first signs appear. Therefore, the patient should be checked by the doctor about once a month. Neuroleptic malignant syndrome is very rare and usually requires emergency treatment in the hospital. Breast milk production is similarly very rare and can be treated by counteracting medication. Loss of menstrual period is not necessarily serious, but the patient should be seen by a gynecologist and dose reduction considered. Patients with a history of epilepsy should take all antipsychotic drugs only under the careful supervision of their psychiatrist and neurologist.

If It Doesn't Work: The problem may be that the patient simply isn't taking the medication. If that is not true and Loxitane has not worked after four weeks, it is usually best to switch drugs.

If It Does Work: Patients with depression or mania placed on Loxitane should keep taking it only as long as needed to eliminate the psychotic symptoms. Schizophrenic patients may have to take Loxitane indefinitely, but frequent attempts should be made to reduce the dose to the lowest possible level that still controls psychotic symptoms.

Cost: Brand, 87 cents/10-mg pill. Generic, 52 cents/10-mg pill.

Special Comments: Loxitane is similar to Trilafon and Moban in being a "middle-of-the-road" antipsychotic drug. It has less tendency than Haldol or Stelazine to produce acute dystonia (sudden muscle stiffness), but is more likely to do this than Thorazine or Mellaril. It is less sedating and causes less of a decrease in blood pressure than Thorazine and Mellaril, but more than Haldol or Stelazine. Therefore, Loxitane is often given to patients who do not tolerate the side effects of whatever antipsychotic drug they are placed on first.

MOLINDONE

Brand Names: Moban, Lidone.
Used for: Psychotic symptoms in patients with mania, depression, or schizophrenia.

Do Not Use if: You do not have psychotic symptoms, you have an enlarged prostate, or you have narrow-angle glaucoma.

Tests to Take First: None required.

Tests to Take While You Are on It: None required.

Usual Dose: The usual starting dose is 50 or 75 mg a day. This is slowly increased over several days to 100 mg, but can go as high as 225 mg to treat severe psychosis.

How Long Until It Works: Although there may be some calming after the first few doses, complete resolution of psychotic symptoms usually takes up to four weeks.

Common Side Effects: (1) Mild sedation. (2) Mild dizziness from lowered blood pressure. (3) Dry mouth, constipation, difficulty urinating, and blurry vision. (4) Akathisia (jumpiness). (5) Parkinsonian syndrome (tremors and stiffness). (6) Akinesia (loss of motivation and decreased movements). (7) Increased sensitivity to the sun.

Less Common Side Effects: (1) Acute dystonia (sudden tightening of muscles). (2) Tardive dyskinesia (involuntary movements after prolonged use). (3) Neuroleptic malignant syndrome (severe muscle rigidity and fever—rare). (4) Loss of menstrual period and sex drive. (5) Breast milk production in men and women.

What to Do About Side Effects: The only remedy for sedation and dizziness is reduction of the dose. The four anticholinergic side effects—dry mouth, constipation, difficulty urinating, and blurry vision—are usually annoying but not dangerous. Dry mouth is best relieved by mouthwash and sugarless hard candies; constipation by eating bran and using laxatives; difficulty urinating by the drug bethanechol (Urecholine); and blurry vision by a new pair of glasses.

The best way to treat the neurological side effects of Parkinsonian syndrome, acute dystonia, and akinesia is with one of the counteracting medications listed in Table 25, such as Kemadrin and Benadryl. Some psychiatrists place the patient on these counteracting drugs as soon as Moban (or Lidone) is started. Sensitivity to the sun is treated by use of at least a No. 15 sunblock and ingestion of plenty of fluids when exposed to the sun. Tardive dyskinesia, the development of involuntary movements in some patients treated with Moban for prolonged periods, usually goes away if the drug

245

is stopped after the first signs appear. Therefore, the patient should be checked by the doctor about once a month. Neuroleptic malignant syndrome is very rare and usually requires emergency treatment in the hospital. Breast milk production is similarly very rare and can be treated by counteracting medication. Loss of menstrual period is not necessarily serious, but the patient should be seen by a gynecologist and dose reduction considered.

If It Doesn't Work: Assuming the patient has been taking the pills as prescribed, if there is no response to Moban after four weeks it is usually best to switch to a different drug.

What If It Does Work: Patients with depression or mania who have been given Moban should stop taking it as soon as the psychotic symptoms resolve. Schizophrenic patients may have to remain on Moban indefinitely, but it is very important to reduce the dose to the lowest possible level that still controls the psychotic symptoms.

Cost: Brand, 55 cents/10-mg pill. Generic, not available.

Special Comments: Moban is very much like Trilafon and Loxitane in having a middle-of-the-road side effect profile between the high-potency antipsychotics (Haldol and Prolixin) on the one hand and the low-potency antipsychotics (Thorazine and Mellaril) on the other hand. Moban has two other interesting features. First, like Prolixin, it is less likely than the other antipsychotic drugs to cause seizures in a patient who has a history of epilepsy. Moban is thus a good choice for treatment of the psychotic patient with a history of seizures, although careful monitoring by the neurologist is still advised. Second, Moban is said to result in less of a weight gain than the other antipsychotic drugs. A patient who gains too much weight with the other antipsychotic drugs might do better on Moban.

PIMOZIDE

Brand Name: Orap.

Used for: The neurological condition Tourette's syndrome, which often begins in childhood and is characterized by uncontrollable tics and a variety of involuntary noises. Occasionally, Orap is used to treat psychotic conditions; it is claimed to be especially useful for patients with the specific delusion that they have a serious abnormality with their physical health (called a "somatic" delusion).

246

Do Not Use if: You do not have Tourette's syndrome or psychosis. The drug company that makes Orap recommends that all patients with Tourette's first be tried on Haldol, and that Orap be reserved for those patients who do not respond to Haldol.

Tests to Take First: Patients must have an electrocardiogram before starting Orap because this drug can exacerbate a rare cardiac problem.

Tests to Take While You Are on It: The electrocardiogram should be repeated at regular intervals to make sure Orap is not causing an abnormality. About 10% of patients treated with Orap show changes on the electrocardiogram, but most of these changes are not clinically significant. Actual heart problems caused by Orap are probably very uncommon.

Usual Dose: Patients are usually started at 1 mg of Orap at night and the dose is raised about once a week by 1 mg until symptoms are controlled. The usual effective dose ranges between about 2 and 10 mg daily.

How Long Until It Works: For treatment of Tourette's, it may take weeks until the proper dose is reached and the tics are under control. For treatment of psychotic conditions, such as somatic delusions, it may also be several weeks before improvement is realized.

Common Side Effects: (1) Acute dystonia (sudden muscle stiffness). (2) Parkinsonian syndrome (tremors and muscle stiffness). (3) Akathisia (jumpiness). (4) Akinesia (loss of interest and decreased movements). *Note: the preceding side effects are defined more fully earlier in this chapter.* (5) Weight gain.

Less Common Side Effects: (1) Neuroleptic malignant syndrome (serious increase in temperature and muscle rigidity—rare). (2) Tardive dyskinesia (involuntary movements after prolonged use). (3) Production of breast milk in men and women. (4) Seizures in people who already have epilepsy. (5) Loss of menstrual period and sex drive. (6) Changes in the electrocardiogram.

What to Do About Side Effects: At the same time Orap is started, patients under age 40 should also be placed on one of the drugs listed in Table 25 to prevent dystonia, Parkinsonian syndrome, and akinesia. Patients over 40 should be given these drugs only if the side effects actually occur. Akathisia is treated with either Inderal, Valium, or Ativan. The only treatment for weight gain is a diet,

247

which sometimes helps. Neuroleptic malignant syndrome is an emergency that requires immediate medical care. Tardive dyskinesia usually occurs only after years of taking these drugs; in most cases it can be controlled by stopping the drug when the first signs occur. Production of breast milk is very rare and can be treated with special medication. Orap is said to produce a change in the electrical activity of the heart, reflected in a change in the electrocardiogram. This is probably rarely of clinical significance and nothing to worry about. Most doctors require periodic electrocardiograms to ensure that no harm is being done; stopping the drug returns the electrocardiogram to normal.

If It Doesn't Work: Tourette's syndrome is very difficult to treat and a great deal more research is needed to understand what causes it. Orap is usually used in psychotic patients only if they have not responded to other drugs for psychosis. If it also doesn't work, the doctor will probably try something else.

If It Does Work: Tourette's syndrome tends to worsen and improve on its own periodically. Also, when the patient with Tourette's reaches adulthood, the symptoms sometimes improve. Therefore, frequent attempts should be made to lower the dose or even discontinue Orap. Some patients, however, must remain on Orap almost continuously to maintain control over their symptoms. The same is true of patients with psychotic illnesses treated with Orap; to reduce the risk of tardive dyskinesia the doctor and patient should constantly try to reduce the dose as low as possible.

Cost: Brand, 53 cents/2-mg pill. Generic, not available.

Special Comments: I have included pimozide (Orap) in this chapter because it is sometimes used to treat patients with psychotic conditions, especially patients who develop somatic delusions. In almost every way, Orap looks and acts like the other antipsychotic drugs, but its main use is the treatment of patients with Tourette's Syndrome, not psychosis.

CLOZAPINE

Brand Name: Clozaril.
Used for: Schizophrenia in patients who do not respond to other antipsychotic drugs or who have developed severe neurological side effects from other antipsychotic drugs.

Do Not Use if: You cannot comply with the absolute need to have weekly blood counts. Patients with a history of convulsions (seizures) may be told not to take clozapine by their doctor.

Tests to Take First: A complete blood count is obtained before initiation of clozapine. In addition, most physicians require a physical examination, blood tests of liver function, and an electrocardiogram.

Tests to Take While You Are on It: A patient on clozapine is required to have a complete blood count (CBC) every week. Only one week's supply of medication is given at a time, and procurement of the next week's supply is contingent on the doctor's review of the previous week's CBC and confirmation of the absence of abnormalities. Repeat blood tests of liver function may also be obtained several times in the first few months of treatment.

Usual Dose: Because clozapine is a relatively new drug, doctors are only now learning what the best doses are. Most patients are started on relatively low doses (25 or 50 mg a day) and gradually increased to between 300 and 500 mg per day over the next several weeks. The recommended top dose is 900 mg.

How Long Until It Works: As with all antipsychotic medications, there may be some immediate relief of severe agitation, but a true decrease in psychotic symptoms may take up to several months.

Common Side Effects: (1) Sedation. (2) Increased salivation and drooling. (3) Rapid heart rate. (4) Dizziness caused by lowered blood pressure. (5) Fever. (6) Nausea and vomiting. (7) Constipation. (8) Dry mouth.

Less Common Side Effects: (1) Blood abnormality involving the white blood cells and technically called agranulocytosis. If not detected and treated by immediate discontinuation of medication, agranulocytosis is fatal. For this reason, patients on clozapine must have a complete blood count (CBC), which includes a count of the white blood cells, every week. The risk of agranulocytosis may be as high as 2%, but will probably turn out to be lower after the drug is extensively prescribed. (2) The risk of seizures while taking clozapine is about 4%, higher than with the other antipsychotic drugs. (3) Sudden loss of muscle strength lasting a few moments, called periodic cataplexy. (4) Bedwetting (enuresis).

What to Do About Side Effects: Although the list of side effects with clozapine seems long, most are tolerable and go away on their own after a few weeks. Sedation, dizziness, nausea, vomiting, and fever are generally transient. Drooling (technically called "sialorrhea") is a mysterious side effect, the cause of which remains unknown. There is no cure for this side effect, which, according to the manufacturer, occurs in about 5% of patients treated with clozapine. Fortunately, it is not serious in most cases. Constipation can be treated by drinking extra fluids or using stool softeners. Dry mouth is treated with mouthwash or sugarless hard candies. Increases in heart rate caused by clozapine are also generally not serious, although sometimes counteracting medication is prescribed.

The less common side effects are clearly more serious. A decrease in white blood cell count is potentially fatal. The blood count must be checked weekly and the drug stopped immediately if this anemia occurs. Since its introduction to the United States in February, 1990, only one death has been associated with Clozapine, and even in this case it is not certain Clozapine was really the cause. Because seizures can be provoked by clozapine, patients with a history of convulsions or epilepsy need to be carefully monitored and take anticonvulsant medications if placed on clozapine. Sudden loss of muscle strength, which can result in falls, is very rare. Bedwetting occurs in less than 1% of patients. Restricting fluids before bedtime is helpful.

If It Doesn't Work: Clozapine sometimes produces dramatic improvements in patients with schizophrenia who have failed to respond to many other antipsychotic drugs. It is not a "miracle drug," and such dramatic reversals in previously refractory patients probably occur only a little over one fourth of the time. If clozapine does not work it should be discontinued.

If It Does Work: Patients should remain on clozapine indefinitely, because such patients are likely to have long-standing schizophrenia that has failed to respond to many other attempts at treatment. When it is time to stop clozapine, the drug should be gradually discontinued over several weeks.

Cost: Because of the expensive blood count monitoring system, the cost of Clozapine can be as high as $9,000 per year. However, arrangements have been made by the manufacturer to permit cheaper monitoring arrangements which should reduce the cost dramatically. Food and Drug Administration in the fall of 1989. It has potentially serious side effects and therefore is now recommended for use in schizophrenic patients who have failed to respond to other antipsychotic drugs or who have developed tardive dyskinesia and therefore should no longer take the other currently marketed drugs. As far as is now known, clozapine does not cause the neurological side effects of dystonia, Parkinsonian syndrome, akinesia, akathisia, and tardive dyskinesia that are common to all of the other antipsychotic drugs. For this reason, clozapine is called the first of the "atypical antipsychotics." At present, it is too early to tell how great of an impact clozapine will have. That will be known only after much more experience is gained. Also, scientists at a number of drug companies and universities are now developing more "atypical" antipsychotic drugs, hoping to find one that works as well as clozapine without producing threatening blood abnormalities.

Other drugs are used to treat schizophrenia, although they are prescribed less frequently than those listed in this chapter. These other drugs include triflupromazine (Vesprin), piperacetazine (Quide), acetophenazine (Tindal), and chlorprothixene (Taractan). These have been omitted from more lengthy discussion only because they are not often prescribed by American psychiatrists. They are perfectly good antipsychotic drugs with the same side effects and precautions as the other medications.

Research in schizophrenia is now the primary mission of the National Institute of Mental Health. It is hoped that this research will lead to new insights and treatments. We must remember that the entire federal budget for research on psychiatric illness is not much more than the cost of one high-technology jet bomber. It is up to all of us to do what we can through pressure on legislators and private foundations to increase funding for schizophrenia research. Until then, we will be left with the drugs discussed in this chapter, drugs that work to control symptoms but also cause many serious side effects.

Chapter 11

Sleeping Pills

For most of us, about two thirds of Americans in fact, our only sleep problem is the morning alarm clock. We work and play hard, get tired at night, and can't wait to get into bed for a good night's sleep.

According to a recent survey, however, about one third of Americans have some degree of insomnia—inability to get enough sleep—and almost one fifth of us find the insomnia severe. People with insomnia often dread getting into bed, anticipating the long and lonely hours of lying awake, tossing and turning, and worrying. The most serious effect of insomnia is daytime sleepiness or anxiety: if you cannot sleep well at night you probably will not function well during the day either.

FACTS ABOUT SLEEP

Many myths about sleep need clarification. Some people believe, for example, that not sleeping will drive them crazy or cause severe physical damage. It is true that people who are kept awake for many days, as done in research experiments many years ago, do show bizarre mental behavior, like hearing and seeing things; however, the insomnia most people suffer from does not seriously harm the brain or the rest of the body. Insomnia is very unpleasant and disruptive, but not life threatening.

People are said to need "at least eight hours of sleep" to function properly. This, too, is entirely untrue. Sleep requirements vary with age and among individuals. A newborn infant sleeps up to 20 hours a day, whereas young children may need 10 to 12 hours to function well during the day.

Parents often tell their children that unless they get to bed on time and sleep through the night they won't "grow to be big and strong." Interestingly, there may be some scientific truth to this statement. Growth hormone, a chemical messenger secreted by a gland in the brain that promotes bone growth and maturation, is typically produced in the largest amounts in growing children during the early phases of sleep each night. Although lack of sleep has not been shown to disturb growth, some parents (myself included) feel they are on somewhat solid scientific ground when cajoling their children to bed, knowing that growth hormone is not actually synthesized during sleep.

The adult's need to sleep is extremely variable and probably is determined by an internal clock located in the part of the brain called the hypothalamus. This internal clock is highly individualized; some people need ten hours of sleep and others do fine with just five. The times at which a person should go to bed and wake up also vary greatly; the internal clock may not be set in the same way as the real clock. For example, some people seem to have an internal clock that operates in a time zone different from the one in which they live. For these people, the day might start naturally when the alarm clock says 4 AM, and by 8 PM, they are tired and ready to sleep. If such a person is forced to stay in bed until 7 AM and remain awake until 11 PM, she will spend three hours in the morning lying awake and three hours at night intolerably drowsy. For others, the internal clock may tick to a day that is shorter or longer than twenty-four hours. These people can become permanently out of sequence with social convention and may constantly feel tired.

Elderly people generally obtain less sleep than younger people. Furthermore, the sleep of older people is often routinely disrupted; a few hours of sleep are interrupted by a few hours of being awake several times through the night. This is common, but many elderly people who have been taught for years that a person is "supposed" to sleep eight hours every night believe there is something wrong with them. They become so worried about sleep that their anxiety keeps them awake. Often, doctors place elderly people on sleeping pills when the proper action would be to reassure them that less sleep is common with increasing age.

The proper amount of sleep for an adult is the amount that makes it possible to remain awake and alert during the day. That is usually somewhere between five and ten hours. No one should be treated for insomnia unless the failure to sleep at night results in an inability to function during the day.

The next myth about sleep has to do with dreaming. Some people think that dreaming is necessary for a night's sleep to be truly restful. Others think that too much dreaming means the sleep has been disturbed and too active to give the body a good rest.

In fact, there is little evidence that the amount of dreaming has anything to do with how restful a night's sleep actually is. Many psychiatric medications, including most antidepressants, reduce or even eliminate dreaming, but patients whose depression is cured by these drugs find the quality of their sleep much improved.

THE NORMAL STAGES OF SLEEP

Before discussing the remedies for insomnia, a characterization of normal sleep would be helpful. Normal sleep comprises two main phases: REM sleep and non-REM sleep. REM stands for "rapid eye movements." During the REM phase, the eyes of the sleeper dart back and forth. It is during the REM phase that dreaming occurs. The first REM period usually begins about ninety minutes after a person first falls asleep at night and lasts about ten minutes. As the night progresses, the REM periods typically grow longer and longer. That is why the alarm clock usually rings in the middle of a

255

dream. Adults spend about 25% of the night in the REM phase.

The remaining 75% of the night is spent in the phase called non-REM sleep. Non-REM sleep is itself divided into four stages. Stages 3 and 4 are also called "deep" sleep. There is more deep sleep in the first half of the night than in the second half. For this reason, waking someone suddenly in the very early hours of the morning is especially disturbing; a person usually feels disoriented and confused if they are suddenly aroused from stage 3 or 4 sleep. When I was an intern, I learned that it was better to remain awake between one and three in the morning instead of getting a few minutes of sleep, because it is especially difficult to be alert and ready to work if awakened during those hours.

Two sleep disturbances can be understood on the basis of these different stages of sleep. *Nightmares* are bad dreams and always occur during the REM phase. *Night terrors* (or *pavor nocturnus*), on the other hand, are sleep disturbances that usually affect young children; the sleeper suddenly awakens, feeling suffocated and terrified, but not in the middle of a dream. Night terrors occur during stages 3 and 4 of non-REM sleep. Nightmares may reflect daytime worries and fears; night terrors are probably a biological phenomenon and often require drug treatment. Other sleep-related problems of childhood, like bedwetting and sleep walking, also occur during non-REM sleep and consequently have absolutely nothing to do with bad dreams.

CAUSES OF INSOMNIA

Insomnia is often a complex problem with several possible causes. Many people, perhaps reinforced by what they see in the movies, think that reaching for a sleeping pill is the first thing to do if they cannot fall asleep. As I will discuss, "sleeping pills" that do not require prescriptions are advertised on television. Taking a sleeping pill sounds so safe and people so badly want to sleep well at night that it may appear simple and harmless.

Now that I have described the different phases of sleep and the many highly individual variations in sleep behavior from person to person, it should be obvious that sleep patterns are a highly regulated physiological function controlled by very complex brain circuits. All sleeping pills, even those bought over-the-counter, disrupt the normal patterns of sleep. Eventually, it becomes pill against brain as the sleep medication attempts to fend off the body's own sleep schedule. Sooner or later, the brain wins out and a person who tries to take sleeping pills every night for several weeks will end up with the problem they started out with: insomnia.

There are many situations in which sleeping pills, which doctors call "hypnotics," are the only solution to disabling sleep problems. In those cases they should be prescribed and used as long as they are needed and continue to work. Before sleeping pills are prescribed, all other means of conquering insomnia should first be tried. Sleeping pills are a last resort, but not a disastrous resort.

What are the possible causes of insomnia? They range from simple and seemingly obvious to some very obscure disorders that require special diagnostic equipment and skills.

The following is what goes through the doctor's mind when a person complains that he or she cannot fall asleep or stay asleep through the night:

1. Nothing is wrong; the patient only *thinks* he can't sleep. It is hard to say why, but some people who claim they can't sleep are just simply mistaken. One way to show this is to ask the person to write down the time he gets into bed and then to make a mark on the paper every hour he remains awake after that. Surprisingly, many people come back a week later with a blank piece of paper. They have actually slept. Perhaps, they had vivid dreams that made them feel they weren't sleeping, or maybe they thought it had taken longer than ten or fifteen minutes to fall asleep. Whatever the reason, nothing is wrong here and the doctor should not prescribe or recommend sleeping pills.

2. The patient is temporarily worried about something. This is a leading cause of not being able to fall asleep. Once the lights are off, the room is quiet, and there are no distractions, an anxious person is left alone with her thoughts. If she is worried, she will not fall asleep. Then she will start to worry about not being able to fall asleep and things will get worse. Worries can even wake a person

up in the middle of the night. Surprisingly, many people are completely unaware that worries are keeping them awake at night. Simply pointing this out sometimes gives the patient an explanation for their insomnia and the problem disappears.

3. The patient has bad sleep habits. Some of these bad habits may seem obvious, but again it is surprising how often people overlook them and come to the doctor looking for sleeping pills. Drinking black coffee an hour before bedtime is almost guaranteed to keep you up. It is best to avoid any beverage containing caffeine up to three hours before bedtime. Other stimulants, like cold remedies and sinus tablets, can also cause insomnia and should be avoided right before bedtime if possible.

Another big mistake is to have a scotch before bed. Alcohol will make you sleepy, but the effect is very short-lived. After two or three hours when the scotch is eliminated from the body, there will occur a sudden, often jolting awakening. Then you will lie awake for an hour. It is best not to drink alcohol for several hours before going to bed. Finally, exercise at night is tricky. Getting a good workout two or more hours before trying to sleeping will actually improve your chances of falling asleep, but exercising immediately before sleep often has the opposite effect. Immediately after exercising, a person is usually aroused and adrenaline is still pouring through the bloodstream. The doctor should take a history to learn what you eat, drink, and do in the evening and thus determine if some bad sleep habit is keeping you awake.

4. A bad sleep environment is less commonly a cause of insomnia, but of course the room in which you sleep should be quiet and at the proper temperature. If you wake up drenched in sweat every night, an internist might worry that you have tuberculosis, and a psychoanalyst may think you are suffering from nightmares; but it also could be that your bedroom is too warm.

5. Sleep changes with aging. As I mentioned earlier, it is very common for people to sleep less as they get beyond age 60. Many older people do fine with just four or five hours of sleep. Often, they fall asleep with no difficulty and then wake up at 4 AM. This is not abnormal and not dangerous. The best remedy is to get out

of bed and be active. Elderly people will find that they are alert and awake at 4 AM and can get a lot of reading done. Giving an elderly person sleeping pills to prolong their sleep in this case is almost guaranteed to produce daytime drowsiness and even more serious sleep disturbances.

6. I recall one patient who complained that he could not fall asleep until 2 AM. I couldn't find any reason until I took a detailed history of his regular daily routine. It turned out that he took a two-hour nap every day after work. The problem at bedtime simply was that he wasn't sleepy. Sleeping during the day will often make it impossible to fall asleep at a "conventional" bedtime. Either eliminate the naps or don't try to fall asleep at night until you really feel tired.

7. Sleeping pills themselves can be the cause of insomnia. Here's how it works: A person can't fall asleep for a few nights for whatever reason. So she buys over-the-counter sleeping pills or takes some Valium from the medicine cabinet. She sleeps fine for a week. Then the effect starts wearing off, so she takes a second sleeping pill in the middle of the night when she wakes up. Soon, her body becomes trained to expect a middle-of-the-night sleeping pill and she automatically wakes up for it. Before long, she awakens regularly several times through the night. She tells the doctor that she can't sleep "even though I am taking sleeping pills." The real danger here is that patient and doctor become misled into thinking that the insomnia is so bad it is breaking through the sleeping pills, and they conclude incorrectly that stronger sleeping pills are needed. In fact, sleeping pills often disrupt a normal sleep cycle and therefore cause insomnia. The only solution is to "bite the bullet," taper off the sleeping pills, and suffer a few sleepless nights. This allows the body to reestablish its own normal sleep schedule.

8. Many medical disorders specifically worsen at night and disrupt sleep, for example, congestive heart failure and some respiratory (breathing) disorders. Even a bad cold can disrupt sleep; when a person lies down, postnasal drip worsens and induces more coughing. Also, a stuffy nose may cause otherwise reasonable people to worry that they will quietly suffocate in the middle of the night. Many of these problems are relieved by sleeping with three or four

259

pillows so the head is propped up and by keeping the room well humidified. Sleeping pills are sometimes advisable, but need careful monitoring for people with serious medical problems.

9. Almost all psychiatric illnesses produce insomnia. One of the cardinal symptoms of depression, for example, is inability to sleep through the night. People with major depressive disorder commonly exhibit early-morning awakening. Anxiety disorders usually make it very difficult to fall asleep. Manic patients feel they don't need sleep at all. A careful psychiatric history often reveals a psychiatric problem requiring treatment to be the cause of the sleep disturbance.

The best treatment for insomnia in these cases is treatment of the underlying psychiatric problem. Short-term use of sleeping pills, however, is often recommended because the psychiatric treatment may take a few weeks to be effective. For example, if a diagnosis of depression is established and an antidepressant recommended, it may be four to six weeks before the medication works to relieve the depression and therefore reverse the insomnia. There is nothing wrong in prescribing sleeping pills for that waiting period. It is still best to avoid taking them every night so that it is easy to stop use once the antidepressant starts to work.

10. What if you and the doctor cannot find any obvious reason for insomnia, like minor worries or bad habits, and no medical or psychiatric illness exists? More and more often, patients with long-standing insomnia who fall into this category are being referred to sleep laboratories for a full evaluation. Sleep laboratories are cropping up in many medical centers and hospitals. Essentially, these laboratories give doctors an opportunity to fully evaluate their patients' sleep patterns. The patient usually must sleep in the laboratory two or three nights. During that time, a trained sleep technician records and videotapes the amount of time the person remains awake, unusual body movements during sleep, and all nighttime awakenings. A continuous recording of brain waves (electroencephalogram or EEG) is made to determine how much time the patient spends in each stage of sleep. Breathing patterns during sleep are also recorded. Many health insurance plans now reimburse patients for the cost of a full sleep laboratory evaluation.

Several disorders can be detected in the sleep laboratory. *Nocturnal myoclonus* is a condition in which the body suddenly undergoes involuntary jerking movements in the middle of the night. This movement will awaken the person with a start and may disrupt sleep several times throughout the night. The patient almost always feels tired throughout the day because of this sleep disruption. Patients with *sleep apnea* actually stop breathing during sleep and wake up immediately. Often, the patient is unaware that she has awakened ten or twenty times during the night because each awakening lasts only seconds. But she has the impression that she did not sleep well the next morning and feels tired all day. Patients with sleep apnea often snore at night and suffer from headaches when they wake up in the morning. Conditions such as nocturnal myoclonus and sleep apnea cause insomnia, can usually be diagnosed only in a sleep laboratory, and require specialized medical treatment. A sleep laboratory evaluation can also detect those people whose biological clock is not synchronized with the real time clock. Such people may think it is nighttime at 12 noon and time to wake up at 1 AM. Sleep experts have worked out a complex but often successful treatment that resets the biological clock more in line with the conventional clock.

Sometimes, however, the sleep laboratory evaluation reveals only what the patient knew all along—she can't fall asleep or stay asleep. No cause is found and no specialized treatment is recommended. In this case, sleeping pills may be the only treatment that works. (Table 27 summarizes the preceding ten points.)

The reason I have explained how sleep works and what causes insomnia is to make it clear that sleeping pills are *always* the last resort. In other chapters I have encouraged the reader to view psychiatric medication as not dangerous and often beneficial; however; sleeping pills are clearly overprescribed in this country and often cause more harm than good. It is so easy to take a pill to fall asleep that many patients and doctors do not bother to find the cause of the insomnia, resulting in two new problems. First, the patient may never have the opportunity to find out what is wrong, such as some unnecessary worries or a psychiatric illness, and, therefore, will never get proper treatment. Second, almost all sleeping pills are habit forming. The body becomes conditioned to their use and

Table 27:

Ten Causes of Insomnia

1. Nothing	The patient only thinks he is not sleeping at night.
2. Minor worries	
3. Bad sleep habits	Ingestion of alcohol or stimulants or exercising immediately before bedtime
4. Bad sleep environment	Excessive noise; increased or decreased temperature
5. Aging	Older people normally do not sleep as much.
6. Daytime napping	A person cannot sleep if she isn't sleepy.
7. Sleeping pills	Interrupt the normal sleep cycle and may cause insomnia
8. Medical illness	Even colds
9. Psychiatric illness	Most psychiatric problems cause insomnia.
10. Sleep disorders	Diagnosis may require a few nights in a sleep laboratory.

eventually refuses to sleep without them. People then have trouble stopping sleeping pills because each time an attempt is made, the insomnia is worse than it was initially. I feel strongly that sleeping pills should be prescribed only if no other solution is possible.

NONDRUG SOLUTIONS FOR INSOMNIA

What solutions can be offered for insomnia other than drugs?

1. If you can't fall asleep, don't stay in bed worrying about it. Get up, do something else for a while, and try again. There is a good chance that eventually your brain and body will get it together and you will finally fall asleep.

2. If you can't sleep at night, don't nap during the day. This only results in more nighttime insomnia.

3. Don't drink alcohol or caffeinated beverages, take stimulant medications like cold remedies, or exercise vigorously less than two or three hours before bedtime.

4. Make sure your bedroom is quiet and not too hot or cold. Use a blanket or fan. Insulate your room against noise. Use a "white noise machine" if necessary.

5. Force yourself to put your worries out of your mind when you get into bed. Tell yourself that you can't do anything at midnight, so you might as well get some rest and be ready to tackle your worries in the morning. Most of the time, the worries mysteriously seem a lot less important the next day. (See Table 28.)

If you still have insomnia despite your best efforts at improved sleep "hygiene," definitely consult your doctor. He or she should take a general medical history, perform a physical examination, and get laboratory tests if indicated.

What if your family doctor wants to prescribe a sleeping pill? Or what if the family doctor says nothing is wrong, but tells you it is alright to take an over-the-counter sleeping pill?

I certainly do not claim that no one should ever take a sleeping

Table 28:

Before You Take Sleeping Pills for Insomnia

1. Remember, insomnia will not hurt you physically or mentally.
2. Do not take naps during the day so you will be sleepy at night
3. Stop taking alcohol, stimulants, or caffeine or exercising three hours before bedtime
4. Make your bedroom as quiet and as comfortable (temperature-wise) as possible.
5. Try to get all your worries taken care of before you lie down.

pill without first consulting a psychiatrist. There aren't enough psychiatrists in the United States to see all the people who think they should take a sleeping pill for a few nights. But there is a very good chance that the sleep problem represents an anxiety disorder or depression or some other psychiatric condition. So I advise two things. First, taking a sleeping pill for two or three nights with the doctor's advice won't hurt. Second, review the chapters in this book on depression, anxiety, and bipolar affective illness (manic depression). Be honest with yourself. Is there any chance you are suffering from even a mild form of one of these disorders? If so, you should definitely see a psychiatrist before getting started on sleeping pills.

WHEN SHOULD SLEEPING PILLS BE TAKEN?

For what reasons should a person take a sleeping pill (Table 29)? Basically, these can be summarized as follows:

1. You are temporarily under tremendous and unavoidable stress and your insomnia makes you so tired during the day that you

Table 29:

Reasons to Take Sleeping Pills

1. Severe stress that produces insomnia and that nothing else can resolve
2. While waiting for treatment for an underlying psychiatric disorder to work
3. A medical problem that gets worse at night and keeps you awake
4. Chronic insomnia of unknown cause that no other remedy resolves

cannot function properly. This is making your life miserable and your problems worse. You have tried everything to relax and fall asleep, but nothing works. You know this stressful time will pass in a week or so, but in the meantime you absolutely have to get at least one good night's sleep. In this case, taking a sleeping pill for a few nights is probably a very wise choice. Take one and don't worry about it.

2. You are suffering from depression or anxiety disorder and your psychiatrist recently began a program of therapy and medication; however, you have been told that it may be weeks before the treatment works and in the meantime you want to sleep at night. Once again, a few nights of sleeping pills won't hurt. You can stop taking them when the underlying psychiatric condition is relieved.

3. You are suffering from a chronic medical problem that regularly makes your nights miserable. You have thoroughly discussed this with your medical doctor, who knows your physical condition well and also knows all of the other drugs you are taking. It is decided that taking a sleeping pill a few nights per week will not make your medical condition any worse and may make you feel better. Patients suffering from terminal illnesses should almost always be given as much medication as they need to sleep at night.

265

4. You are suffering from a sleep disorder like nocturnal myoclonus, or you have chronic insomnia, that is, insomnia lasting months or years, and absolutely no cause has been found. In this case, and this case only, it may be necessary to use sleeping pills on a regular basis.

TYPES OF SLEEPING PILLS

So far, I have used the term *sleeping pills* as if all drugs that makes someone sleep are more or less the same. This is not true. There are different kinds of sleeping pills (Table 30):

Table 30:

Drugs for Insomnia

Benzodiazepine sleeping pills	Dalmane, Restoril, Halcion, Prosom, Doral
Over-the-counter sleeping pills	Nervine, Nytol, Sleep Eze, Sleepinal, Sominex, Unisom, and others
Prescription antihistamines	Vistaril, Atarax
Tryptophan	
Sedative antidepressants	Elavil, Desyrel, Sinequan, Adapin
Drugs to avoid for insomnia	Doriden, Noludar, Seconal, phenobarbital, chloral hydrate, Placidyl

Benzodiazepines

Benzodiazepines are the sleeping pills most commonly pre-scribed by doctors in the United States. This class also includes many of the drugs used to treat generalized anxiety disorder and panic disorder, discussed in Chapter 8. All benzodiazepines de-crease the amount of time it takes to fall asleep and increase the amount of total sleep time. They also suppress stage 4 sleep, the deepest sleep, and therefore usually eliminate such abnormal sleep events as night terrors and sleep walking, which occur only in this stage of sleep. The five benzodiazepines sold specifically for insomnia in this country are ProSom (estazolam), Dalmane (flurazepam), Restoril (temazepam), Halcion (triazolam), and Doral (quazepam).

Dependency may develop to benzodiazepines when taken for sleep. This means that the body becomes used to them eventu-ally requires them to fall asleep. Some people who discontinue benzodiazepines, especially after having taken them continuously for more than two weeks, experience *rebound insomnia,* that is, very bad insomnia usually lasting several nights, until a normal sleep pattern is reestablished. The longer the sleeping pills are continu-ously used, the more severe will be the rebound insomnia. For this reason, these sleeping pills should be used sparingly when possible. Patients should try to fall asleep on their own at least an hour before taking a benzodiazepine sleeping pill and should try not to take it every night.

Benzodiazepine sleeping pills are *not,* however, addicting. There is no physical craving, and no life-threatening events occur after discontinuation. Some patients with chronic insomnia wind up tak-ing benzodiazepine sleeping pills more or less continuously. This is not medically harmful, although it may not work to resolve insomnia after several months. In general, benzodiazepine sleeping pills are the safest and most effective medications for insomnia, but they must be used judiciously and only under medical supervision.

Over-the-Counter Sleeping Pills

Many drugs that do not require a doctor's prescription and are claimed to relieve insomnia are sold in drug stores, health food stores, and supermarkets. Some are simply vitamins and minerals that have no real effect on sleep at all. They probably help a person sleep only if the person is convinced that vitamins and minerals are good for the body and general health. I feel that if it is so easy to convince someone he can sleep at night, he probably doesn't need pills at all.

Most of the over-the-counter sleep products contain antihistamines. These drugs, including Sominex, Nytol, and Nervine, will definitely produce sleepiness. Antihistamines are usually prescribed to relieve allergies and rashes, but long ago most of these drugs were noted to produce the side effect of drowsiness. This side effect, usually unwanted in treatment for hay fever or poison ivy, was exploited by drug companies in formulating over-the-counter sleeping pills. Actually, I think these over-the-counter sleeping pills have more side effects and are less effective than benzodiazepine sleeping pills. Furthermore, if taken several weeks in a row to combat insomnia, they are just as likely to become habit forming. In general, therefore, I feel that over-the-counter sleeping pills should be avoided. If medication is needed, prescription medication is usually superior.

Prescription Antihistamines

Some antihistamines require a prescription and are occasionally prescribed for insomnia. These include Atarax and Vistaril. They are no different from the over-the-counter antihistamines like Sominex and Nytol.

Tryptophan

Tryptophan is a naturally occurring substance found in many foods we eat. It is one of the amino acids, the building blocks of proteins, and is also a key ingredient in the production of a vital brain chemical called serotonin. Originally, it was believed that tryptophan might be useful as an antidepressant, but this proved largely incorrect; however, many people do become drowsy if they take large doses of tryptophan. Its presence in milk may be why drinking a glass of warm milk before bedtime helps some people to sleep. Recently it was discovered that people taking tryptophan may develop a serious, and potentially fatal, problem called eosinophilia-myalgia syndrome. This involves an increase in the number of a type of white blood cell called eosinophils, and muscle aches. It may be due to a contaminant in the preparation of tryptophan and not to the drug itself, but until this is cleared up tryptophan should be avoided.

Sedating Antidepressants

Several antidepressant drugs, especially Elavil, Sinequan, and Desyrel, also make patients feel sleepy. This is usually regarded as an unwanted side effect, but low doses of these sedative antidepressant drugs are increasingly being prescribed for the treatment of insomnia. Although 50 mg of Elavil or Desyrel is too small a dose to treat depression, it will induce sleep in most people. There is some suggestion that sedative antidepressants are less habit forming than benzodiazepine sleeping pills. Therefore, low doses of sedative antidepressants are often a good choice for a patient with chronic insomnia who requires long-term treatment.

Other Sleeping Pills

A large number of prescription sleep medications should generally be avoided, even though they may still be legally prescribed. These drugs are not described individually in the next section because there is almost no instance in which they should be administered, and doctors who prescribe them should become better informed. These medications include barbiturates like phenobarbital and Seconal (although barbiturates may have other legitimate uses besides sedation), Noludar, Placidyl, and Doriden. Chloral hydrate is a sleeping medication sometimes properly used for hospi-

269

talized psychiatric patients, but it has little use for the treatment of insomnia in outpatients.

If drugs are to be prescribed, the best choice for short-term treatment is a benzodiazepine sleeping pill. There are five choices that differ only in the length of action. Dalmane, closely related chemically to Valium, is the oldest pill advertised for treatment of insomnia and the longest acting. It is very effective, but may make the patient feel sleepy the next day. Restoril and Prosom are intermediate in length of action; they may take a bit longer to work than Dalmane or Halcion and their effect lasts up to ten hours. Halcion is ultra-short acting, remaining active only about six hours. With Halcion there is little hangover the next day, but for unclear reasons some patients complain of memory problems while Halcion is still active. This is called anterograde amnesia, which means that things learned from the time the drug is taken until it wears off may be forgotten. There is no permanent "brain damage." Anterograde amnesia can actually occur in some people from almost any benzodiazepine. It may be most troublesome in patients with preexisting memory difficulties, including some elderly patients. If memory problems do occur while on Halcion or any similar drug, it is probably best to avoid it. Patients who take Doral, a recently introduced sleeping pill, do not have a "hangover" effect. The drug's manufacturer claims Doral is more selective in the brain receptors it binds to than the other benzodiazepine sleeping pills, but the significance of this is not known.

Patients who require long-term sleep medication, such as those with an intractable medical illness or chronic insomnia of unknown cause, should be tried on a sedative antidepressant whenever possible. Some medical conditions prevent their use, and these are all discussed in Chapter 7.

Follow these six rules with respect to sleeping pills:

1. Don't take them if there is another way to treat your sleep problem.

2. Don't take over-the-counter drugs more than once or twice. If you need sleeping pills longer than this, see your doctor.

3. If a benzodiazepine sleeping pill is prescribed, take the lowest dose effective for the fewest number of nights possible. Always try to fall asleep before you take the pill and try to skip nights.

4. A low dose of a sedative antidepressant such as Elavil, Sinequan, or Desyrel should be considered for long-term treatment of insomnia.

5. Generally, it is safe to take sleeping pills if you are on other psychiatric medication, as long as you do so under medical supervision.

6. If you are taking sleeping pills, do not drink alcoholic beverages.

Do not let anyone make you feel guilty about taking a sleeping pill. Sleeping pills may not always work but they are generally safe. Certainly, it is better to take a sleeping pill than to get drunk to sleep.

TREATMENT OF JET LAG

Before moving on to describe each individual sleeping pill, a word about a popular new use for sleeping pills is in order. Many people now use sleeping pills to treat jet lag. The idea here is simple: if you have to fly from one time zone to the next, why not take a sleeping pill to help you sleep in the new time zone? This should help you adjust to the new time zone more quickly. Or, if you are flying across time zones, why not take a sleeping pill on the plane and sleep through the trip? You will be wide awake when the plane lands in the morning at your destination.

This type of use makes some doctors uncomfortable, because it represents the use of medication for a non-illness. Jet lag is not a medical disorder and people should not be encouraged to take medicine under these conditions.

There probably is no harm in taking a short-acting sleeping pill, like Halcion, for this purpose. Halcion will put almost anyone to sleep rapidly, and the person usually wakes up six to eight hours later without a hangover. Some people complain that Halcion affects memory, however, and I have heard several anecdotes of people who missed the next plane connection because they forgot where they were going after taking Halcion on the first part of their trip. Personally, I think these stories are somewhat exaggerated. My advice, however, is that medicine should be taken for medical problems. Jet lag is one of those facts of modern life that we should learn to live with and not medicate.

DRUGS USED TO TREAT INSOMNIA

There are five classes of drugs in this section: benzodiazepines, over-the-counter drugs, prescription antihistamines, tryptophan, and sedative antidepressants.

The Benzodiazepine Sleeping Pills

FLURAZEPAM

Brand Name: Dalmane.
Used for: Insomnia.
Don't Take It if: You have a history of addiction to drugs or alcohol or if you think your doctor has overlooked the cause for your sleeping problem.
Tests to Take First: None are required.
Tests to Take While You Are on It: None required.
Usual Dose: Most people take one 30-mg capsule about thirty minutes before going to sleep. Elderly people should try to take half that dose (15 mg) to see if it works.
How Long Until It Works: You should fall asleep about a half-hour after taking Dalmane. The drug remains effective if taken every night for at least a month, and in many people continues to be effective in inducing sleep indefinitely.
Common Side Effects: (1) You may be drowsy the day after because Dalmane has a very long length of action and remains in the body at least a day. (2) You may experience withdrawal symptoms after

272

taking Dalmane nightly for several weeks and then stopping it. The withdrawal syndrome includes anxiety, restlessness, sweating, and severe insomnia, and is very severe in some people and not so bad in others. It always goes away by itself, but can last as long as two weeks. It is not life threatening but can be very disturbing and uncomfortable.

Less Common Side Effects: Elderly people who take Dalmane, particularly for several weeks, may experience dizziness, confusion, and unsteadiness when they walk. Falls have occurred.

What to Do About Side Effects: If Dalmane makes you feel too sleepy the next day, it is probably better to switch to one of the shorter-acting sleeping pills, like Restoril or Halcion. To avoid a withdrawal syndrome, it is best not to take Dalmane every night longer than two weeks. Always try to skip a night here and there and test yourself before taking it by attempting to sleep without it at least one hour before reaching for the pill. Some insomniacs are surprised to find the pill still on the night table the next morning. Sleeping pills should be given very carefully to elderly people. The presence of very serious pain or medical problems that make insomnia insurmountable by any other remedy are valid reasons to give an elderly person small doses of sleep medication. Elderly persons who take Dalmane should be cautioned to get out of bed the next day very slowly and to sit down if they have the slightest sensation of dizziness or unsteadiness. Elderly people with low blood pressure, poor eyesight, or medical problems that make them weak are especially likely to fall if they take sleeping pills. Sleeping pills should almost never be given to alcoholics or older people without very strict medical supervision.

If It Works: After you have had a few nights of good sleep, try doing without the pill. An occasional restless night is worth not getting dependent on sleeping pills.

If It Doesn't Work: If you cannot fall asleep even after you take Dalmane it is unlikely that any other sleeping pill will do much better. Staying awake even after you have taken a drug like Dalmane should alert you that there is a cause of your insomnia that is being overlooked and that a sleeping pill can't cure. You should ask your doctor to refer you to a sleep disorder expert.

Cost: Brand, 49 cents/30-mg pill. Generic, 14 cents/30-mg pill.

Special Comments: Dalmane was the first of the benzodiazepine sleeping pills introduced onto the American market. It is chemically related to other benzodiazepine drugs described in Chapter 8, like Valium and Xanax, that are used to treat anxiety disorder. Dalmane is very safe and highly effective in treating insomnia. It can be used to relieve insomnia experienced by people with depression while they wait for the antidepressant to work. It can also be used to treat a wide variety of sleep problems, including insomnia caused by stress and worry. The major drawback is that like any sleeping pill, it is habit forming. Your body will come to depend on Dalmane to fall asleep, so that if you take it a long time and then stop, your insomnia may be even worse than it was originally. It should be used judiciously and as sparingly as possible.

TEMAZEPAM

Brand Name: Restoril.
Used for: Insomnia.
Don't Take It if: You have a history of drug or alcohol addiction or if you think your doctor may have overlooked the cause of your insomnia.
Tests to Take First: None required.
Tests to Take While You Are on It: None required.
Usual Dose: Most people take one 30-mg capsule about an hour before bedtime. Elderly people should take 15 mg and see if it works. Patients should not take more than 30 mg at night except in very special circumstances under medical supervision.
How Long Until It Works: You should fall asleep an hour after taking a Restoril capsule. The drug remains effective if taken every night for about one month, and longer in most people, but it is always best to avoid taking it every night.
Common Side Effects: (1) You may feel drowsy the next day, but Restoril is shorter acting than Dalmane so this is less of a problem. (2) After taking Restoril night after night for many weeks and then stopping it, you will probably experience a withdrawal syndrome, characterized by anxiety, insomnia, restlessness, and sweating. This is uncomfortable, but not medically dangerous. It will go away by itself, but can last up to two weeks.
Less Common Side Effects: Elderly people who take sleeping pills like

274

Restoril may experience dizziness, confusion, and unsteadiness when they walk. Falls may result.

What to Do About Side Effects: If Restoril makes you feel sleepy during the day you might switch to an even shorter-acting sleeping pill, like Halcion. The best way to minimize withdrawal symptoms is never to get into the habit of taking Restoril every night for more than a few nights in a row. Suffering through a sleepless night here and there is better than getting hooked on a sleeping pill. Sleeping pills like Restoril should be given with great caution to elderly people, who may become confused and disoriented when given for prolonged periods.

If It Doesn't Work: If Restoril doesn't help you to sleep it is unlikely any sleeping pill will do much better. Do not increase the dose. It is better to ask your doctor to refer you to a specialist in sleep disorders and to consider the possibility that there is a reason for your insomnia that cannot be resolved by a sleeping pill.

If It Does Work: After you have slept two or three nights, try taking at least a night off from the pill. Remember, insomnia is unpleasant but never dangerous and staying awake is better than getting dependent on sleeping pills.

Cost: Brand, 50 cents/30-mg pill. Generic, 7 cents/30-mg pill.

Special Comments: Restoril is intermediate between Dalmane and Halcion in its length of action. The drug remains active about 12 hours, less than Dalmane, but longer than Halcion. Originally, there were problems with the capsule material that Restoril was packaged in and the drug was not absorbed into the blood rapidly. This meant that it took hours for a patient to fall asleep. This problem has been corrected and Restoril now works about as rapidly as Dalmane to induce sleep. It is medically safe and habit forming only if taken every night for several weeks. Restoril, like all sleeping pills, is likely to be more habit forming in alcoholics or people with drug abuse problems. They should be given Restoril only in special circumstances and then only under strict medical supervision.

TRIAZOLAM

Brand Name: Halcion.
Used for: Insomnia.

275

Don't Take It if: You have history of addiction to drugs or alcohol or if you think your doctor has overlooked the reason for your insomnia.

Tests to Take First: None required.

Test to Take While You Are on It: None required.

Usual Dose: Most people will fall asleep after taking a single tablet of 0.25 mg. Elderly people should try a tablet of 0.125 mg.

How Long Until It Works: Halcion will make you fall asleep in less than thirty minutes. Some people think it works even faster if you let it dissolve under your tongue instead of swallowing it.

Common Side Effects: (1) Halcion is very powerful and, the morning after taking it, some people find that they have forgotten what happened the night before and are a bit disoriented or even irritable. The drug does not produce permanent memory loss or brain damage as far as is known, and not everyone experiences the effect on memory. Also, some of the memory problems probably arose in persons who took the 0.5-mg dose of Halcion. This dose has been discontinued by the manufacturer and the recommended top dose is 0.25 mg. (2) After taking Halcion every night for several weeks and then stopping it, you will probably experience some degree of withdrawal syndrome, the most pronounced component of which is "rebound" insomnia. Your body will become so used to sleeping with Halcion that it will refuse to sleep without it. You may also experience some anxiety and restlessness. None of this is dangerous to your health, and the withdrawal syndrome will go away on its own, although it may take a few days if you have been taking Halcion nightly for many months.

Less Common Side Effects: (1) Daytime drowsiness is uncommon because Halcion is so short acting and is eliminated from the body by the next morning. (2) Elderly people are prone to develop confusion, dizziness, disorientation, and unsteadiness when they walk if given Halcion or any other sleeping pill.

What to Do About Side Effects: If memory problems arise after taking Halcion or any other sleeping pill, the medication should be discontinued. The best way to avoid a withdrawal syndrome is to avoid taking Halcion too many nights in a row. Always give your body a chance to reestablish its normal rhythm. You may find that after a night or two of taking Halcion you will be able to sleep just fine without it. Try very hard not to convince yourself that the only way you will ever fall asleep is to take the pill. Your body might start to believe you. Elderly people should never be given sleeping pills if it can be avoided, and if they do take Halcion they should be cautioned about the possibility of dizziness or confusion. Medical supervision is always necessary.

If It Doesn't Work: It is unlikely that another sleeping pill will be much better. You should consider the possibility that your insomnia cannot be resolved with sleeping pills. A referral to a sleep disorder specialist might be considered. Above all, do not take extra pills if one doesn't help.

If It Does Work: Always try to skip some nights. Get into bed first and give yourself at least an hour before reaching for the pill. A night of insomnia once in a while is better than getting hooked on sleeping pills.

Cost: Brand, 54 cents/0.25-mg pill. Generic, not available.

Special Comments: Halcion is the shortest acting and most powerful sleeping pill available in this country. Because it is short acting, it is almost completely eliminated from the body by the next morning and therefore is unlikely to cause a hangover. It is medically very safe and very effective. Some people take it on airplanes so they can sleep and prevent "jet lag." This is probably safe, although I have misgivings about using medication to help people with their scheduling difficulties. The memory loss attributed to Halcion involves events that occur in the hours after the drug is taken. Halcion does not cause brain damage. It is important to avoid taking them every night without a break.

ESTAZOLAM

Brand Name: Prosom.

Cost: Brand, 48 cents/1-mg pill. Generic, not available.

Special Comments: Prosom was released for marketing as a sleeping pill in 1991. It is chemically related to Dalmane, Restoril, and Halcion and has about the same length of action as Restoril. The usual adult dose is 1 mg to 2 mg at bedtime.

QUAZEPAM

Brand Name: Doral
Cost: Brand, 41 cents/15-mg pill. Generic, not available.
Special Comments: Recently released, Doral is said to be more selective than other benzodiazepine sleeping pills in the brain receptors it binds to, although whether this is important is not yet known. One 15 mg tablet is usually taken at night.

Over-the-Counter Sleeping Pills

Brand Names: Exedrin P.M. Analgesic/Sleep Aid; Miles Nervine Nighttime Sleep-Aid; Nytol; Sleep Eze; Sleepinal Night-Time Sleep Aid; Sominex; Unisom Nighttime Sleep Aid.
Used for: Insomnia
Don't Take Them if: You have an enlarged prostate gland, asthma, or glaucoma unless your doctor approves. Never take these drugs with alcohol.
Tests to Take First: None required.
Tests to Take While You Are on Them: None required.
Usual Dose: Read the label on the box or bottle. These sleeping pills do not require prescriptions.
How Long Until They Work: You should fall asleep within an hour.
Common Side Effects: Dizziness, disturbed coordination, stomach-ache, and thickening of the secretions normally found in your lungs.
Less Common Side Effects: (1) Patients with narrow-angle glaucoma can get an attack after using these sleeping pills. (2) Patients with an enlarged prostate gland or other problems with urination may find it very difficult to urinate. (3) Confusion and disorientation.
What to Do About Side Effects: Never take more pills than recommended on the label, and do not use them more than one or two nights a month. If you experience dizziness or disturbed coordination, stop taking them immediately. Never give these to children without approval from your pediatrician. If you have asthma, narrow-angle glaucoma, or an enlarged prostate, check with your doctor first.
If They Don't Work: Don't be surprised; my experience is that they frequently don't work. You may need to take a prescription sleeping pill, like Dalmane, Restoril, or Halcion.
If They Do Work: If you find that one of the over-the-counter

278

sleeping pills does help you sleep, you should still use it sparingly. Your body will get used to them after a while and you will find that without them you won't be able to sleep at all. If you are taking them more than once or twice a month, call your doctor and get an evaluation.

Special Comments: These drugs represent one of the rare examples in this book of drugs for which a prescription is not required. All of these sleeping pills, except Unisom, contain the same chemical present in the popular antihistamine Benadryl—diphenhydramine. Unisom contains a related antihistamine called doxylamine succinate. Antihistamines were developed to counteract allergic reactions, but many were quickly noted to have the annoying side effect of making the patient sleepy. This disadvantage was quickly turned into an advantage when drug companies realized they could sell these antihistamines as sleep aids without a prescription.

The fact that they do not require a prescription is their only advantage over prescription sleeping pills. Over-the-counter sleeping pills have side effects, frequently do not work, and are just as likely to become habit forming as prescription sleeping pills. Once the body becomes used to the sleeping pill, it frequently refuses to sleep without it after it is discontinued. These sleeping pills should be taken infrequently. If you require more help to sleep, you should see a doctor anyway, and in most cases a benzodiazepine sleeping pill is safer and more effective.

Prescription Antihistamines

Brand Names: Benadryl, Atarax, Vistaril, and others.
Used for: Treatment of allergies. Insomnia.
Do Not Use if: You have just had an alcoholic beverage. If you have glaucoma, asthma, or an enlarged prostate you should check with your doctor first.
Tests to Take First: None required.
Tests to Take While You Are on Them: None required.
Usual Dose: For Benadryl, a 50-mg capsule about thirty minutes before bedtime is usually sufficient. For Atarax and Vistaril, a 50-mg tablet or capsule is usually sufficient, but 100 mg is also sometimes prescibed.

279

How Long Until It Works: You should fall aleep within an hour.

Common Side Effects: Dry mouth, dizziness, disturbed coordination, and thickening of the secretions normally found in your lungs.

Less Common Side Effects: (1) Asthma attacks in people who already have asthma. (2) Glaucoma attacks in people who have narrow-angle glaucoma. (3) Difficulty urinating in men with enlarged prostate glands.

What to Do About Side Effects: They are usually very mild. If confusion or disorientation occur, stop taking the medication and tell your doctor. If you have asthma, glaucoma, or an enlarged prostate you should not take these medications unless your doctor approves.

If They Don't Work: Do not be surprised. These are really not very good sleeping pills. They may make you drowsy enough to sleep on an occasional bad night, but do not rely on them to resolve serious insomnia. If a prescription antihistamine does not work and sleeping pills are clearly needed, you are probably better off taking a benzodiazepine sleeping pill like Dalmane, Restoril or Halcion.

If They Do Work: Prescription antihistamines, like over-the-counter sleeping pills, should be used sparingly, about one or two nights per month. Although they are medically safe they can still be habit forming. Your body will get so used to them that eventually they will be required for you to fall asleep. Then, if you decide to stop taking these drugs, you may experience worse insomnia than you did originally. If you find you need to take sleeping pills more than occasionally, tell your doctor to evaluate the problem thoroughly and consider referral to a sleep disorder expert.

Special Comments: The chemical ingredients of these prescription antihistamines are identical or almost identical to those of the over-the-counter sleeping pills. So why does one class require a prescription while the other can be obtained merely by walking into a supermarket or a drug store? The reasons have more to do with drug company strategies than real differences in safety or effectiveness. Antihistamines are intended for the treatment of allergies. Many of them have as a side effect sleepiness, and therefore are sold and prescribed as sleeping pills. As sleeping pills they are safe and sometimes effective. Taking them once in a while will not hurt, but if medication for sleep is required frequently, a prescription benezodiazepine sleeping pill like Restoril, Dalmane, or Halcion, is probably a better choice.

Tryptophan

Brand Names: Trofan, Tryptocin, and others.
Used for: Insomnia.
Do Not Use if: You are taking other psychiatric medications, for example, lithium, Prozac, monoamine oxidase inhibitors, and other antidepressants, unless your doctor approves.
Tests to Take First: None required.
Tests to Take While You Are on It: None required. Blood levels of tryptophan are obtained for experimental purposes and are not useful or necessary for patients taking tryptophan at the present time.
Usual Dose: It is best to start with 500 mg about thirty minutes before bedtime. It may take 1,000 mg or more to induce sleep; some patients take up to 12,000 mg every night.
How Long Until It Works: It should make you sleepy within an hour.
Common Side Effects: Tryptophan has been linked to a syndrome of muscle aches and increase in the number of a kind of white blood cell called eosinophils. It is potentially fatal. It is not yet known how common this is or how long tryptophan must be taken before it develops.
Less Common Side Effects: It is possible that too much tryptophan, especially if taken in combination with other psychiatric drugs, will cause what is called the "serotonin syndrome." This syndrome may include intense perspiration, fever, rapid heartbeat, very low blood pressure, and extreme fatigue, and can be a medical emergency. Fortunately, it is extremely rare and limited almost entirely to people who take very large doses of tryptophan along with other psychiatric drugs. There has been one report that administration of very high doses of tryptophan for years produced cancer in mice; it is unclear whether this has any relevance to humans.
What to Do About Side Effects: Tryptophan should be taken in doses of 1,000 mg or less and should not be taken along with other psychiatric drugs unless a physician is monitoring your situation. Until the situation with eosinophilia-myalgia syndrome is resolved, tryptophan should be avoided as a sleeping pill.
If It Doesn't Work: Don't be surprised; it frequently doesn't work.

Tryptophan makes some people very sleepy and does absolutely nothing for others. This high degree of variability in response makes it less than an ideal choice of sleeping pill.

If It Does Work: As with any sleeping pill, if you take tryptophan every night your body will eventually get so used to it that you may not be able to sleep without it. Also, in my experience, the effect of tryptophan wears off after a few nights of continuous use. It is best to use it only two or three nights per week, when you really feel you need to get to sleep. When stopping use, decrease the dose gradually.

Cost: Brand, 22 cents/500-mg pill. Generic, 11 cents/500-mg pill.

Special Comments: Tryptophan is a naturally occurring amino acid, one of the building blocks of protein. It is present in many foods we eat and is used by the brain to make an important chemical called serotonin. It was previously believed that a lack of serotonin causes depression, so many scientists attempted to cure depression by giving patients tryptophan, either alone or in combination with antidepressant drugs. Most of these attempts failed, and it is now widely accepted that tryptophan is not a very effective antidepressant. During these experiments, however, tryptophan was observed to make patients sleepy, and so it has been used as a sleeping pill. It has variable effects and often does absolutely nothing. The fact that it is a "naturally occurring protein substance" should not mislead anyone into believing that it is safer than prescribed medication. Arsenic is also a naturally occurring chemical. My own experience is that tryptophan must be taken in large doses to have any effect on insomnia and that it is not useful for more than one or two nights. The benzodiazepine sleeping pills are at least as safe and more effective. Because of the potential for the serious side effect of eosinophilia-myalgia syndrome, tryptophan has been banned by the Food and Drug Administration and cannot be used for now.

Sedative Antidepressants

Brand Names: Elavil, Desyrel, Sinequan, Adapin.
Used for: Depression. Insomnia
Special Comments: These antidepressants are described in detail in

Chapter 7. They all have the side effect of making a patient drowsy. Recently, doses of these medications lower than those effective in treating depression have been prescribed to help people with insomnia. The usual dose for this purpose is about 50 mg one hour before bedtime. At this low dose, most of the side effects from the medications are minimal but the patient will still feel sleepy. There is some suggestion that these sedative antidepressants may be less habit forming than the benzodiazepine sleeping pills, although this hypothesis requires further testing. I think they are useful in cases where some medication for insomnia is needed many nights in a row, months, or even years. For more short-term treatment of insomnia, the benzodiazepine sleeping pills are superior.

SUMMARY OF DRUGS USED TO TREAT INSOMNIA

In almost all cases of insomnia, if there is no other solution than sleeping pills, the benzodiazepine sleeping pills (Dalmane, Doral, Halcion, Restoril, and Prosom) are the best choice. The only exception is the case in which sleeping medication may be required many months or years. For such cases, I recommend trying a low dose (about 50 mg) of a sedative antidepressant (Elavil, Desyrel or Sinequan) before a benzodiazepine. Over-the-counter sleeping pills and prescription antihistamines should be used only occasionally. The following drugs should almost always be avoided in treating insomnia: Placidyl, Noludar, barbiturates (like Seconal and phenobarbital), Miltown, and Doriden.

Chapter 12

Drugs Used to Treat Drug Abuse

The very idea of giving drugs to stop people from abusing drugs may seem like a complete paradox. How can we tell an alcoholic or cocaine addict that switching to a *different* drug will make him better and win the approval of his family, friends, and doctors?

If you think the concept is strange, you are not alone. Many people involved in the battle against drug abuse are vehemently opposed to prescribing any drug to drug abusers. They feel that programs aimed at complete abstinence—the total drug-free state—are the only ones that make sense.

It is hard to ignore their point. For example, the best current treatment for alcoholism is Alcoholics Anonymous (AA). AA attempts to induce alcoholics to give up drinking entirely; AA views any form of drug therapy for alcoholism as simply addition of another brand of drug dependence.

Although we may all agree that the best treatment for drug and alcohol abuse is to stop the habit entirely, most people with addiction problems find that stopping is more easily said than done. Rates of relapse after treatment for almost every form of drug abuse are very high. Think of all the cigarette smokers who are desperate to stop smoking, make it for a few weeks, and then relapse after the first stressful moment. We do not know how many alcoholics who go to AA remain abstinent for long periods, but there is good reason to believe that their relapse rate is also very high. And we have a very poor track record trying to convince heroin and cocaine users to stop "cold turkey" and remain drug free forever.

THE FEAR OF WITHDRAWAL

Clearly, we do not live in the best of all possible worlds and it is obviously very hard to stop an addiction. One of the biggest reasons addicts do not stop their habits is *the fear of drug withdrawal.* Addiction to cigarettes, alcohol, heroin, or cocaine means that the body is physically dependent on the substance; take it away and there is a violent physical reaction. An alcoholic who suddenly stops drinking will become tremulous and may develop delirium tremens, a syndrome that includes fever, seizures, and sometimes death. Cocaine and amphetamine addicts who stop may develop severe depression and a drug craving so powerful that they will do almost anything—including commit violent crimes—to get more drug. Even sudden cessation of cigarette smoking is accompanied by an irritable, anxious, and depressed state that many find unbearable to the point they must have another cigarette.

One aim of the use of medication to treat drug addiction is reduction of the amount of withdrawal a person must undergo in stopping abuse of the drug. A person who can get through the acute phase of withdrawal, when drug craving is powerful and the physical symptoms unpleasant or even dangerous, has a good chance of remaining drug free forever. Antianxiety drugs, especially Librium, have been administered to alcoholics for almost 30 years to blunt withdrawal effects.

In most hospitals, it is considered dangerous *not* to give an alcoholic trying to detox some Librium for the first few days, because without it the patient might experience seizures or even die. Several years ago, the drug clonidine, best known as a treatment for high blood pressure, was found to reduce the withdrawal syndrome after discontinuation of heroin. The heroin addict given clonidine can stop "shooting up" and experience much less sweating, fever, and shaking than the addict not given clonidine. More recently, in what may be a major breakthrough, Dr. Alexander Glassman at Columbia University presented evidence that clonidine may also blunt withdrawal symptoms, including craving, after stopping cigarette smoking.

Yet, many addicts who get past the withdrawal period still relapse in time. Unfortunately, we do not yet know why. Even after the addict loses the severe physical craving characteristic of the withdrawal period, which usually takes only a few weeks, an inner drive forces her to go back to the abused drug. There is now good evidence that at least in the case of alcoholics, some of this need for the drug is caused by a genetic defect. Strange as it may sound, some addicts apparently are born to be addicts, having inherited what scientists think is an abnormal gene. Different life stresses probably trigger the transformation of the person with the abnormal gene into an addict.

BLOCKING THE HIGH

We do not yet know how to repair such abnormal genes. Instead, several drugs have been developed that prevent addicts from receiving the full impact of their drug of choice or that make addicts sick when they try to take the abused drug. The idea here is that once an addict finds out that his heroin won't produce a high, he will have little reason to continue taking heroin.

Antabuse was one of the first such drugs to be developed. If an alcoholic takes Antabuse everyday and then drinks she will become violently ill. One time is often enough to convince the alcoholic never to take another drink. The problem here, of course, is that the alcoholic has to agree to keep taking Antabuse. The effects of Antabuse last only about one day, so if the alcoholic simply refuses the pill for a couple of days she can resume drinking without getting sick. Antabuse treatment requires a motivated alcoholic, the kind

287

of person who might do just as well attending AA meetings and stopping drinking without drug treatment.

Naltrexone (Trexan) is a drug that blocks the effects of heroin. It is relatively long acting, so the recovered heroin addict need only take it once a day. While the addict is on naltrexone, heroin will have absolutely no effect. A similar claim is made with respect to treatment of cocaine addicts with certain antidepressants. Studies have now shown that the antidepressants imipramine and desipramine may actually block a cocaine high. Once again, the addict must take the medicine every day. When he does so the smoking or snorting of cocaine is reported to produce very little effect. This lack of effect induces some addicts to give up the abused drug.

MIMICKING THE EFFECTS

In addition to decreasing withdrawal symptoms and blocking the effects of abused drugs, there exist medications that mimic the effects of abused drugs but do not produce the same serious health or social risks. The best known of these is methadone, a drug that mimics many of the effects of heroin. Because it is ingested orally instead of injected, methadone does not produce the same devastating physical diseases as heroin, such as infections of the heart and AIDS. Also, because methadone is given out under controlled conditions in clinics, it does not lead to crime and circumvents the drug pushers. Methadone treatment has been successful in treating about one fourth of the nation's heroin addicts, but many people object to it as substitution of one addiction for another. More importantly, there are far too few methadone clinics in the United States to accommodate all of the country's heroin addicts.

Not unlike methadone maintenance, although intended for use over a shorter period, is Nicorette chewing gum. This gum contains nicotine, the addicting substance found in cigarettes. Cigarette smokers are asked to chew the gum several times daily, instead of smoking, to get their nicotine. Although nicotine itself is probably not great for health, chewing the gum is far safer than inhaling the poison into the lungs. After chewing the gum for several weeks some smokers find they are gradually able to give up the gum without starting to smoke again.

TREATMENT OF AN UNDERLYING ILLNESS

There is a fourth way in which medication may help an addict. We now have good evidence that some people who abuse drugs are attempting to treat an underlying psychiatric illness without going to the doctor. In the United States more women have anxiety attacks than men, but there are more male alcoholics. It is likely that some men with anxiety attacks go to the bar instead of going to the psychiatrist. Studies have shown that as many as one third of patients undergoing alcohol detoxification had experienced panic attacks before they became alcoholics. Alcohol is a very powerful although very dangerous medication for anxiety attacks. Dr. Glassman, who showed that clonidine may block the withdrawal effects in persons who stop smoking, also recently showed that smokers who find it the most difficult to stop smoking are more likely to have depression than smokers who successfully quit. The nicotine in cigarettes may act as a stimulant for some depressed people.

Depression and anxiety probably cause many of the cases of cocaine, alcohol, heroin, and cigarette addiction. Cocaine may give the chronically depressed patient a temporary life, alcohol blocks panic attacks and reduces phobias, heroin blocks out almost all painful emotions, and cigarette smoking seems to have some relationship to depression.

Although I do not believe that all cases of drug or alcohol abuse are directly the result of psychiatric illness, it is extremely important that addicts undergo a thorough psychiatric evaluation. If an underlying mental disorder is the root of the addiction problem, successful treatment of that disorder may also eliminate the need for the abused drug.

Psychiatrists have had some success in the use of antidepressant and antianxiety drugs to treat alcoholics, cocaine addicts, and even heroin addicts in whom a psychiatric condition was the real problem. They have even uncovered patients with manic-depressive illness (now called bipolar affective disorder) whose abuse of alcohol or cocaine was an attempt to regulate moods either up or down. Such patients often stop abusing drugs after they are placed on lithium.

In cases of drug abuse, psychiatric medications must be prescribed by an experienced clinician, because some psychiatric drugs do not interact well with abused drugs. Antidepressants of the monamine oxidase inhibitor class, for example, should never be given to people who continue to use cocaine. It would be a serious mistake to prescribe a benzodiazepine-type antianxiety drug, for example, Xanax or Valium, on a long-term basis to an alcoholic patient without very careful monitoring. These drugs are often abused by alcoholics and, in most cases, merely add to their problems.

FOUR RULES FOR DRUG THERAPY

To summarize, there are four ways in which medication may help an addict overcome addiction (Table 31):

1. To block withdrawal symptoms when the abused drug is stopped. This makes it easier to get through the first few weeks.

2. To block the effects of the abused drug or make those effects unpleasant. This reduces the addict's motivation to take the abused drug.

3. To mimic the desired effects of an abused drug with a safer medication. The addict is induced to take a medication that has effects similar to those of the abused drug, but has fewer adverse medical and social consequences.

4. To treat an underlying psychiatric disturbance that is the root of the drug abuse. Once the underlying depression or anxiety disorder is relieved, the addict no long needs to take the abused drug.

Table 31:

Drugs Used to Treat Drug Abuse

STRATEGY	ABUSED DRUG	TREATMENT DRUG
1. Block withdrawal	Alcohol Heroin Cigarettes	Librium, Valium, Ativan Clonidine Clonidine
2. Block effects of abused drug	Alcohol Cocaine Heroin	Antabuse Imipramine, desipramine Naltrexcne
3. Mimic effects of abused drug	Cigarettes Heroin	Nicorette gum Methadone
4. Treat underlying psychiatric disorder	Alcohol, cigarettes, heroin, cocaine	Antidepressants, antianxiety medication

CONVINCING THE ADDICT

Even if we accept that some patients with an addiction are properly treated with medication, there still remains the problem of convincing the addicts that drug abuse is their problem. Psychiatrists miss this point many times. Doctors frequently forget to ask patients about drug and alcohol abuse. Some doctors, including psychiatrists, think that asking their patients about alcohol or drug abuse is insulting. As long as a person doesn't stagger into the office with alcohol on his breath, the doctor refuses to believe the patient has a drinking problem.

With physicians exercising this kind of denial, it is no wonder that many drug abusers with serious addiction problems fool themselves into thinking they are only recreational users. I now offer some simple guidelines to determine if you or someone you care about may have a drug abuse problem.

1. There is never—*absolutely never*—a recreational use for cocaine, heroin, amphetamines ("uppers"), barbiturates ("downers"), Quaaludes, Talwin, or Dilaudid. Most of these drugs are illegal; others are sometimes prescribed by physicians. If you ever take any of these, even once, without a prescription from your doctor, then you have a drug abuse problem.

2. Cigarettes are as harmful as the former Surgeon General Everett Koop said they are. Many people have quit smoking; the remaining smokers are likely to be people who have tried and simply cannot quit. They should see their doctor and try getting into a program that may include clonidine and Nicorette chewing gum.

3. Alcohol is tricky. There is, of course, a legitimate and legal recreational use for alcohol. Most people cannot drink to excess because they do not find it all that pleasant. The average person feels relaxed and happy after a drink or two; more than that makes the person sleepy and then sick. Evidence now suggests that alcoholics tolerate much higher "doses" of alcohol before they feel these unpleasant effects. So an alcoholic can keep on drinking past the point at which the normal person's body says stop. This means that the alcoholic may not recognize she is drinking too much at

first. Later, she insists she is in complete control. Unfortunately, too many people believe her until it is too late.

So here is a simple test. If you think you may have the slightest problem, do not have another alcoholic drink (including beer and wine) for one week. No matter what. Don't make an excuse, like you have to go to a party or business meeting and it will look odd if you don't have a drink. If you cannot last one week without a drink, you have a drinking problem and should get help. If you do last a week it does not mean you are home free, but you have demonstrated that you at least are no longer addicted.

There are other warning signs of an alcohol problem:

1. You drink to fall asleep at night.

2. You drink alone.

3. You drink because you feel you have to calm your nerves.

4. You drink in the morning or the afternoon.

5. You tell yourself you aren't going to have a drink but can't help yourself and have one anyway.

6. You miss work because you are drunk or have a hangover.

7. You have blackouts, that is, you forget everything that happened for several hours after getting drunk.

8. Your body shakes several hours after your last drink (this is a component of withdrawal syndrome; your body is craving alcohol).

9. Someone tells you that you have been drinking a lot.

10. You lie to others about how much you drink or you hide bottles of alcohol so no one will know you are drinking.

If you meet even one of these ten criteria, you should consider the possibility that you have an alcohol abuse problem. Talk to your doctor. Join an AA chapter. Whatever you do, do not ignore the problem.

HOW TO PROCEED

Simply stopping use of the addicting drug is the preferred way to handle the problem. Even insurance companies, who usually resist paying for psychiatric care, are willing to pay for psychotherapies that specifically aim to stop addictions. Everyone knows that it costs far more to treat the medical and social complications of an addiction than to treat the addiction itself. So the first step is to try a drug-free treatment.

If therapy does not work, treatment with one of the drugs listed in this chapter, under the supervision of a qualified doctor, is worth trying. The following strategies are useful:

1. **Alcohol:** Be sure the problem is not an underlying psychiatric disturbance, for example, depression or panic disorder, which should be treated with the proper antidepressant or antianxiety drug. Librium or Ativan may be prescribed for a few days to block withdrawal symptoms. Chronic alcoholics may have to be admitted to the hospital for detoxification, because sudden discontinuation of alcohol can produce life-threatening withdrawal symptoms. Then, consider Antabuse treatment. Always join AA.

2. **Cocaine:** Be sure that the problem is not an underlying psychiatric disturbance, for example, depression or panic disorder, which should be treated with the proper antidepressant or antianxiety drug. Imipramine or desipramine may block the cocaine high. Other drugs, such as buprenorphin, are currently being developed to treat cocaine addiction. Always obtain psychotherapy.

3. **Heroin:** Clonidine is given to block the withdrawal symptoms. Then, naltrexone is administered to block the high from heroin. Alternatively, methadone maintenance mimics the action of heroin without incurring most of the medical and social risks. Methadone-maintained patients can then be switched to clonidine for detoxification.

4. **Cigarettes:** Clonidine may be prescribed to block the severe nicotine craving often experienced during the first few weeks after quitting. During this period, Nicorette chewing gum may be used

to mimic the effects of cigarette smoking with far fewer health risks. Also, be sure that there is no underlying psychiatric disturbance, for example, depression or anxiety, which is producing the need for cigarettes. Nicorette gum is discontinued after a few weeks.

Until more is learned about the causes of addiction, it will fail to be stopped in many cases. Combinations of therapy and medication have saved many people. The following information on the specific drugs used to treat drug abuse should be useful to addicts and to people who care about addicts.

CHLORDIAZEPOXIDE

Brand Name: Librium.
Used for: Blocking the withdrawal symptoms after stopping alcohol.
Note: Librium is one of the many drugs in the benzodiazepine class of antianxiety agents, which are described in detail in Chapter 8. Although Librium has traditionally been used by doctors to prevent serious alcohol withdrawal symptoms, like (delirium tremens), any of the benzodiazepines can be used for this. Ativan is also frequently prescribed.
Do Not Use if: You are not serious about stopping drinking. Alcoholics are at very high risk of getting hooked on Librium. It should be given only for a few days to prevent the serious withdrawal reactions like seizures and heart failure. Librium is not to be taken along with alcohol.
Tests to Take First: Your doctor will do many medical tests as part of the alcohol withdrawal process, including blood tests to determine how much damage alcohol has done to your liver. You will also be given the vitamins and minerals that alcohol usually depletes from the body.
Tests to Take While You Are on It: During alcohol withdrawal, it is important that your pulse, blood pressure, and temperature be checked frequently. Rapid pulse, high blood pressure, and fever are signs that serious and potentially life-threatening alcohol withdrawal reactions may be about to start.
Usual Dose: In many situations, it is best to have a brief admission to the hospital for alcohol detoxification. The first dose of Librium

(50 or 100 mg) is given intramuscularly or intravenously (directly into the vein). Then, 50 or 100 mg is given by mouth every three hours to a maximum of 300 mg per day. The key is to keep agitation to a minimum.

How Long Until It Works: The treatment takes effect immediately. The patient should be relatively sedated and calm throughout detoxification.

Common Side Effects: There are no side effects to the use of Librium in alcohol detoxification. Too much Librium may make the patient too sleepy, but this is probably desirable.

Less Common Side Effects: There is a very small chance that such drugs as Librium, when given intravenously, will cause a temporary (a few minutes) decrease in breathing. Very rarely, the patient actually stops breathing. For this reason, of course, intravenous drugs are only given to patients in the hospital. A doctor or nurse is present when the dose is given, and if a breathing problem develops, a bag is placed over the patient's nose and mouth and air is pumped in by hand for a few minutes. This may sound frightening, but it is actually a very simple procedure (much less complicated than administration of anesthesia during surgery). After a few minutes the patient starts breathing regularly again.

What to Do About Side Effects: If the patient is too sleepy, the dose of Librium is reduced or the interval between doses is extended to more than three hours.

If It Doesn't Work: This is very rare. If given properly, Librium and related benzodiazepines almost always block serious withdrawal symptoms of alcohol detoxification. Sometimes, however, seizures occur even with Librium protection; then, anticonvulsants, for example, Dilantin and phenobarbital, are given.

If It Does Work: The treatment usually lasts about three days. During this time, the dose is gradually decreased and the intervals between doses are increased. At the end of three days, Librium is stopped.

Special Comments: Alcohol withdrawal is very serious. Unlike the situation that results when benzodiazepine use is stopped, patients die during alcohol detoxification. Immediately after abrupt discontinuation of alcohol, many patients become agitated and develop fever, high blood pressure, and rapid pulse. Some hear voices (hallucinations) and have seizures. In delirium tremens, the patient develops severe agitation and hallucinations and signs of hyperactivity of the nervous system. At one time, this medical emergency proved to be fatal in many cases. Use of drugs like Librium now makes this a very treatable condition. A long-term alcoholic ready to quit should be cared for by a physician knowledgeable about alcohol detoxification and withdrawal.

DISULFIRAM

Brand Name: Antabuse.
Used for: Motivating an alcoholic to stop drinking. Drinking while on Antabuse causes a severe and very unpleasant physical reaction.
Do Not Use if: You are not completely serious about stopping drinking and are not ready to begin an alcohol treatment program like AA; you have almost any serious medical problem, for example, heart disease, diabetes, epilepsy, kidney disease, liver disease, and thyroid disease; you are taking other medications, unless your doctor determines that these other drugs do not interact badly with Antabuse; you abuse any drugs besides alcohol, like barbiturates; you have had a drink in the last twelve hours.
Tests to Take First: A complete medical evaluation is necessary, including physical examination, blood tests, urine tests, and an electrocardiogram.
Tests to Take While You Are on It: None are automatically necessary, but your doctor may want to order various blood tests if there is any suspicion that Antabuse is causing side effects.
Usual Dose: First, you must not have ingested alcohol for at least twelve hours. This means alcohol in any form, including cough medicine, mouthwash, sauces, after shave lotion, and back rubs. Then, a dose of 500 mg is given every morning for one to two weeks. Antabuse can also be taken at night if you feel it makes you sleepy during the day. After two weeks, the dose is often cut back to 250 mg.
How Long Until It Works: Immediately. After the first dose of Antabuse you should not ingest alcohol in any form, for example, sauces containing wines and desserts containing liqueurs. If you do, you will develop a violent physical reaction that includes severe

nausea and vomiting, headache, flushing, dizziness, low blood pressure, and rapid heart rate. This can be dangerous, especially if you have a preexisting medical condition, such as heart disease. In many ways, the persons on Antabuse must follow as strict a diet as that followed by persons taking monoamine oxidase inhibitors. Many alcoholics on Antabuse are tempted to try drinking because they don't believe they will actually have these reactions; they are very used to people trying to scare them about the dangers of drinking. **Don't give in to the temptation to drink while on Antabuse.** If you cannot stay away from drinking, do not take Antabuse.

Common Side Effects: There are no common side effects, but some of the less common side effects are serious.

Less Common Side Effects: (1) Neuritis—inflammation of nerves causing pain and difficulty with vision. (2) Liver problems like hepatitis. (3) skin rashes. (4) Drowsiness, headache, impotence, and a bad taste in the mouth; these usually go away after the first two weeks of treatment. (5) Psychosis.

What to Do About Side Effects: Some side effects, like neuritis, psychosis, and hepatitis, are reason to stop the medication immediately. Antihistamines can be given for rashes. The side effects of drowsiness, headache, impotence, and bad taste usually go away on their own. Sometimes, reduction of the dose is necessary.

If It Doesn't Work: If you cannot stay away from drinking, do not take Antabuse. Antabuse works only for the motivated alcoholic who needs the extra impetus of a physical threat to keep from drinking. If you aren't ready to stop drinking completely, you should not take Antabuse. Try Alcoholics Anonymous and other alcohol treatment programs first.

If It Does Work: You may stay on Antabuse as long as you feel you need to. Some patients take it for months or even years. It is hoped that at some point you will feel that you have enough will power to not drink without Antabuse.

Cost: Brand, 53 cents/250-mg pill. Generic, 7 cents/250-mg pill.

Special Comments: Very few doctors prescribe Antabuse anymore. Most of us have learned that a highly motivated alcoholic will stop drinking without the threat of physical harm that Antabuse presents. On the other hand, less highly motivated alcoholics should not be given Antabuse, because the physical reaction is very extreme and sometimes dangerous. Nevertheless, the occasional alcoholic who decides that Antabuse will help his resolve should be allowed to try it. These people should carry a card in their wallet or wear a Medic-Alert bracelet that identifies them as on Antabuse.

CLONIDINE

Brand Name: Catapres.

Used for: Blocking the craving for a cigarette. Blocking withdrawal after discontinuation of heroin or methadone.

Do Not Use if: You have heart disease, unless your doctor tells you it is okay.

Tests to Take First: Clonidine is most commonly used to lower blood pressure in patients with high blood pressure, so it is a good idea to have your blood pressure recorded before starting treatment.

Tests to Take While You Are on It: Blood pressure should be checked every few days during programs to stop cigarette smoking and every day during heroin detoxification.

Usual Dose: The use of clonidine to help people to stop smoking is a relatively recent development. It is safe and probably helpful, but further testing is required. Smokers are usually given a dose of 0.05 mg a day to start. This can be increased by one pill a day to four to six pills daily (0.2–0.3 mg). To block withdrawal symptoms after discontinuation of heroin or methadone, the patient is usually started at 0.1 to 0.3 mg a day three times daily. After two days, the dose is reduced; the patient is treated for a total of one to two weeks.

How Long Until It Works: After the first dose, cigarette smokers may report a reduced "physical" craving for a cigarette. In other words, they still think a cigarette would be nice to have, but they don't get shaky and *crave* one. For heroin addicts who stop shooting up and go on clonidine in a one- to two-week detoxification program, many of the physical withdrawal symptoms—tremors, yawning, sweating, and rapid pulse—are blocked after the first few doses. The patient usually still has a psychological temptation to get heroin. Many heroin addicts are first placed on methadone and then switched to clonidine. Clonidine then blocks the symptoms of withdrawal from

299

methadone, which are much the same as those of withdrawal from heroin.

Common Side Effects: Sedation, drowsiness, dry mouth, and lightheadedness, the latter caused by the lowering of blood pressure.

Less Common Side Effects: Very few. Rarely, nausea and vomiting, skin rash, and a feeling of physical weakness.

What to Do About Side Effects: Some amount of sedation may not be so bad, especially for an addict trying to withdraw from heroin. Reducing the dose usually reverses sedation and low blood pressure.

If It Doesn't Work: (1) Cigarette smoking—it is not yet known how many people can be helped to stop smoking with clonidine. Hence, if it does not work, you will have to try the old-fashioned remedy—willpower.

(2) Heroin detoxification—clonidine is used to block withdrawal symptoms after stopping heroin. It is also used to block withdrawal symptoms after stopping methadone, the drug given to replace heroin for many addicts. If clonidine does not block withdrawal symptoms sufficiently and the patient feels she must have something, she is usually placed back on methadone.

If It Does Work: Patients who are trying to stop smoking are usually treated for one or two weeks. After that, most smokers no longer crave cigarettes and most heroin addicts no longer have withdrawal symptoms. Cigarette smokers may still feel tempted to smoke and should maintain their willpower. Heroin addicts will probably need long-term psychological treatment to prevent relapse.

Cost: Brand, 42 cents/0.1-mg pill. Generic, 3 cents/0.1-mg pill.

Special Comments: Clonidine has been prescribed for many years for treatment of high blood pressure. More recently, it was discovered to block the excess nervous system excitement that occurs when people suddenly stop using substances to which they are addicted. Clonidine is now an established component of detoxification programs for heroin addicts. It is also being tested to help cigarette smokers as well. It is a very safe treatment, although too great a reduction of blood pressure can produce the uncomfortable side effects of dizziness and lightheadedness. Elderly people should use clonidine only under a physician's strict supervision, because these side effects can result in falls.

NICORETTE GUM

Used for: Substitute for cigarette smoking.

Do Not Use if: You continue to smoke, you have serious heart disease, or you are pregnant.

Tests to Take First: None required.

Tests to Take While You Are on It: None required.

Usual Dose: Chew one piece slowly when you feel like having a cigarette. Do not exceed thirty pieces a day.

Common Side Effects: Dizziness, nausea and vomiting, stomachache, mouth or throat soreness, aching jaw, hiccups.

Less Common Side Effects: Insomnia, headache, decreased appetite, increased salivation.

What to Do About Side Effects: Most side effects are caused by chewing Nicorette gum too fast. Chew slowly, stopping every few seconds for a brief rest.

If It Doesn't Work: Keep trying. You can't do anything much better for yourself than to quit smoking. You can stay on Nicorette for up to six months.

If It Does Work: After you have used the gum without smoking for three months, try stopping the gum. You may be free from nicotine forever!

Cost: Brand, $29.40/96 pieces. Generic, not available.

Special Comments: If you cannot quit smoking without help, try Nicorette with your doctor's supervision. It doesn't work for everyone, but it is worth a shot.

NALTREXONE

Brand Name: Trexan.

Used for: Blocking the high from heroin.

Do Not Use if: You are not serious about stopping use of heroin or you have liver disease.

Tests to Take First: Blood tests for liver problems are necessary. Because you should not start naltrexone until at least a week has passed since you used heroin, a blood or urine test is required to confirm the absence of heroin in your body.

Tests to Take While You Are on It: Blood tests to confirm that naltrexone is not hurting your liver should be done periodically.

Usual Dose: Treatment is not begun until the patient has been off heroin at least one week. This fact is often confirmed by obtaining a blood or urine test. Then, 50 mg can be given every day to block the high from heroin. Because naltrexone has a very long length of action, many patients eventually take it only three times a week. One schedule, 100 mg on Monday and Wednesday and 150 mg on Friday, seems to offer sufficient blockade.

How Long Until It Works: The effect is immediate. If, after taking naltrexone, a patient shoots up with heroin, he will not get high. This quickly discourages the patient from shooting up.

Common Side Effects: Nervousness, insomnia, low energy, headache, joint and muscle pain, nausea and vomiting, difficulty ejaculating, impotence, dizziness, diarrhea, constipation, rash, increased thirst, decreased appetite, and chills.

Less Common Side Effects: If a person is mistakenly prescribed naltrexone while she is still addicted to heroin, she will experience an acute withdrawal syndrome. In other words, naltrexone will suddenly block all of heroin's effect and the patient will be in the same boat as if she had suddenly stopped heroin. The withdrawal syndrome includes tremors, sweating, shaking, runny nose, tearing, and rapid pulse.

What to Do About Side Effects: The abrupt withdrawal syndrome induced by mistakenly prescribing naltrexone to someone still addicted to heroin can be treated with methadone or, in some cases, with clonidine. It is best to wait a week before trying naltrexone again. The common side effects are not dangerous and may subside in time on their own. In actual practice, few former heroin addicts are very bothered by the side effects of naltrexone.

If It Doesn't Work: Patients who cannot stop injecting heroin even though they are taking naltrexone to block the high should probably be placed on methadone.

If It Does Work: Treatment can continue indefinitely, although liver problems can rarely occur which warrant stopping naltrexone. It is hoped that psychological treatments will work so that the patient can ultimately stop naltrexone without returning to heroin.

Cost: Brand, $4.18/50-mg pill. Generic, not available.

Special Comments: Naltrexone treatment requires a motivated heroin addict who really wants to quit. It is easy to stop taking naltrexone at any time and start injecting heroin again. After about a week off naltrexone, the effects wear off and the addict is able to get high again. Naltrexone treatment is promising but, unfortunately, has not really made a big dent in the number of people who continue to use heroin. Naltrexone is very expensive, but usually is not taken on a daily basis.

METHADONE

Brand Name: Dolophine.

Used for: Substitution for heroin in long-term maintenance treatment. Methadone is also sometimes used for severe pain in patients with cancer and other serious medical problems.

Do Not Use if: You have serious respiratory (breathing) disease. Some people with thyroid, liver, and kidney disease, Addison's disease, an enlarged prostate gland, or other serious medical problems also should not take methadone. Of course, they should not take heroin either, and there is almost no situation in which remaining on heroin is better than taking methadone.

Tests to Take First: A complete physical examination and routine blood tests should be done.

Tests to Take While You Are on It: At least once a year most patients on methadone are required to have a physical examination and routine blood tests.

Usual Dose: Dosage varies greatly and is controversial. Most patients are started at 20 mg a day. The dose is increased to the point where the patient has no withdrawal symptoms and no desire to take heroin. Some patients take as much as 80 to 100 mg per day in a single dose.

How Long Until It Works: After the first dose or two of methadone, the patient should feel little desire to take heroin.

Common Side Effects: Most side effects wear off in time. These include lightheadedness, dizziness, sedation, nausea, vomiting, and sweating.

Less Common Side Effects: These occur mostly in people who also have other medical problems and include respiratory and heart problems.

What to Do About Side Effects: The more common side effects usually go away in time. Reducing the dose may help. Less common—and more serious—side effects almost always require reduction of the dose or even discontinuation of methadone.

If It Doesn't Work: It often doesn't. Many heroin addicts drop out of methadone programs and return to heroin. An equally serious problem is the shortage of methadone clinics in large cities in the United States. Most heroin addicts cannot get into methadone treatment because of the long waiting lists.

If It Does Work: Being on methadone is always superior to injecting heroin. Some patients stay on methadone the rest of their lives. Many attempt to get off methadone, often by taking clonidine to block withdrawal symptoms (see earlier in this chapter) and then naltrexone to block the heroin high (see earlier in this chapter).

Cost: Brand, 11 cents/10-mg pill. Generic, 9 cents/10-mg pill.

Special Comments: By taking methadone every day, a heroin addict loses the need or desire to take heroin. Methadone is much safer than heroin; AIDS or heart infections cannot be contracted by drinking methadone, as they can by injecting heroin. Methadone is also safer for society: heroin addicts must often engage in criminal activities to obtain heroin; methadone is legally available from special clinics and can be given free of charge to indigent patients. As methadone can also be abused and sold on the street, methadone clinics have strict regulations controlling the dispensing of methadone. By law, most methadone clinics offer counseling to their patients and always attempt to get them off all drugs. Methadone maintenance is often successful and certainly superior to heroin injection.

IMIPRAMINE

Brand Name: Tofranil.
Used for: Blocking the high from cocaine.
Note: Imipramine (Tofranil) is one of the class of drugs called cyclic antidepressants, which are described in more detail in Chapter 7. Desipra-

mine is another cyclic antidepressant that may be useful in treating cocaine addicts.

Do Not Use if: You have narrow-angle glaucoma; you have an enlarged prostate; you have epilepsy (seizures), unless your doctor determines that you are properly treated; or you have a heart condition, unless your doctor determines from the electrocardiogram that it is okay.

Tests to Take First: For patients over 50, an electrocardiogram to rule out a rare heart problem should be done first.

Tests to Take While You Are on It: None required.

Usual Dose: Dose is still being worked out, but up to 300 mg a day may be necessary to block the cocaine high. Most patients are started on much lower doses, about 50 mg a day, and worked up to the 200 to 300 mg a day range over two to three weeks.

How Long Until It Works: The effect may take several weeks. After that, some cocaine patients report less craving for cocaine or failure to get high if they do use cocaine. With the high blocked, the addict has less motivation to use cocaine.

Common Side Effects: Dry mouth, dizziness after getting up fast, constipation, difficulty urinating, weight gain, increased sensitivity to the sun (see Chapter 7 for complete details).

Less Common Side Effects: Problems with heart rhythm, confusion (especially in the elderly), seizures, blurred vision, and loss of menstrual period (see Chapter 7 for complete details).

What to Do About Side Effects: (See Chapter 7 for details.) Most of the side effects are annoying rather than dangerous and go away in a few weeks. There are a variety of antidotes to some of the side effects. Patients over 50 should have an electrocardiogram periodically.

If It Doesn't Work: This would not be surprising. Good treatments to stop cocaine use are still lacking, which is why cocaine addiction has become such a serious problem in the United States. Use of imipramine or desipramine to block the cocaine high probably works in only a small percentage of patients.

If It Does Work: It is not yet known how long treatment for cocaine abuse with imipramine or desipramine should last—probably at least until the patient feels she is under control and can resist the temptation to take cocaine.

Special Comments: Cocaine can be snorted or injected. A very addicting and potent form of cocaine, called "crack," is usually smoked. Cocaine produces a very powerful and immediate high, which disappears in minutes. Once patients are hooked, they may have an unbearable craving for more cocaine several times a day. Unless they get more cocaine they suffer severe withdrawal, involving mostly a psychological feeling of extreme depression and fear. There is some evidence that imipramine and desipramine block the high; therefore, a person who is motivated to stop cocaine may find these drugs helpful. At best, this partial solution probably helps no more than 20% to 30% of cocaine abusers. One of the biggest public health needs in this country today is a treatment for cocaine abuse.

Part III

SPECIAL TOPICS ABOUT PSYCHIATRIC DRUGS

13. Treating the Violent Patient   309
14. Family, Environment, and Genetics   315
15. Weight Loss and Weight Gain   323
16. Sex and Psychiatric Drugs   331
17. Treating the Elderly   337
18. Psychiatric Drugs and Pregnancy   345
19. AIDS: Dealing with Psychiatric Problems   351
20. Generic Versus Brand: What's in a Name?   359
21. How Psychiatric Drugs Work   365

Chapter 13

Treating the Violent Patient

It is a popular notion, perpetuated by television and the movies, that people with psychiatric illnesses are violent and dangerous.

For the most part, this view is absolutely false.

Certainly, the vast majority of patients with depression, bipolar depression, and anxiety disorder are no more violent, and probably less so, than anyone else. There are a few psychiatric syndromes associated with violence, although violence among psychiatric patients is not nearly as common as we are often lead to believe.

Certain forms of schizophrenia may predispose people to violence. Paranoid schizophrenic patients—those schizophrenics who develop delusional ideas that people are out to harm them—may feel threatened and believe they need to defend themselves by violent means, as in this example:

Roger, a 22-year-old chronic schizophrenic patient, decided to stop taking his antipsychotic medication one day. Three days later he began to feel that people on the street were talking about him. Then, he became convinced that his next-door neighbor had been hired by the Mafia to kill him. He attempted to avoid the neighbor, but voices told him the neighbor was about to shoot him. One afternoon he saw the neighbor in the lobby of his apartment building. When the neighbor put his hand in his pocket, Roger was sure he was reaching for a gun to shoot him. Roger suddenly screamed and threw a small table in the lobby at the neighbor, then ran out the door into the street. Once in the street, he began screaming for police and throwing garbage cans at the door of the apartment building, hoping to hit his neighbor in case he ran out after him. Police were indeed called and they immediately restrained Roger and brought him to the emergency room.

Roger's violent behavior was motivated by fear, not a real or malicious desire to hurt anyone. Schizophrenics do not routinely plot murders and are not vicious. They should not be shunned on the false belief that they are all killers.

Direct injury to specific regions of the brain and some types of neurological illness can unleash violence, although this is not common. A form of epilepsy variously called temporal lobe epilepsy, psychomotor epilepsy, and partial complex seizures (the official name used by neurologists) is sometimes cited as a cause of violent behavior. Patients with this type of epilepsy are said to commit violent acts as part of an involuntary seizure. This behavior has never been well documented and if true must be extremely rare. Most patients with temporal lobe epilepsy engage in purposeless behavior of a nonviolent nature during seizures.

The next example is of violent behavior that is the direct result of brain injury:

Jonathan was a hard-working electrician, devoted father of three children, and regular churchgoer until one fateful day when he tried to change a tire on his car. While kneeling next to the tire to remove the bolts, the car suddenly fell off the jack, propelling the tip of the jack handle directly into Jonathan's head. He was knocked unconscious, bleeding severely, and rushed by ambulance to the hospital. Miraculously, he survived the injury, but two days after regaining consciousness a marked disturbance in his behavior became apparent. The formerly mild-mannered Jonathan began using profane language, screaming at people, and throwing things around the room. He violently attacked a nurse's aid. Eventually, he was transferred to the psychiatric unit for management of his violent behavior.

310

Sometimes, a psychiatric illness is used as an excuse to commit a violent crime. A person who can convince a judge or jury that she is "insane" by virtue of brain damage, drug abuse, or psychosis may not be held criminally responsible for her crimes. Obviously, this book is not the place to debate this point. I merely want to reiterate the point that psychiatric illness is rarely the cause of violence. Psychiatric patients have enough stigma with which to deal.

Drug abuse is probably the only psychiatric condition that regularly produces violence, for two reasons. First, drug addicts are so desparate to get drugs that they often commit acts of violence to obtain the money to buy drugs. Second, drugs like cocaine and amphetamines produce violent feelings in patients, and drugs like heroin and alcohol may unleash violent feelings that are already there but usually under control. Unlike schizophrenic patients, a person driven crazy by cocaine may carefully plot a violent crime to get the money for drugs.

MEDICATIONS FOR VIOLENCE

In some instances, medications are needed to treat violent behavior when it is caused by a mental disturbance, as in these situations:

Agitated Schizophrenic Patients

Antipsychotic medication should be given as soon as possible to the agitated schizophrenic patient, by injection if the patient will not take the medicine by mouth. Many civil libertarians and patients' rights advocates have correctly questioned administration of antipsychotic drugs to patients against their will. Almost everybody agrees, however, that in the face of a dangerously violent situation, medication should be given immediately. It is not doing the patient any favor to let him continue being violent. Schizophrenics become violent when they feel threatened and this is almost always a treatable condition. All the drugs used are described in detail in Chapter 10.

Brain-Damaged Patients

In the acute, emergency situation, the antipsychotic drugs are appropriate to stop violent behavior in a patient with brain damage. If it is determined that the violence is actually part of a seizure, anticonvulsant medication is given. For longer-term management of chronic violent eruptions in patients with brain damage, especially in cases in which antipsychotic medications do not work sufficiently to control violence, many other drugs have been tried. These include anticonvulsants (Tegretol and Dilantin), lithium, and propranolol. Propranolol (Inderal) can be especially valuable. Its use in treating violence was pioneered by Dr. Stuart Yudofsky. Propranolol is usually given to treat such medical conditions as high blood pressure, angina, and migraine headaches. It has been observed that propranolol, often in very high doses (more than 320 mg and as high as 1,000 mg a day) reduces violent behavior in brain-damaged patients. It can be given in combination with antipsychotic drugs like Thorazine or Haldol. Blood pressure and pulse must be carefully monitored because propranolol lowers both.

Drug Abusers

The situation of the drug abuser is very difficult because drugs that produce violence often interact badly with drugs used to control violence. Cocaine, amphetamines, and Angel Dust (phencyclidine, PCP) can induce a violent state. This state can be treated with antipsychotic drugs, but should be done in an emergency room under careful medical supervision. The best treatment for violence in a drug abuser is physical restraint until the effects of the abused drug have worn off.

A few tips to family members: If your son, daughter, husband, wife, or other relative has a psychiatric problem and becomes violent you should almost always call the police or an ambulance. It is very easy to say the wrong thing to a psychotic patient and make her even more frightened and confused. Psychosis, by its very nature, makes a person difficult to reason with and resistant to logic.

312

In a psychotic state a frightened patient can be unbelievably strong: he truly believes that his life is threatened and that everybody, even his closest relatives, are enemies. As difficult as it may be, it is best to get help quickly.

Also, *do not let your love for your relative stand in the way of quick and effective treatment.* Violent patients can hurt people and can themselves be hurt. It is best to allow trained people to restrain and medicate a violent patient quickly. There will be plenty of time, after the acute situation is resolved, to decide calmly on a proper course of treatment.

Finally, even in a person with a clear-cut diagnosis of schizophrenia or other mental disorder, always suspect alcohol or drug abuse if violence suddenly becomes a problem. Schizophrenic patients tolerate alcohol, cocaine, and heroin especially badly and are very prone to lose control when intoxicated.

Most violence does not involve psychiatric patients and should be taken care of by police and courts, not psychiatrists. A rapid response, however, to a psychiatric patient who is out of control with physical restraint and medication is both humane and effective.

Chapter 14

Family, Environment, and Genetics

A mother came to see me about her 35-year-old daughter. For about two years I had been treating her daughter with lithium for bipolar affective illness (formerly called manic-depressive illness). Recently, the daughter had developed a mild depression despite the lithium treatment and I had prescribed an antidepressant as well. The mother was very concerned.

"Does this mean she is getting worse and lithium won't help anymore?" she asked me.

"No," I answered. "It is very common for lithium-treated patients to develop occasional breakthrough depressions. If treated quickly enough, these depressions usually resolve without any serious consequences. I do not think it means the lithium has stopped working."

"That's good to know. Is there anything we, my husband and I, should be doing? I mean, we never know whether to leave her alone when she gets depressed or urge her to go out and do things. Sometimes it's very frustrating when all she wants to do is stay in bed. And should we say anything about her weight? She's gained a lot since you put her on lithium."

These are all very common questions from family members of patients with psychiatric illness. Here was my answer:

"The most important thing is not to get angry at your daughter and make her feel you blame her for her problems. You have been very supportive in the past and I think part of the reason she has done so well is the way you have treated her with respect and encouragement. When people get depressed it's natural that they don't feel like doing things and sometimes they really can't. So I wouldn't go overboard pushing her. Try to help her do the things that are essential and leave it at that. When the depression is over she will pick up on her own. The weight gain troubles me too. It is a side effect of lithium, and also, depressed patients sometimes overeat. Right now I wouldn't make a big deal about it, but when her depression resolves, I definitely think we should encourage her to go on a diet."

Then the mother asked me the question that is probably on the mind of every parent of a patient with psychiatric illness.

"Doctor, how did she get to be this way in the first place? Do you think it is because I had to go back to work when she was 2? I think we always had good babysitters, but I wasn't home all day. My husband might have been a little gruff with the children in those days. He is really a good father, but you know how it is. He was just starting his business when my daughter was born, and at first it didn't go so well. Maybe he wasn't, you know, emotional enough with her. Could that do it?"

This kind of question breaks my heart. People have been brainwashed into believing that parents are responsible for mental illness. So mothers and fathers carry a tremendous burden of guilt and shame when their children require psychiatric care.

I explained what we know about the roots of mental illness to my patient's mother. "We really do not know what causes any psychiatric illness. That's what the research is aimed at right now. There are a few things you should know. First, if working mothers and less than the most gushingly emotional fathers were the cause of mental illness, about half the world's population would be seeing psychiatrists right now. From what I have heard from you and your daughter, you were as good parents as most and the things you mentioned are not the cause of mental illness. It is possible that an abnormal

316

gene causes some forms of psychiatric illness and there is even some evidence for that with the specific problem your daughter has. But for all we know, it might be a virus, a toxin in the air, or just bad luck. I think bad parents can make mental illnesses worse and good parents can help make them a lot better, but parents don't cause schizophrenia, bipolar illness, serious depression, or panic attacks."

Did the mother feel relieved by my answer? Only partially. She felt better to know that I don't blame her and that scientists do not believe that bad parenting causes psychiatric illness. But do most of her friends and acquaintances know that? Or will she feel blamed by the people with which she ordinarily comes into contact?

Furthermore, I could not give her a definite answer. I could not say, "your daughter's illness is the result of a childhood viral infection that affected her brain." People are most reassured when they know the cause of an illness. Vague answers—the only kind that can honestly be given in psychiatry—are only partially helpful.

GENES AND MENTAL ILLNESS

Do genes cause psychiatric illness? There is good reason to think so, at least in part. The first step in determining whether a particular disease, psychiatric or otherwise, is inherited is to see whether it runs in families. In so-called "family history" studies, a group of patients with a disorder is selected along with a group of people without the disorder. The latter group is called the "normal controls." Then the history of psychiatric illnesses in first-degree relatives of the patients and of the normal controls is ascertained, either by asking the patients and control subjects about their families or, even better, by interviewing family members directly.

Through these studies, it was determined that such psychiatric disorders as schizophrenia, bipolar affective illnesses, serious (major) depression, panic disorder, obsessive-compulsive disorder, and alcoholism clearly run in families. These disorders occurred in more relatives of patients than in relatives of normal subjects.

Nevertheless, this only tells us that if a parent has a psychiatric condition there is a greater likelihood that his or her children will have it also. Is that because an abnormal gene is passed down or because the children learn to adopt the parent's behavior? Is it nature (genes) or nurture (the experience of being raised by a parent with a psychiatric condition)?

One way to try and tease this apart is to look at psychiatric conditions in twins. There are two types of twins: identical twins (scientists call them monozygotic) have the same genes; fraternal twins (called dizygotic) share the same genes as do ordinary brothers and sisters. In other words, monozygotic twins are genetically identical, and dizygotic twins are genetically similar.

If a disease is truly genetic, if one identical twin has it the other twin should also have it, because they have the same genes. On the other hand, if one fraternal twin has the disease the other fraternal twin need not also have it, because they may not have both inherited the abnormal gene. Scientists say that if a disease is genetic, the "concordance" rate should be higher for monozygotic twins than for dizygotic twins.

One excellent place to study twins is in the Scandanavian countries where very complete health records, including twin registries, are maintained. By studying the inheritance of psychiatric conditions in twins from these countries, it has been shown that schizophrenia, bipolar affective illness, and panic disorder are probably, at least in part, genetic illnesses. I say in part because genes do not explain all cases of these disorders.

Now, there exist even more powerful scientific methods for determining whether a disease is genetic. These methods involve molecular biology, a field that opened up with the discovery in 1953 by Watson and Crick of DNA, the genetic molecule. Molecular biology is a very complex field and I will not try to describe it in detail here. Basically, scientists can now take DNA from blood cells, chop it up in test tubes, and find out whether people with a particular illness have a similar DNA pattern. By doing this, it is possible to determine on which of the twenty-three human chromosomes an abnormal gene for a given disorder resides.

Using molecular biology, scientists localized the gene for the neuropsychiatric disorder Huntington's disease to chromosome 4. They have also found that part of the cause of the dementing disease of the elderly called Alzheimer's disease is probably a gene on chromosome 21.

There is now also evidence that some other psychiatric illnesses may be associated with abnormal genes. One group, studying Amish families, found evidence that bipolar affective disorder may be associated with chromosome 11, although follow-up studies have failed to confirm this finding. Another group, working in Israel, linked bipolar illness to the X chromosome, one of the two chromosomes that determines sex. It is possible, indeed very likely, that both groups are correct and that there are different genetic routes to bipolar illness.

An English group found a link between schizophrenia and a gene on chromosome 5. Further study is required before this finding is deemed correct.

All of this work, which has occurred with remarkable speed, has the field of psychiatry at a high pitch of excitement. Molecular biology is now one of the top priorities of the National Institute of Mental Health's research program. There is good reason to expect that within the next decade, genes responsible for specific mental illnesses will be located.

Once a gene is located, it is not a long road before it is known what the abnormal gene does. It may make an abnormal substance that produces the illness or it may be unable to make a necessary substance that normal genes make. This leads to obvious attempts to treat genetic mental illness either by blocking the action of abnormal genes or by giving patients necessary substances that abnormal genes fail to produce.

Genetics clearly will not provide all the answers. Even in those conditions that we are pretty certain have a genetic basis, like schizophrenia, we sometimes find that only one member of an identical twin pair is affected. How did the other member escape the illness? One possibility is that he does have the abnormal gene but for some reason it is not expressed. Another possibility is that to get the disease, there must be a combination of abnormal genes and other factors. These other factors could be viruses, poisons, or stress. Obviously, we have a long way to go before we know how all these factors come together to produce an illness.

BLAMING GENES FOR EVERYTHING

With all the emphasis on genes and biology in psychiatric research, some people wonder if family and environment are ever factors in psychiatric illness. In some situations, it may truly be harmful to blame everything on biology. A good example occurred to me after reading a very sad story in the newspaper.

A mother and father were suing the local school system for negligence. Their teenage son had recently committed suicide. The parents claimed that the school should have known their son was depressed and gotten help for him. After reading the story, I wondered if the parents believed that the school personnel should have known their child better than they did? Didn't they notice their son was depressed? Should families be entirely "off the hook" for psychiatric problems?

I can only offer my own opinion. The major psychiatric illnesses like schizophrenia, bipolar affective illness, major depression, panic disorder, alcoholism, and obsessive-compulsive disorder probably have genetic roots. Without an abnormal gene I do not think it is possible to develop these conditions.

But stress, including a poor home environment while growing up, can probably influence the degree to which these abnormal genes are expressed. And this must vary from illness to illness. Schizophrenia is probably among the least influenced by stress. Warm, supportive treatment will make the life of a schizophrenic easier, but I do not think it can prevent or cure the illness. The same seems to be true of bipolar illness. On the other hand, a good childhood with relatively little stress may prevent a person with a gene for alcoholism from becoming an alcoholic.

Certainly, the burden remains on family members to recognize a psychiatric problem promptly so that it can be treated. Depression may not be preventable, but suicide almost always is if the depressed patient receives prompt and humane care.

Parents should not feel guilty or ashamed if their children develop psychiatric problems. They should not believe they are bad parents or made horrible mistakes; however, they are responsible for getting their children help and for giving them as much support and encouragement as possible. Until the exact causes of mental illness are known and the cures are found, family members will continue to be the psychiatrist's most powerful allies in treatment.

Chapter 15

Weight Loss and Weight Gain

While reading through the side effects caused by psychiatric drugs, you may have noticed that one side effect crops up unusually often—weight gain. This side effect is a plague for psychiatric patients and their doctors. Often, it seems that just when everyone is happy with the way a drug is working and the patient is ready to resume life, someone notices the patient is gaining weight.

At first, it may not appear to be a major problem. During the acute part of a psychiatric illness, many patients lose their appetite, stop eating, and lose weight. So the first few pounds gained may seem like a breakthrough, a simple return of healthy appetite and eating habits.

Soon, however, the patient realizes that he is continuing to gain weight without seeming to eat all that much extra. Often, doctors fail to realize this weight gain as a side effect of the drug and mistakenly tell the patient he *must* be eating more. "Stop eating cake and cookies," the doctor pompously insists, "and the weight will disappear."

So the patient stops eating dessert, but the weight gain continues.

Soon, the patient believes the treatment is worse than the disease. Everyone accuses the patient of being a glutton.

DRUGS CAUSE WEIGHT GAIN

The fact is that many psychiatric drugs—including most antidepressants, lithium, and most drugs for psychosis—cause weight gain. We really do not understand why. As it turns out, however, we understand a lot less about obesity in general than we once thought.

Physicians, nutritionists, and scientists used to insist that how much a person weighed was almost entirely a function of how much she ate and how much she exercised, with an emphasis on the former. The more calories consumed, the more weight gained. Vigorous exercise burns calories and eliminates a few pounds, but not enough to offset a high caloric intake. So overweight people were told it was all up to them; diet and exercise or your fatness is your fault.

Things are not so simple. Evidence now exists suggesting that weight is in part determined by *metabolic rate,* the rate at which the body burns calories and uses exercise. Each person apparently has a specific set point for weight, something akin to body temperature. A regulator, probably located in the part of the brain called the hypothalamus, controls how fast the body uses calories in almost the same way that body temperature is maintained at 98.6 degrees.

Overeating will absolutely cause weight gain. Decreasing calories causes weight loss. Below a certain point, however, scientists now believe, the hypothalamus will not permit any further burning of calories. Once a certain weight is reached through dieting, the body's metabolism slows and further weight loss becomes impossible. The only way to overcome this appears to be through absolute starvation, which is why patients with illnesses like anorexia nervosa can reduce their weight to the point that they come close to death.

Psychiatric drugs may cause weight gain by artificially slowing the metabolic rate. They may do this by tricking the hypothalamus into somehow changing its set point, or they may affect the way fat cells throughout the body burn fat. All of this is speculation. What is clear is that many psychiatric drugs produce weight gain, even if the patient does not eat a lot.

Because so many psychiatric drugs have this unfortunate side effect, it is easier to list the drugs that do *not* cause weight gain (Table 32).

Keeping in mind the large number of drugs reviewed in this book, it is immediately obvious that the list of psychiatric drugs that do not produce weight gain is comparatively small. Patients taking cyclic antidepressants (for example, Tofranil, Elavil, Norpramin, Pertofrane), monoamine oxidase inhibitor antidepressants (for example, Parnate and Nardil), antipsychotic drugs (for example, Thorazine and Mellaril), and lithium may all gain weight.

Table 32:

Psychiatric Drugs That Do Not Cause Weight Gain

  I. Antidepressant Drugs
     Prozac (fluoxetine)
     Vivactil (protriptyline)
     Dexedrine (amphetamine)
     Welbutrin (bupropion)
 II. Antipsychotic drugs
     Moban (molindone)
III. Drugs for bipolar affective disorder
     Tegretol (carbamazepine)
     Depakene (valproic acid)
 IV. Drugs for anxiety
     All benzodiazepines (for example, Valium, Librium, Ativan, and Xanax)
     BuSpar (buspirone)

COMMONLY ASKED QUESTIONS

Ten questions are frequently asked with respect to drugs:

Is the weight gain always severe? No, it varies tremendously from patient to patient. Some people gain very little, only a few pounds. This is usually acceptable. Other patients, however, gain ten, twenty, or even more pounds.

Is dieting while on psychiatric drugs useless? No. Staying on a diet often limits the amount of weight gained. It is just not fair to blame a patient who gains weight on a psychiatric drug for not dieting enough. Some of the weight gain may not be preventable, even with strict caloric reduction.

Does weight gain continue as long as the drug is continued? No. After a few months, it usually stops and weight levels off.

Can any of the drugs that do not produce weight gain on the list be used to help with dieting and weight loss programs? Unfortunately, no. Amphetamines like Dexedrine were once widely prescribed for the sole purpose of weight loss. It is true that they speed up metabolism and curb appetite and, if taken regularly, cause weight loss at first. But the effect is very transitory and most people quickly gain back what they lose, probably because the hypothalamic set point is reset to slow metabolic rate. Furthermore, the patient who uses amphetamines for weight loss quickly becomes addicted and cannot stop the drug without suffering withdrawal depression. Consequently, amphetamines should not be prescribed for weight loss. On rare occasions, described in more detail in Chapter 7, they are useful as antidepressants.

When Prozac was first tested as an antidepressant, many depressed patients were observed to have lost some weight. Sometimes this loss was substantial, five to ten pounds. Rumors quickly spread that Prozac would be effective and safe as a weight-reducing pill for overweight people. Although the company that makes Prozac did not contribute in any way to the spread of these rumors, there is no doubt that some physicians initially prescribed Prozac to nondepressed patients to help them lose weight. As it turns out, most patients do not lose very much weight from Prozac and the little they do lose is usually regained in a few months.

What is important to remember about Prozac, Vivactil, and Welbutrin is that they are unique among antidepressants in *not* causing weight gain. This makes them distinctly advantageous for many patients. Similarly, if a monoamine oxidase inhibitor is recommended, Parnate appears to induce less weight gain than Nardil.

The other drugs on the list are more or less neutral when it comes to weight gain and loss. Tegretol and Depakene do not cause weight gain the way lithium often does, but they usually do not induce weight loss either. Benzodiazepine antianxiety drugs and BuSpar also do not affect weight one way or the other.

Are any psychiatric drugs useful for treating anorexia nervosa? Anorexia nervosa is an illness affecting mainly young women in which the patient develops a fixed idea that she is overweight. No matter how thin she becomes, she still looks in the mirror and sees herself as fat. The patient stops eating and abuses water pills (diuretics) and laxatives to try to lose more weight. Often, the patient with anorexia nervosa becomes an exercise fanatic and makes herself vomit after meals, both attempts to lose weight. The illness can be fatal, as the sad case of the popular rock star Karen Carpenter made clear to the world.

Many psychiatric drugs have been used to treat anorexia nervosa. Some clinicians have observed the high rate of depression in anorexics and tried antidepressants. Others have likened patients' insistence that they are fat when in fact they are wasting away to a psychotic delusion and prescribed antipsychotics. There is little evidence that antipsychotics work in anorexia nervosa. Patients with anorexia nervosa are often extremely anxious, and for this reason antianxiety drugs are sometimes used.

There is some evidence that antidepressants do help anorexics. These include Tofranil, Elavil, and Norpramin among the cyclic antidepressants and Nardil among the monoamine oxidase inhibitor antidepressants. Whether these drugs relieve the depression or directly treat the cause of anorexia nervosa is not known. It is pretty clear that they do not work simply by causing weight gain. Furthermore, these drugs are only partial answers: relatively infrequently will an antidepressant alone reverse all of the symptoms of anorexia nervosa. Many psychiatrists prescribe antidepressants to patients with anorexia nervosa, particularly if these patients also have depression, as part of a comprehensive treatment package that includes psychotherapy and family counseling. More research is needed before it is known when and for which patients with anorexia nervosa antidepressants should be prescribed, but they should always be considered as part of a comprehensive treatment program.

Can any of the drugs that do not produce weight gain be used to treat bulimia? Like anorexia nervosa, bulimia is an "eating disorder" that affects primarily young women. Recent reports indicate that college students are especially prone to developing bulimia, although many experts suspect that this hypothesis is more the result of who is surveyed than the true prevalence of bulimia. The primary feature of bulimia is binge eating. Bulimics seem periodically to develop uncontrollable urges to eat as much as they possibly can, often consuming jars of peanut butter, gallons of ice cream, and boxes of cookies at a single sitting. Many make themselves vomit immediately after binging, so only a proportion of bulimics actually gain weight. Some patients go through periods of bulimia and anorexia nervosa in cycles.

Prozac, Vivactil, and Welbutrin are antidepressants that curb appetite and even induce modest weight loss in some patients. Monoamine oxidase inhibitors are antidepressants that are particularly useful in atypical depression (see Chapter 7) in which the patient usually overeats. Desyrel, Elavil, Tofranil, and Norpramin have all been tried with some success in bulimic patients. Although there are many reported successes, more research is needed before it is known if bulimics should be routinely treated with psychiatric drugs. As with anorexia nervosa, it is reasonable to include antidepressant medication as part of a comprehensive treatment plan for bulimia.

Is weight gain important enough to warrant switching drugs or even stopping a psychiatric drug? Absolutely. Being overweight is unpleasant and bad for your health. Sometimes, a small weight gain is a reasonable price to pay for freedom from a debilitating psychiatric illness. Like any side effect, a balance must always be struck between the harm a drug does and the benefit it provides. Some people gain a lot of weight from psychiatric drugs and this may mean that switching to a different drug is in order. For example, many depressed patients who gain too much weight from a cyclic antidepressant like Tofranil or a monoamine oxidase inhibitor like Nardil can be switched to Prozac and maintain the depression-free state while losing the drug-induced weight gain. Keep in mind that there are rules for switching from one drug to another that must always be observed. A patient must wait for two weeks after stopping Nardil before trying Prozac, for example.

When a psychiatric drug is stopped, will the weight be lost? Any weight gained because of a psychiatric drug is usually lost once the drug is stopped. It may take a few months, however, to return to baseline weight.

Are there medical disorders that produce both weight gain and psychiatric illness? There are several, but probably the most important is an underactive thyroid. This condition, called hypothyroidism, results in weight gain, lethargy, fatigue, hair loss, intolerance to cold, and constipation, among other symptoms. It is increasingly recognized that some very subtle forms of hypothyroidism can be associated with chronic depression. For this reason, psychiatrists should always order blood tests of thyroid function when treating patients with psychiatric illness. Also, if a depressed patient fails to respond to the usual antidepressant drug therapy, more extensive thyroid tests are recommended because hidden thyroid problems may be the reason.

Lithium, the primary drug used for patients with bipolar affective illness (manic-depressive illness), causes both hypothyroidism and weight gain. Sometimes, but not always, lithium causes weight gain *because* it causes a decrease in thyroid gland function. Therefore, it is important to undergo thyroid tests every six months to a year while on lithium.

Are there medical conditions that cause weight loss and psychiatric illness? Yes, and many of these are serious. Many forms of cancer, for example, produce weight loss and depression. Another illness that can do this is AIDS. As depression itself results in a reduced appetite and therefore weight loss, it is very common for depressed patients to report weight loss; the vast majority do not have serious underlying medical problems. Any patient with depression and weight loss should, however, be evaluated by a medical doctor to rule out the possibility of an underlying medical problem. Often, the doctor can do this simply by taking a good medical history and ordering routine blood and urine tests, but sometimes a more in-depth medical workup is needed.

Chapter 16

Sex and Psychiatric Drugs

Psychiatrists are supposed to be the doctors that people can tell anything and everything to without feeling embarrassed. Maybe that is true, but it is surprising how reluctant people are to reveal to their doctor that a psychiatric drug is producing a side effect that interferes with sex and sexual function.

Today, most medical schools teach young doctors to obtain a sexual history from every patient they see. Medical students are told it is their responsibility to bring this subject up, not the patient's. Most people are reluctant to reveal they have a sexual problem or to ask questions about how illness or medications may affect their sex lives.

Unfortunately, many doctors—psychiatrists included—are also embarrassed to discuss sexual issues. Elderly patients are especially likely to leave the doctor's office without discussing sexual concerns or difficulties because even physicians maintain the ridiculous myth that old people do not have sex.

SEX AND PSYCHIATRIC ILLNESS

Many psychiatric illnesses have a profound effect on sexual functioning. One of my professors used to insist that "if a depressed person still has a good sex drive, you know they aren't too far gone." As general rules, depressed patients usually lose their interest in sex at least to some degree, anxious patients have a sex drive but cannot calm down long enough to have sex, and manic patients want to have sex all day long.

For diagnostic purposes, then, a psychiatrist should also ask at least a few basic questions about a new patient's sex life. Here is a typical discussion about sex I might have during the evaluation of a 35-year-old married woman complaining of depression:

"You've told me so far that you have lost your appetite and have felt blue most of the time for the last six weeks or so. You also do not have interest in a lot of things you used to enjoy. How about your interest in sex?"

"Forget it," the patient replies emphatically. "We haven't had sex in six months."

"You mean you and your husband haven't had sex at all in the last six months?"

"That's right, if you could call what we have sex."

"Is the problem that you have lost your interest in having sex—your sex drive is low—or that you and your husband are having trouble with your relationship?"

"I'm not interested."

Obviously, everything doesn't quite fit together with this story. "You told me you have been feeling depressed for about a month and a half, but you haven't had sex with your husband for six months. What was the problem before you started feeling depressed?"

Now I get the story. "He's never home, so how can we have sex?" my patient explained. "And when he does come home in the middle of the night he usually just wakes me up and wants to get it over with. That's not sex. I would like a little more romance."

After some more discussion, I was able to figure out that the patient really had maintained her sex drive. She still thought about

332

sex and often became aroused. The problem here had to do with her relationship with her husband. Although she was clearly depressed, loss of libido (sex drive) was not one of her symptoms, as it often is with depressed patients.

This woman's sexual difficulty required counseling and therapy, not antidepressant medication. Other times, however, a loss of interest in sex is a direct result of depression.

Patients with anxiety disorders, for example, generalized anxiety disorder, may be so nervous that they can't take their minds off their troubles long enough to enjoy sex. These patients may suffer from impotence or difficulty with vaginal lubrication. Anxiety disorder may make it difficult to relax enough during sex to maintain an erection or have an orgasm.

A cardinal symptom of mania, on the other hand, is increased sex drive. Manic patients often speak incessantly about sex, sometimes at inappropriate times or places. They become sexually irresponsible, often forgetting about the risks of pregnancy or sexually transmitted diseases. Although psychiatrists are not interested in spoiling someone's good time, the increased sex drive of manic patients usually leads to unfortunate consequences and requires treatment.

DRUGS AFFECT SEX

Treatments, however, sometimes produce more sexual impairment than the original illness. A number of psychiatric drugs, particularly the antidepressants, can produce sexual side effects (Table 33).

Antidepressants of the monoamine oxidase inhibitor class (see Chapter 7) are notorious in this respect. These drugs are used most often for patients with atypical depression. The patient with atypical depression can feel profoundly depressed but maintains the ability to be cheered up temporarily if something favorable occurs. Patients with atypical depression usually overeat and oversleep. They do not look forward to sex, but frequently enjoy it if their partner takes the initiative.

Monoamine oxidase inhibitors like Nardil and Parnate are very

Table 33:

Sexual Side Effects of Psychiatric Drugs

SYMPTOM	DRUG
Delayed orgasm	Many antidepressants, especially monoamine oxidase inhibitors (Nardil, Parnate) and Prozac
Priapism (prolonged erection)	Trazodone (Desyrel)
Retrograde ejaculation (ejaculation into the bladder)	Many antidepressants and antipsychotics (for example, Mellaril)
Hypersexuality	Any antidepressant that produces manic behavior, including Nardil, Parnate, and Prozac

effective in treating this kind of depression. About four weeks after beginning treatment with one of these drugs, the patient with atypical depression typically feels more energetic and hopeful, stops overeating, and begins to anticipate events with pleasure, including sex.

Usually about one month after this good feeling, however the patient often (about 20% to 30% of the time in my experience) notices a problem. Both men and women find the length of time needed to achieve an orgasm lengthens. Men are usually not concerned at first. They are able to maintain erections for long periods and view this effect as good. But then the frustration sets in.

Unfortunately, patients are often embarrassed to discuss such subjects as orgasms with the doctor, so they suffer. They sometimes think there is something wrong with them and do not realize that delayed orgasm is a fairly common side effect of monoamine oxidase inhibitors. It also occurs with use of other antidepressants, including Prozac and the cyclic antidepressants like Tofranil and Elavil.

Antidepressants, then, do not usually cause impotence or decreased sexual desire. If anything, they increase sex drive by relieving depression; however, they may cause delayed orgasm. It is important to discuss this problem with the doctor, because several solutions are possible. First, it is important to know that delayed orgasm often goes away with time, so sometimes, realizing it is a side effect and waiting for it to go away is the best solution. Second, reducing the dose of the drug may help. If these remedies do not work, a counteracting medication can be added. Some psychiatrists have found that the drug Urecholine (bethanechol) relieves delayed orgasm caused by antidepressants; others prescribe an antihistamine called Periactin (cyproheptadine).

Retrograde ejaculation is another sexual side effect that occasionally occurs with psychiatric drugs. This means that the male ejaculation goes the wrong way, back into the bladder instead of out of the penis. This effect should be reported to the doctor immediately. Usually, dose reduction or switching to another drug is required.

Patients who take benzodiazepine antianxiety drugs (like Valium and Librium) for prolonged periods occasionally complain of reduced sex drive. Very occasionally, men on lithium complain of difficulty in maintaining an erection.

One final rare, but potentially dangerous, side effect should be mentioned. Some men taking the antidepressant drug Desyrel (trazodone) develop prolonged erection, a condition called priapism. It is estimated to occur in only 1 in 1,000 to 1 in 10,000 men who take Desyrel. This can be an emergency because erection lasting more than an hour may result in serious damage to the penis. Men who take Desyrel should be warned about this side effect and should call the physician immediately if they have a sustained erection for no apparent reason.

DRUGS TO IMPROVE SEX

What about the use of psychiatric drugs to improve sexual function? Many people find that alcohol, marijuana, cocaine, amyl nitrate, Quaaludes, and other "recreational" drugs make sex more intense or more enjoyable. Are there prescription drugs that also do this?

This is a tricky area because the potential for abuse is obvious. Of course, a depressed patient who takes an antidepressant will realize improved sexual performance and desire once the depression abates; however, this is not treatment of a sexual problem, but rather treatment of a sexual impairment caused by underlying depression.

In some situations, extreme anxiety surrounding sex can be treated with antianxiety agents. Some patients, for a variety of reasons, develop intense anxiety about sex. This may stem from unconscious prohibitions about sex learned in childhood or from performance anxiety and fear of failure. It may stem from negative feelings about the sexual partner that the patient is unable to recognize and deal with. Most of these call for psychotherapy; medications are generally unwarranted, but short-term prescription of small doses of benzodiazepine antianxiety drugs like Valium or Xanax may be helpful. It is important not to prescribe these too liberally or the patient may come to feel that he or she cannot have sex without them. It thus can become a psychological dependency.

Psychiatrists, psychologists, and psychoanalysts are often portrayed as being preoccupied with sex. Some people think that everything they say to the psychiatrist will be interpreted with respect to sex. Therefore, they resist discussing sexual problems and sexual side effects openly. Let me emphasize the two main points of this chapter: The doctor must obtain a sexual history as part of the initial psychiatric evaluation, and second, any possible sexual side effects of psychiatric drugs must be brought to light.

Chapter 17

Treating the Elderly

The problem with discussing the use of psychiatric drugs for elderly patients is that too many doctors become frightened and refuse to prescribe them, and thus many elderly patients with psychiatric illness remain untreated.

This problem has recently been made worse by media attention to overprescription of psychiatric drugs to patients in nursing homes. It is clear that many nursing home patients are given drugs without proper medical supervision, often resulting in serious side effects.

There also exists the prevailing misconception that it is somehow normal for older people to feel depressed and anxious. After all, younger people reason, it is depressing to grow old, so what is there to treat with medication?

It is important to set the record straight on these issues. First, it is not dangerous to prescribe psychiatric drugs to elderly people who have treatable mental disorders. Certain skills and knowledge are required, but treatment should not be avoided just because someone is over 65.

Second, what goes on in some nursing homes is bad medicine and should be corrected. The appropriate solution, however, is better medical care, not abandonment of psychiatric treatment for the elderly.

Third, depression, psychosis, and anxiety disorder are absolutely never normal, no matter how old someone may be. This does not mean that psychiatric drugs always cure these disorders, but some form of treatment should always be considered. Most elderly people do not become depressed, although the incidence of depression does rise in the elderly.

RULES FOR TREATING THE ELDERLY

There are three important features to stress in treating elderly people with psychiatric drugs:

1. The diagnosis of psychiatric illness may be complicated.

2. There may be preexisting/coexisting medical problems that pose particular challenges.

3. Elderly people are very sensitive to all drugs and may experience more side effects than younger people.

These points require further explanation.

Diagnosis

Whenever an elderly person develops a psychiatric symptom, the first consideration must be that a medical problem exists. With age, the chance of developing medical problems increases, as does the possibility that a new psychiatric problem is really a symptom of medical disease. All persons over age 65 who complain of depression, loss of interest, decreased appetite, constipation, change in sleep habits, or anxiety or exhibit abnormal behavior (for example, hallucinations and delusions) need a complete medical and neurological workup.

The list of medical problems that can cause psychiatric symptoms in the elderly is very long and includes all forms of cancer, hormonal disturbances, heart problems, unrecognized strokes, and Alzheimer's dementia. Note these examples:

Mrs. C., an 80-year-old widow, complained to her married children on several occasions that she felt dizzy and lightheaded quite frequently. Sometimes she experienced a fluttering in her chest and broke out in a sweat. Her internist examined her, drew some routine blood tests, and performed an electrocardiogram. All the tests were normal, so Mrs. C. was told it was her "nerves" and sent home with a prescription for a tranquilizer.

Fortunately, one of her daughters felt a second opinion was in order and referred her to another physician who performed a twenty-four-hour monitor test of her heart. This revealed a serious, but intermittent, irregularity in Mrs. C.'s heart rhythm. A simple electrocardiogram, which monitors heart rate for only a few minutes, can easily miss this kind of problem. Mrs. C. required a pacemaker which solved her problem. Tranquilizers were clearly the wrong treatment.

Mr. B., a 66-year-old retired shopowner, complained of trouble sleeping and seemed listless and bored to his wife. She also noted that he had been picking at his food for several weeks and often seemed distracted. His family doctor found nothing wrong, so Mr. B. was referred to a psychiatrist. Here is how the beginning of the consultation went:

> "How are you feeling today, Mr. B?"
> "I'm okay, I guess. About the same as before."
> "Your wife says that you have not seemed yourself lately. Have you noticed that yourself?"
> "Yeah, maybe for about a month or so."
> "When exactly did it start?"
> "Oh, maybe a month ago, September I guess."

The problem was that it was February and a "month ago" would have been January. The psychiatrist then gently tested Mr. B.'s memory by asking him questions about what he had done the day before, what he had had for breakfast, and where his children were living. Mr. B. seemed confused and could not answer most of the questions. As he tried to answer, he became visibly upset, then clammed up and seemed disinterested in the rest of the interview.

Further testing revealed that Mr. B. was suffering from Alzheimer's dementia, not depression. This devastating illness is the most common form of dementia and results in progressive loss of memory and other intellectual functions. There is no treatment, but intense research has indicated the strong possibility of a genetic basis to the disorder. Frequently, demented patients are first thought to be depressed or psychotic. Antidepressants and other psychiatric drugs often make the memory ability of patients with dementia even worse, so the diagnosis is particularly important.

On the other hand, everyone was convinced that Mrs. G. was suffering from dementia because at age 71, she started to forget things and act confused. She talked very little, looked glum, and seemed disinterested. A psychiatrist noted, however, that Mrs. G. did well on memory tests but seemed to have trouble concentrating. Careful questioning revealed that she also had crying spells, loss of appetite, and insomnia, and felt that she had raised her children so badly that now they were all suffering. In fact, Mrs. G.'s children were happy and well adjusted. Mrs. G. was suffering from major depression. What seemed like a memory problem was really the result of poor concentration, a common symptom of depression. Mrs. G. was treated with an antidepressant and made a full recovery.

A final case is Mr. R., a vigorous 80-year-old man who had continued to walk five miles and spent at least one hour daily in his garden until he began complaining that the neighbors were stealing his gardening tools. Then he refused to walk his usual five miles because he became convinced that his wife was having an affair while he was gone. Finally, he accused his grandson of hiding his glasses on purpose to confuse him. These clear signs of paranoid delusions often occur in elderly patients with Alzheimer's disease,

340

but the curious thing about Mr. R. is that his memory seemed fine. Paranoid delusions also occur in patients with major depression, but Mr. R. had no other symptoms consistent with depression. Paranoid delusions are also a component of schizophrenia, but this disorder rarely manifests for the first time in someone of Mr. R.'s age. A neurological examination revealed a number of abnormalities that turned out to be secondary to a brain tumor. Fortunately, the tumor was benign, and with the proper treatment, Mr. R.'s paranoid delusions disappeared completely.

Another problem in deciding what is and is not a psychiatric illness in the elderly is the effect of the various drugs they frequently must take for medical problems. Many medications prescribed to treat common medical problems, like high blood pressure, can produce serious psychiatric symptoms. As elderly people are more likely to take medications, development of a psychiatric symptom should be carefully analyzed with respect to initiation of a new drug for a medical problem.

All of this is not to say that a diagnosis of psychiatric illness in an elderly person is impossible. It merely reinforces the need for careful attention to many factors, especially the possibility of underlying medical illness.

Preexisting/Coexisting Medical Problems

Medical problems can make psychiatric drug treatment of the elderly tricky. Although a medical problem may not be the *cause* of an elderly person's psychiatric symptoms, an elderly person is more likely than a younger person to have some medical problem that will interfere with a psychiatric drug. For example, heart conditions that make the use of cyclic antidepressants like Tofranil and Elavil more risky are relatively rare in young adults but become more common with age. Some psychiatric drugs, like monoamine oxidase inhibitors, may cause problems in patients with diabetes, which also is more common in elderly people. Most cyclic antidepressants and many antipsychotic drugs (like Thorazine and Mellaril) can result in a serious medical problem in an older man with an enlarged prostate. Hence, medical problems—and the

341

drugs used to treat them—may interfere with the use of psychiatric drugs.

Again, this does not mean that psychiatrists should be frightened into not treating the depressed or anxious elderly patient. It does mean that the psychiatrist and the medical doctor treating an elderly patient should work together to find the safest treatment plan.

Increased Sensitivity to Side Effects

Many psychiatric drugs produce a drop in blood pressure when the patient stands up quickly. This is particularly serious in elderly patients, who can experience significant decreases in blood pressure when taking many antidepressants and antipsychotic drugs. This decrease in pressure may cause dizziness and lightheadedness and result in serious falls. Many psychiatric drugs also cause drowsiness. Again, elderly people are more sensitive to this side effect than younger people. In general, elderly people are more sensitive to drugs of any kind than younger people because the capacity to metabolize ("break down") drugs declines with age. A younger person given a drug will rapidly break it down, but in elderly people, the drug may hang around in the body for a longer period.

With very few exceptions, elderly people should always be given lower doses of medication and should be evaluated for side effects more frequently than younger people. Some medications may be safer than others for elderly people, as shown in Table 34.

In general, for any drug, it is prudent to start the elderly patient with half the dose that a younger person would start with. Lower doses may actually work well in elderly patients. If it is recommended that blood levels be obtained for a drug for safety reasons, for example, lithium blood levels, these should be obtained about twice as often in elderly people as in younger people.

One of the most tragic situations is the elderly person left to suffer with psychiatric illness. A major problem here at present is the terrible Medicare rule that limits people over 65 to the barest minimum of outpatient psychiatric care. An older person essentially has to become so sick with a psychiatric problem that they need hospitalization before Medicare will pay for treatment.

Table 34:

Some Drugs That Are Comparatively Safe for Elderly Patients

ILLNESS	DRUG	ADVANTAGE
Depression	Nortriptyline[a]	May not lower blood pressure as much as other cyclic antidepressants
	Prozac[a]	Does not affect blood pressure, heart rate, bowel function, or urinary function
Psychosis	Haldol, Navane, Prolixin, Stelazine	Causes less sedation, smaller drop in blood pressure, less constipation, and less urinary retention than such drugs as Thorazine and Mellaril
Anxiety	Xanax, Ativan, Serax	May be more easily metabolized by elderly people than Valium, Librium, or Tranxene

[a]See Chapter 7.

Elderly people can and should be treated for psychiatric illness with medications. Careful diagnosis, skillful prescription, good communication between psychiatrist and internist, and vigilance for potentially serious side effects are required. In other words, it takes good medical practice.

Chapter 18

Psychiatric Drugs and Pregnancy

Scientists, especially those who work for drug companies, have expended many years and great effort in engineering drugs with the special properties necessary to cross from the blood into the brain. After all, unless a drug can gain access to the brain, it probably will not be much help in treating a psychiatric problem.

Unfortunately, many of the properties that enable a drug to cross the blood-brain barrier also enable the drug to cross the placenta and enter the unborn fetus. Therefore, when taken by the pregnant woman, most psychiatric drugs will gain access to her baby.

Since the 1950s and thalidomide, we have become acutely aware of the potential dangers to the fetus of a pregnant woman who takes medications. We also know that alcohol, cigarettes, and cocaine are bad for the unborn baby.

In evaluation of the potential harm a psychiatric drug may do to a fetus, special problems arise. These drugs affect the brain and it is hard to determine right away if a newborn infant has subtle brain damage because its mother took psychiatric medications during pregnancy. Infants exposed to psychiatric drugs in utero will not

345

show lower intelligence, learning disabilities, hyperactivity, or any of a number of behavioral problems for years.

Admittedly, we do not know if maternal psychiatric illness has a bad effect on the fetus either. It is quite possible that the changes in brain chemicals and hormones that depressed, anxious, and psychotic patients experience may also be harmful to the unborn baby.

Drug companies and medical textbooks usually offer the following vague advice: When contemplating use of a psychiatric drug in a pregnant woman, the benefits of the treatment must be weighed against the risks to the fetus. I cannot think of a more useless sentence. Without evidence one way or the other, what can actually be weighed? Who decides when treating a psychiatric illness in a pregnant woman if it is worth risking even the most remote possibility of harm to the fetus? In this age of rampant malpractice suits, psychiatrists are going to be very reluctant to make such a decision. Can a pregnant woman with severe depression or panic attacks or psychosis be expected to decide and make a well-informed decision? Should we involve the lawyers?

WHAT WE DO KNOW

Let me first go over the few things we do know about psychiatric illness and psychiatric drugs during pregnancy with some certainty.

In general, pregnancy seems to be a time when psychiatric illness is relatively quiet. Although there exist limited scientific data to support this position, psychiatrists have noted for many years that depression, panic attacks, mania, and even schizophrenia seem relatively quiescent during pregnancy. Often, a woman who experiences severe panic attacks stops having these attacks when she becomes pregnant, remains panic free during the pregnancy, and then relapses after her baby is delivered. We can thus offer some reassurance to a woman contemplating pregnancy that she may be spared a relapse of her illness if she stops taking the prescribed drugs.

Only lithium among the psychiatric drugs is definitely known to cause birth defects. The risk is greatest during the first three months (first trimester) of pregnancy. The defects caused by lithium appear to involve the heart. This does not mean that benzodiazepine antianxiety drugs, buspirone, antidepressants, and antipsychotic drugs have been proven safe during pregnancy, only that there is no proof yet that they definitely cause birth defects.

Integrity of spermatazoa and viability of the embryo have not been observed to be affected by psychiatric medications. A side effect that some men may encounter is delayed ejaculation.

SOME RECOMMENDATIONS

I recommend the following guidelines to women on psychiatric drugs who want to get pregnant:

1. It is best to try to get off the drug before you try to conceive. The first step is to taper off the medication; most psychiatric drugs should never be stopped abruptly. Then stay off the medication for several weeks before trying to get pregnant to ensure the body has completely eliminated the drug.

2. Most psychiatric illnesses do not return immediately upon discontinuation of the drug, so there is a "safety zone" between your last pill and the time you get pregnant.

3. The most critical time for fetal development is the first trimester. Do everything possible to avoid drugs during this period. I would even venture to say that a suicidally depressed pregnant woman in the second month of pregnancy should be hospitalized and observed around the clock rather than being given an antidepressant. This may sound cruel, but I do not know of any way at present to say with certainty that the antidepressant will not harm the fetus. Although I fully recognize how awful panic attacks and other anxiety symptoms are, I again advise trying to live with them during the first trimester of pregnancy.

4. Should a serious psychiatric disturbance develop after the first three months of pregnancy, medication can be considered. It is a

lot to ask a person to live with mania, severe depression, panic attacks, or hallucinations and delusions for six months. Furthermore, some of these illnesses can themselves potentially be dangerous to a fetus. If a depressed woman cannot eat and loses weight, the fetus may be malnourished. If a psychotic woman abuses alcohol or cocaine or becomes paranoid and refuses routine medical care, the consequences can be serious for the newborn baby. Many women have taken cyclic antidepressants, antipsychotic drugs, and benzodiazepine antianxiety drugs during pregnancy and delivered normal babies. Originally, it was believed that use during pregnancy of the antianxiety drugs like Valium and Librium caused cleft lip or cleft palate in the infant, but this has recently been disputed. One would think that by now if any of these drugs did produce serious birth defects, we would know about it, although it is possible that subtle defects have been missed. The best advice is, if a psychiatric disturbance is so severe that the mother's and/or the unborn baby's life and health are jeopardized, it is reasonable to prescribe medication in small doses after the first trimester.

5. If psychiatric medication is prescribed, it should be one of the drugs that has been on the market for twenty or more years. In other words, avoid newer drugs like Xanax, Prozac, Desyrel, Welbutrin, Halcion, Restoril, Clozaril, Ludiomil, and Asendin. There is no theoretical reason to think that these drugs would be more harmful to a fetus than other drugs in their classes, but it is certain that fewer pregnant women have used them and therefore there is a greater chance that they cause birth defects we do not yet know about.

6. Lithium should probably be avoided during the entire pregnancy, but I am also not secure in prescribing the other drugs (Tegretol and Depakene) used to treat bipolar affective disorder (formerly manic-depressive disorder) during pregnancy. There is mounting evidence that these medications are also harmful to a fetus. A bipolar patient who becomes depressed during pregnancy and absolutely needs medication might be better off taking an antidepressant temporarily; a bipolar patient who becomes manic during pregnancy and absolutely requires medication should probably be given an antipsychotic temporarily.

348

7. Despite the bad press it has received, electroconvulsive (shock) treatment is probably the safest way to treat depression in a pregnant woman. It causes seizure activity in the brain much like the activity that occurs during epileptic seizures, and we know that women with epilepsy have normal babies. Although it is usually hard to convince patients and their families of this, it is probably true that shock treatment is safer than antidepressant medication for a depressed pregnant woman.

The following case history may illustrate these recommendations best:

Joan had serious emotional disturbances as a teenager and young adult. At age 17 she experienced her first serious depression and began psychotherapy. She went to college, but took six years to graduate because of two more severe episodes of depression, one of which required hospitalization. After graduation from college she had a manic episode and again required hospitalization. Unfortunately, she was not placed on lithium until she had two more manic episodes and a depression that resulted in a serious suicide attempt.

When at age 24 Joan was finally placed on lithium, her life was in disarray. She had never held a job for any length of time, lost many of her friends during her episodes of highs and lows, and never had a serious romantic relationship. Over the next ten years, because of her courage and intelligence, she went to graduate school, got a job, reestablished friendships, met a man, and got married. Now, at age 34, she is happily married and successful. She also is stable on lithium with ten years of no mood swings. Understandably, she wants to get pregnant, but should she risk a severe depression or manic episode to have a child? Although her husband is very understanding and loves her, he has never seen her in the middle of a high or low. Joan wonders how it will affect her relationship with her husband if she becomes ill. Will she lose all the ground she has gained in her career over the last ten years if she needs a hospitalization once taken off lithium and appears unstable to her bosses?

It would be a tragedy for a woman like Joan to deny herself the opportunity of having a child in these circumstances. Naturally, no one can predict what will happen. It is possible that she will become depressed or manic once off lithium. Given the stigma attached to mental illness, it is also possible that her husband, friends, and co-workers will have a negative attitude toward her if she becomes psychiatrically ill. The alternative, however, is to voluntarily give up the chance of having a baby.

I would tell Joan that there is a good chance she will not relapse during the period between stopping lithium and getting pregnant and a reasonable chance that she will remain well through the pregnancy. I would advise her to see me with her husband so that he understands the warning signs of approaching mania and depression. And I would maintain more frequent contact with her, at least with weekly phone calls and monthly appointments, during the pregnancy.

There are many situations, psychiatric and otherwise, when couples are well advised to forgo having children. But, whenever possible, we should not further stigmatize psychiatric patients by making this an absolute rule for everyone who needs psychiatric medication. For many of us, having children is the best thing we can do to improve our mental health.

Chapter 19

AIDS: Dealing With Psychiatric Problems

Patients suffering from many different medical diseases can develop psychiatric problems. Sometimes, as I have stressed many times in this book, a hidden medical illness is actually the *cause* of a psychiatric symptom like depressed mood, panic attacks, or hallucinations.

All of this is true with respect to AIDS—the acquired immune deficiency syndrome. AIDS is generally thought to be caused by a virus, called HIV (or human immunodeficiency virus), which slowly destroys the infected patient's immunological system. Stripped of its natural defenses, the body becomes susceptible to a host of serious infections and tumors. Scientists now think that most, if not all, people infected with HIV will ultimately develop AIDS, but the period between infection with HIV and development of AIDS varies greatly and can be ten years or longer.

At the beginning of the AIDS epidemic there was much talk about "high-risk groups"—specific groups of people who seemed most likely to be infected by HIV. We now know that anyone who engages in *high-risk behavior* can be infected with HIV. The most common behaviors are unprotected sex (sex without using a condom) and intravenous drug use. Although drugs like AZT (zidovu-dine) and pentamidine can prolong the life of someone with AIDS, the only way to avoid infection with HIV is to change sexual and drug use behavior.

Psychiatrists and their mental health professional colleagues have therefore become very involved in the AIDS epidemic because they are the experts in behavioral change. The Alcohol, Drug Abuse, and Mental Health Administration (ADAMHA) is spend-ing millions of dollars annually to fund research aimed at learning how to change behavior and stop the spread of HIV.

It might seem logical that the person infected with HIV, knowing the high likelihood that he or she will develop AIDS and die, would become highly anxious or depressed. So far, however, several ex-cellent studies have failed to find high rates of any psychiatric disorders among persons infected with HIV. The emotional reac-tion seems to follow a pattern: The person who thinks she or he may be infected usually feels very anxious undergoing the HIV blood test and awaiting the results. If the results are positive—the person is indeed infected—depression and suicidal thoughts often occur: "I'll kill myself before I get sick." "I'll never let myself suffer and die a slow, painful death." "I'd rather be dead than have anybody know I have AIDS."

As far as we can tell, however, these reactions are temporary. Within two weeks of hearing the test results, patients with HIV infection seem to begin making peace with themselves. They recog-nize that it may be years before any medical symptoms develop from the HIV infection and that scientists throughout the world are working to find a cure. HIV-infected patients often develop hope and optimism at this point, channeling negative thoughts and en-ergy into work, family, and various altruistic efforts. In fact, in my own research work with people infected with HIV, I have been consistently impressed with their fortitude, courage, and resilience.

During the period in which the HIV-infected patient remains medically asymptomatic, he or she may develop psychiatric symp-toms at about the same rate as an uninfected person. The treatment of these patients, however, may not be the same.

Patients with HIV infection have an immune system that is pre-carious at best. Many drugs—prescribed and not prescribed—can affect the immune system. The last thing we want to do is give patients antidepressant or antianxiety drugs that might harm their immune systems.

On the other hand, we do not wish to leave HIV-infected patients to suffer with anxiety disorder or depression. We want infected patients to lead normal lives while awaiting the scientific breakthrough that will cure them.

So, a few commonsense principles are in order. First, whenever possible, I think that a person with HIV infection who becomes depressed or develops anxiety disorder should be treated with brief, nonpharmacological methods. Support groups, counseling, and cognitive therapy are all good choices. If these are going to work for the depressed or anxious patient, they should do so in a few weeks.

If medication is needed to treat depression or anxiety disorder I recommend starting with low doses and monitoring the number of immune cells once or twice while the person is on the drug to ensure that no harm is being done. HIV infection destroys a particular immune cell called the T4 or T helper cell. Normally, a person has about 800 of these cells per microliter of blood. A patient with HIV infection may eventually have none. Many viral infections can temporarily lower the number of T4 cells, but only HIV causes a progressive and permanent loss. Therefore, I recommend a simple blood test to check the number of T4 cells at baseline, two weeks after starting the medication, and a month or so thereafter. Several research studies are now underway to determine if any of the commonly used psychiatric drugs depress the number of T4 cells; until these studies are complete, it is best to check each patient.

Followers of a relatively new field, called psychoneuroimmunology, believe that treating depression and anxiety disorder may actually *improve* immune function. Some research has shown that stress and depression may themselves harm the immune system; therefore, it might be expected that reversing these psychiatric conditions will lead to improvement. These assumptions are largely unproven. For now, it seems reasonable to recommend that depression and anxiety disorder be treated in patients with HIV infection, but that caution be exercised.

To understand my recommendations on selection of antidepres-

353

sant and antianxiety drugs, it is necessary to understand one more facet of HIV infection. HIV affects one other system besides the immune system: it invades the brain. No one yet knows exactly how the virus crosses into the brain or how it destroys brain cells, but it is now clear that patients with HIV are susceptible to two kinds of serious nervous system attack. First, the virus itself infects the brain, causing in some patients a progressive loss of intellectual ability. Late in the course of infection some patients develop what is frequently called AIDS-related dementia. Their mental faculties are slowed, their memory is reduced, and their powers of reasoning are weakened. It is extremely important to stress that this is a late event in most patients and occurs after other medical problems have arisen. Asymptomatic patients rarely have serious problems with dementia.

The second impact HIV has on the brain is indirect, but no less serious. By weakening the body's immune system, HIV also makes the brain susceptible to infections and tumors. Patients with HIV can develop brain infections such as toxoplasmosis, cyptococcosis, and cytomegalovirus. They can develop brain tumors like lymphoma. Many of these are treatable, but they must first be diagnosed.

Patients with HIV infection may develop psychiatric symptoms later in the course of the disease that are the direct result of brain infection, either by HIV, other agents, or brain tumor. What may seem like depression can actually be the loss of motivation, decreased appetite, and inability to concentrate caused by AIDS dementia. The sudden onset of hallucinations, delusions, and bizarre behavior could be the result of a brain tumor caused by the AIDS virus.

Any patient with HIV infection who develops psychiatric symptoms must therefore be evaluated medically. Although we say this for almost all psychiatric patients, it is especially important for HIV-infected patients. Many times a neurologist is asked to evaluate the patient, and brain x-rays, including CAT and MRI scans, are required.

Let us say that a brain infection or tumor is ruled out. Even so, it is still possible that the depressed patient with HIV infection has some degree of subtle brain invasion by the AIDS virus. Whether this is the cause of depression, anxiety, or other psychiatric symptoms is not yet known, but we do know that such patients are very sensitive to the side effects of psychiatric drugs. A drug that is sedating will often make the HIV-infected patient especially sleepy. A drug that produces decreased appetite may cause the patient to lose dangerous amounts of weight. Perhaps most important, psychiatric drugs with *anticholinergic* side effects (dry mouth, constipation, blurry vision, difficulty urinating) can cause memory problems in patients with HIV infection.

Therefore, we want to treat the HIV-infected patient with psychiatric problems with medications that produce the least number of side effects. Here are some recommendations (Table 35):

Table 35:

Some Recommended Psychiatric Drugs for Patients With HIV or AIDS

I. Depression
 Patients who are medically asymptomatic—Prozac or desipramine
 Patients with serious medical symptoms—Ritalin or Dexedrine
II. Anxiety
 Low doses of Xanax, Ativan, or Serax
III. Psychosis
 Low doses of Haldol, Prolixin, Stelazine, or Navane

Depression

Anticholinergic antidepressants such as Tofranil (imipramine), Elavil (amitriptyline), Sinequan (doxepin) and Pamelor (nortriptyline) should be avoided. A full list of these drugs is provided in Table 11 in Chapter 11. The new antidepressant Welbutrin (buproprion) should be avoided for now because it appears more likely to produce seizures than other antidepressants and therefore is not recommended for patients with brain infection. A good choice might be the new antidepressant Prozac (fluoxetine), which does not have anticholinergic side effects. It may curb appetite, however, and the patient's weight needs to be watched. Desipramine, a cyclic antidepressant with relatively fewer anticholinergic side effects, is also sometimes chosen.

To treat depression in patients with AIDS, many clinicians now recommend the stimulant antidepressants Ritalin (methylphenidate) and amphetamines (Dexedrine, Biphetamine, Desoxyn). Surprisingly, these drugs produce few side effects, although weight loss may be a problem. The main problem with stimulant antidepressants, as discussed in more detail in Chapter 7, is that they are addicting; however, it seems reasonable to offer the best possible treatment available to someone with a late-stage medical illness.

For depression, then, I recommend Prozac or desipramine (Norpramin, Pertofrane) for relatively asymptomatic patients and Ritalin or Dexedrine for patients with AIDS. The T4 cell count should be checked several times in the first few months of treatment. Low doses should be used and the patient's weight monitored carefully. The emergence of any new neurological symptoms should prompt reevaluation and consideration of discontinuation of the medication.

Anxiety

A review of Chapter 8 might be useful at this point to understand the many different forms of anxiety disorder. If antianxiety drugs are necessary for generalized anxiety symptoms, I recommend low doses of the short-acting benzodiazepine drugs—Xanax (alprazolam), Ativan (lorazepam), and Serax (oxazepam). These drugs are more rapidly cleared by the body than the long-acting benzodiazepines (Valium, Librium, and Tranxene). Relief of chronic anxiety may be a blessing to someone suffering with HIV infection. Benzodiazepines are quite safe, even though they may produce sedation, hence the recommendation to keep doses low. To my mind, it would be cruel to deny an anxious patient with HIV infection safe and effective treatment. Once again, the T4 cell count should be checked once or twice in the month after starting a new drug.

Psychosis

Psychotic symptoms like hallucinations and delusions (see Chapter 10 for a discussion of these symptoms) are fairly uncommon in patients with HIV infection or AIDS. When they occur they are almost always the result of viral infection of the brain. Such patients should be treated with antipsychotic medications. The best choices are the high-potency drugs with few anticholinergic side effects, given as usual in very low doses: Haldol (haloperidol), Prolixin (fluphenazine), Stelazine (trifluoperazine), and Navane (thiothixene). These drugs are usually given for very short periods (a few days) to relieve psychotic symptoms and severe agitation. They may produce other side effects (described in detail in Chapter 10). Careful medical supervision is required.

It must be stressed that these are only recommendations. The psychiatric complications of HIV infection and AIDS are only now being studied, and treatment recommendations may change radically, very quickly, as psychiatrists gain more experience and researchers publish the results of ongoing studies. At present, the best advice is to try nondrug treatment first, but never permit the HIV-infected patient to suffer with psychiatric symptoms when medication might help. Always remember the possibility of brain infection and observe the patient very carefully for drug-induced side effects.

Most importantly, the psychiatric treatment of an HIV-infected patient should be coordinated with the other doctors involved in the patient's care. Psychiatric symptoms should never be passed off as the "expected" or "understandable" reaction to life-threatening illness. It is bad medicine to ignore the emotional suffering of patients with HIV infection or any other serious illness.

357

Chapter 20

Generic Versus Brand: What's in a Name?

Despite the fact that millions of Americans take some form of medication every day, most haven't the slightest idea how all these drugs get on the market. Many of us simply take it on faith that the government makes sure that medication is safe and effective before doctors are allowed to prescribe it.

One of the biggest areas of confusion for doctors and patients alike is whether to take brand name or generic drugs. Every drug usually has three names: (1) the formal chemical name useful almost exclusively to scientists; (2) the generic name, a shortened version of the chemical name; and (3) the brand name, the name given to the drug by the company that wants to market it.

As an example, let's take the antianxiety drug Xanax. The scientific name for Xanax is (8-chloro-1-methyl-6-phenyl-$4H$-s-triazolo[4,3-a][1,4]benzodiazepine)—not something that rapidly falls off the tongue! When the compound was first discovered and thought to be potentially useful, it was given the generic name alprazolam. A drug company then assigned the name Xanax. A drug can have many brand names if different companies obtain the right to market it, but it can have only one generic name and one chemical name.

359

DEVELOPING A NEW DRUG

Once a person discovers a compound that he thinks may be useful in treating a medical condition, he usually applies for a patent to ensure exclusive rights over the compound. In most cases today, new drugs are discovered by scientists working in the laboratories at the large drug companies. Relatively few drugs are discovered by scientists working in medical school laboratories.

A patent on a drug is good for seventeen years, but usually, many years pass before a new drug is ever prescribed to an actual patient. Once the patent is issued, the company must run the drug through exhaustive tests according to the regulations of the U.S. Food and Drug Administration (FDA). First, there must be tests on animals that indicate the drug is not likely to cause serious harm to humans. If mice or rats develop cancer or liver failure from the new drug, it is probably the end of the road.

If nothing terrible happens to the animals, the drug company submits an application to the FDA to receive permission to test the drug in humans. There are three mandated phases of this testing. In phase 1, patients and normal volunteers are given the drug to establish its safety, the best doses, and its usefulness in specific medical problems. In phase 2, several hundred patients are entered into controlled trials of the drug. In a controlled trial, some patients receive the active drug and others are given an inactive placebo. Phase 2 testing must determine whether the drug works better than a placebo to treat the targeted condition. Finally, phase 3 usually involves thousands of patients in controlled trials and must result in data that prove the drug is safe and effective. After all three phases are completed, the company submits a New Drug Application (NDA) to the FDA, which must include all of the results from the three phases.

It takes an average of almost three years between submission of an NDA and FDA approval to market a new drug. As many as two thirds of the NDA applications are returned to the drug company by the FDA with requests for more information or even more studies on patients.

During all of this time, the clock on the patent is ticking. Companies spend millions of dollars getting through the regulatory process, so if they are lucky enough to get FDA approval for a new drug, they want to make a profit quickly before the patent runs out. Until the patent does run out, only the drug company that received permission from the FDA can market the new drug.

For the first few years, then, most new drugs are marketed only under one brand name. At the time of this writing, for example, the antidepressant drug fluoxetine is available only under the brand name Prozac. If a doctor prescribes fluoxetine to a patient, the patient is automatically given the Prozac brand.

With the lack of competition and the need for drug companies to recover the expenses incurred in developing the drug, it is clear why companies charge a lot for their brand name drugs. Doctors rarely have any idea how much the drugs they prescribe actually cost, so they are not much help in keeping the cost to the patient for medications at a minimum. For that reason I have given prices per pill of brand name and generic drugs in this book so the consumer can make comparisons.

Once a patent for a drug expires, the situation changes dramatically. Now, any drug company that meets FDA standards can manufacture and market the drug. Because it has been such a successful drug, it is inevitable that in 1993, when the patent for Xanax expires, scores of drug companies will line up to manufacture and sell generic alprazolam.

Furthermore, the government actively encourages generic drug prescription. The federal government's maximum allowable cost (MAC) program limits the reimbursement for drugs to patients on Medicare, Medicaid, and similar programs.

At the end of a patent's life, therefore, the generic drug becomes available. Now there is competition among companies and the price of the drug usually, but not always, falls. The generic drug companies have an important advantage over the brand name companies that makes it possible for them to charge less for the drug: the generic company did not spend millions of dollars developing the drug and therefore does not have to recover those expenses.

ARE GENERICS AS GOOD?

So it is almost always the case that the generic drug is cheaper than the brand name drug. But are generic drugs as good as brand name drugs? That depends on whom you ask.

The brand name drug companies obviously want doctors and patients to believe that generic drugs are inferior. One of their main arguments is the so-called "70/70 rule." FDA policy says that a generic drug should be equivalent to a brand name drug in 70% of people tested 70% of the time. Also, generic drugs are allowed to be 30% as potent as brand name drugs for the antipsychotics and 20% for most other psychiatric drugs. For example, if we take as the standard 100 mg of brand name drug, a 100-mg tablet of the generic drug must be equivalent in activity to between 70 and 130 mg of the brand name drug.

In actual fact, say generic drug manufacturers, most generic drugs are much closer in strength to brand name drugs. Furthermore, they insist, there are very few reported situations in which a patient has experienced trouble after switching from the brand name drug to a generic medication.

Not so, say the brand name drug manufacturers. They are quick to cite examples of patients well stabilized on a brand name drug who become sick or develop new side effects when switched to a generic drug. They also claim that generic drugs are associated with more allergic reactions and do not taste as good as brand name drugs. Recent scandals in the generic pharmaceutical industry involving submitting false data to the Food and Drug Administration are frequently cited as evidence that generic drugs are not reliable. Hopefully, however, this is not a widespread problem.

Many state governments do everything they can to encourage doctors to prescribe generic drugs. In New York State, for example, even if a doctor writes a brand name on the prescription, the pharmacist is required to fill the prescription with a cheaper generic unless the doctor completes another part of the prescription with the initials "daw." But state governments have ulterior motives too. Many drug prescriptions are paid for by state-funded insurance programs, so obviously the state wants patients to get the cheaper treatment.

Doctors usually start prescribing a medication when it is still patented and therefore get to know it by its brand name. They are visited regularly by representatives of drug companies, called "detail men," who encourage prescription of their company's brand name drugs. Generic drug companies do not have the money for "detail men" and do not spend money on advertisements in medical journals. So physicians usually become accustomed to writing prescriptions using brand names.

The brand name drug companies also lobby doctors to prescribe their drugs by pointing out that they use part of the profits they make to pay scientists and equip laboratories so that new drugs can be discovered. At this point, the bulk of new drug development in the United States takes place at the brand name drug companies; without them, there is no question that new drug development would virtually grind to a halt, and diseases for which cures might be found would remain untreated.

All of this explains why brand name companies think your doctor should always prescribe a brand name drug and why insurance companies, state governments, and generic drug companies would like your doctor to prescribe less expensive generic drugs. What is best for you?

I have two recommendations:

1. When your doctor writes a prescription, ask him or her if there is any medical reason why you shouldn't take the generic instead of the brand name drug. Many times, the doctor will acknowledge there is no good reason and write down the generic name.

2. Do not switch from a brand name drug to a generic or among different generics in the middle of a treatment period. If you are started on a generic drug and stabilized, and need to continue the drug, it is okay to stay with the generic variety. But switching midstream from the brand name to the generic may mean getting a preparation that is not as active, which increases your risk of relapse, or that is more active, which increases your risk of developing new side effects. If a generic is prescribed, ask your pharmacist

whether he or she has been told about an increased rate of side effects from that preparation and whether it is likely the pharmacy will continue to carry the same generic preparation during the entire course of your treatment.

Also, check to see if the generic form really is cheaper than the brand name. Generic amitriptyline can be ten times cheaper than Elavil, but generic perphenazine costs about the same as Trilafon.

And shop around. Drug stores sometimes charge wildly different prices in the same community for the same drugs.

If blood level testing is available for a drug, it is always a good idea to check the level a week or two after switching from a generic to a brand or from one generic to another. For example, lithium is available as many brand name and generic preparations. For the most part, these all have the same activity because lithium is a very simple drug and easy to manufacture. So switching from Eskalith to Lithonate, both brand names for lithium, should make no difference. Nevertheless, it is a good idea to recheck the lithium blood level about two weeks after the switch to make sure there is no dramatic change, up or down.

I have included price information about drugs in the drug information sections of this book because of all the things doctors should know about the medications they prescribe, cost is the one item they are most likely to be ignorant about. I know of no medical school courses on this topic and the *Physician's Desk Reference* does not say a word about price either.

There is absolutely no reason why a patient should not take the price of treatment into consideration, and generic drugs, when they are available, are almost always cheaper. So by all means, ask your doctor if you can take the generic and make him or her provide a logical reason if you are told no. The reason may be correct, but it's your dollar that is at stake.

Chapter 21

How Psychiatric Drugs Work

It is not at all necessary to know how psychiatric drugs work in order to take them safely and benefit from them. Some people would just as soon be spared the biological details and for them I advise skipping this last chapter entirely.

But the way the brain works is really one of the most fascinating aspects of science and also one of the great scientific frontiers ahead of us. The brain is by far the most complex and mysterious organ of the body. I would venture to say that the human brain is the most complicated thing in all of nature. It has billions of individual nerve cells. In fact, there are more nerve cells in one human brain than there are people who have ever lived on Earth. If we took the brain of a single person and stretched the cells out in a straight line, the line would go to the Moon and back. We are now in the midst of a neuroscience revolution in which more top scientists and laboratories and more funds than ever before are directed at research to learn how the brain functions. Every week our journals, and sometimes our popular newspapers, magazines, and television news reports, are crammed with exciting new discoveries about the scientific basis for human behavior.

So if you have a lively scientific curiosity, you might want to read on. Furthermore, many patients find it helpful to know a little of the specifics of drug action to understand what the drugs are actually doing to them and what benefits and risks they can expect. It gives everything a grounding in nuts and bolts facts.

Although the brain is indeed nearly impossibly complex to understand, no one has to be a scientist to understand the basics of brain function and the way in which psychiatric drugs work. To explain the important features, it is first necessary to describe a little bit about how the human brain looks and works.

A LITTLE ABOUT THE BRAIN

In the broadest sense, any drug that affects the brain can be called a psychiatric drug. Alcohol and marijuana were among the first such drugs discovered, both obviously having profound effects on the brain and emotions. A wide variety of medications prescribed for nonpsychiatric conditions similarly have effects on the brain, although physicians are often unaware of this. Such commonly prescribed drugs as propranolol, used in the treatment of high blood pressure and angina; cimetidine, used for ulcers; and prednisone, used to treat many different diseases involving the immune system, all can produce marked changes in mood and behavior.

The ability of a drug to have an effect on mood and behavior is dependent on its ability to move from the digestive tract into the blood and then into the brain. The first step is relatively easy and scientists have known for many years exactly how to prepare orally administered medications so that they eventually are absorbed into the bloodstream. The second step, crossing from blood into brain, is problematic. Brain scientists often talk about a drug's ability to cross the "blood-brain barrier." Perhaps appropriately, out of self-protection, the human central nervous system has evolved in such a way that many substances are blocked from getting into the brain, as if a wall stands between blood vessels and brain tissue. In general, drugs that are very fat soluble (technically called lipophilic), not bound to protein, and electrically uncharged have the best chance of getting into the brain. Furthermore, often, the concentrations of drug necessary to have an appreciable effect on the brain are much larger than those needed to affect another organ of the body. For example, in relatively low doses, a commonly prescribed antidepressant drug, imipramine, dries mucous membranes in the body, causing dry mouth; however, doses of the drug as much as ten times higher than the mouth-drying dose may be needed to get an antidepressant effect. This is probably because of the difficulty drugs have in getting into the brain. Making drugs that safely affect mental processes is clearly a difficult task.

Once in the brain, a drug faces the most intricate, complex, and mysterious organ of the body. Nothing in the universe comes close to the human brain in complexity. Sometimes, psychiatric researchers complain that whoever designed the brain did so just to frustrate their attempts to understand it. Like other parts of the body, the brain is a collection of cells, the most important of which for our purposes are called neurons. These brain cells or neurons send out long filaments or branches called axons and dendrites that entangle each other in an endlessly complex web of connections and interconnections. A dendrite from one neuron may communicate with an axon, dendrite, or cell body of another neuron. But at each point of communication, there is an empty space between the two neurons, called the synapse. Brain cells essentially communicate by sending electrical signals, sometimes called action potentials. When a signal reaches the end of one neuron—just before the synapse—it causes the cell to secrete a chemical messenger into the synapse. This chemical messenger, called a neurotransmitter, floats across the synapse and binds to a receptor on the surface of the cell on the other side, the postsynaptic neuron. The binding of the neurotransmitter to the receptor on the other cell initiates a chemical process in that cell that either excites it and makes it continue to transmit the electrical signal or inhibits it and stops further transmission of the electrical impulse. Whether the process is excitatory or inhibitory depends on a number of complicated factors, including the kind of neurotransmitter involved. Once the neurotransmitter has done its job, it either is degraded by enzymes or is reabsorbed into the cell that originally secreted it (the presynaptic neuron). The most important components of this system are the pre- and postsynaptic neurons, the synapse, the neurotransmitter, the receptor on the surface of the postsynaptic neuron, and the degrading enzymes (Figure 2).

This process may seem simple and one may wonder at this point why I marvelled earlier at the complexity of the brain. But consider the following. There are at least one hundred billion synapses in the human brain. There are about thirty different known neurotransmitters, but at the rate new ones are being discovered, some speculate that there are probably hundreds. Many neurons make or respond to two or more neurotransmitters. Finally, a host of cofactors, such as calcium and chloride ions, have an effect on the strength of neurotransmitter responses.

Scientists are also beginning to learn that many things can affect the sensitivity of the postsynaptic neuron's receptors for neurotransmitters. Starve these receptors of neurotransmitter for a while and they become supersensitive to the chemical's effect the next time around. Or the postsynaptic neuron may actually produce new receptors. It is quickly becoming apparent that the process by which receptor binding of a neurotransmitter leads to excitation or inhibition of the neuron depends on a very complicated chain of chemical reactions. In many cases, it involves chemicals called "second messengers" that work within the postsynaptic cell once it has bound the neurotransmitter on its surface.

Most psychiatric drugs exert their effects at the level of the synapse and therefore affect neurotransmitter binding to receptors in one way or another. For example, most of the drugs used to treat psychotic illnesses like schizophrenia attach to postsynaptic receptors that normally bind the neurotransmitter dopamine. By doing so, these antipsychotic drugs prevent dopamine from getting to the receptor, and therefore stop nerve cell activity that depends on dopamine to maintain signal transmission.

The group of antidepressants called cyclics, on the other hand, blocks the reabsorption or reuptake of the neurotransmitters noradrenaline and serotonin into the presynaptic neuron after they have bound to the postsynaptic receptor. This prolongs the life of the neurotransmitter in the synapse and allows it to reattach to the receptor, thus increasing neurotransmission. The new antidepressant drug Prozac (fluoxetine) specifically and potently blocks the

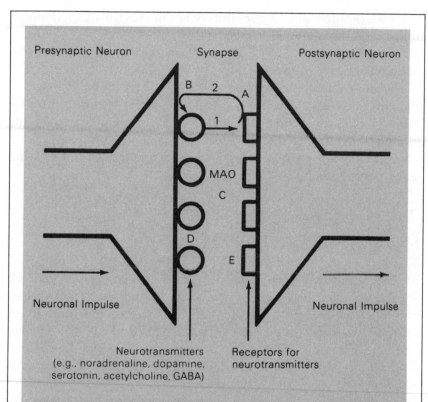

Neurotransmitters
(e.g., noradrenaline, dopamine,
serotonin, acetylcholine, GABA)

Receptors for
neurotransmitters

A. Antipsychotic drugs (e.g., Thorazine) block dopamine from binding to its receptor.

B. Many antidepressants (e.g., Tofranil, Elavil, Prozac) stop reuptake of neurotransmitters to the presynaptic cell thus prolonging their life in the synapse. This increases neuronal flow.

C. MAO destroys many neurotransmitters. MAO inhibitor antidepressants (e.g., Nardil, Parnate) inhibit MAO, thus prolonging the life of the neurotransmitters. This increases neuronal flow.

D. Amphetamines and cocaine cause increased release of some neurotransmitters from the presynaptic neuron.

E. Some antianxiety drugs (e.g., Valium, Librium, Xanax) and sleeping pills (e.g., Dalmane, Halcion) increase the effectiveness of the neurotransmitter GABA at its receptor. This *quiets* the postsynaptic neuron and decreases neuronal flow.

reuptake of serotonin. Other kinds of antidepressants, called mono-amine oxidase inhibitors, reduce the amount of one of the degrading enzymes in the synapse, again increasing the life of the neurotransmitter in the synapse.

The benzodiazepine antianxiety drugs, for example, Xanax and Valium, increase the activity of an inhibitory neurotransmitter called gamma-aminobutyric acid (GABA) that is released by the presynaptic cell. This has the effect of reducing neuronal transmission and probably explains why these drugs reduce anxiety and make people sleepy.

HOW THE DRUGS WORK

At first, scientists believed that psychiatric drugs exerted their effects mostly by increasing or decreasing the amount of neurotransmitter available in the synapse. By increasing the amount of serotonin available, for example, it was reasoned that tricyclic antidepressants improved neural transmission and cured depression. For a variety of reasons, it now seems pretty clear that this explanation is too simple. Instead, researchers are now focusing more and more on the effects psychiatric drugs have on receptors for neurotransmitters and on the second messengers. Exciting new findings suggest, for example, that lithium may exert its complex effects for patients with bipolar affective disorder by working on one of these second messenger systems.

Almost immediately after the introduction of medication into psychiatric practice, major scientific effort was expended to determine if the actions of these drugs on the brain could tell us anything at all about the cause of psychiatric disease. This may sound a little like the tail wagging the dog, and indeed that is an apt analogy. The usual procedure in medicine is to first find out what causes an illness and then develop a drug for it. For example, once it was known that some forms of pneumonia are caused by bacteria, scientists developed antibiotics to kill the bacteria and cure the pneumonia. In psychiatry, however, the procedure has been exactly the opposite. The first step has almost always been the accidental discovery of a drug, usually through the astute and persistent work of a careful observer. Next, some knowledge of what the drug does is gained, and finally an attempt is made to relate drug action to cause of disease.

To use the example of the antipsychotic drugs, these were discovered mostly by anesthesiologists who first used them to anesthetize surgical patients and observed their calming effect. Then they were shown to have a specific effect in relieving certain psychotic symptoms, like hallucinations and delusions, commonly seen in schizophrenic patients. Next, the discovery was made that these drugs block the dopamine receptor. Could that mean that any part of schizophrenia is the direct result of an excess of dopamine?

Similarly, could the cause of depression be related to an insufficiency of the neurotransmitters serotonin and noradrenaline? Or could anxiety be caused by too little GABA?

We do not yet have answers to these questions, although as mentioned earlier, it already seems certain that simple theories based on too much or too little neurotransmitter will not be adequate to explain such complex, common, and variable illnesses as depression, anxiety disorder, and schizophrenia. But psychopharmacology has certainly turned attention to the real possibility that many of these illnesses are caused at least in part by biological rather than psychological defects. The capacity to make images of the brain and its activity using sophisticated technology and the recent major breakthroughs in molecular genetics will certainly help us find out what is wrong in the brains and the genes of people with psychiatric illness. For now, we must be content with the knowledge that psychiatric drugs are often of great benefit and the promise that research will someday tell us why.

WHAT RESEARCH WILL TELL US

There has probably never been a more exciting or productive time in the history of brain science research as we are now experiencing. Almost every day scientific journals and mass media announce a significant new breakthrough in our understanding of how the mind works.

These new findings will undoubtedly have a great impact on the way patients with psychiatric illness are treated, but the effect will probably not be seen for at least another decade. Right now, scientists are using new technologies to figure out how the brain actually works.

One of the most significant advances in recent years is the capacity to image the living, intact brain. Scientists studying psychiatric disease have long been hampered by the inaccessibility of the brain. Other organs of the body can be seen quite well with ordinary x-rays or can be biopsied so that tissue can be studied directly. Blood tests reveal a great deal about the function of such organs as the kidneys, liver, and heart. There is, however, little chance to obtain pieces of brain tissue from a living person, and the previously described blood-brain barrier means that little information about brain chemicals can be learned through blood tests.

Recently, and in rapid progression, new methods of seeing the brain have been developed. The first of these, called computerized axial tomography, or CAT scanning, reveals brain structures in great detail, allowing examination of small structures of the brain without harming the patient. Next, an even more sophisticated way of looking at the fine details of brain structure was developed, this time using no radiation. Magnetic resonance imaging (MRI) depends on the creation of magnetic fields and gives highly refined pictures of the brain. Perhaps most exciting of all are the techniques called positron emission tomography (PET) and its close relative, single photon emission computed tomography (SPECT). These methods not only reveal brain structure but also show the degree of metabolic activity in various parts of the brain and allow visualization of brain chemicals and their receptors. For the first time, scientists can label drugs and chemicals with tiny, safe amounts of radioactivity, inject them into a person's bloodstream, and see exactly where in the brain they go and to what they bind.

Imaging techniques are already being used to describe abnormalities in the brains of patients with various psychiatric diseases, including panic disorder, obsessive-compulsive disorder, and schizophrenia. They have taught us something about the receptors for antipsychotic and benzodiazepine antianxiety medications. And they have shown us the patterns of tissue destruction in Alzheimer's dementia and AIDS.

Another very exciting area in psychiatric research involves the powerful new tools of molecular geneticists. It was only a little over thirty years ago that Watson and Crick first described the structure of the genetic molecule deoxyribosenucleic acid (DNA) and began a scientific revolution. At that time, it was probably unthinkable to most people that psychiatric disease would ever be found to have a genetic basis that could be linked to abnormalities on human chromosomes. Yet at least four neuropsychiatric disorders have now been linked to abnormal genes—schizophrenia, Huntington's disease, Alzheimer's disease, and bipolar affective disorder (formerly called manic depression). Once discovered, knowledge about abnormal genes can lead to a complete understanding of the cause of an illness and ultimately to its cure.

Molecular genetics and brain imaging techniques are two dramatic examples of powerful research technologies being applied to the study of psychiatric illness. But other new approaches to psychiatric research, although not always so dramatic, also promise to provide important information that will change our treatment strategies. I have stressed the differences of opinion that have traditionally existed in psychiatry between pharmacologically and psychotherapeutically oriented practitioners. More recently, scientists have developed methods for studying psychotherapies under rigorous, controlled conditions. They can compare drug therapies directly to psychotherapies for specific conditions. This has already been done in a large study of depression and is planned for a treatment study of panic disorder. The end result is a more scientific understanding about the indications and limits of both kinds of treatment. We can expect that in the near future, doctors will have scientific information upon which to base treatment decisions, rather than relying on dogma or tradition.

NEW DRUGS ON THE HORIZON

It is hard to predict which new classes of drugs will be most important in the future, but two are excellent candidates: the so-called "atypical" antipsychotics and the drugs that affect the serotonin nervous system.

Antipsychotic drugs like Thorazine and Haldol, described in more detail in Chapter 10, are used mostly to treat patients with the devastating illness schizophrenia. Although effective in many patients to calm the most obvious symptoms, like hallucinations and delusions, these drugs cause many side effects, including one that can permanently affect the nervous system—tardive dyskinesia. Recently, a new antipsychotic drug called clozapine (Clozaril) has been developed that apparently works even in schizophrenics who are not helped by the older antipsychotic drugs. More importantly, clozapine does not seem to cause any of the neurological side effects common to drugs like Haldol and Stelazine. It is therefore called an "atypical" antipsychotic drug. Unfortunately, clozapine causes serious side effects of its own, limiting its usefulness. Many companies are on the verge of introducing new atypical antipsychotics that promise to be as effective as clozapine without any serious side effects. This development is eagerly awaited.

Serotonin is one of the important neurotransmitters believed to play a particular role in depression and anxiety disorders. Prozac (fluoxetine), an antidepressant that is also very effective in treating many anxiety disorders, interacts specifically with the serotonin system. It has proven to be very effective and has far fewer side effects than most of the antidepressants previously available. Because of Prozac's success in treating depression, obsessive-compulsive disorder, and panic disorder, there is great activity among scientists to develop more drugs that regulate brain serotonin. Again, this class of medications will be carefully watched by psychiatrists and their patients over the next few years.

Perhaps of greater importance, we now appear to be approaching an era in which psychiatric disease is less stigmatized, and scientists who study mental illness can receive adequate support and funding for their work. For the first time, private citizens, foundations, and special interest groups are focusing on the problems of the mentally ill and raising money for psychiatric research. Rather than blaming parents for causing mental illness, it is now understood that much psychiatric illness is the unavoidable result of abnormalities of brain function. Patients with the devastating diseases of schizophrenia or Alzheimer's dementia are now felt as worthy of our help and understanding as patients with multiple sclerosis or diabetes.

A Final Note

It is perfectly reasonable to expect that before much longer we will finally know what causes some psychiatric diseases and therefore have more specific remedies. In the meantime, we already have many treatments that are extremely effective and others that can at least help to reduce the suffering and social disturbance of psychiatric illness. In the preceding chapters, I have tried to be completely honest about the limitations of medications for emotional disturbances, even as I attempted to convey the great excitement shared by many psychiatrists about our ability to make a real difference in treating mental illness. It will always be impossible to describe every possible situation because in psychiatry, more than any other medical specialty, individual differences are of paramount importance. But the more the patient understands about psychiatric illness and treatment, the better he or she will be able to participate with the doctor in making good decisions.

If there is any overriding principle to this book, it is simply that the object of psychiatric treatment should always be to make the patient better. That may sound ridiculously obvious, but in fact will be challenged by many. Some feel the object of treatment is to make the patient understand more about him or herself, to be better able to "deal" with complex emotions like anger and envy, or to follow societal rules and regulations better. I am not going to argue these points, because that would require another book. But I will bluntly assert that the object of psychiatric drug treatment has nothing to do with self-understanding or self-realization; it is a medical procedure intended to relieve symptoms and sometimes even cure disease. Thus, a patient can always ask himself a simple question when evaluating the usefulness and success of a drug treatment: Do I feel significantly better now than before I started taking the medicine?

In the historic Virginia village called Williamsburg stands the oldest continuously operating hospital dedicated to the care of patients with mental illness in the United States. The history of this Public Hospital serves as a metaphor for the changing attitudes toward mental health care in this country.

377

In the colonial period and through the early nineteenth century, the hospital resembled a prison. Rooms were tiny and had formidable bars on the windows. Patients, or "inmates" as they were called, rarely left their rooms. There was no attempt at treatment. The patients were approached like criminals and kept in cells to protect society from their supposed irrational acts.

But through the years it was noticed that some of these "inmates" actually got better. Often, they were able to leave the hospital and return to their former lives. Some subsequently worked and raised families. By about 1830, attitudes had changed and for the first time the patients in the Public Hospital were regarded as suffering from potentially treatable illness.

Doctors began to visit the patients regularly. Rooms were made larger, cleaner, and less prisonlike. The bars were replaced by fine wire mesh, which still kept the patient from escaping but were less intimidating. Patients were let out of the rooms and every effort was made to rehabilitate them and return them to society as soon as possible. This was an era of great hope that with proper care and kindness, patients with mental illness could get better and leave the hospital.

This era too came to an end. Despite their best efforts, the physicians and other staff increasingly became discouraged by the numbers of patients who did not get better. As the hospital became a more humane place for the mentally ill, it also became a more popular place. The census increased dramatically through the nineteenth century, and with that increase came larger numbers of chronically ill patients who could never leave the hospital. By the end of the nineteenth century, the Public Hospital again became a place dedicated mainly to chronic institutionalization rather than to treatment of patients with psychiatric disease. When the hospital burned down in the first half of the twentieth century, most of the optimism that mental illness was treatable had waned.

Clearly, we are now in a new age of hope. The reasons for the loss of optimism at the end of the nineteenth century are clear. Despite their best and noblest efforts, the doctors of that era had no idea what caused mental illness and no scientific basis for its treatment. Patients with time-limited illness like some forms of depression got better on their own; patients with chronic illnesses like schizophrenia remained ill. The ability to differentiate among these different diseases was rudimentary.

Today we have sharpened our diagnostic skills and introduced powerful scientific methods to the study of the brain and its dysfunction. Scientific journals are replete with new and exciting findings that will lead the way to improved treatments. If the Public Hospital in Williamsburg, Virginia, were today a functioning hospital instead of a museum, it might look like any other general hospital, with doctors, nurses, social workers, x-ray machines, and laboratories. And it would be full of the belief that a combination of compassion and science will show us the way to relieving the pain and suffering of mental illness.

Glossary of Terms

ANHEDONIA   Loss of interest in life, often experienced by depressed patients.

ANOREXIA   Loss of appetite.

ANOREXIA NERVOSA   An illness in which the patient has a fixed idea that she is fat and therefore must starve herself to lose weight. In addition to self-imposed starvation, patients with anorexia nervosa often abuse water pills (diuretics) and laxatives, induce vomiting, and become fanatical about exercise. The illness is potentially fatal.

ANTICHOLINERGIC   Generally refers to a set of side effects caused by many psychiatric drugs. The major anticholinergic side effects are dry mouth, constipation, difficulty urinating, and blurry vision. Many antidepressants and antipsychotic drugs cause anticholinergic side effects.

ATYPICAL DEPRESSION   A form of depression in which the patient can usually be temporarily cheered up if something good happens. Often associated with overeating and oversleeping. Generally responds best to antidepressants of the monoamine oxidase inhibitor class and possibly to Prozac.

BIPOLAR AFFECTIVE DISORDER   Formerly called "manic-depressive illness," in this psychiatric illness the patient alternates between states of depression and states of hypomania or mania. A patient with four or more depressions and/or manic episodes in a year is said to have "rapid cycling" bipolar illness.

BLOOD-BRAIN BARRIER   A wall-like separation between the brain and the bloodstream that carefully modulates what substances, including drugs, cross into the brain.

BULIMIA   An illness characterized by episodic binge eating, sometimes followed by self-induced vomiting.

CYCLIC ANTIDEPRESSANTS   The class of antidepressants that includes Tofranil, Norpramin, Aventyl, Pamelor, Pertofrane, Elavil, Endep, Sinequan, Adapin, Vivactil, Surmontil, and Ludiomil. They are used mainly to treat major depression.

DELUSION   A false belief that no amount of reality, facts, or hard evidence will shake. This is a psychotic symptom.

DIZYGOTIC TWINS   Another name for fraternal twins. Dizygotic twins are as genetically similar as ordinary brothers and sisters.

DSM-III-R   The revised third edition of the *American Psychiatric Association's Diagnostic and Statistical Manual.* It gives precise instructions on the symptoms and signs needed to make every psychiatric diagnosis. Most psychiatrists and many other mental health professionals use it, and many insurance companies now require a DSM-III-R diagnosis on their forms. A fourth edition (DSM-IV) is due in the early 1990s.

DOPAMINE   A chemical neurotransmitter in the brain. Most of the antipsychotic drugs block the binding of dopamine to its receptors.

ELECTROCONVULSIVE THERAPY (ECT)   A treatment for major depression in which the patient is given a small current of electric shock, inducing a seizure. It is called *bilateral ECT* if electrodes for the shock are placed on both temples of the head and *unilateral ECT* if the electrodes are placed on only one temple.

EUTHYMIC   Normal mood.

GAMMA-AMINOBUTYRIC ACID (GABA)   A neurotransmitter that generally reduces brain activity. Benzodiazepine antianxiety drugs usually increase the effects of GABA in the brain.

GENERALIZED ANXIETY DISORDER (GAD)   An anxiety disorder in which the patient feels continuously anxious for no apparent reason for at least six months.

GLAUCOMA   A condition involving increased pressure in the eyes. There are two types, chronic wide-angle and acute narrow-angle glaucoma. Patients with acute narrow-angle glaucoma should not take psychiatric drugs with anticholinergic effects.

HALF-LIFE   A measure of how long a drug remains in the body after it is taken. Some drugs are broken down and eliminated very fast by the body and therefore are said to have a short half-life. Some drugs remain in the body for days or even weeks after they are taken and therefore have a long half-life.

HALLUCINATION   Hearing, seeing, or feeling things that are not really there. A psychotic symptom. Auditory hallucinations are common to patients with schizophrenia.

HYPERTENSIVE CRISIS   A sudden and severe increase in

382

blood pressure produced when a person on a monoamine oxidase inhibitor antidepressant eats or drinks something on the restricted list.

HYPNOTIC DRUGS Sleeping pills.

HYPOMANIA A relatively mild "high" that may come on spontaneously in patients with a form of bipolar affective disorder (formerly called manic depression) or may be produced by taking antidepressants. When hypomanic, the patient is unusually energetic and talkative, may be irritable, and is overly optimistic often with bad judgment.

HYPOTHALAMUS The part of the brain that controls many important "vegetative" functions including appetite and sleep. Some abnormalities in the functioning of the hypothalamus may occur in psychiatric illness, especially depression.

HYPOTHYROIDISM A condition in which the thyroid gland is underactive.

INSOMNIA Inability to fall asleep (also called initial insomnia) or stay asleep (also called middle insomnia) or waking up too early in the morning (also called terminal insomnia or early-morning awakening).

LIBIDO Sex drive.

MAJOR DEPRESSION A form of depression in which the patient cannot be cheered up, even temporarily. Often associated with loss of appetite and concentration and insomnia. Responds to cyclic antidepressants and electroconvulsive therapy.

MANIA A serious psychiatric condition in which the patient is "high." This usually occurs as part of bipolar affective disorder (formerly called manic depression), but can be caused by drugs. The patient with mania is extremely energetic, hyperactive, and talkative. He or she has an increased sex drive and very little need for sleep, and becomes grandiose. In very severe forms, the patient talks so fast and the mind races so rapidly that nothing she says makes much sense. The patient may hear voices (auditory hallucinations) or develop delusions.

MONOAMINE OXIDASE An enzyme in the brain that breaks down neurotransmitters.

MONOAMINE OXIDASE INHIBITORS Antidepressant/ antianxiety drugs that interfere with the brain enzyme monoamine oxidase. They are used to treat atypical depression, as well as major depression and panic disorder that do not respond to other medications.

MONOZYGOTIC TWINS   Another name for identical twins. Monozygotic twins have identical genes.

NEGATIVE SYMPTOMS   A cluster of symptoms observed in some schizophrenic patients that include loss of motivation, apathy, and loss of emotion. Although controversy exists, it is said that negative symptoms do not respond to antipsychotic drugs as well as other symptoms of schizophrenia such as hallucinations and delusions.

NEUROLEPTIC   A term sometimes used for antipsychotic drugs.

NEURON   Brain cells.

NEUROTRANSMITTER   The chemicals in the brain that cross the space (or synapse) between one brain cell and the next to enable communication between cells. Examples of neurotransmitters are noradrenaline, serotonin, and dopamine. Psychiatric drugs often effect the levels of neurotransmitters.

NIGHT TERRORS (PAVOR NOCTURNUS)   A sleep disorder in which the person, usually a child, wakes from stage 4 (deep) sleep in a state of terror with rapid breathing and heart rate. By definition, night terrors do not involve nightmares and the patient never remembers dreaming.

NORADRENALINE   A neurotransmitter that may be involved in depression and anxiety disorders. Many antidepressant drugs affect the level of noradrenaline in the brain.

OBSESSIVE-COMPULSIVE DISORDER (OCD)   An anxiety disorder in which the patient suffers from the need to complete seemingly meaningless rituals, like handwashing, over and over again or must incessantly entertain meaningless and anxiety-provoking thoughts.

ORTHOSTATIC HYPOTENSION   A drop in blood pressure resulting in a dizzy or faint feeling that is produced after suddenly sitting up or standing up. Many psychiatric drugs cause orthostatic hypotension. It can be a serious side effect in elderly patients.

PANIC DISORDER   An anxiety disorder characterized by sudden unexpected anxiety attacks that occur at least once a week and usually more often. Patients with panic disorder may also develop worries about having panic attacks, called *anticipatory anxiety,* and may avoid situations in which they fear they will not be able to get help quickly in case of a panic attack, a situation called *agoraphobia.*

PARANOIA A feeling or state in which someone believes others are trying to harm him when this is absolutely untrue. Some schizophrenic patients suffer from paranoid delusions: they persistently believe there are plots against them and nothing can convince them otherwise. Uneasiness with or mistrust of other people is not the same as paranoia.

PLACEBO An inactive sugar pill used in research to test the effectiveness of new drugs. In a drug trial, a new medication must be shown to work better than the placebo to prove it is truly effective.

PSYCHOPHARMACOLOGY The branch of medicine that specializes in medications to treat psychiatric illnesses. Practitioners are called psychopharmacologists and usually are medical doctors with special training in psychiatry and psychopharmacology.

PSYCHOSIS A severe psychiatric abnormality often defined as involving a break with reality and comprising hallucinations, delusions, thought disorder, and markedly bizarre behavior. It can occur as part of many psychiatric illnesses or may be caused by some drugs.

RAPID CYCLING A form of bipolar affective disorder in which the patient experiences four or more episodes per year of mania or depression. It is said to be less responsive to lithium than regular bipolar illness.

REM (RAPID EYE MOVEMENTS) The stage of sleep in which almost all dreaming occurs. During this stage the eyes dart rapidly back and forth.

SCHIZOAFFECTIVE A diagnosis for patients who combine features of schizophrenia and abnormal mood, either depression or mania.

SEROTONIN A neurotransmitter that may be involved in depression and anxiety disorders. Many antidepressant drugs affect the level of serotonin in the brain.

SIDE EFFECTS Unwanted physical and emotional changes

caused by drugs that have nothing to do with their ability to treat an illness. Also called "adverse effects."

SIMPLE PHOBIA   An anxiety disorder in which a patient, for no good reason, fears and avoids specific objects to the point that it interferes with her ability to function normally. Examples are phobias of small animals, heights, and close spaces.

SOCIAL PHOBIA   An anxiety disorder in which the patient has anxiety symptoms only in specific social situations, such as giving a presentation in front of a group, talking to people at a party, and answering a question in class.

SYNAPSE   In the brain, the space between one nerve cell and the next.

TAPERING   The process of slowly decreasing the dose of medication over several days or weeks until the medication is completely discontinued. This is done to reduce or avoid withdrawal symptoms.

TARDIVE DYSKINESIA   A serious side effect of the antipsychotic medications (and possibly the antidepressant Asendin) characterized by abnormal and involuntary movements. It usually does not occur until the patient has taken the drug many months and usually years, but elderly people can develop it more quickly. The first symptoms usually involve movements of the face, mouth, and tongue. It is sometimes irreversible, even when the drug is stopped.

TEMPORAL LOBE EPILEPSY   A form of epilepsy involving the temporal lobe of the brain. Also called "psychomotor epilepsy" and "partial complex seizure disorder." During seizures the patient engages in some usually purposeless activity like banging on things, twirling around, or stomping his foot. As with all seizures, the behavior is involuntary. Anticonvulsant medication is given to control this.

WITHDRAWAL SYMPTOMS   New symptoms that arise because a drug is discontinued. These almost always go away within two weeks of drug discontinuation. Tapering a drug rather than abruptly discontinuing it reduces and sometimes even eliminates withdrawal symptoms.

Suggestions for Further Reading

Agras, W. Stewart. *Panic: Facing Fears, Phobias, and Anxiety,* W. H. Freeman, San Francisco, 1985.

Andreasen, Nancy. *The Broken Brain: The Biological Revolution in Psychiatry,* Harper and Row, New York, 1984.

Barlow, David H., and Jerome A. Cerny. *Psychological Treatment of Panic,* Guilford Press, New York, 1988.

Benson, Herbert. *The Relaxation Response,* Avon Books, New York, 1975.

Bruno, Frank J. *The Family Mental Health Encyclopedia,* John Wiley and Sons, New York, 1989.

Burns, David D. *Feeling Good: The New Mood Therapy,* New American Library, New York, 1981.

Campbell, Robert J. *Psychiatric Dictionary,* 6th ed., Oxford University Press, London/New York, 1989.

Carroll, David L. *When Your Loved One Has Alzheimer's: A Caregivers Guide,* Harper and Row, New York, 1989.

Diagnostic and Statistical Manual of Mental Disorders, Third Edition, Revised (DSM-III-R), American Psychiatric Press, Washington, D.C., 1987.

Duke, Patty. *Call Me Anna,* Bantam Books, New York, 1987.

Ehret, Charles F., and Lynne Waller Scanlon. *Overcoming Jet Lag,* Berkley Books, New York, 1983.

Fieve, Ronald. *Moodswings,* Bantam Books, New York, 1982.

Fisher, Richard B. *A Dictionary of Mental Health,* Academy Chicago Ltd., Chicago, 1983.

Gold, Mark. *The Good News About Depression,* Bantam Books, New York, 1988.

Goodwin, Donald W. *Anxiety,* Oxford University Press, New York, 1986.

Graedon, Joe: *The People's Pharmacy,* St. Martin's Press, New York, 1985.

Greist, John H., and James W. Jefferson. *Depression and Its Treatment,* American Psychiatric Press, Washington, D.C., 1984.

Greist, John H., James W. Jefferson, and Isaac Marks. *Anxiety and Its Treatment,* American Psychiatric Press, Washington, D.C., 1986.

Hobson, J. Allan. *The Dreaming Brain,* Basic Books, New York, 1988.

Katcher, Brian S. *Prescription Drugs,* Avon Books, New York, 1988.

Klein, Donald F., Rachel Gittelman, Frederic Quitkin, and Arthur Rifkin. *Diagnosis and Drug Treatment of Psychiatric Disorders: Adults and Children,* 2nd ed., Williams and Wilkins, Baltimore, 1980.

Klein, Donald F., and Paul H. Wender. *Mind, Mood, and Medicine,* New American Library, New York, 1982.

Klein, Donald F., and Paul H. Wender. *Do You Have a Depressive Illness?* New American Library, New York, 1988.

Kline, Nathan S. *From Sad to Glad,* Ballantine, New York, 1981.

Knauth, Percy. *A Season in Hell,* Harper and Row, New York, 1975.

Kovel, Joel. *A Complete Guide to Therapy,* Pantheon Books, New York, 1976.

Liebowitz, Michael. *The Chemistry of Love,* Little, Brown, Boston, 1983.

Lithium and Manic Depression: A Guide, Lithium Information Center, Madison, WI, 1982.

Luria, S. E. *A Slot Machine, A Broken Test Tube,* Harper and Row, New York, 1984.

Marks, Isaac M. *Living With Fear,* McGraw-Hill, New York, 1980.

Morrison, James R. *Your Brother's Keeper: A Guide for Families Confronting Psychiatric Illness,* Nelson-Hall, Chicago, 1981.

Papolos, Demitri F., and Janice Papolos. *Overcoming Depression,* Harper and Row, New York, 1987.

Piersall, Jim, and Al Hirshberg. *Fear Strikes Out: The Jim Piersall Story,* Little, Brown, Boston, 1955.

Rapoport, Judith L. *The Boy Who Couldn't Stop Washing,* E. P. Dutton, New York, 1989.

Rush, John. *Beating Depression,* Facts on File, Inc., New York, 1986.

Schau, Mogens. *Lithium Treatment of Manic Depressive Illness: A Practical Guide,* Karger, 1989.

Sheehan, David. *The Anxiety Disease,* Bantam Books, New York, 1986.

Silverman, Harold M. *The Pill Book: Guide to Safe Drug Use,* Bantam Books, New York, 1989.

Torey, E. Fuller. *Surviving Schizophrenia: A Family Manual,* Harper and Row, New York, 1983.

Walsh, Maryellen, *Schizophrenia: Straight Talk for Families and Friends,* William Morrow, New York, 1985.

Index

Abnormal affect, 203
Abnormal Involuntary Movements Scales
    (AIMS), 221
Acetophenazine (Tindal), 251
Acute dystonic reaction, 218
Adapin (doxepin), 41, 73, 75–76,
    282–284
Addiction
    benzodiazepines and, 131–135, 267
    drugs that cause, 39–40, 107–108
    drugs to treat, 285–306
    violence and, 311–313
Aging. See Elderly
Agoraphobia, 123–124
AIDS, psychiatric problems of, 207,
    351–357
Akathisia, 218
Akinesia, 221
Akineton (biperiden), 218, 220–221
Alcoholics Anonymous (AA), 285,
    293–294
Alcoholism and drug abuse
    causes of, 317, 320
    drugs to treat, 24, 189, 285–306
    violence and, 311
Alprazolam (Xanax), 41, 105, 121, 123,
    129, 131, 135, 142–144, 147,
    151–153, 359, 361. See also
    Benzodiazepines
Alzheimer's disease, 206–207, 213–214,
    319, 340
Amantadine (Symmetrel), 218, 220
American Psychiatric Association Diagnostic
    and Statistical Manual (DSM-III-R).
    15–16
Amitriptyline (Elavil, Endep, others), 41,
    69–71, 185, 269, 282–283
Amoxapine (Asendin), 100, 104–105,
    221
Amphetamines (Dexedrine, Biphetamine,
    Desoxyn, others), 36, 40, 42,
    107–110, 292, 311–312, 326
Anafranil (chlomipramine), 41, 125, 127,
    148, 164–166
Anesthesia when taking psychiatric drugs,
    43
Angel Dust (phencyclidone, PCP), 312
Anorexia nervosa, 327–328
Antabuse (disulfiram), 287, 294, 297–299
Anterograde amnesia, 270
Anticipatory anxiety, 122, 146–147
Antidepressants, new, 63, 99–107. See also
    Depression, drugs to treat

Antihistamines, 268, 278–280
Antipsychotic drugs. See Schizophrenia,
    drugs to treat (antipsychotics)
Anxiety
    drug abuse and, 289–290
    drugs to treat, 23, 41–43, 117–172
    forms of, 118–121
    HIV-infected patients and, 356
    sex and, 332–333
Anxiety disorders, 120–127, 129
Artane (trihexyphenidyl), 218–219, 221,
    223
Asendin (amoxapine), 100, 104–105, 221
Atarax, 268, 279–280
Atenolol (Tenormin), 125, 156, 158–162
Ativan (lorazepam), 41, 43, 121, 123,
    131, 140–141, 147, 186, 220, 294.
    See also Benzodiazepines
Attention deficit disorder
    and amphetamines, 108
    and Ritalin, 110–111
Atypical depression, 17, 49–50, 55–57, 61
Atypical antipsychotics, 226, 248–251,
    374
Auditory hallucinations, 202
Aventyl (nortriptyline), 41, 71–73, 123,
    148

Barbiturates, 130, 133, 269, 283, 292
Barlow, David, 150
Bedwetting and imipramine, 65
Benadryl (diphenhydramine), 218–219,
    221, 279–280
Benzodiazepines, 40, 43, 121, 123,
    129–144, 147–148, 186, 267,
    270–277, 290, 335, 370
    long- and short-acting, 136
    symptoms of withdrawal from, 132
Benztropine (Cogentin), 218–219, 221,
    223
Beta adrenergic blockers, 157
Beta blockers, 124–125, 149, 157–162
Bilateral ECT, 114
Biologists, radical, 7
Biperiden (Akineton), 218, 220–221
Biphetamine (amphetamines), 36, 40, 42,
    107–110, 292, 311–312, 326
Bipolar affective disorder, 39, 54–55, 60,
    175–199, 206, 348
    causes of, 317–320
    drug abuse and, 290
    order in which drugs are prescribed,
    199

Bipolar affective disorder *(cont.)*
  treating the patient with, 184
  vs. schizophrenia, 176–184, 212–213
Birth defects and psychiatric drugs,
  345–350
Blocadren, 159
Blocking the high, 287–288
Borderline personality disorder, 216, 235
Boy Who Couldn't Stop Washing, The,
  (Rapoport), 125
Brain
  HIV infection of, 354
  psychiatric drugs and, how they work,
  365–375
Brain-damaged patients and violence,
  310–312
Brand names vs. generic drugs, 359–364
Breakthrough depressions, 185–186, 188,
  315
Breakthrough mania, 188
Bromocriptine (Parlodel), 220, 222
Bulimia, 106, 328
Bupropion (Welbutrin), 105–107, 185,
  327
BuSpar (buspirone), 35, 122, 136,
  144–145

Cade, John, 193
Calan (verapamil), 149, 184–185, 189,
  199
Carbamazepine (Tegretol), 184–185
Catapres (clonidine), 149, 189, 199, 218,
  286–287, 292, 294, 299–300
Centrax (prazepam), 139. *See also*
  Benzodiazepines
Chlomipramine (Anafranil), 41, 125, 127,
  148, 164–166, 172–174
Chloral hydrate, 267
Chlordiazepoxide (Librium), 23, 41, 43,
  121, 129, 131, 138–139, 147, 286,
  294–297. *See also* Benzodiazepines
Chlorpromazine (Thorazine), 41, 186,
  188, 223–224, 230–232
Chlorprothixene (Taractan), 251
Cholinergic nervous system, 41
Cigarette addiction, drugs to treat,
  285–292, 294–295, 299–301
Clonazepam (Klonopin), 123, 131, 148,
  184–185, 188–189, 197–199. *See
  also* Benzodiazepines
Clonidine (Catapres), 149, 189, 199, 218,
  286–287, 292, 294, 299–300
Clorazepate (Tranxene), 40, 129, 131,
  139. *See also* Benzodiazepines
Clozapine (Clozaril), 226, 248–251, 374
Cocaine addiction
  drugs to treat, 285–292, 294, 304–306
  violence and, 311–312

Cogentin (benztropine), 218–219, 221,
  223
Command hallucinations, 202
Compulsions. *See* Obsessive compulsive
  disorder (OCD)
Confidentiality, 28
Controversies about psychopharmacology,
  7
Corgard, 159
Cyclic antidepressants, 26, 54, 62, 57,
  65–82, 123, 148, 185, 368
  side effects of, 74–75
  summary of, 82
Cylert (pemoline), 42, 107, 111

Dalmane (flurazepam), 267, 270,
  272–274
Dantrium (dantrolene), 218, 220
Delirium tremens, 286
Delusions and schizophrenia, 202–203
Dementia, 206–207, 213–214, 340, 354
Depakene (valproic acid), 184–185,
  188–189, 195–197, 327
Deprenyl (selegiline), 99. *See also*
  Monoamine oxidase inhibitors
  (MAOIs)
Depressed bipolar patient, treating,
  185–186
Depression
  checklist of, 62–64
  drug abuse and, 289–290
  drugs for use as sleeping pills, 269,
  282–283
  drugs to treat, 10, 16–18, 24, 26, 28,
  38, 47–115, 206, 368
  features of different forms of, 52–53
  HIV-infected patients and, 355–356
  sex and, 332–335
  terms to classify, 50
  treatment plans for, 60–61
  See also Bipolar affective disorder
Desipramine (Norpramin, Pertofrane), 41,
  67–69, 123, 148, 151–153, 288,
  305
Desoxyn (amphetamines), 36, 40, 42,
  107–110, 292, 311–312, 326
Desyrel (trazodone), 100, 103–104, 269,
  282–283, 335
Dexedrine (amphetamines), 36, 40, 42,
  107–110, 292, 311–312, 326
Diagnosis, importance of, 15–20, 151,
  177
  elderly and, 338–340
Diazepam (Valium), 23, 40–41, 43, 121,
  129, 131, 135, 137–138, 147, 218,
  220. *See also* Benzodiazepines
Dilantin, 312
Dilaudid, 292

Diphenhydramine (Benadryl), 218–219, 221, 279–280
Disulfiram (Antabuse), 288, 294, 297–299
Dogmatic psychologists, 7
Dolophine (methadone), 288, 294, 303–304
Dopamine, 217, 368
Doral, 278
Doriden, 133, 269, 283
Double depression, 57
Doxepin (Sinequan, Adapin), 41, 73, 75–76, 269, 282–283
Doxylamine succinate (Unisom Nighttime Sleep Aid), 278–279
Drug abuse, 128, 132
    drugs to treat, 285–306
    violence and, 311–313
DSM-III-R (American Psychiatric Association Diagnostic and Statistical Manual), 15–16
Dystonia, 218

Eating disorders, 327–328
Elavil (amitriptyline), 41, 69–71, 185, 269, 282–283
Eldepryl (selegiline), 85, 99. See also Monoamine oxidase inhibitors (MAOIs)
Elderly
    prescribing drugs for the, 214, 224, 337–344
    sleep patterns of, 255, 258–259
Electroconvulsive therapy (ECT), 54, 111–115, 349
Endep (amitriptyline), 41, 69–71
Environment, family, and genetics, mental illness and, 315–321
Eosinophilia-myalgia syndrome, 269, 282
Equanil (meprobamate), 130, 133, 145–146
Eskalith and Eskalith CR (lithium), 39, 54–55, 182–193, 212–213, 312, 315, 329, 335, 346–347, 364
Estazolam (Prosom), 267, 269, 277
Euresis and imipramine, 65
Euthymic bipolar patient, treating, 1877–189
Eutonyl (pargyline), 85, 96–99. See also Monoamine oxidase inhibitors (MAOIs)
Excessive anxiety, 119–120, 129
Exedrin P.M., 278–279

Family
    causes of mental illness and, 315–321
    importance of involvement, 27–29
Fenfluramine (Pondomin), 167

Fluoxetine (Prozac), 57, 83, 100–102, 123, 125, 127, 149, 158, 166–167, 185–186, 326–327, 368–369, 374
Fluphenazine (Prolixin, Permitil), 223, 225, 237–238
Flurazepam (Dalmane), 267, 270, 272–274

Generalized anxiety disorder (GAD), 121–122, 136–146, 333
Generic drugs vs. brand names, 359–364
Genetics, family, and environment, mental illness and 315–321
Glassman, Alexander, 287, 289
Granulocytosis, 226, 249
Growth hormone and sleep, 254
Guidelines for getting psychiatric drugs, 29

Habit-forming drugs, 39–40, 107–108
    benzodiazepine as, 131–135, 267
    See also Drug abuse, drugs to treat
Halazepam (Paxipam), 139–140. See also Benzodiazepines
Halcion (triazolam), 267, 270–272, 275–277
Haldol (haloperidol), 186, 223, 228–230
Haldol Decanoate (haloperidol), 225, 228–230
Hallucinations and schizophrenia, 202
Haloperidol (Haldol), 186, 223, 225, 228–230
Health insurance coverage for psychiatric care, 26, 294
Heroin addiction
    drugs to treat, 285–292, 294, 299–304
    violence and, 311
High, blocking the, 287–288
High-potency antipsychotic drugs, 223–224
HIV infection, psychiatric problems of, 207, 351–357
Hollander, Eric, 167
Hospitalization
    for bipolar affective disorder, 187
    to stop using psychiatric drugs, 43
Huntington's disease, 207, 318
Hyperactivity. See Attention deficit disorder
Hypertensive crisis and monoamine oxidase inhibitors, 83
Hypnotics. See Sleeping pills
Hypomania, 26

Imipramine (Tofranil, Janimine, others), 41, 65–67, 123, 148, 151–153, 185, 288, 294, 304–306

Inderal (propanolol), 125, 149, 156, 158–160, 220, 312
Insomnia, 36, 40, 253–283
  before taking sleeping pills for, 264
  ten causes of, 262
Isocarboxazid (Marplan), 85, 93–95. *See also* Monoamine oxidase inhibitors (MAOIs)
Isoptin (verapamil), 149, 184–185, 189, 199

Janimine (imipramine), 65–67, 151–153, 288, 294
Jet lag, treatment of, 271–272

Kemadrin (procyclidine), 218–219, 221
Klein, Donald F., 56
Klonopin (clonazepam), 123, 131, 148, 184–185, 188–189, 197–199. *See also* Benzodiazepines

Lecithin, 199
Levodopa, 220, 222
Librium (chlordiazepoxide), 23, 41, 43, 121, 129, 131, 138–139, 147, 286, 294–296. *See also* Benzodiazepines
Lidone (molindone), 244–246
Limbitrol (Librium and amitriptyline), 139
Lithium (Lithonate, Lithane, Lithobid, Eskalith, Eskalith CR, others), 39, 54–55, 182–193, 212–213, 312, 315, 329, 335, 346–347, 364
Long-acting benzodiazepines, 136
Long-term treatment, 38–39
Lopressor, 159
Lorazepam (Ativan), 41, 43, 121, 123, 131, 140–141, 147, 186, 220, 294
  See also Benzodiazepines
Low-potency antipsychotic drugs, 223–224
Loxapine (Loxitane), 41, 242–244
Ludiomil (maprotiline), 41, 80–82

Maintenance ECT, 114
Major depression, 17, 49–52, 55, 60, 112, 315
Manic bipolar patient, 186–187, 333
Manic depression. *See* Bipolar affective disorder
Maportiline (Ludiomil), 41, 80–82
Marplan (isocarboxazid), 85, 93–95. *See also* Monoamine oxidase inhibitors (MAOIs)
Medical problems and psychiatric drug treatment, 341–342
Medicare and psychiatric care, 342
Medium-length treatment, 37–38
Mellaril (thioridazine), 41, 223, 232–235

Memory loss and electroconvulsive therapy, 113–114
Mental illness, causes of, 315–321
Meprobamate (Miltown, Equanil), 130, 133, 145–146, 283
Mesoridazine (Serentil), 235
Methadone (Dolophine), 288, 294, 303–304
Methylphenidate (Ritalin), 42, 107, 110–111
Miltown (meprobamate), 130, 133, 145–146, 283
Molindone (Moban, Lidone), 244–246
Monoamine oxidase inhibitors (MAOIs), 26, 43, 57, 63, 83–99, 123, 125, 149, 153, 157, 162–163, 185, 333–335, 370
  foods and drugs to avoid while taking, 84–85, 290
  headaches and, 88
Mood, reactive vs. nonreactive, 49
Mood log, 180–181, 183

Naltrexone (Trexan), 288, 294, 301–303
Narcolepsy and amphetamines, 108
Nardil (phenelzine), 41, 85–89, 123, 125, 149, 153, 156, 162–163, 325. *See also* Monoamine oxidase inhibitors (MAOIs)
National Alliance for the Mentally Ill, 205
Navane (thiothixene), 184, 241–242
Negative symptoms of schizophrenia, 211
Nervine, 268, 278–279
Neuroleptic malignant syndrome, 222
Neuroscience and psychiatric drugs, 365–375
New antidepressants, 63, 99–107
Nicorette chewing gum, 288, 292, 294–295, 301
Night terrors (pavor nocturnus), 137, 256
Nightmares, 256
Nocturnal myoclonus, 261, 266
Noludar, 133, 269, 283
Normal anxiety, 118–119, 129
Norpramin (desipramine), 41, 67–69, 123, 148, 151–153, 288
Nortriptyline (Aventyl, Pamelor), 41, 71–73, 123, 148
Nytol, 268, 278–279

Obsessive compulsive disorder (OCD), 125–127, 164–172, 317
Orap (pimozide), 246–248
Over-the-counter sleeping pills, 268, 278–279
Oxazepam (Serax), 41, 131, 141–142. *See also* Benzodiazepines

Pamelor (nortriptyline), 41, 71–73, 148
Panic control therapy, 150
Panic disorder, 10, 122–123, 128–129,
    146–155, 317–318
  features of, 147
  treatment of, 152–153
Paranoid delusions, 202, 209, 309,
    340–341
Parenting and mental illness, 315–321.
    See also Pregnancy and psychiatric
    drugs
Pargyline (Eutonyl), 85, 96–99. *See also*
    Monoamine oxidase inhibitors
    (MAOIs)
Parkinsonian syndrome, 218
Parlodel (bromocriptine), 220, 222
Parnate (tranycypromine), 85, 89–93,
    123, 149, 153, 162, 325. *See also*
    Monoamine oxidase inhibitors
    (MAOIs)
Partial complex seizures, 310
Pavor nocturnus (night terrors), 137, 154
Paxipam (halazepam), 139–140. *See also*
    Benzodiazepines
PCP (Angel Dust, phencyclidine), 312
Pemoline (Cylert), 42, 107, 111
Permitil (fluphenazine), 223, 237–238
Perphenazine (Trilafon), 41, 188,
    239–241
Personality disorder, 216, 235
Pertofrane (desipramine), 67–69, 148,
    151–153, 288
Phencyclidine (Angel Dust, PCP), 312
Phenelzine (Nardil), 41, 85–89, 123,
    125, 149, 153, 156, 162–163, 327.
    See also Monoamine oxidase
    inhibitors (MAOIs)
Phenobarbital, 269, 283
Phobias, 123–125, 146–147, 155–163
Physicians Desk Reference (PRD), to look
    up side effects, 32–33
Pimozide (Orap), 246–248
Piperacetazine (Quide), 251
Placidyl, 133, 269, 283
Pondomin (fenfluramine), 167
Post, Robert, 195
Prazepam (Centrax), 139. *See also*
    Benzodiazepines
Pregnancy and psychiatric drugs, 345–350
Procyclidine (Kemadrin), 218–219, 221
Prolixin (fluphenazine), 222, 237–238
Prolixin Decanoate (fluphenazine), 225,
    237–238
Propanolol (Inderal), 125, 149, 156,
    158–160, 218, 220, 312
Prosom (estazolam), 267, 270, 277
Protriptyline (Vivactil), 41, 78–80, 327

Prozac (fluoxetine), 57, 83, 100–102,
    123, 125, 127, 149, 158, 166–167,
    185–186, 326–327, 368–369, 374
Psychiatric drugs
  brand names vs. generic drugs,
    359–364
  deciding a need for, 9–13, 127–129
  elderly and, safest for the, 343
  finding a practitioner to prescribe,
    21, 30
  guidelines for getting, 29
  for HIV-infected patients, 357
  how they work, 365–375
  length of treatment with, 25–43
  psychotherapy and/or, 15–20, 25
  sexual side effects of, 334
  weight gain not caused with, 325
Psychiatrists
  choosing a, 21–30
  features of, 18
  rules to consider before seeing, 10–13
  seeking one for help with anxiety,
    127–129
  views on psychopharmacology, 7
Psychologists, 7, 9
Psychomotor epilepsy, 310
Psychoneuroimmunology, 353
Psychopharmacology, 6, 7, 22
Psychosis, treatment of for HIV-infected
    patients, 356–357
Psychostimulants. *See* Stimulants
Psychotherapist, choosing a, 19–20
Pscyhotherapy and/or psychiatric drugs,
    15–20, 25
Psychotic depression, 53–55, 61
Psychotic episodes, 209, 312–313
Psychotic symptoms of schizophrenia,
    202–204

Quaaludes, 292
Quazepam, 278
Quide (piperacetazine), 251
Quitkin, Frederick, 57

Radical biologists, 7
Rapoport, Judith, 125
Rapid cycling, 185, 195
Reactive depressions, 58
Rebound symptoms, 41
Rebound insomnia, 267, 270
REM sleep, 255–256
Reserpine (Serpasil), 220, 222
Response blocking, 167
Restoril (temazepam), 265, 270, 274, 275
Retrograde ejaculation, 335
Ritalin (methylphenidate), 42, 107,
    110–111

Schizoaffective disorder, 177–178, 184
Schizophrenia
    bipolar affective disorder vs., 176–184,
        212–213
    causes of, 317–320
    drugs to counteract side effects of
        antipsychotics, 219–220
    drugs to treat (antipsychotics), 10–11,
        201–251, 368
    HIV-infected patients and
        antipsychotics, 356–357
    summary of antipsychotic drugs, 224
    treating violent patients, 309–313
Schou, Mogens, 183, 193
Seconal, 269, 283
Second opinion, getting a, 25–26
Selegiline (Eldepryl, Deprenyl), 85, 99.
        See also Monoamine oxidase
        inhibitors (MAOIs)
Serax (oxazepam), 41, 131, 141–142. See
        also Benzodiazepines
Serentil (mesoridazine), 235
Serotonin syndrome, 281
Serpasil (reserpine), 220, 222
Sex and psychiatric drugs, 331–336
Shock treatment. See Electroconvulsive
        therapy (ECT)
Short-acting benzodiazepines, 136
Short-term treatment, 37
Side effects, 27–28, 31–33, 39, 342. See
        also Pregnancy and psychiatric
        drugs; Sex and psychiatric drugs;
        Weight loss and weight gain,
        psychiatric drugs and
Simple phobia, 124
Sinequan (doxepin), 41, 73, 75–76, 269,
        282–283
Sleep, facts about, 253–256
Sleep apnea, 261
Sleep Eze, 278–279
Sleepinal, 278–279
Sleeping pills, 36, 40, 253–283
    drugs used as, 266
    reasons to take, 265
Sleep laboratories, 260–261
Social control with psychiatry, 182
Social phobia, 124–125, 155–163
Social workers, 19
Somatic delusion, 246
Sominex, 268, 278–279
Stelazine (trifluoperazine), 186, 223,
        235–237
Stimulants, 42, 64, 107–111
Stress and mental illness, 320. See also
        Anxiety
Suicide, 24, 48, 54, 58, 108, 176, 187,
        320

Surgery when taking psychiatric drugs,
        42–43
Surmontil (trimipramine), 76–78
Symmetrel (amantadine), 218, 220

Talwin, 292
Tapering schedule, 42–43, 135
Taractan (chlorprothixene), 251
Tardive dyskinesia (TD), 211, 221–222
Tegretol (carbamazepine), 184–185,
        188–189, 193–195, 312, 327
Temazepam (Restoril), 267, 270,
        274–275
Temporal lobe epilepsy, 310
Tenormin (atenolol), 125, 156, 158–162
Tetracylic drugs, 80–82
Therapist. See Psychotherapist
Therapy. See Psychotherapy
Thioridazine (Mellaril), 41, 223,
        232–235
Thiothixene (Navane), 186, 241–242
Thorazine (chlorpromazine), 41, 186,
        188, 223–224, 230–232
Thought disorder, 203
Thyroid hormone and lithium, 186, 188,
        329
Tics, 207
Tindal (acetophenazine), 251
Tofranil (imipramine), 41, 65–67, 123,
        148, 151–153, 185, 288, 294, 304
Tolerance, 35–36
    benzodiazepines and, 130
    stimulants and, 107–108
Tourette's syndrome, 207, 246–248
Tranxene (clorazepate), 40, 129, 131,
        139. See also Benzodiazepines
Tranycypromine (Parnate), 85, 89–93,
        123, 149, 153, 162, 327. See also
        Monoamine oxidase inhibitors
        (MAOIs)
Trazodone (Desyrel), 100, 103–104, 269,
        282–283, 335
Treatment with psychiatric drugs, length
        of, 35–43
Trexan (naltrexone), 288, 294, 301–303
Triavil (Trilafon and Elavil), 240–241
Triazolam (Halcion), 267, 270–272,
        275–277
Tricyclic drugs, 65–80, 370
Trifluoperazine (Stelazine), 186, 223,
        235–237
Triflupromazine (Vesprin), 251
Trihexyphenidyl (Artane), 218–219, 221,
        223
Trilafon (perphenazine), 41, 188,
        239–241
Trimipramine (Surmontil), 76–78

Tryptophan (Trofan, Tryptocin, others), 268–269, 281–282
Tyramine and monoamine oxidase inhibitors, 83–85

Unilateral ECT, 114
Unisom Nighttime Sleep Aid (doxylamine succinate), 278–279

Valium (diazepam), 23, 40–41, 43, 121, 129, 131, 135, 137–138, 147, 218, 220. See also Benzodiazepines
Valproic acid (Depakene), 184–185, 188–189, 195–197, 327
Verapamil (Calan, Isoptin), 149, 184–185, 189, 199
Vesprin (triflupromazine), 251
Violent patient, treating the, 309–313
Visken, 159

Vistaril, 268, 277–280
Vivactil (protriptyline), 41, 78–80, 327

Warning signs that a psychiatric drug may be needed, 12
Weight loss and weight gain, psychiatric drugs and, 323–330
Welbutrin (bupropion), 105–107, 185, 327
Withdrawal symptoms, 41–42
benzodiazepine and, 131–133
fear of and drug abuse, 286–287

Xanax (alprazolam), 41, 105, 121, 123, 129, 131, 135, 142–144, 147, 151–153, 359, 361. See also Benzodiazepines

Yudofsky, Stuart, 115, 312

Antipsychotics:
Zyprexa- antipsychotic
risperdal